DISSERTATIONS SR

Volume 1

The Social Setting of the Ministry as Reflected in the Writings of Hermas, Clement and Ignatius

Harry O. Maier

Published for the Canadian Corporation for Studies in Religion/Corporation Canadienne des Sciences Religieuses by Wilfrid Laurier University Press

1991

BR
195
.P36
M35
1941

Canadian Cataloguing in Publication Data

Maier, Harry O., 1959-
  The social setting of the ministry as reflected
in the writings of Hermas, Clement and Ignatius

(Dissertations SR ; v. 1)
Includes bibliographical references.
ISBN 0-88920-995-2

1. Church polity − History − early Church, ca. 30-600.
2. Pastoral theology. 3. Christianity − Early
church, ca. 30-600. 4. Hermas, 2nd cent.
5. Clement I, Pope. 6. Ignatius, Saint, Bishop of
Antioch, d. ca. 110. I. Canadian Corporation for
Studies in Religion. II. Title. III. Series.

BV648.M35 1991   253   C91-094300-1

© 1991 Canadian Corporation for Studies in Religion/
         Corporation Canadienne des Sciences Religieuses

Printed in Canada

The Social Setting of the Ministry as Reflected in the Writings of Hermas, Clement and Ignatius has been produced from a manuscript supplied in electronic form by the author.

Order from:
WILFRID LAURIER UNIVERSITY PRESS
Waterloo, Ontario, Canada N2L 3C5

To my Father

Edmund Maier

Was du ererbt von deinen Vätern hast,
erwirb es, um es zu besitzen.

— Goethe

Contents

This book was published with the
support of the Dissertation Series prize
of the Canadian Corporation for
Studies in Religion.

Acknowledgments

Foremost among the many people I should like to thank for contributing to this thesis is my supervisor Professor M. F. Wiles. Since I embarked on this topic three years ago he has provided me with both personal support and constructive criticism, without which the following chapters would not have been possible. I have been privileged to study under him and am grateful for his excellent supervision.

I should also like to thank Dr. Bryan R. Wilson who supervised the sociological portions of this thesis. The contemporary sectarian phenomena to which he drew my attention stimulated my imagination and led me to a new approach of early Christian texts. The Reverend Robert Morgan kindly read the New Testament chapter. He was generous with his time and provided valuable criticisms. It was under his tutelage that this topic first took shape and I am grateful for his active interest as it has developed.

To David J. Reimer I also express my heartfelt thanks. By plodding through pages of often rebarbative prose and suggesting more fluent ways of stating my case, he helped remove many stylistic asperities.

A Commonwealth Scholarship has enabled me to study in the United Kingdom. I thank the Association of Commonwealth Universities for supporting my academic endeavor in this university.

Finally, I should like to thank my wife Faith. She has faithfully supported and cared for me during our stay in Oxford. Her confidence in me and enthusiasm for my topic, as well as the hours she sacrificed to type revisions and proofread, contributed greatly to the completion of this project. I am thankful for her dedication, and for sharing in my passion for early church history; sola fide.

H.O.M.

Oxford
23 July 1987

Introduction

A Topic With a Long History

This essay is an attempt to provide an account of the origins and development of the ministry in the Christian communities represented by the writings of Hermas, Clement, and Ignatius. Although its approach is new, the topic has a long and distinguished if laboured history. From an early date there has been debate over the origins of the office of bishop and elder. Jerome contended that originally the titles of elder and bishop were interchangeable, and that only later did monarchical episcopacy arise.[1] Theodore of Mopsuestia, however, argued for an original monarchical episcopate first occupied by apostles and later by appointees who distinguished themselves from elders.[2]

During the Middle Ages what has become the traditional Roman Catholic view emerged and was proclaimed as orthodoxy. Thomas Aquinas (c. 1225-74) argued that the orders of bishop and presbyter were different from the start.[3] Luther objected to this theory and cited Jerome in support of an original equivalence of bishops and elders.[4] The Council of Trent declared those who argued for an original equivalence "anathema."[5] The battle lines thus drawn, a war of words issued forth for over three centuries. In Britain, where Puritans were unhappy with the reconciliation of episcopal forms with Reformation ideals, the debate was especially vigorous. Others, such as Milton (1641), Blondel (1646), Saumaise (1641, 1645), Vitringa (1696 English translation 1842), and Daillé (1661), argued for an original identity of bishops and presbyters. Alternatively, British divines, such as Hall (1628, 1639, 1640, 1644), Ussher (1641, 1644), Hammond (1651), Pearson (1672), and Bingham (1708), pressed for a "monarchicall [sic] Reformation."[6] Much of the debate centred on the trustworthiness of Ignatius' letters, an edition of which was published by Ussher in 1644. In the eighteenth century, these divisions continued on the Continent with little deviation. Böhmer (1711), for example, cited the arguments of Blondel and Saumaise for an original identity of presbyters and bishops.[7] Thomassin (1703) and the Dominican Alexander (1762) defended the traditional Roman position.

Many nineteenth-century scholars attempted to overcome this *impasse*. In 1803, Planck argued that bishops and elders were originally distinct but equal positions.[8] And in 1837, Richard Rothe, a Lutheran, contended that after the destruction of Jerusalem the remaining apostles founded a new order of monarchical episcopacy in their respective imperial provinces.[9] Vitringa's investiga-

Notes to the Introduction appear on pp. 11-14.

tion into the synagogue and his argument, that the church modelled itself after and derived the presbyterate from it, influenced many nineteenth-century scholars.[10] Baur's theory of a Petrine-Jewish Christian thesis and Pauline-Gentile Christian antithesis synthesized in second-century hierarchical Catholicism assumed that the office of elder was derived from the synagogue.[11] Ritschl, after distancing himself from Baur his teacher, argued for an original Jewish-Christian and Gentile-Christian episcopate.[12] The questioning of the reliability and authenticity of New Testament sources also provided impetus for reflection on the development of leadership in the early church. Holtzmann argued in his work on the Pastorals[13] that an original Pauline charismatic church order was gradually replaced by a legalistic office structure derived from the synagogue. This theory is similar to those put forward by twentieth-century German scholars such as von Campenhausen,[14] Schweizer,[15] and Käsemann.[16]

Nineteenth-century study of Graeco-Roman clubs led Renan,[17] then Weingarten[18] and Heinrici[19] to argue that the early church patterned itself after pagan associations. They claimed that there was not sufficient evidence to argue that the early church derived the office of presbyter from synagogues, a point repeated by Schürer[20] (and restated by contemporary scholars[21]). In 1880, Hatch argued that the titles and functions of the early Christian ministry must be seen in the same way as similar titles used in pagan *collegia* contemporary with the early church.[22] The ἐπίσκοπος as financial overseer of the early church was especially important because of the great number of poor and destitute Christians. The presbyters, as in Palestinian synagogues and secular Graeco-Roman government, occupied their position in the community on the basis of their seniority. The distinction between presbyters and bishops was one of function and rank. While the bishops and deacons took an active role in the eucharistic celebration, the elders enjoyed a position of honour in the worship service without taking an active part in it. In the daily life of the community, these presbyters exercised discipline and jurisdiction in matters of dispute between Christians. Monarchical episcopacy did not emerge fully until the third century, although it began to develop from the time of Ignatius through the church's battle with gnosticism. The weak link in Hatch's argument, as Loening and Lietzmann pointed out,[23] is his assumption that the office of ἐπίσκοπος in Graeco-Roman *collegia* always denoted financial oversight. Recent scholars have pointed to *collegia* as more or less distant analogies for the early Christian church.[24]

Harnack embraced Hatch's theory, but expanded it slightly after the appearance of the Didache in 1883. In 1884,[25] and again in 1886,[26] Harnack put forward his theory of the twofold ministry of the church.[27] He argued that there were two levels of government in the early church: rulership by wandering apostles, prophets, and teachers who were not tied to individual churches, and by congregationally elected bishops and deacons, responsible for the administrative and cultic leadership of the individual community. With the disappearance of charismatic itinerants, bishops and deacons took over their duties (pp. 58f.). Ἐπίσκοποι and πρεσβύτεροι were originally coterminous – one denoting administrative tasks, the other patriarchal. But when the duties of bishops became more important, as a result of taking over the functions of prophets and teachers, a distinction arose between them. Deacons became separate from presbyters through the deacon's role in taking care of the poor and assisting in worship (pp. 66-67). In England, Harnack's application of the Didache as the key to solving a centuries-old debate led Turner to observe that the able German had "prophets on the brain."[28]

Rudolph Sohm was Harnack's central opponent in Germany.[29] Denying his double organization, Sohm argued that the apostolic church was purely charismatic, ruled entirely by apostles, teachers, and prophets (pp. 28-51). As these charismatics disappeared, the threefold ministry arose in order to celebrate the eucharist (p. 68). Bishops and deacons were elected from the honoured members of the congregation (i.e., presbyters) for this task (pp. 108-13, 121-28). The monarchical episcopate arose as the result of the challenge presented by false prophets to administer the sacraments correctly (p. 38, ch. 2). This first occurred in Rome: through *I Clement* the church was brought to a new era in which a special priesthood took the place of the priesthood of all believers. Sohm's theory of an original charismatic organization of the church influenced many German theologians including Bultmann (1948 English translation 1965), Greeven (1952/53), Campenhausen (1953 English translation 1969), Schweizer (1959 English translation 1961), and Käsemann (1964, pp. 63ff.; 1969, pp. 236ff.).[30]

In England, Hatch's theories provoked a severe response from Charles Gore, who argued for the appointment of bishops by apostles.[31] C.H. Turner presented similar views,[32] as did all the essays in Swete's book in which Turner's essay appeared.[33] Lightfoot (1888) argued that the threefold ministry developed out of the ministerial structures which the earliest church had in common with the Jewish synagogue. He argued that the original communities were synagogues with presbyters chosen to direct the church's religious life and administer its affairs (p. 191). Originally ruled by the Twelve, as the church expanded from Jerusalem, the office of presbyter emerged as a chief administrative position, and the first elders were joined to the apostles to form a hierarchy. The title ἐπίσκοπος was taken over by Gentile churches from the name of the directors of non-Christian *collegia* which, at the same time, maintained the older title πρεσβύτερος, joining the two titles synonymously (p. 193). An ἐπίσκοπος acted as a president of a council of πρεσβύτεροι. In the Jerusalem Church, James, the Lord's brother, was elevated from the presbytery to become the first monarchical bishop (p. 196). In other churches, the episcopal position was first occupied by apostles and then, apostolic delegates (p. 199). Towards the beginning of the second century, John and the remaining apostles divided the empire amongst themselves and travelled about establishing monarchical bishops (pp. 201f.). The view that the synagogue influenced the shape of the early ministry may be described as the consensus of British scholarship; it was reasserted by Dix[34] and other contributors to Kirk's book of essays on the ministry in 1946,[35] and most recently by Frend.[36]

All of these theories presume a relative degree of uniformity in earliest Christianity. But this view has been called increasingly into question. Streeter anticipated later scholars when he argued for varying forms of ministries in different areas of the Roman Empire, instead of a relatively straightforward development from Jerusalem outwards.[37] Bauer assumed a similar early diversity when he argued that "orthodoxy" and monarchical episcopacy were minority positions in the second century; he argued that it is more appropriate to speak of "ministries" and "churches" and "developments" in this period than to refer to them in the singular.[38] Since the discovery of the Nag Hammadi corpus in 1945, scholars have again addressed the question of what constituted normative Christianity in this period of origins.[39] The "orthodox" second-century church Father is cross-examined,[40] the "heretic's" position freed from the detractor's interpretations.[41] A view which sees early Christianity as constituted by relatively independent and dynamic "trajectories,"[42] rather than an unchanging "Wesen des Christentums" handed down from above, dominates much of contemporary scholarship.

The Early Ministry and the Household: A House-Church Trajectory

By referring to the role of house-church patrons as hosts of the worshipping community, the development of leadership structures in the churches addressed by Hermas, Clement, and Ignatius will be explicated. We shall argue that the church meeting in households provides the social setting of the development of leadership structures in these early churches. It is presented as a "trajectory." We are not attempting to provide a universal explanation: patterns and influences in Alexandria, Palestine, and Syria may have been different. The trajectory we are here arguing for begins before or with Paul and extends to Rome, Corinth, and the Asia Minor communities addressed by Ignatius (it may also extend to Philippi at the time of Polycarp but the evidence here is inconclusive). These were all communities or areas where Paul was active and although we cannot say that these were "Pauline" churches, there is a *prima facie* case for arguing that similar patterns of meeting were present in other communities associated with his activities. In the case of Asia Minor (especially Ephesus) we may also have to do with communities associated with Johannine patterns. We shall argue that the typical leaders of the communities here analysed were *patresfamilias* with houses large enough to accommodate meetings in their homes. They were the wealthier members of the church, and their social position is an important factor to be taken into account in any attempt to understand the problems to which these selected documents testify and the efforts of their writers to solve them. It will be argued that not enough attention has been paid to social factors by those using other methodologies to provide an explanation of the development of ministerial structures in certain early churches.[43] We are not attempting to supplant theological explanations altogether by suggesting that social structures are the only significant factors, but rather to argue that ideas in and of themselves are not sufficient to explain how the ministry evolved.[44] At best they provide a two-dimensional picture which gains depth only when it is realized that the people who formulated them were motivated by a number of social concerns. We are aiming at an "interactionist" account between ideas and social structures.[45]

A recognition that the early church met in houses is not new. In 1696, Vitringa, who may be called the father of the socio-historical approach to early Christianity, argued that the earliest church patterned itself after house synagogues.[46] In 1753, Mosheim presented a similar line of argument.[47] As we have seen, most subsequent scholars focused on the parallels Vitringa made between the Jewish and Christian presbyterate. Kist, however, cited Vitringa in support of his contention that the earliest Christians met in the houses of its wealthier members who acted as its first leaders.[48] Baur[49] and Weingarten[50] presented similar arguments. This approach was short-lived. Although scholars such as Kirsch,[51] Hauck,[52] and Leclerq[53] continued to argue that the early church met in houses, deductions regarding leadership were not drawn from this fact.[54] After the discovery of the house church at Dura-Europas in 1930-31,[55] however, Filson postulated that the development of the ministry could not be understood without reference to the house church.[56] In 1945 Dix noted that the early eucharist took place in private houses.[57] And Farrer in 1946 argued that the apostolic church's hospitable patrons were its bishops.[58] In 1962, Telfer argued that bishops lived in "church houses" commonly owned by the community, and were responsible for offering hospitality to travellers.[59] In 1949, Wagner, in a thesis which unfortunately has remained unpublished, assessed the importance of the household in the development of the eucharist, again without attempting to determine how it influenced the ministry.[60]

Social-historical studies since 1960 have attempted to assess the importance of the household for leadership in Pauline churches,[61] but there is often little reference to the extra-canonical evidence. Hans-Josef Klauck, in what is becoming the authoritative work on house churches in the New Testament, provides a fruitful account of the impact of the household on the earlier churches, but is disappointingly reticent about identifying a similar setting in later canonical and extra-canonical evidence.[62] Most recently, Ernst Dassmann has painted in very broad strokes a house-church setting of Ignatius' letters.[63] Literary and archaeological evidence suggests that Christians met in private homes at least until the beginning of the third century.[64] This field is relatively untouched; although the New Testament data has been investigated with enthusiasm in recent years, no scholars of whom I am aware, Dassmann excepted, have ventured outside its limits.

The Methodology

Subsequent chapters employ insights gleaned from the social sciences, especially sociology. Sociological explanations of early Christianity have become increasingly popular amongst New Testament scholars.[65] The application of sociological tools to early Christian evidence is not an entirely new venture; in 1925 Cullmann argued that the success of Form Criticism was dependent on "une *branche spéciale de la sociologie [soit] consacrée à l'examen des lois de l'évolution des traditions populaires.*"[66] In the first quarter of this century, Shailer Mathews, Shirley Jackson Case, and Donald Riddle, members of the so-called Chicago School, argued for careful attention to the social background and dynamics of early church history.[67]

Cullmann's request, however, remained unheeded, and the work of the group at Chicago is often burdened by a crude form of sociological functional-ism.[68] Sociologists and historians over the last two centuries have often been uneasy bedfellows, the historian accusing the sociologist of butchering the English language with dressed-up pseudo-scientific language which only states the painfully obvious, the sociologist accusing the historian of being, as Auguste Comte (1798-1857) charged, "the blind compilers of sterile anecdotes,"[69] unable to transcend their parochialism and stubbornly resisting potential insights offered by investigating comparable social phenomena.[70] This is surprising: sociology initially developed out of the attempts by Comte, Dur-kheim, Weber, and others to understand historically the development and struc-tures of European civilization.[71] Max Weber, for example, was a noted Roman historian and regarded the collection of historical data as integral to his sociolog-ical task. In fact, he did not distinguish between sociology and history. In the 1950s and 60s, it became generally accepted to regard the tasks of both disci-plines as distinct but complementary. Lipset, a central figure in the creation of this *détente* describes the new relationship as follows:

> History must be concerned with the analysis of the particular set of events or processes. Where the sociologist looks for concepts which subsume a variety of particular descriptive categories, the historian must remain close to the actual happenings and avoid statements which, though linking behaviour at one time or place to that elsewhere, lead to a distortion in the description of what occurred in the set of circumstances being analysed.[72]

When the two tasks are divorced from each other there is a danger, on the one hand, of ending with an armchair "great-men" approach to history, wholly atomistic and isolated from the flesh and blood of real life, and, on the other, a crude reductionism which ignores the creativity of individuals to transcend roles and social expectations.

The sociologist concerns himself less with what is historically idiosyncratic than with what is "typical, recurrent, general,"[73] less with "singular conditions of a specific situation than with structural relationships which apply to several situations."[74] The problem for the investigator who hopes to identify such phe-nomena in early Christian texts is that early Christian writers and the com-posers of the New Testament wrote for the most part not about typical, recur-rent or general issues, but about special concerns. Moreover, an educated per-son such as Paul or Clement of Rome may not be a typical member of his com-munity. The researcher using sociological methods to investigate Christian ori-gins must therefore learn "to read between the lines" and recognize what are the typical social variables underlying a text and what are not. Gerd Theissen identifies three procedures to facilitate this task: constructive, analytic, and comparative.[75]

Constructive methods pay particular attention to expressions in the text which describe the social situation in which the document has been composed. Such expressions include descriptions of groups, institutions, and organizations and those of individuals — their roles, background, and status.

Analytic methods infer underlying social realities from historical events, social norms, or religious symbols. By describing conflicts, for example, a writer often inadvertently identifies differing attitudes, customs, and social assumptions which shape opposing opinions. Norms such as those contained in the *Haustafeln* or truisms such as "the love of money is the root of all evils" often help one to identify the assumed role expectations and more general social structures exerting an influence on the group. The analysis of religious symbols facilitates one's understanding of the group's identity, challenges, and ideals.

Finally, comparative procedures analyse texts which are not derived from the Christian group being investigated. Here the investigator looks outside the Christian milieu to its contemporary society, to such institutions as synagogues, philosophical schools, and Graeco-Roman clubs in the hope of gaining insights into what Christianity has in common with its greater environment and how it differs from it. Or he or she seeks what early Christianity has in common with sociological phenomena of other periods. Maurice Duverger identifies two categories of comparison: close and distant.[76]

Close comparison is used to compare phenomena relatively proximate temporally and culturally; it aims at precision, thoroughness, and detail; it seeks to identify differences between data and to explain those variations by reference to possible differences of context and structure. For historical research, close comparisons are only helpful where there is a wealth of detailed information concerning the social phenomenon under investigation. Because this is not available for investigators of the early church, they must rely upon Duverger's second kind of comparison: distant comparison.[77] Here, rather than differences between phenomena, resemblances are sought:

> Different types of structures or institutions from different cultural contexts or of different dimensions or of different significance, are compared. They are either historical comparisons covering widely separated periods or ethnological comparisons.[78]

The researcher is interested in the degree to which they are similar and the significance of their resemblances. The comparison is not rigorous (it cannot be), but there must be sufficient proximity to be able to draw analogies. Such analogies then become the basis of hypotheses for further research. The point of a distant comparison, therefore, is not so much to identify social phenomena of various epochs and cultures, but to provide, as Duverger says, "one means amongst others of provoking shock which produces discovery."[79]

Researchers attempting to make distant comparisons between phenomena have two tools available to them: ideal types and models. The ideal type is especially associated with Max Weber (1864-1920). Weber, as one historian among many who attempt to understand contemporary society by comparison with past and culturally different societies, developed this device to locate differences between groups which could then be subjected to further hypotheses and research. "An ideal type," Weber explained,

> is formed by the one-sided *accentuation* of one or more points of view and by the synthesis of a great many diffuse, discrete, more or less present and occasionally absent *concrete individual* phenomena, which are arranged according to those one-sidedly emphasized viewpoints into a unified *analytical* construct. In its conceptual purity, this mental construct cannot be found anywhere in reality.[80]

More simply, ideal types are logically integrated mental constructs of specific phenomena arising from the observation of a wide range of similar data drawn from a wide variety of periods and cultures. They are purely heuristic devices designed to enable a researcher to focus his attention on similar phenomena, identify differences between them, and generate hypotheses for further research. They are very useful in the construction of distant comparisons. In subsequent chapters we shall make use of Bryan Wilson's sect type and Weber's type of charismatic leadership. Used as heuristic tools, these ideal types will help to discover social aspects associated with the leadership of the early church.

The word "heuristic" is used with emphasis; it is unsound to allow types to generate data or make predictions where the text is silent. This is a point Robin Scroggs forgets when he sets out to treat early Christian communities as sectarian communities.[81] He first identifies seven aspects of sects and then seeks to locate them in the available data. The methodologically fateful step comes when he argues that where evidence is lacking it may be assumed that the typical elements were present.[82] Thus he uses the type to generate evidence and argues in a vicious circle. The proper course is to note that there are enough similarities to draw an analogy between contemporary sects and early Christian groups, and then to use contemporary evidence about sects to formulate questions to bring to the ancient sources. Another instance of a misuse of the methodology is committed by James A. Wilde in his discussion of Mark's gospel. He uses Bryan Wilson's sevenfold typology of sectarianism to help to understand the group behind the gospel by arranging characteristics inferred from the text according to the different types of sects Wilson identifies. He then argues that Mark's community constituted a "vector," i.e. a combination of characteristics drawn from different sect types.[83] The problem is that Wilde's attempt fits together too closely contemporary types and ancient data, and confuses description with explanation. In order for types to be fruitful in analysis it is imperative that they be used as more than descriptive boxes: their chief value lies in their ability to stimulate the investigator's imagination, to see the data in a new light, and to ask questions which have not been raised before.

The second tool available to researchers studying a text using a comparative procedure is the model. Models are schematized abstractions formulated on the basis of theories.[84] They are created to help formulate hypotheses to test theories. Bruce Malina describes models as

> abstract, simplified representations of more complex real world objects and interactions. . . . [T]hey are approximate, simple representations of more complex forms, processes, and functions of physical and non-physical phenomena.[85]

Like ideal types, they cannot be used to generate data — otherwise theories would never be able to be falsified or verified — but unlike ideal types, they predict relationships between entities and outcomes when elements of the model are changed. They are "blueprints"[86] for further study. As in the case of ideal types, models are also heuristic devices when applied cross-culturally; they help to generate questions concerning relationships between various phenomena adduced from the text. The social models potentially available to the historian are manifold, but it is necessary to recall Duverger's warning before distant comparisons are drawn between phenomena: there must be good reason to suppose that the data which the model describes and the topic of investigation are analogous. Most, if not all, historians make use of models of one form or another (although not all use comparative models); as Carney has noted, the question is not so much *whether* historians employ models, as *which* models to use and whether they will choose to be conscious of them in the future.[87] One of the aims of this study is to show that the traditional ways in which the Shepherd and 1 Clement are treated lead to inaccurate conclusions because of the use of inappropriate models.

The chief model which we shall employ is Berger and Luckmann's concept of legitimation.[88] Again, there is a timeless aspect to their model; examples they use to illustrate various points are drawn widely from different cultures and periods. Legitimation is defined by them as a process which arises after institutions have been created. It arises because of the need to justify and explain those institutions to individuals whom they affect but who did not initially construct them, or to explain their validity to those who are questioning their validity. Berger and Luckmann describe four levels of legitimation; the most important is that of the symbolic universe.[89] It is described as a "canopy" under which the individual, his past and future, his relationships, and all institutions are placed, and which gives them all a place and a meaning.[90] By referring to it an individual knows who he or she is, where he or she belongs, and why. When the legitimacy of institutions is questioned, this results in the creation of new symbols or the explication of old ones. This model has great value when one attempts to understand the development of the ministry. Clement and Ignatius, for example, may be described as legitimators of leadership institutions which have come under attack. We shall be interested to see how they use symbols shared with the group to justify the authority of local leaders, and how they contributed to the building of further institutions, i.e., the extension of the canopy.

As in the case of ideal types, models have also been misused in the attempt to apply insights from the social sciences to the early church. John G. Gager is a good example of a scholar who has forgotten that models are a heuristic means to help understand early data.[91] In his book entitled *Kingdom and Community: The Social World of Early Christianity*, Gager argues that the social sciences can provide new data concerning the early Christians.[92] This is false: they can only help raise new questions which then may facilitate the discovery of data which were always there but which had been passed over. More importantly, however, he forces the New Testament data to fit the model he chooses for comparative analysis. The model he uses is borrowed from L. Festinger and others. Festinger argues that contemporary, socially deprived millenarian groups often engage in greater mission activity rather than disintegrate when their prediction of a certain date for the Second Coming is proved incorrect; this results in what he calls "cognitive dissonance" and he argues that this is overcome by increased proselytism.[93] Gager argues that a similarly disappointed expectation in the early church accounts for its emphasis on mission. He contends that the death of Jesus presented a crisis for his disciples, which disconfirmed their belief in him as Messiah and resulted in a vigorous mission campaign to overcome their "cognitive dissonance."[94] For the model to fit he must first establish that the early Christians were constituted by the proletarian poor.[95] In doing this, however, he overlooks all the evidence to the contrary; he selects his data to fit the model. Secondly he must establish that Jesus had clear perceptions concerning his ultimate fate — a topic about which there is insufficient evidence to arrive at any firm conclusions. Further, he must show that the early Christians expected Jesus to return on a specified date. It is most important that there be a parallel here or the entire enterprise fails; that the early Christians had strong eschatological beliefs is without doubt, but there is no evidence that they specified a time of Christ's return. Indeed one may draw the opposite conclusion from the evidence; in Mark 13:32 Jesus admits ignorance of the precise time of the Parousia and 2 Pet. 3:8 ("with the Lord one day is as a thousand years, and a thousand years as one day" — a text Gager quotes as evidence of a revision arising from the initial disconfirmation) may be equally interpreted as testimony to the fact that short of a global catastrophe the Christian doctrine of Christ's Second Coming is in fact non-falsifiable. However one interprets this Petrine passage, there is no evidence that the earliest Christians predicted the Parousia with the precision demanded in order for cognitive dissonance to arise. Thus Gager postulates connections where there are none and forces the evidence to fit his models, which are then used to fill the lacunae of historical evidence.

Both ideal types and models enable one to engage in comparative sociological research of the early Christian church. They cannot generate data; they can only help us to ask new questions. In subsequent chapters we hope to show that they help us to raise valuable questions unasked by scholars who have employed other methodologies in their attempts to discover the origins and development of the ministry.

The Strategy

To gain a full appreciation of the role of householders in the communities selected for investigation here, it will be necessary first to provide a survey of the household in antiquity. We shall concentrate first on the traditional Graeco-Roman household, and then turn to a discussion of pagan and Jewish groups organized along household lines. This will provide a *prima facie* case for looking to house-church patrons as the church's early leaders. This is followed by a chapter on the evidence of house churches and house-church leadership contained in the Pauline corpus. This chapter will provide us with a relatively firm setting from which to approach the later documents. Hermas provides the most direct evidence to substantiate our thesis. Here we shall analyse the problems facing the community arising out of leadership by well-to-do patrons as challenges to its sectarian identity, and Hermas' efforts to establish group boundaries. 1 Clement will provide us with an opportunity to discuss the institution-building role of Clement's letter for the Corinthian community, and the development of house-church leadership. Finally, Ignatius will be discussed as a charismatic leader who used his privileged position as a potential martyr for Christ to establish more defined leadership structures in the Asia Minor communities by giving impetus to social forces inherent in the house-church setting of the community, and to protect these groups from perceived false teaching.

Notes

1 *Comm. in Tit. 1:3* (*Migne Bibliotheca Patrum Latina* 30, p. 880A); *Epistle* 146 (*Corpus Scriptorum Ecclesiasticorum Latinorum* 56).

2 *Ep. ad Tim. I 3:8* (H.B. Swete, ed., *Theodori Episcopi Mopsuesteni in Epistulas B. Pauli Commentari. The Latin Version with the Greek Fragments*. Vol. II. (Cambridge: Cambridge University Press, 1882), pp. 117ff.

3 *Summa Theologica* II,2 *quaest. 184, art. 6.*

4 *Schmalkaldic Articles* (1547) *Tractatus de potestate et primatu papae* n. 60ff.

5 Sess. XXIII canon 7.

6 Hall, 1640, pp. 17f.

7 Pp. 303f.; also Pfaff, 1727, pp. 69f.; 1770; Hildebrand, 1745, pp. 9f.; Mosheim, 1753, pp. 125f.

8 Vol. 1, pp. 24-33.

9 1837, pp. 351-92; similarly, Bunsen, 1847, pp. 85f., 129f.; Lightfoot, 1888; Telfer, 1962, pp. 69f.

10 1696, pp. 467ff., 609ff. (English translation 1842, pp. 145ff.; 169ff.).

11 1835, pp. 84f.; 1838, pp. 59f.; first published 1863 (English translation 1873, Vol. 2, pp. 16ff.).

12 1857, pp. 415f., 432f., 441f.

13 1880, pp. 194ff.

14 First published 1953 (English translation 1969, pp. 76ff.).

15 First published 1959 (English translation 1961, pp. 70f., passim).

16 1964, pp. 63ff.; 1969, pp. 236ff.

17 1866, pp. 351f. In 1869 (Paulus, p. 257) Renan argued that parallels could be drawn between household, *collegia* and Christian house churches; cf. also Liebenam, 1890, p. 272 n. 4.

18 1881, pp. 453f.

19 1876, pp. 465ff.; 1877, pp. 89ff.; 1880, pp. 20-29; 1887, p. 556.

20 1879, pp. 542-46.

21 Schürer (rev. and ed. Fergus, Millar, Black, and Goodman), Vol. 2, 1973f., pp. 427-39; also Harvey, 1974, pp. 318-32 (who overstates his case). The modern evidence is listed by Brooten, 1982, pp. 41-56, but her conclusions are far too strong. Evidence for πρεσβύτεροι (male and female) in some localities (notably Alexandria) is insufficient to allow scholars to draw the strong parallels which have been drawn between the synagogue and the early church. It is difficult to determine in much of this evidence whether the title was used honorifically or to describe membership in a council. Such theories leave unexplained the entire lack in the early church of titles most common in the Jewish epigraphic and literary evidence. The exception is Epiphanius who notes that Palestinian Ebionites(!) possessed ἀρχισυνάγωγοι and πρεσβύτεροι (*Panarion* 30:18.2; cf. *Haer.* 30:11 for ὑπηρέτης = ‏ ו ו ה ?).

22 Especially lectures two to four; Hatch also argued for the influence of the synagogue.

23 Loening, 1889, pp. 21f.; Lietzmann, 1914, pp. 101-106; Porter, 1939, pp. 110ff.

24 Wilken, 1972, pp. 268ff. (although he is somewhat equivocal: compare pp. 279 and 280); also Countryman, 1977, pp. 135ff.; Meeks, 1983, pp. 77-80; Malherbe, 1983, pp. 89-91. In our view the analogy holds, as we shall see in Chapter One, where both church and *collegia* relied upon wealthy patrons for the success of their communal activities, and the leadership drawn from these ranks.

25 Pp. 88-151.

26 Pp. 31ff.

27 For what follows we shall outline the position presented by him in 1920; for further discussion see Linton, 1932, loc. cit.

28 1912, p. 10 (first published 1887); for criticism of Harnack's use of evidence see pp. 10f.

29 1892; 1895; cf Linton, pp. 49f. for further discussion. References are to his 1892 publication.

30 See Holmberg, 1980b, pp. 187f.; for further discussion and criticism and Chapter Four below.

31 1900, esp. pp. 57-197.

32 Turner, 1921, pp. 93-214.

33 Swete, 1921, pp. xiif. lists the conclusions of the collected essays; more succinctly, see 1912, pp. 13ff.

34 Dix, 1947, pp. 183ff., esp. pp. 227-74; 1978 (first published 1945), pp. 19ff., 48ff. Dix pursued a unique line of argument by contending that the ministry arose out of liturgical practice, much of it borrowed directly from the synagogue. Dix's conclusions, especially those about *1 Clement*, upon which much of his argument rests, are criticized by Jay, 1981, pp. 125ff. Dix (1978, pp. 82f.) also generalizes too broadly from Hippolytus' *Apostolic Tradition* to make a case for earlier liturgical practice. His argument that the early eucharist was *mutatis mutandis* a *chabûrah* which everywhere took on normative characteristics from this Jewish religious meal exceeds the bounds of the evidence. His contention (pp. 50f.) that the Last Supper was a *chabûrah* becomes circular when he uses evidence drawn from later *chabûrôth* prayers to fill in gaps where evidence concerning Jesus' prayer is lacking (see especially pp. 54-5).

35 Kirk, 1946, especially the essay by Farrer, pp. 113-82. This whole approach has come under increasing attack; see, e.g., Burke, 1970, pp. 499ff.

36 1984, pp. 106, 120ff.; Frend is also influenced by Harnack: cf. pp. 139f.

37 1929, pp. 50f.; note also the methodological assumptions established in Chapter One.

38 1934 (ET 1971); further discussion of his theories appear in subsequent chapters.

39 The fruit of such labours may be discovered in Wilken, 1971.

40 For example Vallée, 1981 (short version, 1980, pp. 174ff.).

41 For example Pagels, 1979.

42 Robinson and Koester, 1971, esp. pp. 13-16, 114ff.

43 Linton, 1932, pp. 132-35 groups twentieth-century approaches to the problem of early church leadership into four categories and provides examples of each: lexigraphical (focusing on key terms), theological (emphasizing the transcendent and often ideal origins of the church), historical (centring on recoverable data and chronology), and sociological. Our approach falls within Linton's fourth general category and will be explicated in the next section.

44 Philosophical questions of reductionism, the implications of sociology for a doctrine of Providence, and the relation between social determinism and free will are large topics which fall outside the confines of this discussion. While many nineteenth-century sociologists like Durkheim were reductionist, contemporary sociologists make more modest claims. A discussion (not always convincing) of the topic of free will can be found in Berger, 1967, pp. 142ff; Berger and Kellner, 1981, pp. 92ff. Berger also discusses the relationship between sociological explanations and the ultimate reference of theological statements: see 1967, pp. 179ff.

45 Gill, 1977, has coined this term in his discussion of Berger and Luckmann's sociology of knowledge.

46 Pp. 145ff.; 429ff. (ET pp. 10f.) He refers to Beza (1519-1605) and Erasmus (1469-1536) in partial support (pp. 430, 431).

47 Pp. 76ff., especially 116.

48 1832, pp. 54ff. (Vitringa, 1696, p. 258).

49 1835, pp. 82, 84f.; 1838, pp. 86f.; 1863 (English translation 1879, Vol. 2, p. 16).

50 1881, pp. 444f.

51 1897, pp. 6ff.

52 1901, pp. 774ff.

53 1921, Vol. 4, pp. 2279ff., esp. 2287.

54 Harnack, 1884, p. 142 argued that presbyters were often the church's patrons, but he did not draw a connection between hospitality and episcopacy.

55 Kraeling, 1967, provides an exhaustive account (summarized in Snyder, 1985, pp. 68-71); cf. also Hopkins, 1979, who postulates too confidently that it was a private place of worship before its conversion in the third century; similarly, von Gerkan, 1964.

56 1939, pp. 105ff.

57 1978, pp. 16ff.

58 1946, pp. 147f.

59 Pp. 57, 86, 165, esp. 165f., 171. This conclusion seems to be drawn primarily from the letters (especially *Epistle* 7) of Cyprian (d. 258), but is it not highly suspect to argue from such later evidence to account for an earlier setting? The burden of the proof is on those who contend that the earliest Christians owned buildings from the start. White, 1982, adducing pagan analogies for support, argues convincingly for a development from private-household meetings to semi-public house churches like that at Dura to the *domus ecclesia* of the third and fourth century.

60 Especially Chapters One and Two.

61 For reference see Chapter Two below.

62 Klauck, 1981, pp. 63ff.

63 First in 1984, pp. 82ff., and again in 1985, pp. 886-901.

64 A discussion of the literary evidence may be found in Rordorf, 1964, pp. 110ff. and Dassmann, 1985, pp. 886ff.; the archaeological evidence is discussed by Snyder, 1985, pp. 67ff., where relevant literature is also cited.

65 Gerd Theissen is a contemporary pioneer who began offering essays employing a sociological methodology in 1973 (most collected in 1982). His conclusions regarding the well-to-do status of some early Christians were anticipated by Judge, 1960b and restated by Gülzow, 1974, pp. 189ff. See Meeks, 1983 and Elliott, 1985, pp. 27-34, for bibliography.

66 P. 573 (his italics).

67 Their concerns are summarized by Funk, 1976, pp. 4-22, esp. pp. 15-16.

68 Their methodology is criticized by Keck, 1974, p. 437.

69 Cited by Burke, 1980, p. 19.

70 Burke, 1980, pp. 13-29 provides a useful summary of the relationship between the disciplines over the years; cf. Hofstadter, 1968, pp. 3ff. for the relationship in America.

71 Martindale, 1959, pp. 59f.

72 Lipset, 1968, p. 22.

73 Theissen, 1982, pp. 176-77.

74 Ibid., p. 177.

75 For what follows cf. ibid., pp. 177ff.

76 1964, pp. 261f.

77 Ibid., pp. 266f.

78 Ibid., p. 266.
79 Ibid., p. 267.
80 1949, p. 90.
81 1975, pp. 1-23.
82 Ibid., p. 14; cf. Tuckett, 1987, pp. 146f. for further discussion.
83 1978, p. 62.
84 For thorough discussion see Willer, 1967.
85 Malina, 1981, p. 17; cf. also Elliott, 1985, pp. 1-10.
86 Roth, 1971, p. 91.
87 1975, p. 5.
88 The model is set out in 1971, pp. 110ff. It is presented more fully in Chapter Four.
89 Ibid., p. 114.
90 Ibid., p. 79.
91 The review by Thomas, 1979, pp. 95-96 offers similar criticisms.
92 Gager, 1975, p. 4.
93 The theory is described in ibid., pp. 39f.
94 Ibid., p. 41.
95 Ibid., pp. 24, 217f.

Chapter One

The Household in the Ancient World

In this chapter we shall present a general discussion of the Graeco-Roman household in antiquity. A large topic such as this must be limited here to a brief survey, which will provide a more general context for the argument presented in subsequent chapters. The discussion will be divided into two parts. First, the general contours of the traditional Greek and Roman household will be presented. Here, literary evidence will be largely relied upon. In the second part we shall also turn our attention to epigraphic evidence and argue for the importance of the household and its patrons in the life and organization of various Graeco-Roman groups.

The Traditional Graeco-Roman Household

The basic economic, political, and religious social unit of antiquity was the household. Generally speaking, the ancient household was composed of two elements: the οἶκος and the οἰκία. The οἶκος was constituted by the habitation with all of its property, power, and possessions and the οἰκία consisted of the relatives, *clientela*, and servants.[1] The Latin equivalent of the οἶκος/οἰκία unit is the *domus/familia*. Finley defines *familia* as "all the persons, free or unfree, under the authority of the *paterfamilias*, the head of the household, or all the descendants from a common ancestor; or all one's property; or simply all one's servants. . . ."[2] The Septuagint translates the Hebrew word בּיִת by both οἶκος and οἰκία.[3] Οἶκος/οἰκία is used in the Septuagint to designate a physical dwelling (Esther 2:3; 7:8), the family of a patriarch (Gen. 50:8; 1 Sam. 1:21) including his wife, concubine, sons and daughters (Gen. 36:6), dependent relatives (Gen. 13:1), servants (Gen. 15:2), vassals (Gen. 14:14) and slaves (Gen. 17:13-27), a clan (2 Sam. 9:4), or domestic property with its privileges, tools, slaves, and livestock (Dt. 20:17; Esther 8:1).[4] It is important to note, especially in the case of the Roman *familia*, that the family was not a static social phenomenon, but underwent a significant development in the course of antiquity.[5] Still, the household remained an important institution economically, politically, and religiously throughout the period of Graeco-Roman civilization.

Notes to this chapter appear on pp. 24-28.

The basic element in Greek social, economic, and political life was the household.[6] Aristotle (*Politics* 1252a f.) argues that the household is the smallest social unit of the state. Several households bound together make a village, and several villages the crowning association — the polis.[7] The "complete household" (1253b) consists of slaves and free men alongside the husband, wife, and children. Each of these has his or her appropriate place in the household and they are to be governed by proper relationships with one another. The householder rules his slave (animate property) as a master, his wife (a free member of the house) as a statesman, and his children, who are subject to him, as a monarch (1255a f.; 1259 f.). Economy is presented as a matter of household management. This is evident in Xenophon's *Oeconomicus*, where the proper relations between different members of the household are outlined.[8] The household also provided a powerful ideological instrument to protect and maintain society. "Ethically, politically, and religiously," writes Elliott,

> the *oikos* provided the framework for viewing and distinguishing the native (*oikeios*) from the stranger (*metoikos, paroikos = allotrios*), hence the citizen from the quasi- or non-enfranchised, the correligionist from the "heathen."[9]

The household in ancient Greek society was also the cultic centre of the family. The household religious cult, of which the patriarch was head, had a central role in the family's daily life.[10] "Der 'oikos' ist zugleich eine Kult- und eine Lebensgemeinschaft. Der häusliche Kult und die F(amilie)grabstätte halten die Verbundenheit selbst über den Tod hinaus noch aufrecht."[11] The length of one's afterlife depended upon memory, and so was ensured above all through the remembrance at the grave, which carried the name of the dead. With the advent of the belief that the soul or spirit went to heaven after death, arose the idea that the spirit lived in heaven as in its earthly house.[12] In heaven, as on earth, the household provided psychological comfort, certainty, and protection from chaos.[13]

As in Greece, so also in Rome the household community constituted the basic social unit of society. The ancient Roman family is described by Betti as a "Schicksalsgemeinschaft."[14] "Die archaische, bäuerliche F(amilie)," writes Gaudemet, "wird charakterisiert durch ihren festen Zusammenhalt, ihre Unterordnung, unter das Oberhaupt, ihre Treue gegenüber den Verfahren."[15]

Like the Greek οἶκος, the Roman *familia* provided a psychologically and existentially satisfying social setting for its individual members.[16] At the head of the *familia* was the *paterfamilias*, his power traditionally defined by Roman law in three parts: *potestas*, the power over his children, his grandchildren, and his slaves; *manus*, the power over his wife and his sons' wives; and *dominium*, the power over his possessions.[17] The term *pater* connoted more than generation, it also implied authority and protection.[18] The result of this, during the Republican period, was a society in which the family was the "irreducible unit in law, economics, religion, as well as other functional areas."[19] Early Roman society was comprised of a number of households, each under its own *paterfamilias*, in whom was vested absolute authority over its members and the responsibility of executing justice.[20] It was with the growth of the city-state and republican institutions that the autonomy of the family became more circumscribed.[21] But while such institutions attempted to subordinate the autonomy of the household to the public interest, "the household in its broader sense remained a rival body."[22] In fact, where republican ideals had never been established, the autonomy of the household remained intact under the *paterfamilias*.[23]

In the political sphere, the Roman *familia* continued to exercise great influence even in Republican times. The competition and allegiances of Roman aristocratic families to achieve political ends in the autumn days of the Republic, testify to the importance of the household in this period.[24] *Amicitia* and *clientela*, both extensions of the Roman *familia*,[25] formed the basis of political manoeuvring in the Republic, and then provided a structure for the *princeps* to establish an imperial system finally accountable to him alone. It was the alignment and realignment of the Roman aristocracy, thereby reducing Republican institutions to "the aggrandizement of the household community,"[26] which resulted in rule by Caesar.[27]

The household was also the location of the family cult, whose priest was the *paterfamilias*.[28] Roman religion in the Republic consisted largely in "a spiritualization of family life, reaching back to earliest ancestors and forward to the unborn."[29] "Nothing," Nisbet comments,

> violated the priestly authority of the Father over his hearth, and religion was deemed as inextinguishably a function of kinship as was life itself. Birth, marriage, and death were the ceremonial highpoints, and in each ritual the authority and unity of the family were, in effect, reaffirmed. No child was born into the family, he had to be accepted. What else were death rites but the means whereby one left the earthly members of the family to join the departed — who were deemed not the less living for their eternal stay elsewhere?[30]

This last point is supported by the fact that in some cases the Romans decorated their sarcophagi with representations of the household and its activities and sometimes even a doorway, in relief, to Hades. Petronius' Trimalchio, who believed he would live longer in the grave than in his earthly home, took great care with the erection and decoration of his grave.[31] The departed soul depended for its preservation on the food offered by the householder still on the other side of the grave to the household gods, and especially his maintenance of the sacred flame. To allow strangers into the religion of the hearth was equally to risk the alienation of the departed.[32]

As in other aspects of Roman life, household religion followed a hierarchical pattern.[33] Cicero prescribes that the performance of private rites is the duty of the *paterfamilias*.[34] Cato reminds wives that it is the master who "attends to the devotions for the whole household"[35] and Columella prohibits slaves from offering any sacrifice without the permission of the master.[36] Their religious role in the household cult was confined mainly to menial tasks.[37] Proper maintenance of the cult and homage to the *genius* of the master provided an important means for slaves to express their loyalty.[38] While traditional household religion was increasingly threatened by the intrusion of new cults, throughout the imperial period the *paterfamilias* continued as the head or priest of the traditional household cult.[39]

The success of Augustus can largely be ascribed to his ability to capitalize on the household in its religious, social, and political manifestations. The penetration of the image of Caesar, for example, into the private hearth — the sanctum of the family community — and alongside the Lares and Penates, established Augustus as a household god and won for him a place at the centre of Roman family life.[40] The importance of the family in the early Empire can be seen in Augustus' use of domestic ideology and the existing patronage system derived from the extended household structure for his own benefit. Augustus was anxious to restore society in such a way that each part was connected to himself. By the time of the Principate the traditional Roman family was in a state of decay.[41] Augustus sought to re-establish family values, but in a way that fostered devotion to the Empire and to himself. He prohibited marriage between partners of unequal status, he sought to curtail divorce through punishment, and he attempted to stop the decrease of the Roman population through legislation in which unmarried widows or widowers, or widowed heiresses without children, were kept, at least in part, from their inheritance. In contrast to this, large families gained certain remunerative advantages.[42] Augustus' more far-reaching strategy, however, was to incorporate the entire Empire under his authority. In 2 B.C. he was acclaimed *pater patriae*, although he was seen as this long before winning the title.[43] With this came the appropriate *potestas*. "Loyal subjects would be, henceforth, favoured sons and daughters of the 'father of the fatherland.'"[44] It is in this greater context that the *Lex Papia Poppaea* is to be understood.[45] So also at the conclusion of the *Res Gestae Divi Augusti*, after recounting his great works, the Emperor recalls that he is hailed *"pater patriae"* by "the entire Roman people."[46] "This paternalism reveals the emotional basis upon which the power of the Caesar rested."[47] Tiberius did not forget this,[48] nor did successive emperors.[49] This was no abstract relationship. It was established by formal oaths of allegiance to the house of Caesar.[50] Imperial power was extended throughout the empire by a web of personal servants, slaves, and freedmen under the *potestas* of Caesar, forming his οἶκος (cf. Phil. 4:22). The picture of the ideal empire was, therefore, that of a harmonious household, protected, maintained, and supervised by the ideal *pater patriae*. If the state was a *familia*, the emperor was its *paterfamilias*.[51] "The perpetuation of the Caesarian system" Judge writes, "was not the result of sinister dynasticism: it was the product of the characteristic Roman sentiments of the family's obligation to its own tradition, and the loyalty of dependants to the patron household."[52]

The Household and Mystery Religions and Foreign Cults, Philosophical Schools, Associations, and Jewish Synagogues

So far we have relied to a large extent on the opinions of the ancient *literati* to fill out a picture of the Graeco-Roman household. But it would be methodologically dangerous to leave the matter here. The opinions of a Cicero, Cato, or Pliny were formed within a social stratum which constituted a minuscule fraction of ancient society. And it would be misleading to present the ancient household as a static phenomenon. Its central interest for us in this thesis is its adaptation for the use of groups which extended beyond the traditional family boundaries. Samuel Dill suggests that no other age "felt such a craving for some form of social life wider than the family and narrower than the state."[53] In the rest of this chapter we shall discuss the role of the household and its members in particular types of ancient groups. We shall interest ourselves particularly in the role of the household and patronage in four broad areas: the mystery religions and foreign cults, the philosophical schools, the Graeco-Roman associations, and the Jewish synagogue. This will provide a more general context for our discussion of the early Christian movement and show what kind of social expectations were present when a group met in an individual's house, or when a group drew sustenance from its wealthier members.

Mystery Religions and Foreign Cults

Reciting the history of a plague which swept down upon Rome in 430-427 B.C., Livy states that not only bodies were infected with disease, but the minds of Romans, too, were polluted by a horde of foreign superstitions as a result of the intrusion of a certain class of (unspecified) individuals who "introduced strange rites into their homes." In response, the leading citizens rose up and reasserted the practice of the traditional household cult.[54] This was a theme to which the Roman historian was to return; on the eve of Hannibal's invasion the Romans awoke to find themselves again infested with superstitious practices so that "within the walls of houses were Roman rites abandoned."[55] Two centuries later Cicero was to echo Plato in his condemnation of the worship of private gods.[56] All in vain; one of Augustus' achievements during his war against Antony was the expulsion of Egyptian deities — first from Roman households, later one mile from the official city boundaries.[57] From the start, foreign cults won adherents through household channels.[58]

It is a commonplace to see mystery religions and foreign cults described as mission religions.[59] How were adherents won? Plato describes one way. In *Republic*, Book II (364C) he describes two mythical Orphic mendicant priests, Musaeus and his son Eumolpus, who knock on the doors of rich men and make available heavenly powers and an initiation for the price of a dinner.[60] The practice was evidently still popular among various groups half a millennium later; Origen describes a sect of Ophites who enter the houses of unsuspecting females and propagate their ideas.[61]

But this was not the only way. There is also evidence of patrons establishing conventicles in their own homes and inviting others to participate. A fourth to fifth century A.D. manuscript instructs an Orphic to prepare as he is able a private room for the introduction of the god.[62] We know of three villas in Italy with wall murals from the cycle of Dionysian mysteries and rites, perhaps suggesting that the cult met in private homes of well-off property owners.[63] How such domestic cults may have been organized can be adduced from an inscription from Torre Nova near ancient Rome which contains a long list of members of a Dionysiac cult who erected a statue to the priestess Pompeia Agrippinilla. Originally from Lesbos, this woman brought the cult with her to Italy after she married a man who was proconsul in Asia Minor in A.D. 150.[64] The list of members describes the dependants and clients of Agrippinilla's great household — her husband, children, relatives, *clientela*, servants, and slaves. Thus we see the hierarchical order of the household maintained in the cult.

Mystery cults showed an affinity to the household community when they tended toward association on a family basis or met in secret. Of the 53 excavated mithraea, only ten appear to be specially constructed buildings. The rest are backroom or subterranean chambers in pre-existing private houses or public buildings.[65] Laechuli coined the term "mithraic house church" to describe the small single-room mithraea of private houses.[66] Scholars note that the establishment of a mithraeum depended upon the leadership and beneficence of wealthier individuals who were attracted to the cult.[67] This is evidenced by the household mithraea of Callinicus, the "Mithraeum of the Painted Walls," both at Ostia,[68] and the Dura Mithraeum,[69] all dating from the second century. In the first case Callinicus invited his confrères into his home; in the second, evidence of architectural modifications to segregate the mithraeum from the rest of the private house may be interpreted as evidence of a host establishing a house conventicle, but attempting to protect his privacy. The Durene evidence is more ambiguous. This mithraeum was originally established in one room of a private house — possibly that of one of its Roman military founders — although it is also possible that an already existing house was purchased to establish a meeting place. Perhaps most significant is the evidence that the wealthier hosts and patrons, as a result of their beneficence, were given positions of leadership and titles betokening a high rank within the cult. The titles *pater, pater patrum, pater sacrorum*, and *sacerdos* were commonly ascribed to benefactors, and Vermaseren has suggested that the term *pater* was equated with patron, i.e. one who owned or donated the cult's property.[70]

The Sarapis cult took place in a more open setting, as is indicated by the spacious temple complexes which have been unearthed. But the private household also served as a setting for its religious practices. This may be adduced from evidence of common meals, where meat was sacrificed to the god, or sacrificial food was eaten.[71] Invitations sent to members in the name of the god indicate that members of the cult believed Sarapis himself was both guest and host at the meal.[72] Where there were no existing temples, all cult activities probably took place in households. In fact, we are able to trace the development of a Sarapis cult at Delos, from its foundations in a local household in 200 to 180 B.C. to the construction of a Sarapeum and temple complex on the site of the original house.[73] The inscription recounts the importation of the Sarapis cult to Delos by one Apollonios (I), a hellenized Egyptian priest, who brought a statue of the god from Memphis in the mid-third century B.C. and established the cult in the rented quarters where he resided. His son Demetrius succeeded him as priest and continued to host the cult in his home. Later, when the number of adherents increased and the cult became more prosperous, his grandson, Apollonios (II) built a temple complex — its dining hall retaining its original position at the site of Apollonios I's residence. Here is a clear example of a priest acting as both patron and missionary of a cult.[74]

Less well-known cults spread in similar ways. A private cult in Philadelphia in Lydia (100 B.C.), dedicated to the Attic goddess Agdistis, probably consisted of the members of a well-to-do household.[75] The goddess Agdistis, the "mistress of the house," dictates the rules of the cult to Dionysios, the ruler of the house and patron of the cult. The statute includes moralizing rules for its members, among whom are included οἰκέται (probably household slaves) and the inclusion of an oath to be taken by Dionysios and his extended family. As in the inscription from Torre Nova, the household cult probably helped to reinforce allegiances to the household community and its patron. From Priene in Caria comes evidence of what perhaps constituted a similar cult. Archaeological evidence of a household was unearthed here at the end of the last century.[76] The remains of the so-called *hieros oikos*[77] suggest that it was partly renovated for cultic use, but also continued as a domicile. It is not clear whether a cult community was attached to the household, and it is possible that adherents were drawn solely from members of the household community. Again, this time in the case of the Durene Temple of Gadde, archaeologists have identified four periods of construction. Established *c.* 150 B.C., the cult originated with Palmyrene merchants, among whom was a prominent family who perhaps established the cult in its home. They continued as leaders in the cult for several generations.[78] As in the case of the Sarapeum of Delos, this house later became the location of the sanctuary and subsequent expansion. The host family later built a house adjacent to the temple for its own dwelling.[79]

Philosophical Schools

Like many of the foreign cults of ancient Greece and Rome, the many philosophical schools often had their origin in the households of teachers or their patrons. There were exceptions; Diogenes, for example, resided in an earthenware jar in the Athenian agora[80] — a famous ancient tourist attraction. But for most a domestic setting provided a more conducive environment for philosophy and debate. Plato's *Protagoras* opens in the house of the wealthy Athenian Kallias, where Sophists are gathered in various corners, debating in small groups (314C-315E). The *Parmenides* takes place in the house of Antiphon. The *Symposium* assumes a similar setting. Wycherley cites with approval the contention that "a Greek philosophical school was essentially a specialized extension of the Hellenic household."[81] Friends and pupils lived with Epicurus[82] and he bequeathed his house and garden to his pupils, which provided a quiet atmosphere for philosophical pursuits and the basis for a school.[83] Teaching in one's own home remained an attractive option for many philosophers throughout the Hellenic and Imperial period.[84] Even Justin seems to have plied his philosophical trade in his own rented quarters.[85]

Many philosophers remained unattached to such settings. Some, like the more extreme Cynics, forsook home and patronage and lived in public buildings, such as temples, stoas, and gymnasia.[86] Aulus Gellius may be describing one of these when he recounts the meeting of a mendicant philosopher "in a cloak, with long hair and a beard that reached almost to his waist."[87] The begging philosopher was a popular target of Lucian's satire; the *bel esprit* repeatedly rails against those who seek to make a fortune from the charity of the rich.[88] If begging was too extreme, residing at the home of a well-to-do patron as the household educator or resident intellectual must have been an attractive alternative. Epictetus describes the ideal symbiotic relationship between a willing young pupil and a household educator.[89]

There are also cases of Christian teachers setting up schools in the houses of wealthy patrons and patronesses.[90] But others were less taken with the idea. Lucian is especially disgusted at the resident philosopher who becomes wealthy through patronage.[91] When he describes the mishaps that befall a resident philosopher who relies for his livelihood on the good will of a patron he is not engaging in mere merriment.[92] The philosopher who allows himself to be seduced into waiting on the tables of his patron's guests in order to keep his post is indeed dubious.[93] More sober arguments are put forward in the first century A.D. Cynic letters attributed to Socrates and his disciples. A *cause célèbre* of the Cynics was how a philosopher was to make his living. Should he beg, accept posts at the homes of the wealthy, or ply his own trade?[94] Important in the debate was whether or not Plato, Aristotle, and other philosophers accepted gifts and positions at court.[95] The argument among Cynics reveals the importance of the role of the household and patronage in the pursuit of philosophy and the problems to which that setting could give rise.

Associations

The Graeco-Roman *collegia, thiasoi,* and *eranoi*[96] represent the most widespread type of gathering to which we shall address ourselves in this chapter. Among the varied groups which dotted the Graeco-Roman world, some may be described as family clubs. The most famous example telling of a household *collegium* is the inscription which records *"collegium quod est in domo Sergiae Paullinae."*[97] This may have been a *collegium* formed by the slaves and clients of a well-to-do family. *Patresfamilias* often acted as patrons of such *collegia domestica,* hosting them in their own homes, or providing buildings for them.[98] There are also examples of Greek clubs established along household lines.[99] The degree of exclusiveness of membership varied with different household associations. The third century B.C. κοινόν of Epikteta at Thera was constituted primarily but not entirely by household dependants;[100] that of Diomedon at Kos (third to second century B.C.), however, was made up exclusively of family members.[101] In most cases, the association was established by the patron in specially provided quarters and was governed by dependants, who used the funds provided by the householder for various banquets in his (or her) honour. In some instances, however, the patron or a blood relative of the founder took over various aspects of leadership in the club. Epikteta, for example, established her daughter's son as priest to her family club. And there are other instances where the founder was the acting head of the club.[102]

Of course, most clubs were not domestic. But the hierarchical pattern of the household and Graeco-Roman society favoured more prosperous club members as its leaders. In name, Graeco-Roman clubs were democratic and egalitarian; in practice, by the time of the Empire, they were often something quite different. Dill has noted that ". . . the college . . . of the Antonine age cannot be relieved of the charge of purchased or expectant deference to mere wealth."[103] Tertullian, writing in ca. A.D. 197, reveals, by means of an implied contrast between the Christian church and clubs, the deference to wealth among the pagan associations: "Our presidents . . . have gained their distinction not by money but by merit. For money counts not in the things of God" (*Apology* 39). One may speak of "charities" in Graeco-Roman society only with qualification, and the "charitable" help which individuals offered the clubs to which they belonged is no exception: wealthier members of clubs donated sums of money in return for *honor*[104] – a coveted commodity. *Honor virtutis praemium*. In a monetarist age it is easy to forget that it has not always been the case that money makes the world go round. In the early empire, it was expected that club officials would go out of their way to earn their *honneur*, by using their own resources to pay for the banquets, building projects, and ornamentations the club could not otherwise afford.[105] There is evidence that where it was possible such norms existed even in the *collegia funeratica*, the more humble burial associations of the poor.[106] Thus, those most suited for these tasks, the relatively well-to-do, were elected (and re-elected) as its leaders.[107] In the Roman *collegia*, the strata of leadership were often named after and ranked according to political office.[108] This aping of the political sphere spilled over into the choice of leaders, for higher ranking officials were often its well-to-do patrons.[109] The use of secular titles was not as prevalent in the Greek *thiasoi* or *eranoi*, but a similar parallel between wealth and importance of position prevailed there as well.[110] Alongside the "mothers" or "fathers" of the club – the donors or *patroni*, whose names head the lists of charters of Graeco-Roman associations[111] – the well-to-do officer had a central role to play in the maintenance of the club.

The Household Synagogue

Klauck comments, "So lange die judische Familie, das judische Haus intakt ist, droht dem Judentum keine Gefahr."[112] Of the six known Diaspora synagogues, two, at Dura[113] and Priene,[114] were almost certainly domestic meeting places; another, at Stobi,[115] probably originated as a house; and of the remaining three – Sardis, Delos,[116] and Ostia[117] – only Sardis and Ostia were clearly monumental structures. The household evidently played a central role in the common life of the Jewish community during the Hellenistic and Imperial periods.[118]

We shall focus our discussion on the inscriptional evidence recovered from the house synagogues at Dura and Stobi. From the Durene synagogue we have third century A.D. epigraphic evidence that the owner of the house, Samuel ben Yeda'ya, not only funded and supervised the conversion of his home into a synagogue, but was also πρεσβύτερος and ἄρχων, probably the highest authority of the community.[119] Kraeling argues that Samuel continued to live in the domestic suite of the enlarged complex.[120] The evidence is clearer in the case of the household synagogue at Stobi. Tiberius Polycharmus, "father of the synagogue," converted his villa into a Jewish community centre, with prayer hall, eating hall, and portico, reserving for himself and his successors the right to reside in the upper story of the complex.[121] "Fathers" (and "mothers") of synagogues were not always its leaders, but the expectation of a synagogue leader (ἀρχισυνάγωγος) was to use private funds for renovations, ornamentations, and maintenance of the community hall.[122] At Teos in Asia, for example, Proutioses (Publius Rutilius Joses) the ἀρχισυνάγωγος, built the synagogue

from its foundations.[123] Sometimes the title ἀρχισυνάγωγος was given honorifically[124] for services rendered,[125] but we may assume that leadership and
patronage went hand in hand, especially when a member's generosity extended
to the gift of his home for communal use.

Summary

This discussion suggests that the household played a central role in shaping
Graeco-Roman civilization — both in its political and social institutions and in
the hopes and expectations of its members. Literary and archaeological evidence
indicates that the ancient household was a major influence in the shaping of
ancient groups. The householder's power over the affairs of his own home
often extended to a wider sphere when he acted as patron and benefactor of
groups broader than the household. The primary social universe in which the
member of Graeco-Roman society lived was the household. The early church
could not exist in such a milieu without something of that environment leaving
its mark upon it.

Notes

1 These terms are used here only to help to identify the various elements constituting the household; they were not used consistently in the ancient world to define
these respective social relationships; cf. Gaudemet, 1969, pp. 312f.

2 Finley, 1973, p. 18.

3 For example Jos. 24:15, where בית in "as for me and my house . . ." is translated
with οἶκος in Codex A and οἰκία in Codex B.

4 For a discussion of the Old Testament evidence see Klauck, 1981, pp. 4f.; Elliott,
1981, pp. 182-86.

5 This is a point Elliott, 1981, pp. 170-82, has not taken fully enough into account in
his discussion of the household in Graeco-Roman times. See Gaudemet, 1969,
pp. 286-358, for a more balanced discussion. For different uses of οἶκος terminology see van Buren, 1937, 2119-23.

6 Elliott, p. 173; see p. 244, n. 42, for further literature. For the Homeric period see
Finley, 1977, pp. 51-107; Lacey, 1968, Nilsson, 1940, pp. 65f.; Gaudemet, 1969,
pp. 303-319.

7 For the state as modelled on the household in ancient Greece see Nilsson, 1940, p.
75; Lacey, 1986, pp. 125f. argues that the cult of Vesta, goddess of the hearth, as
part of official Roman state religion implies a similar modelling; cf. Ovid *Fasti*
6.308-318 for the connection of Vesta with the hearth.

8 For the moral responsibilities of the householder, see *Oec.* 2:5-7; for the proper
relations between husbands and wives: 3:10-16; 7:3-43; 8:2-33; for the responsibilities of overseers: 12:1-15:1; cf. also Finley, 1973, p. 17.

9 Elliott, 1981, p. 174.

10 This is evinced by the many courtyard and portable household terracota altars
excavated on the site of fifth to fourth-century B.C. Olynthus in Macedon. See
Robinson, 1938, p. 321 for courtyard altars, pp. 322-23 for portable ones; for pic-
tures see plates 73, 81; idem., 1946, plates 40, 169-173, 39, 181-183, 188. See Plato
Rep. 328C for a courtyard sacrifice. For further discussion of the Mediterranean
housecult see Wachsmuth, 1980, pp. 34-75.

11 Gaudemet, 1969, p. 314. This is well illustrated by reference to the stone relief

presented by Lacey, 1968, p. 17, where a mother, father, and child are seen before a household altar which is set before Zeus (the traditional god of the household cult); behind the family in miniature appear their ancestors, also facing Zeus; cf. Aeschylus *Pers.* 609, 620; *Coreph.* 15. For a condemnation of house shrines see Plato *Laws* 909B, but for high regard for gods of the family and class see 729C. For traditional Greek household deities see Nilsson, 1940, pp. 65f. Dionysius Halicarnassus *R.A.* 1:673 lists the Greek parallels to the Roman household gods (Penates). For ancient Roman practice of propitiation of the spirits of the dead, which continued into the imperial period, see Livy 1:20; Ovid *Fasti* 535f., 541.

12 Stommel, 1969, p. 116.

13 Ibid., p. 119.

14 Betti, 1954, p. 16.

15 Gaudemet, 1969, p. 332.

16 Ibid., p. 328.

17 Finley, 1973, p. 19. This threefold division was theoretical and these spheres of power were subject to much development and change during the Republic and early Empire.

18 Nisbet, 1968, p. 206; Gaudemet, 1969, p. 320.

19 Nisbet, p. 210.

20 See ibid., pp. 208f. This lasted until 149 B.C., when *Lex Calpurnia de Repetundis* was established and the first *Quaestia Perpetua* — a permanent commission for the examination of public crimes. Before this, offences were dealt with by the Senate and execution of justice left to the familia. But traditional values may have lingered for some time: Aulus Gellius (*N.A.* 10:23.4) cites Cato in support of the power of life and death of a husband over a wife who drinks too much wine and Seneca (*Ben.* 3:11) describes the authority of a father as *magistratus domesticus*.

21 See Gaudemet, 1969, pp. 332f.

22 Judge, 1960b, p. 31. For a description of republican ideals see Cochrane, 1957, especially 1-113; Hammond, 1951. For the breakdown of republican ideals and a discussion of the mutual comfort of the household see Judge, op. cit., pp. 29f.

23 Ibid., p. 30. Even where they were pursued, traditional values asserted themselves, as may be seen in Cato's *De Re Rustica* and Columella's work of the same title.

24 Syme, 1939, pp. 10-27, summarily sketches the domestic and political *mise en scène* on the eve of the first triumvirate. See also Judge, 1960b, p. 32.

25 Judge, 1960a, pp. 6f.

26 Idem., 1960b, p. 30.

27 Hammond, 1951, pp. 89f.; Judge, 1960b, pp. 32f.

28 For general discussion see Halliday, 1922, pp. 24-40; Ogilvie, 1986, pp. 100-105.

29 Nisbet, 1968, p. 209.

30 Loc. cit.

31 *Satyricon* 71:7; Stommel, 1969, p. 117 comments that the grave existed "als Behausung des Totes, in der sein Weiterleben gesichert werden soll unter Verhältnissen, die im allgemeinen den irdischen Lebensbedürfnissen entsprechen."

32 Nisbet, 1968, p. 209.

33 Mantle, 1978, pp. 137ff.

34 *Laws* 2:10.19; cf. 2:19.48; *De Domo Sua* 41:109.

35 *Rust.* 5:143.

36 *Rust.* 1:8.

37 Cato *Rust.* 5:143 describes such tasks.

38 Williams, 1978, p. 15.

39 Ibid., pp. 8f. notes that this is suggested by continuing inscriptions to the genius of the paterfamilias: e.g., *CIL* 4, 1679. In Judaism, too, household religious festivities were led by the head of the family. Cf. *RAC* Haus II for further discussion.

40 Pelham, 1911, p. 109.

41 Satires of the period, which ridicule liberated women who cannot be kept silent at banquets, or who gad about neglecting their household tasks, testify to a period of social change (cf. Juvenal *Sat.* 6). *Laudatio Turiae* provides a more sober account of shifting family ideals: here a woman in the absence of her exiled husband proves herself more than able to protect the *familia* and provide for her husband's needs. For discussion of shifting patterns see Rawson, 1986, pp. 1-57.

42 See Gaudemet, 1969, p. 335 for further discussion and Dio Cassius 56:10; examples of these laws are *Lex Iuliae* (*de maritandis ordinibus or de adulteriis coercendis*; cf. Berger, *PW* 122, 2362f.) and *Lex Papia Poppaea* (cf. Schiller, *PW* Suppl. 6, 227-32).

43 Syme, 1985, p. 519; see pp. 509-24 (especially 520), 459-75 for the creation of ideology in Augustus' reign.

44 Elliott, p. 175.

45 For Augustus' use of family ideology, see his speech to married and unmarried men in the Forum in Dio Cassius 56:1-10.

46 *Res Gestae Divi Augusti* 35.

47 Judge, 1960b, p. 33.

48 See Tiberius' eulogy of Augustus in Dio Cassius 56:41.9f.

49 See Pliny's description of Trajan as a father in Lewis and Reinhold, 1966, p. 99.

50 See ibid., 20, pp. 85-88 for oaths of allegiance. Judge, 1960b, p. 34 provides an oath sworn by Paphlagonians and Roman businessmen to the house of Caesar.

51 For the state as a family see Lacey, 1986, pp. 125f.

52 Judge, 1960b, p. 33; political and household authority were similar even in Republican times: for the power of imperium as similar to patria potestas in the first century B.C. see Lacey, 1986, pp. 131f.

53 Dill, 1904, p. 267, writing in the context of collegia but also applicable more generally.

54 Livy 4:30.

55 Livy 25:1.

56 *Laws* 2:10.25-26.

57 Cited by Nock, 1933, p. 74.

58 Ibid., pp. 116f.

59 Thus, e.g., Moore, 1920, pp. 236f.; Nock, 1964, pp. 11f.

60 Though mythic the practice probably had some basis in fact; cf. Burkert, 1982, pp. 3f. for a discussion of wandering Orphic priests.

61 Origen *Contra Celsum* 6:24.; cf. 2 Tim. 3:6-7.

62 *Papyri Graecae Magicae*[2] (ed. K. Preisedanz), I.84f. (Preisedanz I,6). For evidence not later than A.D. 300: III.192 (I, 40); IV.1859-1862 (I, 130)

63 I.e. Villa Item, Casa Omerica in Pompei; Villa Farnesina in Rome; similarly, the so-called "House of the (Isiac) Mysteries at Antioch-on-the-Orontes," where there seems to be a portrayal of Isiac initiation, but there is no evidence for actual cultic activity. (See A.M.G. Little, *Roman Bridal Drama at the Villa of the Mysteries*, 1972.)

64 Text in Vogliano, 1933; English abstract, pp. 264-70 by Christine Alexander.

65 Among the more famous examples is the mithraeum under San Clemente at Rome, dating from the third century and consisting of a transformed private courtyard (for further discussion and literature see Snyder, 1985, p. 76), and that

under Sta. Prisca, from the second century (see Vermaseren and van Essen, 1965, pp. 111f. for the history of the mithraeum and MacMullen, 1984, pp. 39-40 and notes for further discussion and literature). MacMullen's dating of the house church is unconvincing; Vermaseren and van Essen, p. 114, n. 3 place it in the third century).

66 Cited by White, 1982, p. 414.

67 Ibid., p. 420.

68 Vermaseren, 1960, Vol. I, nos. 216-23. For further literature and discussion see MacMullen, 1981, pp. 118-19 and notes; White, 1982, pp. 423ff.

69 Vermaseren, 1960, Vol. I, nos. 34-70. For further discussion see Dura Report VII-VIII. An earlier mithraeum founded at the end of the first century may have met in the house of Epinicus and his son Alexander, successive priests of the cult; the absence of a temple in the area of the inscriptions may suggest a household cult. See ibid., pp. 128ff. for inscriptions.

70 *The Secret God*, p. 56, cited by White, 1982, p. 421, n. 82.

71 Cf. Smith, 1977, pp. 212-16 for a sarapeum in a converted stoa-domicile.

72 For example *SIG³* 985.

73 *IG* 9:4, 1299; the inscription together with a commentary may be found in Osers, 1975.

74 For further discussion see White, 1982, pp. 380f.; Tinh, 1982, pp. 110f.

75 *Syll.³* 3, 985.

76 Wiegand and Schrader, 1904, pp. 172-178.

77 Ibid., House XXII.

78 May this be an analogy for the curious description of Polycrates as eighth in a line of seven bishops who were also his relatives (Eusebius *Historia Ecclesiastica* 5:24.6)?

79 White suggests this reconstruction of the archaeological and inscriptional evidence. For further discussion see Dura Report VII-VIII, pp. 278ff., inscr. 907-8; 257f. and n. 31.; 398, n. 35 (for the family of Nasor and Hairan as prominent figures in the cult and the owners of a large house comprising part of the precinct).

80 Diogenes Laertius 6:2.23.

81 Wycherley, 1961, p. 155.

82 Diogenes Laertius 10:10.

83 Ibid., 10.17; for further comment see Wycherley, 1959, pp. 73-7; 1962, p. 15.

84 Seneca *Ep.* 76:1-5; Epictetus *Diss.* 4:1.177; Dio *Orations* 15:1; Lucian *Nigr.* 1-7; Aulus Gellius *A.N.* 2:2.1-2; 2:11.1.

85 *Acts of Justin* 3.

86 Dio *Orat.* 4:12-13; 6:14; 8:4-5; 9:4; Diog. Laer. 6:22.

87 *A.N.* 9:2.1-11; cf. also Epictetus *Diss.* 3:22.10; Dio *Orat.* 32:9; Lucian *Runaways* 14.

88 He was especially fond of ridiculing the mendicant Cynic who amassed fortunes from begging from the wealthy; cf. *Timon* 56-7; *Fisherman* 33-4; *Runaways* 17. These were regarded as heroes in other circles: cf. Diog. Laer. 6:83,86,99; Plutarch *Cons. ad Ux.* 609C describes the reception of wandering philosophers.

89 *Diss.* 4:11.35.

90 See the description of Paul of Antioch, presumably instructing disciples in the home of Origen's patroness (Eusebius H.E. 6:2.13-14); for further discussion see "Scholars and Patrons: Christianity and High Society in Alexandria" by L.M. White in *Christian Teaching. Studies in Honor of Lemoine L. Lewis* (ed. E. Ferguson), Abilene, Texas, 1981, pp. 328-42, unavailable to me. Cf. also *Contra Celsum* 3:55.

91 Lucian's *Career* 15,18; similarly, Dio *Orat.* 77/78:34-35.

92 *On Salaried Posts* 1-4.

93 Lucian *The Lover of Lies* 14.

94 For further comment see Hock, 1976, pp. 41-53; Malherbe, 1982, pp. 48-59.
95 *Ep.* 8; Diog. Laer. 3.9, passim; Dio *Orat.* 2:79; cf. also Philostratus *Lives of the Sophists* 600.
96 The titles of Graeco-Roman clubs were various; for further discussion see Poland, 1909, loc. cit.; Waltzing, Vol. 1, 1895, pp. 32ff.
97 *CIL* 6, 9148, 10261-63.
98 Waltzing, Vol. 1, 1895, p. 215; cf. n. 2 and Vol. 3, 1899, pp. 342f. for inscriptions; cf. also Liebenam, 1890, pp. 272f.
99 See Ziebarth, 1896, pp. 6f.; Poland, 1909, pp. 87-88, passim, for further discussion.
100 *CIG* 2448; cf. Poland, p. 87 for further discussion.
101 *Syll²* 734, cf. Poland. loc. cit. for further discussion; see also *Syll²* 641 for the family association of Poseidonius (third to second century B.C.; made up of the entire household community).
102 Ziebarth, 1896, p. 9.
103 Dill, 1911, p. 270.
104 Hands, 1968, pp. 52, passim; MacMullen, 1974, p. 76.
105 For the wealth required of a leader see Waltzing, Vol. 1, 1895, pp. 397f, 406f.
106 Müller, 1905, p. 185 cites an example of an official using his private funds to renovate the club's *columbarium*.
107 Poland, 1909, pp. 421, 498 for the treasurer as founder or well-to-do and re-elected several times; also Liebenam, 1890, pp. 217f.
108 MacMullen, 1974, p. 76 and notes.
109 Kornemann, 1901, p. 422.
110 Especially in the case of treasurers: cf. Poland, 1909, pp. 366, 377f.
111 For further discussion see Waltzing, Vol. 1, 1895, pp. 425ff.; these patrons were often given titles of higher ranking club officials, but these were usually purely honorific.
112 Klauck, 1981, p. 93; for the importance of Jewish family life in the preservation of religious identity see Edersheim, 1985, pp. 86-181; for further general discussion of Diaspora Judaism see Meeks, 1983, pp. 32-39.
113 See Kraeling, 1956, for the Dura report.
114 Mistaken for a house church by Filson, 1939, p. 108; for archaeological discussion see Wiegand and Schrader, 1904, pp. 480f.; also, Klauck, 1981, p. 95.
115 Hengel, 1966, pp. 145-83.
116 Ibid., p. 161.
117 For Sardis and Ostia cf. Kraabel, 1981, pp. 79f.; White, 1982, pp. 440f.
118 For discussion see Gutmann, 1975, pp. xiif.; Kraabel, 1981, pp. 81f.
119 Kraeling, 1956, pp. 331f.; 263-64; Tiles 23, 24, p. 277.
120 Ibid., p. 11.
121 *CIJ* I, 694.
122 See Theissen, 1982, pp. 74-5 for discussion and examples.
123 *CIJ* II, 744; cf. also *CIJ* I, 720, 722, 723; *CIJ* II, 1404 for other examples and White, 1982, p. 451f. for further discussion.
124 As was apparently the case with the title πρεσβύτερος (cf. Frey, 1936, pp. lxxxvi-lxxxvii).
125 See *CIJ* II, 741, 756 for female ἀρχισυνάγωγαι probably given the title for patronage; further examples are cited by Meeks, 1983, p. 35 and notes.

Chapter Two
The Pauline Epistles

Part One: The Genuine Pauline Epistles

This section reviews the work of recent New Testament scholars who have employed sociological methodology in their study of the churches represented by the genuine Pauline epistles (Romans, 1 and 2 Corinthians, Galatians, Philippians, 1 Thessalonians, and Philemon).[1]

First, we shall locate Paul's churches in a sectarian milieu. A discussion of the house church setting of the Pauline sect will follow. Finally, we shall attempt to identify the leaders of the local communities.

The Early Pauline Churches as Sectarian

Recent students of the New Testament have become increasingly aware of the benefits of treating early Christianity as a sectarian movement. The term "sect" has been applied to New Testament communities in various ways. Christopher Rowland in his book *Christian Origins*, for example, entitles the section in which he discusses the development of early Christianity, "The Emergence of a Messianic Sect."[2] Rowland uses the term appropriately to place the earliest Christian groups in a milieu of Jewish religious plurality, i.e., as a sect among sects. This is one possible use of the term. But it has also been employed to describe the self-definition of early Christianity *vis-à-vis* contemporary Graeco-Roman society.[3] Applied in this way, the early church is placed not only in the context of its more defined religious environment, but also in a broader and more general societal one. A decade ago, Robin Scroggs contributed to the consideration of the earliest church as a sect by identifying the use of the term in contemporary sociology, and by showing how sociological models of sectarianism can help to illuminate certain aspects of the early church.[4] More recently two scholars, Elliott and MacDonald, have successfully applied Bryan Wilson's typology of sectarianism to 1 Peter and the genuine Pauline letters.[5] They have shown that Wilson's sect typology helps to situate early Pauline communities in their contemporary environment and to identify and account for certain challenges which confronted them. In the following discussion we shall present Wilson's

---

Notes to this chapter appear on pp. 47-54.

sect type and show how closely evidence from early Pauline communities is in accord with it.

According to Wilson, sects typically possess many of the following features:

> The sect is a clearly defined community; it is of a size which permits only a minimal range of diversity of conduct; it seeks itself to rigidify a pattern of behaviour and to make coherent its structure of values and ideals, and against every other organization of values and ideals, and against every other social context possible for its adherents, offering itself as an all-embracing, divinely prescribed society. The sect is not only an ideological unit, seeking to enforce behaviour on those who accept belief, and seeking every occasion to draw the faithful apart from the rest of society and into the company of each other. . . . The sect, as a protest group, has always developed its own distinctive ethic, belief and practices, against the background of the wider society; its own protest is conditioned by the economic, social, ideological and religious circumstances prevailing at the time of its emergence and development.[6]

Whilst we must be careful not to force first century social phenomena to fit contemporary sociological models, there are many aspects of the earliest Pauline communities which reflect several of the characteristics listed by Wilson.

Judging by Paul's language, an event of profound significance for members of the communities he founded was baptism. As an initiation ritual, baptism probably served as a preeminent boundary-creating and community-defining symbol. In 1 Cor. 12:13 Paul states that baptism marks entry into "one body," and in 6:11 this is presented as a washing which has sanctified and justified community members. He uses the language of life and death in Rom. 6:3-4 to indicate the radically new life which the baptized have begun to enjoy. Paul's reference to "outsiders" (οἱ ἔχω) in 1 Cor. 5:12, 13 and 1 Thes. 4:12 indicates a consciousness of being "inside." And the terms he uses to describe his fellow Christians as "saints" (ἄγιοι), or a predestined and called elect (Rom. 8:30), also arise from an awareness of being a group separate from the world. The language of separation is present where Paul contrasts the present state of the baptized with their former lives of worldly vice (1 Cor. 6:9-10). Lists of virtues and vices, such as those found in Gal. 5:19-25, define what attitudes and behaviour the person who has new life in Christ is to avoid and pursue. The apostle exhorts the sect not to be "conformed to this world" (αἰών – Rom. 12:2). And he contrasts the true monotheistic belief with the corruption and deceit of pagan polytheism; in Rom. 1:18f., the creation of gods by humankind is linked with immorality and disobedience toward the true God. The former pagan beliefs of Christians are presented as a form of bondage (Gal. 4:8).

Members are exhorted to control their relationships with outsiders. In 1 Cor. 6:1f., for example, they are admonished not to seek the legal advice of outsiders to solve problems within the group. How can saints seek the advice of the unrighteous outsider? How can those who are to judge angels rely on the world's judgments? Another example is the advice concerning marriage with outsiders. Paul does not encourage divorce when only one member of a married couple is a believer (1 Cor. 7:12-16), but he forbids marriage with an unbeliever. In 2 Cor. 6:14-15, Paul supports his advice by piling up an extraordinary series of opposing descriptions to portray the differences which exist between believers and unbelievers: righteousness – iniquity, light – darkness, Christ – Belial, the temple of God – idols. "Come out from them, and be separate from them" Paul quotes (v.17). The Pauline sect is constituted by people who have broken with the world.

The baptized belong to a new community, where distinctions between slave and free, male and female, Jew and Greek – normative indices of contemporary society – are relativized in the face of a dynamic new communal identity (Gal. 3:27-28). To be "in Christ," a favourite expression Paul uses to describe the identity of members of the community, implies a whole new set of relationships – not only the destruction of old significations of status and social identity, but also the creation of new ones. Paul's description of members as brothers and sisters and his description of himself as father (1 Cor. 4:15) or mother (Gal. 4:19) of the community are examples of what Meeks has called the language of belonging.[7] Entry into the community implies inclusion in a new family – new social patterns, which, if not entirely supplanting the old ones (e.g. 1 Cor. 11:2-16; 7:21-22), reconstructs them according to the new life in Christ.

Wilson further identifies seven subtypes of sectarianism within his more general sect type. Each subtype represents a different pattern of sectarianism arising out of different characteristic responses to the world. The "conversionist sect" is a type which Elliott and MacDonald employ in their discussion of 1 Peter and Paul. By defining further the sectarian pattern adduced from Paul letters, they are able to assess more accurately challenges to the sectarian identity of the group and its place in the contemporary society.[8] Wilson defines the conversionist sect as follows:

> The world is corrupt because men are corrupt; if men can be changed then the world will be changed. Salvation is seen not as available through objective agencies but only by a profoundly felt, supernaturally wrought transformation of the self. The objective will not change but the acquisition of a new subjective orientation to it will be salvation.
>
> Clearly this subjective conversion will be possible only on the promise of a change in external reality at some future time, or the prospect of the individual's transfer to another sphere. This is the ideological or doctrinal aspect of the matter, but the essential sociological fact is that what men must do to be saved is to undergo emotional transformation – a conversion experience. This is the proof of having transcended the evil of the world. Since it is a permanent and timelessly valid transcendence, some future condition of salvation is often posited in which objective circumstances come to correspond to the subjective sense of salvation, that he is saved *now*. Thus he can face the evil of the world, the processes of change that threaten men with decay and death, because he is assured of an unchanging condition *and feels this*. This response is the *conversionist* response to the world.[9]

If any person be in Christ, Paul says in 2 Cor. 5:17, "he or she is a new creation." The central parallel between the conversionist type and the Pauline sect is the emphasis which Paul places on the transformation or conversion of the members of the community because of their belief in Christ. The burden of Paul's argument in Romans 6-8 is to show that belief in Christ represents a transformation of the individual, no longer under the constraints of the Law, but renewed with the life of the Spirit. This is a divinely wrought salvation. "God has sent the Spirit of his Son into our hearts, crying, 'Abba! Father!'" (Gal. 4:6; Rom. 8:15-16). This salvation is in the present tense: "Behold now is the acceptable time; behold now is the day of salvation." (2 Cor. 6:2) But if now, there is also a vital element of "not yet." What believers have begun to experience now foreshadows the more complete state of salvation which is imminent. Creation groans for the eschatalogical adoption of the sons and daughers of God and its freedom from decay (Rom. 8:19-25). If some of the sisters and brothers have already died before the full revelation of the sons of God, there is no cause for alarm; the "children of light" are to remain vigilant and wait with eager expectation for their destined salvation (1 Thes. 4:13-5:11).

Wilson warns that it is a futile exercise to use a sect typology merely to classify; it is necessary to move beyond classification and to see how the type helps to illuminate "the expectable logic of the social arrangements of a given genus of phenomena."[10] In the remainder of this section we shall indicate briefly how Wilson's conversionist sect type helps to enlighten our understanding of tensions within the Pauline communities, a topic to which we shall return in subsequent chapters. The pressure to evangelize and to draw others into the fold raises particular difficulties for the conversionist sect, and these will be discussed in more detail in our treatment of the Shepherd of Hermas. But it is enough to state here that the tension between reaching out to and separating itself from the world is intensified in the conversionist sect. MacDonald has cast light on tensions which arose within the Paul's churches as a result of their sectarian identity and goals.[11] For example, the organization of the mission around the households of well-to-do patrons not only contributed to the success of Paul's mission, but also resulted in a certain ambiguity about group boundaries. Are patrons to leave off from their business associations, indeed their business ventures, or are the sect's values and identity of separation to be compromised? Paul's inconsistent remarks regarding the consumption of meat offered to idols reveals a similar tension: in 1 Cor. 6:12-20, where Paul focuses on the moral purity of the Christian sect, he seems to discourage the consumption of food offered to idols. But in 1 Cor. 8 he offers a more liberal interpretation (cf. also the differing statements on this issue in 1 Cor. 10:1-22 and 23-33). As Theissen has shown, the rough and tumble of daily life in the world dictates that the more prosperous members of the community be permitted to indulge in banquets where meat offered to idols is inevitably served.[12] Ambiguity in group boundaries is even promoted by Paul when he advises spouses of non-believers not to seek divorce. Instead, they are to use their relationship as an opportunity for evangelization (1 Cor. 7:16). Comparison of such group challenges with the more specific tensions which contemporary conversionist sects undergo, has enabled scholars to show that Paul's teaching was not formulated as an exercise in doctrine, but as a response to particular social situations.

The Household Context of the Christian Sect

New Testament scholarship is increasingly recognizing the Graeco-Roman household as an important element in the rise, growth, and institutionalization of the early Christian church.[13] Malherbe argues that we will never really understand the early Christian church unless we attempt to understand it from within, and the fact that this statement occurs in a chapter entitled "House Churches and Their Problems" indicates that he thinks house churches are the place to enter.[14] He is correct. Writing nearly fifty years ago, Floyd Filson stated that although early Christian worship was indebted to Jewish practices the house church made possible "a distinctly Christian worship and fellowship from the very first days of the apostolic age."[15] We shall try to understand the growth and organization of the Pauline sect by analysing the role of households and household leaders in the apostle's mission.

Hospitality and Gospel Transmission

In an article contemporary with that of Filson, D. W. Riddle noted that the spread of the Gospel in the early church depended upon the hospitality of householders who received Christian missionaries and permitted them to use their homes as bases for their work.[16] The portrait painted of Paul in Acts presents the apostle as a traveller who converts households of the relatively well-to-do and then stays with them for varying periods of time (Acts 16:14-15,40; 17:1-9; 18:5-8).[17] Luke's portrayal of Paul as a man on the move shows him relying on the hospitality of fellow and sister Christians (Acts 18:1-4; 20:6-12; 21:4,7,8; 21:15,17).

A similar picture emerges from Paul's letters.[18] In Rom. 16:23, Paul mentions Gaius, "host to me and to the whole church." Again, he asks Philemon, another host of the church (Phlm. 2), to prepare a guest room for him (v.22); Paul evidently is planning to lodge with him. A similar reference to hospitality is probably behind Paul's reference to Phoebe as his "patroness" (προστάτις – Rom. 16:2).[19]

There is other indirect evidence that household hospitality played an important role in the life of the earliest church. Theissen correctly argues that hospitality is part of the social backdrop assumed in Paul's vilification of the "super-apostles" in 2 Cor. 10-12.[20] In short, Paul's opponents were itinerant Christian missionaries who had taken literally Christ's injunction to leave all and follow him, and so relied for their livelihood on the hospitality of members of the Corinthian community. Letters of recommendation gained them welcome and access to the community's resources (2 Cor. 3:1; 10:12).

The conversion of households with their dependants also helps to account for the growth of the community. The references in Acts to the salvation or baptism of entire households (10:2; 11:14; 16:15, 31-34; 18:8) are in accord with Paul's reference to the household (οἰκία) of Stephanas as the first converts in Achaia (1 Cor. 16:15; cf. 1 Cor. 1:16 where οἶκος is used to define the family). This may be interpreted as evidence that Stephanas and his dependants were baptized together. But there is also evidence that entire households were not always baptized; Philemon's runaway slave, Onesimus, was probably not a Christian at the time of his escape from his master (Phlm. vs. 11, 15-16).[21] L. M. White argues with justification that the extended household community provided a network for further expansion into the community, a factor which helps to account for Christianity's rapid spread throughout the Roman

Empire.[22] Judge speaks of "networks" in this regard — namely, social factors such as patronage networks arising from the conversion of well-to-do house-holders.[23] The conversion of such a householder allowed access to members of the extended household community, which in turn provided opportunities for contact with other networks.[24] Three such networks in Corinth, for example, were probably the extended households of Gaius, Crispus, and Stephanas — all very likely well-to-do patrons whom Paul baptized (1 Cor. 16:15-16).[25]

Household units similar to those associated with these three members also help to explain the tendency of the apostolic church to split into factions.[26] Interpreters may be claiming too much when they argue that the followers of Apollos, Peter, and Paul represented various household groups (1 Cor. 1:12),[27] but we will see in later chapters that the household setting of the early church helps to account for community schisms.[28]

Hospitality was important not only for the initial proclamation of the Gospel; willing hosts also provided the necessary locale for the continuation of the group during Paul's absence. In fact it is with reference to the establishment of house churches that Theissen and others have called Paul a "community-organizer" or "founder" or "minor founder."[29] Paul's references to churches in the homes of certain individuals suggest that he laid the foundations of his churches in the household. This is indicated in Rom. 16:5, 1 Cor. 16:19, and Phlm. 2, where he links the church by use of the phrase κατ' οἶκον ἐκκλησία to the household of particular hosts. In Rom. 16:23, a similar association is implied. Scholars have inferred the presence of other house churches in Paul's communities from further passages: the reference to Phoebe as "patroness" of Paul and the church in Cenchreae (Rom. 16:1);[30] Paul's recommendation of Stephanas and his household as devoted to the service of the saints (1 Cor. 16:15);[31] greetings to various groups in Rom. 16:14 and 15.[32]

The number of house churches in a given locale is a topic of debate.[33] Klauck, for example, argues that the preposition κατά in Rom. 16:5, 1 Cor. 16:19, and Phlm. 2 should be understood distributively, i.e. "die sich hausweise konstituierende Kirche."[34] Gielen, however, argues that Klauck and others are guilty of eisegesis. Contemporary papyrological evidence, as well as the fact that the formula occurs in the context of a greeting, indicates that the preposition should be interpreted simply as ἐν, i.e., "the church in the house of X."[35] Gielen is correct to point to some form of common meeting in Corinth, as the reference to Gaius as ὁ ξένος ... ὅλης τῆς ἐκκλησίας would seem to imply, but this does not exclude the possibility of further meetings or even eucharists in Corinth. Afanassieff's contention that only one eucharist could have been celebrated because of Paul's theology of the church reads concerns of a later period into his ecclesiology. Both Gielen and Afanassieff fail to account successfully for the greetings in Rom. 16:14-15, where separate groups seem to be indicated, as well as the evidence concerning the household of Stephanas in 1 Cor. 16:15. In our view, while there were probably meetings of the whole community in *some* places (e.g. Corinth), in other places this may not have been the case (e.g. Rome[36]).

Wealth, Patronage, and the Pauline House Church

The traditional picture of the early Christian church as a movement consisting solely of the dregs of society has been challenged in recent scholarship.[37] Both Acts and Paul's letters contain evidence which indicates that a small number of relatively wealthy individuals belonged to churches associated with Paul. Theissen identifies four criteria with which to assess the degree of wealth of individuals mentioned by Paul: to be active in a civil or religious office; to possess a house; to have served Paul or the church or both; to be able to make a journey.[38] (Theissen notes that the last two criteria of themselves do not point to wealth).

He concludes from his analysis of members described in the Corinthian epistles that the persons in leading positions (such as Gaius, Crispus, and Stephanas) were well-to-do, and from this he infers that Paul actively sought to convert the relatively wealthy, who could then provide a house large enough to act as a base for a church and also act as leaders in his absence. The instances of the wealth of Gaius and Crispus are relatively straightforward. Gaius was presumably wealthy enough to own a house of a size sufficient to accommodate a meeting of the whole community (Rom. 16:23), and, assuming that the description of Crispus in Acts 18:8 as an ἀρχισυνάγωγος is accurate,[39] it is probable that he too was wealthy.[40] But Malherbe criticizes Theissen's interpretation of Stephanas' social status. He doubts that Stephanas was the patron of a house church and this leads him to question wealth as a criterion for leadership in Paul's churches.[41] The cumulative weight of the evidence with respect to the wealth of Stephanas, however, is against him, and, as we shall see, the case for wealth as an important determining factor in local leadership is stronger than Malherbe admits. It is true that Paul does not state directly that the church met in Stephanas' home, but the fact that Paul singles out Stephanas with Crispus and Gaius in 1 Cor. 1:14-16 as the only individuals whom he baptized — both wealthy and one certainly offering his home as a meeting place, combined with his reference to Stephanas' household as devoted to the service of the church — makes Theissen's interpretation of the role of Stephanas as a house-church patron compelling. Because Paul mentions Stephanas' household twice (1 Cor. 1:16; 16:15), refers to the service of Stephanas' household to the community, and exhorts the local church to be subject to individuals such as him, Meeks locates Stephanas' social status "fairly high on the scale of wealth."[42]

How did the presence of relatively wealthy members affect life in the sect? Research into the status of the members associated with Paul's churches has led scholars to conclude that Paul did not seek to upset existing household and patronage arrangements. He certainly relegated them to a secondary position when he sought to define the identity of the sect: in the light of the imminent return of Christ, for example, Paul urges wives to live as though they had no husbands, and those who have dealings with the world to act as though they had none (1 Cor. 7:29-31). This is one face of Paul. But there is also a more conservative one: earlier in the same chapter he instructs slaves to remain in their servile state (v. 21),[43] elsewhere he tells women to cover their heads as a sign of submission to men (11:2-13), and he respects the rights of the slave-owner Philemon over his slave Onesimus (Phlm v.14). If in Christ there is no longer male nor female, slave nor free, the expression of this in the community is not to deny the validity of these distinctions, but to transform them into vehicles of community cohesion. Philemon is not only the master of Onesimus, but also his brother (Phlm. v. 16). Theissen, following Ernst Troeltsch, names Paul's community ethic "love patriarchalism." He writes:

> love patriarchalism takes social differences for granted but ameliorates them through an obligation of respect and love, an obligation imposed upon those who are socially stronger. From the weaker are required subordination, fidelity, and esteem. Whatever the intellectual sources feeding into this ethos, with it the great part of Hellenistic primitive Christianity mastered the task of shaping social relationships within a community which, on the one hand, demanded of its members a high degree of solidarity and brotherliness and, on the other, encompassed various social strata.[44]

While this was a laudable ideal, it was fraught with difficulty, as one may imagine if one tries to conceive how a slave could also be a brother or sister. But for all its attendant problems, it continued to be invoked, as we shall see when we discuss the *Shepherd of Hermas* and *1 Clement*.

The ideal of love patriarchalism is well illustrated by reference to Paul's advice regarding meat offered to idols (1 Cor. 8:9ff.; 10:25ff.). Here, in the face of status-specific behaviour, Paul's advises wealthier members to accommodate their behaviour to less prosperous Christians, while at the same time preserving the factual privileges of their status.[45] Similarly, the conflict surrounding a eucharist at Corinth (1 Cor. 11:17-34), where, again, class-specific practices seem to have disrupted the *esprit de corps* of the Corinthian community, is not resolved by denying that wealthy members are entitled to privileges, only by his insistence that they are not to exercise them at the common table.[46] And more generally, the pattern of leadership exercised by a well-to-do householder is in accord with this pattern. It is to this topic of leadership that we now turn.

House-Church Leadership

If the Graeco-Roman household was the backdrop for the daily life of the Pauline communities, which members occupied roles of leadership? This is a topic which has continued to occupy the attention of New Testament scholars. But more recent studies have noted that important roles of local governance are to be found in the household leadership offered by house church patrons. Filson foreshadowed the contemporary discussion when he noted that the host of a house church, "almost inevitably a man [sic] of some education, with a fairly broad background and at least some administrative ability," was a likely candidate for local leadership.[47] Much earlier, in 1909, Ernst von Dobschütz identified ten types of actions a local house church patron undertook on behalf of the local church:

> (1) Hergeben des Lokals für die Gemeindeversammlung, (2) vielleicht auch Herstellung der nötigen Ordnung dabei, (3) Vorbeten, (4) Vorlesen, (5) Vorsingen, (6) Gewährung von Unterkunft und Unterhalt für zureisende Brüder, (7) von Unterstützung für Arme, (8) Stellung von Kaution (vgl. Jason Apg. 17:9), (9) Vertretung vor Gericht (Patronisieren!), (10)

gelegentlich vielleicht eine Reise im Interesse der Gemeinde, kurz alle Pfli-
chten, sie später dem Vorsteher, dem Bischof zufielen, aber alles als freiwil-
lige Leistung, ohne rechtlichen Auftrag, ohne gehaltsmässige Vergütung. . . .[48]

Holmberg, a contemporary scholar, comments that with the exception of points
3 to 5 these functions are recognizable in Paul's letters and Acts. Stephanas, for
example, owns a house (probably 1 and 2), he makes a journey on behalf of the
church (10), and he serves the church in various ways (probably 6 and 7). And
he argues further, that apart from functions 3 to 5 all these listed tasks presup-
pose a certain degree of wealth and social standing.[49] Similarly, Elliott argues
that the heads of the households where Christians met for worship were the
most obvious candidates to assume the responsibilities of the management of
community affairs because of their already existent social status and economic
resources.[50]

Bryan Wilson has commented that newly emerging religious sects are often
marked by a surprising versatility and fluidity of institutional structures. In the
case of the earliest Pauline communities, there is evidence that at least one
church (Corinth) was challenged by certain religious manifestations which
threatened to undermine the solidarity of the group. Even if Corinth was a
"problem church" (it is probably for that reason that we learn so much about it,
not because Paul saw in it an ideal "charismatic church order" as many German
scholars are wont to interpret Paul's corrective statements in 1 Cor. 12 and
14),[51] we should not underestimate the power of various social manifestations,
such as those demonstrated by the πνευματικόί (1 Cor. 12:1), to steer the community down new paths. But having stated this, one should also note that Paul
recommended certain individuals as leaders within the communities he
founded and recognized the legitimacy of their oversight. Most easily identifiable among these are the apostles, prophets, and teachers mentioned in 1 Cor.
12:28.[52] But alongside these there are also other leaders who are mentioned in 1
Cor. 12:28 and 16:16, Rom. 12:8, and 1 Thes. 5:12, and Phil. 1:1. In 1 Cor.
12:28, Paul mentions κυβέρνησις as a gift, and when he mentions a
προϊστάμενος in Rom. 12:8 he probably has a similar function in mind. When
one compares the use of this term in 1 Thes. 5:12, it seems likely that
προϊστάμενοι were in some position of leadership. Paul exhorts the Thessalonians to "respect" (RSV; εἰδέναι) those "over them."[53] If one compares the
RSV translation of προϊστάμενος in Rom 12:8 and 1 Thes. 5:12, one discovers
different nuances of the same term. In the former passage the term is translated
as "he who gives aid," where "aid" refers to material help.[54] In the latter passage, however, the translators emphasize the aspect of the term which indicates
leadership. In fact, in contemporary usage the term connotes meanings of both
patronage and leadership.[55] If we interpret the term keeping both of these
nuances in mind, then a probable inference is that those who act as patrons are
in some sense also involved in the governance of the community. The evidence
which we have concerning Stephanas is in accord with this interpretation. Paul
urges that the Corinthians submit themselves (ὑποτάσσεσθαι) to men like
Stephanas, who have devoted themselves to the ministry of the community (1
Cor. 16:15). The exhortation to submit to "such men" (οἱ τοιούτοι) is a general description and is not necessarily restricted to patrons (Paul may also have

in mind apostles, prophets, and teachers, for example[56]), but the evidence listed above suggests that one group he was probably referring to was the community's patrons. As Meeks notes, the evidence of 1 Thes. 5:12, 1 Cor. 12:28 (and, we add, 1 Cor. 16:15) indicates that "a position of authority grows out of the benefits that persons of relatively higher wealth and status could confer on the community."[57] Similarly, Holmberg cautiously suggests the following summary of the evidence presented above,

> in most of Paul's churches we have a group of persons who teach, guide, transmit divine revelations, expound the scriptures and formulate God's will in concrete, everyday life, and here we find the prophets and teachers. . . . Beside this group we find another, not so clearly defined, consisting of people with sufficient initiative, wealth, and compassion to care for the sick and poor, to receive travelling missionaries and other Christians, to be able to accommodate the worshippers and the communal meals of the church in their own houses, sometimes travelling on behalf of the church and generally taking administrative responsibility.[58]

In the case of the reference to ἐπίσκοποι and διάκονοι in Phil. 1:1, the reference is too general to determine whether these leaders fit into this pattern. But in our discussion of the Pastoral epistles we will see that in that community, overseers were probably wealthier members of the community. The cumulative evidence permits one to speculate that a similar situation prevailed in Philippi.

How "official" were the various functions of leadership in Paul's churches? David Moberg's model of contemporary sect development, used heuristically, helps us identify various forces which encouraged and retarded the institutionalization process in the early Pauline churches.[59]

Moberg calls the earliest stage of institutionalization of sects "incipient organization." This term describes the earliest days of the community, in which the group is dominated by a "charismatic, authoritative, prophetic leader"[60] and structures are relatively formless. The second stage, "formal organization," refers to a period of increased efforts by leaders to consolidate the membership through the formulation of ethical codes, the definition of belief, or the development of rituals.[61] Now the evidence of the New Testament indicates that Paul's churches were probably somewhere between Moberg's first two stages of institutionalization. Holmberg and, more recently, MacDonald argue that Paul was a "charismatic" (using the term sociologically) leader and that, as long as he was alive and available to the churches he founded, there was no fully fledged institutional structure of the type we find developing within a generation after his death.[62] Paul's letters bear testimony to the authority he enjoyed even while absent and to the fact that he continued all the time to be the primary source of direction. While Paul does recommend certain individuals as leaders, there is good reason to suppose that local authority structures were relatively fluid while the apostle was still alive: the fact that he feels obliged to call for obedience to particular people; the variety of nomenclature he uses to describe what were probably similar functions of governance in 1 Thes. 5: 12, 1 Cor. 12:28, Rom. 12:8 and Phil. 1:1; the variety of functions in the Corinthian church; the lack of division between local leadership, leadership for the maintenance of contact between different churches, and leadership for evangelization.[63]

However fluid institutions may have been, Paul looked to local members to solve internal disputes; there must have existed individuals in a position to expel immoral members from the meetings (1 Cor. 5:1-5), or to help resolve antagonisms between members (1 Cor. 6:1-5). He does not give precise instructions concerning how these tasks are to be accomplished; he assumes they will be done, and presumably relies on the community to take the appropriate steps. He is a parent (e.g., 1 Thes. 2:7; 1 Cor. 4:14) and, consonant with the paternal metaphor, he expects his children to grow up and take control of their own affairs (1 Cor. 3:1-4). In a situation like this we may assume that institutions would have quickly developed to provide the kind of community governance necessary for the continuation of the church.

How did leaders arise? Paul states that Stephanas and his household appointed themselves (ἔταξαν ἑαυτούς) to the service of the saints (1 Cor. 1:15). Did Paul appoint them as leaders, or did they volunteer their services?[64] This question has been a topic of much debate.[65] And it has tremendous significance for one's interpretation of *1 Clem.* 42:4 and 44:2, where the community's first leaders are treated as appointees. But perhaps the way the question is traditionally phrased is misleading. For even if Paul did not establish formal leaders when he left communities, those who acted as leaders nonetheless gained their legitimacy from recognition by the apostle.[66] It is fair to argue that in Paul's presence, as in his absence, household leadership emerged "from below" in the community and was legitimated "from above" by the apostle.[67]

The evidence in Paul's letters, then, suggests that the process of institutionalization[68] was relatively open while Paul was still alive. Whatever authority householders possessed, it is unlikely that there was a single leader of the community. The openness with which Paul expects instructions to be carried out in 1 Cor. 5:5, 6:5., and 16:3 suggests that at this date the Corinthian church did not possess an integrated body of leaders. We cannot expect that all communities developed in the same way; Phil. 1:1 may indicate that in some communities more patterned organization developed more quickly and perhaps with less turmoil. But the evidence generally suggests that while Paul was still alive the process of institutionalization was in its early stages. The passage of time, the growth of the group, the physical absence of the apostle, the repeated action of certain members — all these factors encouraged the development of organizational patterns, however informal.[69] Some positions, such as those of apostles, prophets, and teachers, were relatively well defined. Others, such as household leaders, though identifiable and possessing a degree of permanency, were probably not functionally discrete. But because house-church patrons provided the group with relative continuity in a period of development and with structure in a time of flux, it seems likely that their position was an important focus point, even if not the only one,[70] of relatively rapid institutionalization.[71] Their administrative talents, the practical benefits of their hospitality, and their natural position in Graeco-Roman culture favoured their emergence as leaders in Paul's absence and their increasing importance with the passage of time.[72]

Part Two: The Pseudonymous Pauline Epistles

Colossians and Ephesians

Our discussion of the pseudonymous Pauline writings will be divided into two parts. First we will treat Colossians and Ephesians, and then turn to the Pastoral epistles. Our discussion naturally divides in this way because of obvious affinities between Colossians and Ephesians, and because the Pastorals probably belong to a much later date, perhaps as late as the first quarter of the second century. The Pastorals also contain what appear to be more developed institutions of leadership. Our purpose in this section is to review the evidence concerning house-church meetings and leadership in the interim between Paul's death and the documents we have chosen for investigation in subsequent chapters.

The Authorship and Date of Colossians and Ephesians

The authorship of Colossians and Ephesians continues to be a topic of debate in contemporary scholarship. We do not propose to defend scholars who argue for pseudonymity,[73] but will assume it as the basis for our discussion.[74] The cumulative force of the arguments for non-Pauline authorship of Colossians (differences of language and style from the non-contested letters, theological differences, literary dependence on the genuine Pauline corpus[75]), at least justifies our treatment of it as pseudonymous. And if Colossians was not written by Paul, the probability that Ephesians was written after Colossians[76] and contains passages dependent upon it indicates that it too is pseudonymous.[77]

The dates of Colossians and Ephesians are also difficult to determine. The greetings in Colossians may indicate that it was composed soon after Paul's death, or even toward the end of his life when he was no longer available to the community (Onesimus, for example, is now evidently a freedperson).[78] Ephesians is more difficult to locate and date. The omission of the prepositional phrase ἐν Ἐφέσῳ in several early and important manuscripts has led scholars to treat the epistle as an "encyclical" of Pauline teaching.[79] Affinities between Ignatius' epistle to the Ephesians and New Testament Eph. 1:1-19, probably indicate that Ignatius associated the letter with Ephesus, and the ascription by many manuscripts connecting it with this city may indicate that it originated there.[80] If Ignatius knew the letter, this indicates that it was written before ca. 113 A.D. Mitton dates it near to 90 A.D.[81]

The Household Setting of Colossians and Ephesians

In Colossians and Ephesians household language and descriptions of the church are linked together. The chief example of this occurs in Eph. 2:19-20, where the writer describes his audience as "members of the household of God" (οἰκεῖοι τοῦ θεοῦ). Again, in both Colossians and Ephesians a household code appears household of God.

(Col. 3:18-4:1; Eph. 5:21-6:9). The use of these rules as paraenetic devices to order life within the community probably indicates that there were local church cells whose form and identity were closely connected to that of the household. Recent studies have correctly called into question the view often put forward by scholars that the household rules constitute an independent, self-contained paraenetic unit which had little to do with the particular challenges, norms, and organization of early Christian communities.[82]

Verner summarizes an emerging consensus concerning the alternative interpretation of these codes as reflecting particular community realities when he writes, "The form of the Haustafeln . . . strongly suggests that they address real, concrete, and in some cases persistent social needs within the church."[83] More particularly, MacDonald comments that the Haustafeln in Colossians and Ephesians probably arose out of a close connection between household and church.

> The Haustafeln exhibit an interest in household relationships on the one hand, and in the church understood on the model of the household on the other. If a slave is instructed to be subject to his or her master in the Lord, this carries with it certain implications for the slave's behaviour not only in the outside society, but also within the sect. The slave of a believing householder would respect the leadership of the one who places his home at the disposal of the member of the household of God. . . . [I]t is evident from Paul's letters that the household may have acted as an important model for the formation of the ecclesia. Meetings were held in individual house churches and one's position in the household was probably related to the role in community life. In Colossians and Ephesians one discovers signs of the continued articulation of the implications of household-rooted life.[84]

John Elliott comes to a similar conclusion in his discussion of 1 Peter (a writing roughly contemporary with Ephesians[85]). The description of the church as a "spiritual household" (οἶκος πνευματικός) in 1 Pet. 2:5, together with the appearance of a Haustafel (2:18-3:9) leads him to conclude,

> The household formations of the early Christian movement . . . made the ecclesiological adaptation of this image (i.e. "the household of God") for the Christian community possible. The household formations of the early Christian movement, moreover, made this embracing symbol for the early Christian community sociologically plausible.[86]

Given the appearance in these writings of Haustafeln and the description of the Ephesian community as a household of God, it is probable that the church and local households were closely related.[87]

This impression gains more direct support in Col. 4:15, where the church in Nympha's house is greeted. We have already met the formula κατ᾽ οἶκον ἐκκλησία in the genuine Pauline epistles. It is most likely that its appearance here reflects a community arrangement similar to that found at an earlier date. The question of roles of leadership by patronesses, a topic already indirectly addressed in our discussion of the reference to Phoebe in Rom. 16:1-2, presents itself here in a more acute form.[88] It is probable that contemporary norms helped to promote the authority of patronesses. Banks comments, concerning the authority of Nympha in the church meeting at her home:

If, as seems most natural, Nympha was a relatively wealthy woman who, like Gaius at Corinth, acted as host to a local group of believers, it seems unlikely that she, presumably a widow who conducted her family, managed her slaves and welcomed her friends all week, would take an insignificant part in the proceedings in favour of socially inferior male members who were present. To do that would be socially unacceptable whereas, in the absence of a husband it would be perfectly legitimate, in the eyes of others for her to behave in home and church *as her husband would have done* if present. Most probably male heads of other households also belonged to this church and had an influential role in its activities but, given her position, Nympha would have functioned alongside them in similar sorts of ways, not in a subordinate capacity. This acts as a reminder that Paul generally talks about the relation of wives to husbands: where no husband is in view, quite different arrangements become possible.[89]

It seems likely that the link between household and house church continued to exert an influence on community life and church leadership in this period.

The number of house churches in Colossae and Laodicea is difficult to determine, but the possibility of a plurality of household meetings cannot be excluded; the house church associated with Nympha may have been one of many.[90] The ascription of the title of church to Nympha's house does not necessarily indicate that the "church" is being given a well-defined and permanent location, or that it refers to the whole Colossian or Laodicean community. At the time of these documents, the church meeting in a patron or patroness's household was probably a relatively informal arrangement.[91]

Community Leadership

The quotation by Banks indicates that in Laodicea and Colossae patrons and patronesses of house churches probably enjoyed positions of leadership. This is consistent, as the quotation cited above from MacDonald states, with the use of household rules to establish hierarchical social arrangements as a basis for community life. The writer of Colossians is not explicit about the nature and functioning of this local leadership, but in Ephesians 4:11, he presents a list of various kinds of leaders. Apostles, prophets, evangelists, pastors and teachers probably represent various kinds of leaders who exercise various forms of control in the community or communities represented by this letter. The precise functions of those referred to in this list cannot be reconstructed with any certainty, but it is probable that there were several types of leadership in this period.

Margaret MacDonald presents an intriguing line of argument concerning patterns of leadership at the time when Colossians and Ephesians were written.[92] She argues that the death of Paul presented a kind of crisis for the communities represented by these two epistles. Because the churches addressed by these letters probably relied upon the apostle's guidance when faced with problems and divisions within the community, it was necessary to fill the vacuum left by his absence with other forms of guidance. MacDonald puts this forward as an explanation for the use of Paul's name in the composition of these documents; they represent what Paul would have said about contemporary problems. She argues further that several kinds of members were well placed to adopt positions of guidance at this time, but the fact that not all seem to have survived into the second century leads her to argue compellingly that these were communities "in transition."[93] She seems only to apply this insight to Ephesians and to the importance of teaching or teachers in the guidance of the community,[94] but it is applicable on a more general level. It is probable that after Paul's departure and death his personal retinue helped to guide the local communities.[95] The references to Epaphras (Col. 1:7; 4:12-13) and Tychicus (Col. 4:7; Eph. 6:21-22), for example, may either refer to apostolic delegates who continued to guide communities — probably, like Paul, at a distance — or function as legitimating descriptions of other more local individuals in similar roles of guidance.[96] There is no evidence that institutions developed to perpetuate the roles of guidance exercised by apostolic delegates and it seems likely that while they fulfilled interim needs, other institutions grew to replace them.[97]

One of the categories of leaders named in Eph. 4:11 calls for special comment — that of pastor (ποιμένες). Again, it is difficult to come to any firm conclusions concerning the function and nature of this form of leadership, but the term itself provides some clues. In several instances, roughly contemporary Christian literature associates the roots ποιμεν- and ἐπισκοπ- together. The linking of these two terms together may derive from the Septuagint.[98]

In Acts 20:28, a document which has certain affinities with Ephesians,[99] elders are exhorted with images of both shepherding and overseeing. Again, in 1 Peter a similar connection occurs: in 2:25 Christ is presented as ἐπίσκοπος of the "sheep"; in 5:2 (in some manuscripts) elders are described as overseeing (ἐπισκοποῦντες) the sheep. Elders were probably in positions of administration in the Petrine and Lucan communities and given this apparently wide-spread association, it is possible to infer tentatively that the reference to pastors in Eph. 4:11 implies some form of governance.[100] Any conclusions concerning the status of these pastors are also tentative. Given the use of household rules to establish norms within this community, it is at least probable that hosts of the community carried out tasks of pastoring and that the reinforcement of hierarchical social arrangements within the community, as a result of the application of this code, promoted the authority of house-church hosts.

The Pastoral Epistles

Authorship, Location and Date

There is less debate concerning the pseudonymity of the Pastoral epistles: vocabulary, chronology, theology, degree of organization — all these make authorship by Paul highly unlikely.[101]

A brief discussion of the location of the community behind the Pastorals is necessary because it is often assumed that they are the product of an Ephesian Christian community.[102] If this is the case, it has great import for our discussion of the evidence for the ministry in the Ignatian corpus, since Ignatius addresses one of his letters to the Ephesians. The evidence for Ephesus as the place of origin, however, is not clear. True, in 1 Tim. 1:3 (cf. 2 Tim. 1:18) the author mentions Ephesus as the place where Timothy is to remain. And a further piece of evidence which scholars adduce for Ephesian provenance is the apparent use of the Pastorals by Polycarp.[103] Some even suggest that Polycarp composed them.[104] But this evidence is not enough to establish Ephesian authorship. In Tit. 1:5, the presumed setting is Crete and, assuming that these letters come from the same hand, it is impossible to determine which (if either) place refers to the writer's community. Neither is the second argument, based on Polycarp's probable use of the Pastorals, strong enough to connect them with Ephesus (or Smyrna); borrowing can be (but is not necessarily) an indication of provenance. In our view the question of location must be left open.

Scholars have dated these epistles from soon after the death of Paul to the mid-second century.[105] The later date seems unlikely because of the lack of reference to monepiscopacy in these letters, but the evidence of more formal institutions of leadership suggests that some time has passed since Paul's death. Most scholars date the Pastorals between 90 and 110.[106]

The Household Setting of the Pastorals

The use of household language to describe the church is more prominent in the Pastorals than in Ephesians and Colossians. In 1 Tim. 3:15 the church is described as the "household of God" (οἶκος θεοῦ), and in a manner consonant with this image, the author in 2 Tim. 2:20-21 describes various members of the church as vessels of a great house (μεγάλη οἰκία). Again, the author uses household language when he describes the bishop as God's οἰκονόμος, i.e. his household steward (Tit. 1:7). Finally, as in the two documents discussed above, household rules are used as a means of promoting a certain community ethos (1 Tim. 2:8-15; 6:1-2; Tit. 2:1-10), and on the basis of stylistic similarities Verner argues compellingly that the prescriptions for overseers and deacons (1 Tim. 3:1-13; Tit. 1:5f.) are based on elements of a *Haustafel*.[107] As in Colossians and Ephesians, the predominance of this language is best explained by households acting as the setting for the community's house churches.

More direct evidence that households constituted various local house churches is the description of the author's opponents. In 2 Tim. 3:6 "Paul" describes these individuals as those "who make their way into households" (οἰκίαι), and in Tit. 1:11 he describes them as upsetting whole households (ὅλοι οἶκοι) by their teaching.[108] These references may imply a variety of house-church meetings to which the author's opponents have gained access.

Wealth and Leadership

The Pastorals contain more direct evidence of the presence of wealthy Christians than Ephesians and Colossians. In 1 Tim. 2:9 exhortations against the flaunting of material wealth is best interpreted as assuming a degree of material wealth among some female members. The writer is acquainted with members who have allowed the pursuit of wealth to undermine allegiance to the community; in 1 Tim. 6:9-10 he refers to those who have fallen away because of the desire to be rich. Of course, greed is not a vice necessarily reserved for the rich. It seems likely, however, that this instruction was addressed more precisely to prosperous members. Again, the author's instruction to slaves to please believing slave-owners (1 Tim. 6:2) implies that there were members wealthy enough to possess slaves. If the reciprocal duties of slave owners are omitted here, the exhortation to the rich not to place their hope in "uncertain riches," but to be content with doing acts of benevolence (6:17-19), describes a positive ethic of love patriarchalism. This, again, assumes a degree of wealth.

The kinds of community service which the wealthier members could provide are well illustrated by the description of the activities of Onesiphorus in 2 Tim. 1:16 (cf. 4:19), a person otherwise unmentioned in the Pauline corpus. The household of Onesiphorus is presented in a way which suggests that its patron was relatively prosperous: he is congratulated for refreshing Paul (i.e. probably offering him accommodation) and he is in a position to travel and use his journeys in the service (διακονεῖν) of the community. Whether or not this is a contemporary figure, the description of him provides a window through which we can see the kinds of activities the well-to-do were probably expected to perform for the community.

The descriptions of the characteristics expected of local leaders also assume the presence of wealth. The writer prescribes that overseers[109] should not be greedy or out for gain (1 Tim. 3:3; Tit. 1:6). The need to include such a warning is best understood if overseers were drawn from the rank of more prosperous members. The argument for the presence of a wealthy stratum gains further support from 1 Tim. 3:1f., where the author uses a "true saying" (πιστὸς ὁ λόγος) which describes the task of ἐπίσκοπος as a καλὸν ἔργον. This saying is probably drawn from Hellenistic municipal life and it is likely that its inclusion here indicates that the position was regarded as "a public service to be undertaken by the comparatively well-to-do."[110] The evidence regarding proper characteristics for deacons implies a similar scenario. In 1 Tim. 3:12, the description of the ideal deacon as a man who not only governs his children but also his household well probably indicates that the οἶκος included both slaves and children. Verner's statement concerning the wealth of deacons may be applied more generally as true for the profile presented for bishops as well:

> the author betrays his assumption that prospective church officers will be householders with sufficient means to own household slaves. This fact in itself locates these householders in the higher social strata of the Asian cities. It is most important to recognize that relatively high social standing does not appear here as a requirement which the author is intent on imposing on would-be office holders, but as a casual assumption that he makes about them. Thus it is not the author's special program or prejudices that are reflected here, but the actual situation in the churches. He apparently accepts this situation without question and pursues his own aims within it.[111]

A similar assumption lies behind the household rules contained in 1 Timothy and Titus. If one compares the exhortation to slaves in the household rules in Colossians and Ephesians, for example, one finds both slaves and masters mentioned. In the instructions to slaves in 2 Tim. 6:1-2 and Tit. 2:9-10, however, "Paul" is looking "from the top down"; only slaves are exhorted to be faithful to their master, the reciprocal duties of masters are not mentioned. This may indicate that the writer was part of the upper stratum of the community. Whatever the author's social status, it is evident that he promoted the authority of the well-to-do as an unquestioned norm. Dennis MacDonald calls the overseers, presbyters, and deacons in these communities "the respectable household-ers."[112] Countryman's conclusion from the rules set out for bishops and deacons in 1 Tim. 3:1ff and Tit. 1:5f. reiterates this description. The important thing is that all ranks of ministers are expected to display the virtues appropriate to prosperous householders; they are to be drawn from among the elite of the church.[113] He argues further that the profile of the appropriate bishop in these passages is a hospitable *paterfamilias* who keeps his household affairs under control. "When such men were ordained," he writes, "the local elite and the clergy would become identical."[114] One may add to the characteristics adduced by Countryman the criterion of being well-thought of by outsiders (1 Tim. 3:7); for a community evidently seeking the approval of the wider society, a good candidate for leadership was a prosperous and civil householder.

In their commentary on the Pastorals Dibelius and Conzelmann argue that the adaptation of Hellenistic household rules to establish norms within the community arose as a result of the delay of the Parousia. The profile of the bishop and the members of the community as "good citizens" belongs to a church whose eschatalogical hope has been replaced with moral codes and a church order, adapted for consolidation in the world.[115] They contend that the delay of the Second Coming necessitated a shift in the church's "conceptual structure" from imminent expectation and separation from the world to the re-orienting idea of good citizenship.[116] Dibelius and Conzelmann are correct to argue that as time passed ecclesiological institutions developed, but it is unsatisfactory to explain this development wholly by reference to the delay of the Parousia or solely by the application of ideas. A fuller explanation of the institutional development evident in these letters should include the continuing impact of social phenomena, such as the organization of the community in Graeco-Roman households, and the influence of leaders drawn from the upper stratum of the church on the formulation of group symbols and ideals. It is not enough to speak of "the concept of 'good Christian citizenship' . . . understood in the context of a transformed self-understanding of the church."[117] It is also necessary to refer to the social structures or social world which contributed to the community's picture of itself.

There is indirect but good evidence that house-church patrons continued to exercise oversight of the groups which met in their homes. One of the characteristics of a bishop is that he be hospitable (1 Tim. 3:2; Tit. 1:8). References to hospitality are often interpreted as descriptions of the reception of travellers. We will discuss this in more detail when we turn to the setting of the *Shepherd* and *1 Clement*. The term φιλόξενος is also used in 1 Pet. 4:9 to describe the reception of local members,[118] and this is the implication of the term ξένος in Rom. 16:23. The inclusion of hospitality among the characteristics of a bishop may be interpreted as an indication that overseers invited the community into their homes.[119] This virtue probably implied a form of patronage. In 1 Tim. 5:10, the context of the passage indicates that the hospitality of widows was a form of patronage;[120] hospitality is included as a "good deed" and elsewhere in the Pastorals (1 Tim. 6:18; Tit. 3:14) the phrase καλὸν ἔργον implies material help. Further, Abraham Malherbe, Raymond Brown, and Judith Lieu (whose treatments we shall discuss in more detail in our discussion of the setting implied in

Ignatius' letters) argue convincingly that the inhospitality of Diotrephes described in 3 John includes not only his unwelcoming attitude toward travellers, but also his exclusion of certain community members from the local meeting. They observe that Diotrephes' exclusion and reception of members is best explained if he was the host of a house church. This insight helps to explain why it was important for the community that bishops be hospitable: its viability probably depended to a great extent on the willingness of bishops to receive members into their homes. Further, it is notable that management (προΐστασθαι/προστῆναι) of the bishop's own household is linked with management of the church (1 Tim. 3:4-5). It seems likely that proper management of the household is linked with successful oversight of the house church because both overlap; the host is not only householder but also bishop and the success in one occupation has direct implications for success in the other.[121]

Summary

This brief review of the Pauline evidence indicates that the Graeco-Roman household played a central part in the establishment, growth, and leadership of the early church. The evidence for leadership by house-church hosts is more direct in the genuine epistles, but even in the pseudonymous letters, where it is more circumstantial, a similar pattern emerges. During Paul's lifetime and after it, the household shaped the identity and governance of communities established by him. There were, of course, patterns of leadership other than the type offered by householders. But it is probable that such patrons carried out important administrative tasks which contributed to them prevailing over other possible patterns. The host who possessed the wealth and initiative to invite the church into his or her own home had important leadership responsibilities, probably occasioned by the patronage he or she offered. This discussion provides a general setting in which to place the social descriptions and assumptions of the documents treated in subsequent chapters.

Notes

1 See Kümmel, 1975, pp. 250-387 for discussion of dating and authorship problems of the various books ascribed to Paul. We will assume this list as a datum of New Testament scholarship, recognizing that these topics continue to be debated.

2 Rowland, 1985, pp. 109ff., 75f.; similarly, Nickelsburg, 1985, pp. 73-91.

3 Meeks, 1983, pp. 84ff.; idem., 1972, pp. 44-72 with reference to the Johannine community; Tidball, 1983, pp. 106f.

4 Scroggs, 1975, pp. 1-23.

5 Elliott, 1981, pp. 73f.; MacDonald, 1986, pp. 46ff.; also Esler, 1984, pp. 83-108, who employs Wilson's sect typology in his analysis of Luke-Acts; Wilde, 1978, pp. 47-70, who employs it (in an unsatisfactory way) in his discussion of Mark.

6 Wilson, 1961, p. 1; Elliott, 1981, p. 75; see also Wilson, 1982, pp. 89ff. for a more detailed discussion.

7 Meeks, 1983, pp. 85f.

8 Elliott, 1981, pp. 76f.; MacDonald, 1986, pp. 49, 54f.; cf. also Meeks, 1983, pp. 85, 169.

9 Wilson, 1973, p. 22.

10 Wilson, 1982, p. 105.
11 MacDonald, 1986, pp. 54f.
12 Theissen, 1982, pp. 121-43, esp. 129f. For criticism see Malherbe, 1983, pp. 79f., but he agrees (p. 84) that social status probably exacerbated problems within the Corinthian community.
13 There is a plethora of material on this topic. What follows is a list of the chief works in which attention is devoted to New Testament house churches: Afanassieff, 1974; Banks, 1980; Brown, 1982; Elliott, 1982; Filson, 1939; Fiorenza,1983; Gielen, 1986; Gnilka, 1982; Gülzow, 1974; Hainz, 1972; Holmberg, 1980a; idem., 1980; Jaubert, 1974; Judge, 1960a; 1960b; 1966; Klauck, 1981a; 1981b; Lemaire, 1974; Lieu, 1986; Lührmann, 1981; Malherbe, 1983; Meeks, 1983; Petersen, 1985; Rordorf, 1964; Stambaugh and Balch, 1986; Stuhlmacher, 1975; Theissen, 1982; Verner, 1983; Wagner, 1949; White, 1985/86; Wiefel, 1970.
14 Malherbe, 1983, pp. 60-91, esp. p. 60.
15 Filson, 1939, p. 109.
16 Riddle, 1938, pp. 141-54; this position echoes earlier opinions: e.g., Hatch, 1888, pp. 430-46; Harnack, 1904, Vol. 1, pp. 219f.
17 For a discussion of Luke-Acts as a writing with its own theological interests and composed *c.* A.D. 80-100 see Barrett, 1961, p. 62; Esler, 1984; Haenchen, 1971, p. 164; Juel, 1983, p. 119; Maddox, 1982, p. 9; Martin, 1986, pp. 95-112; O'Neill, 1961, p. 173; Tiede, 1980, p. 120.
18 Hock, 1980, pp. 26ff., and 1978, pp. 555ff. argues that Paul supported himself by means of his trade and used the workshop as his mission venue (e.g., the workshop of Prisca and Aquila — Acts 18:3) but he ignores the evidence of Paul in the household of patrons. It seems more likely that the apostle adapted his mission to suit the needs of the church; if Acts 19:9 is historically accurate, he may also have made use of a "lecture hall" (σχολή).
19 For προστάτις as *patrona* see Kearsley, 1985, pp. 124-30; Fiorenza, 1983, pp. 48-49; Meeks, 1983, pp. 60, 79; Judge, 1960b, pp. 128f.
20 Theissen, 1982, pp. 27-67, esp. 46f.
21 It is unsatisfactory, as Strobel attempts to do (1965, pp. 91-100), to decide the question of what the terms οἶκος/οικία refer to by appeal to contemporary legal definitions. Gaudemet, 1969, pp. 312f., points out the nonuniformity in legal sources at this time, as does Theissen, 1982, pp. 83-87. Each case must be assessed separately. See also Weigandt, 1963, pp. 49-74.
22 White, 1985/86, pp. 97-127; cf. MacMullen, 1984, pp. 37f. (but he overemphasizes the role of daily contacts among the poor and ignores the evidence of movement from upper ranks downward in Christian writings contemporary with the later New Testament documents).
23 Judge, 1960b, pp. 59f.; cf. Meeks, 1983, p. 30.
24 White, 1985/86, p. 119.
25 Meeks, 1982, pp. 57-58; Malherbe, 1983, p. 77 (for Gaius and Crispus).
26 Filson, 1939, p. 110.
27 Ibid., p. 105; Meeks, 1983, p. 76; Klauck, 1981a.
28 A less ambiguous scenario of divisions between household conventicles is the description by Paul of the separation in Antioch of Jewish Christians from Gentiles for a common meal (Gal. 2:11f.). Jewish and Gentile Christians probably met in separate households for their common meal or eucharist, but gathered together for other communal events; for a similar interpretation see Holmberg, 1980a, pp. 32f. Such divisions may have occurred in some communities even in the second

century (cf. *Dialogue* 66, where Justin alludes to Jewish-Christians who do not offer hospitality to their Gentile brethren).

29 Theissen, 1982, pp. 35f.; Grelot, 1974, p. 43; Holmberg, 1980a, pp. 70-72; cf. also Stark, 1969, Vol. 4, p. 84.

30 Fiorenza, 1983, pp. 181f.; Klauck, 1981. p. 30; Gülzow, 1974, pp. 201-202.

31 E.g., Klauck, 1981, p. 33; Holmberg, 1980a, pp. 103f.; Theissen, 1982, pp. 104f.; Meeks, 1983, pp. 75,76.

32 Klauck, 1981a, pp. 27f.

33 The majority of scholars contend for a plurality of meetings (Banks, 1980, p. 38; Gnilka, 1982, p. 25; Hainz, 1972, pp. 195, 346; Judge, 1960b, p. 37; Klauck, 1981a, pp. 35f.; Meeks, 1983, p. 75; Stuhlmacher, 1975, p. 71; Wagner, 1949, pp. 2ff.; among these, Klauck (p. 38) argues explicitly that in Corinth only one common eucharist was celebrated.

34 Klauck, 1981a, p. 21.

35 Gielen, 1986, pp. 109ff.

36 For Romans 16 as addressed to the Roman church see Klauck, 1981a, pp. 24f. Donfried, 1977, pp. 50ff., also presents a strong case for its inclusion in Paul's Roman epistle. The objection that Paul's greetings reveal an acquaintance with Christians he could not possibly have had were they at Rome (since he had not yet been there), does not recognize the mobility of early Christians (especially Prisca and Aquila!). Even if he did not know those whom he greeted personally, such greetings would have had the effect of marshalling support for him among the Roman brethren. The textual evidence for a fifteen-chapter form is relatively weak and the inclusion of the sixteenth chapter provides the greetings typical of the ancient letter. For a highly speculative discussion of the emergence of the Roman church from a Jewish synagogal milieu to a setting of various house churches see Wiefel, 1970, esp. pp. 75-81 and Judge and Thomas, 1966, pp. 81ff., esp. p. 91.

37 For a discussion of the earlier literature see Countryman, 1980, pp. 1-18, who argues for the presence of the wealthy among the early Christians. Kautsky, 1925, p. 9 presents the traditional interpretation, but there were exceptions to this consensus: see e.g., Knopf, 1900, pp. 325-47, who argued for a minority of well-to-do Christians in Paul's churches. Some scholars still insist incorrectly that all early Christians were impecunious: e.g. Gager, 1975, pp. 93ff.; Lee, 1972, p. 126. The following is a select list of major scholars who argue that some members were relatively wealthy: Banks, 1980; Elliott, 1981, pp. 189f.; Grant, 1977, pp. 88, passim; Gülzow, 1974, pp. 195f.; Hengel, 1974, pp. 60ff.; Holmberg, 1980a, pp. 103f.; Judge, 1960b, pp. 49ff.; Kee, 1980, pp. 96-97; Klauck, 1981a; Malherbe, 1983, pp. 60ff.; Meeks, 1983, pp. 51ff.; Theissen, 1982, pp. 69ff.; Tidball, 1983, pp. 90ff.

38 Theissen, 1982, pp. 73f.

39 For the reliability of Acts concerning Crispus' status see Malherbe, 1983, p. 73, n. 27.

40 See Theissen, pp. 73-75, for further discussion of the prosperity of synagogue rulers in this period.

41 Malherbe, 1983, pp. 73f., esp. n. 27.

42 Meeks, 1983, pp. 57-58.

43 See Bartchy, 1973, for detailed discussion and a similar conclusion.

44 Theissen, 1982, pp. 107-108; cf. Troeltsch, 1931, pp. 69-89; also Hengel, 1974, pp. 61f.

45 Theissen, 1982, pp. 121-144, esp. p. 139.

46 Ibid., pp. 145-174, esp. p. 164.

47 Filson, 1939, p. 111; also, Lemaire, 1974, pp. 65f.; Holmberg, 1980a, pp. 105f.

48 Cited and numbered by Holmberg, 1980a, p. 101.

49 Ibid., pp. 101-102.

50 Elliott, 1981, pp. 189-90.

51 Brockhaus, 1975, pp. 7-94, summarizes the discussion in German scholarship of the last one hundred years and speaks of a consensus in regard to this. Contemporary examples of this interpretation can be found in von Campenhausen, 1969, pp. 55-76, esp. 58f., 70f.; Greeven, 1952/53, pp. 1ff.; Käsemann, 1971 and 1969; Schweizer, 1961, pp. 89-104, (7a-7o), esp. 102 (7m). For further literature and discussion cf. Holmberg, 1980b, pp. 192f. and Chapter Four below. The chief criticism of the interpretation of the problems mentioned in 1 Cor. 12 and 14 as indicative of a Pauline church order is that it overlooks the occasional purpose of these chapters. For further discussion see Brockhaus, 1975, pp. 210-18; Holmberg, 1980a, pp. 120f.

52 For these members as defined groups see Greeven, 1952/53, pp. 3-31.

53 The appearance of one article with the three participles κοπιῶντες, προϊστάμενοι, and νουθετοῦντες in 1 Thes. 5:12 probably indicates that these terms refer to various functions of the same role; see Meeks, 1983, p. 134; Greeven, 1952/53, p. 33.

54 The term appears in a triad indicating roles of material. The term appears in a triad indicating roles of material helper; cf. Meeks, 1983, p. 135 (see also the footnote, p. 234) who translates the triad ὁ μεταδιδούς ... ὁ προιστάμενος ... ὁ ἐλεῶν as "the donor," "the patron," and "the one who shows mercy." This triad also echoes to a certain extent the pair ἀντιλήμψεις – κυβερνήσεις in 1 Cor. 12:28, where "helps" probably implies material succour, Holmberg, 1980a, p. 100.

55 See Meeks, 1983, p. 234, n. 75 for further discussion and literature; also Brockhaus, 1975. p. 107.

56 It should be clear from this discussion that Greeven, 1952/53, p. 37 and Kertelge, 1972, pp. 125f. are incorrect to infer from 1 Cor. 12:28 that the reference to governance refers exclusively to prophets; prophets probably had some role in the guidance of the community, but in the daily life of the group individuals such as patrons and patronesses also had an important leadership role. For criticism of Greeven see Holmberg, 1980a, pp. 113-14, n. 90.

57 Meeks, 1983, p. 134; also, Rowland, 1985, p. 258; Petersen, 1985, pp. 296f.

58 1980a, p. 116.

59 Moberg, 1962, pp. 100ff. This model is also used by Tidball, 1983, pp. 123f.

60 Moberg, p. 119.

61 Ibid., pp. 119-20.

62 Holmberg, 1980a, p. 116; MacDonald, 1986, pp. 62ff.; cf. also Pesch, 1971, p. 446; Martin, 1972, pp. 29f.; Schürmann, 1968, p. 331, n. 120; Goppelt, 1970, p. 92. We shall return to a fuller discussion of this in our treatment of 1 Clement.

63 For the final point see MacDonald's (1986, pp. 74f.) description of the variety of activities members such as Stephanas (1 Cor. 16:15,17) and Epaphroditus (Phil. 2:25-30; 4:18) undertake. One may add Prisca and Aquila who appear in different places at different times (1 Cor. 16:19; Rom. 1 6:3), but continue to invite the church into their homes. Gnilka, 1969, pp. 96ff., adduces Phil. 1:1 as evidence that by the end of Paul's life a collegium of bishops had already developed (cf. also Martin, 1972, p. 26). But it is not clear that Philippians is one of Paul's later letters. For further criticism see Brockhaus, 1975, p. 80.

64 Luke portrays Paul as appointing leaders (Acts 14:23), but it is probable that he is reading his contemporary church structure back into the earlier period; thus, e.g., Haenchen, 1971, p. 436; Käsemann, 1965, p. 86; Martin, 1986, p. 161.

65 Barrett, 1968, p. 395; Goppelt, 1970, p. 197; Roloff, 1965, p. 134; Martin, 1972, pp. 27f.; Pesch, 1971, p. 444 argue against appointment by Paul; Ellis, 1971, p. 451; Grelot, 1971, pp. 457f.; Hainz, 1972, p. 46 argue for appointment; Gnilka, 1968, p. 34 states that the question must be left open.

66 The interaction between Paul, willing individuals, and recognition by the wider community is discussed by Lemaire, 1974, pp. 67-68; cf. also Holmberg, 1980a, pp. 106-109.

67 Laub, 1976, pp. 34-35 speaks of "eine orginäre Unter- und Uberordnung."

68 Institutionalization will be discussed more fully in Chapter Four.

69 For further discussion of these variables see Budillon, 1971, p. 486; Martin, 1972, pp. 29, 33-34, 45; Grelot, 1971, pp. 454, 461-62; Pesch, 1971, pp. 444f.; Gnilka, 1969, p. 103; Goppelt, 1970, p. 187; Barrett, 1968, pp. 24-25.

70 There is evidence that teachers had a permanent role in the local community (Gal. 6:6). But Acts 18:24-26, where house-church patrons are presented in a teaching role, suggests that the boundaries between these two groups may not always have been distinct.

71 Pesch, 1971, p. 446 comments on this basis that the function of members described as προϊστάμενοι (1 Thes. 5:12; Rom. 12:8) and carrying out functions of κυβέρνησις (1 Cor. 12:28) were the first to be subject to institutionalization; cf. also Hainz, 1972, p. 345-46; Brockhaus, 1975, pp. 107f.

72 For the appropriation of apostolic functions and authority by local leaders as time passed, see Hainz, 1972, pp. 349f.; Jaubert, 1974, p. 27; Ellis, 1971, pp. 440f. and 1974, pp. 139-40. Note for example the use of συνεργός to describe the household leadership of Philemon (v. 1), Stephanas (1 Cor. 16:16), and Prisca and Aquila (Rom. 16:3), and the root κοπ- used to describe the contribution of Stephanas and his household (1 Cor. 16:16; cf. 1 Thes. 5:12) and Paul's missionary labour (1 Cor. 15:10; Gal. 4:11; Phil. 2:16).

73 Guthrie's (1963, pp. 282-94) arguments against pseudepigraphy in the New Testament are unconvincing; a more balanced treatment is provided by Kiley, 1986, pp. 17-35.

74 For Colossians as pseudonymous: von Campenhausen, 1969, pp. 53f.; Kertelge, 1972, pp. 132f.; Kiley, 1986; Lohse, 1971; Lührmann, 1981, pp. 83-97 (argues on the basis of the Haustafeln); Meeks, 1983, p. 125; Schweizer, 1982. For Colossians as genuine: Bruce, 1984, pp. 28-33; Cannon, 1983, pp. 175ff.; Kümmel, 1975, pp. 340-46; Martin, 1974, pp. 32-41; Scott, 1958.

75 Kiley, 1986, pp. 38-73 summarizes the arguments; cf. also Lohse, 1971, pp. 177-83; Schweizer, 1982, pp. 15-24.

76 Which document borrows from which has been debated but most accept the priority of Colossians; for further discussion cf. Goodspeed, 1933; Mitton, 1976, pp. 11f.; Kiley, 1986, pp. 37f.

77 For Ephesians as genuine: Barth, 1974, pp. 36-50; Bruce, 1984, pp. 229-33; Scott, 1958, pp. 119-23. For Ephesians as pseudonymous: Goodspeed, 1933; Kümmel, 1975, pp. 357-63; Meeks, 1983, p. 126; Mitton, 1951; 1976, pp. 2-11; Sampley, 1971.

78 Thus, Schweizer, 1982, pp. 24-6; Meeks, 1983, p. 125.

79 Thus Goodspeed, 1933; Mitton, 1976, pp. 25f. Many who argue for Pauline authorship also argue for the "encyclical" nature of the letter: e.g., Bruce, 1984, pp. 250-51.

80 For parallels between Ignatius's *Eph.* and New Testament Eph. see Schoedel, 1985, p. 37. For Ephesian origin see Goodspeed, 1933; Mitton, 1976, pp. 40f.; Barth's (1974, p. 51) view that it originated in Rome is unconvincing.

81 Mitton, 1976, pp. 24-25; similarly, Kümmel, 1975, p. 366.

82 For a description and critique of scholars who argue for this position see Crouch, 1972, pp. 9-31.

83 Verner, 1983, p. 91; cf. also Crouch, 1972, pp. 144-45. A detailed discussion of this debate falls outside the scope of this thesis. For further discussion see Balch, 1981; Cannon, 1983, pp. 95-131; Crouch, 1972; Elliott, 1981, pp. 208-20; Sampley, 1971, pp. 17-28; Verner, 1983, pp. 83-125.

84 MacDonald, 1986, pp. 185-86; similarly, Klauck, 1981a, p. 96.

85 Kümmel, 1975, dates it *c.* 90-95 A.D.; Elliott, 1981, p. 87, places it between 73 and 92 A.D.

86 Elliott, 1981, p. 200.

87 Similarly, Klauck, 1981a, p. 66.

88 For MSS differences see Bruce, 1984, pp. 182-83; Lohse, 1971, p. 174; Schweizer, 1982, p. 241, who argue that the feminine form may have been changed by a later scribe.

89 Banks, 1980, p. 127-28; for further discussion see Fiorenza 1983, pp. 51, 177-78; for females in public secular office in this period see Kearsley, 1985, pp. 124ff.; Thraede, "Frau," *RAC*, 297-69.

90 A plurality of meetings is assumed by several scholars: Bruce, 1984, p. 183; Lohse, 1971, p. 174; Schweizer, 1982, pp. 241-42 (admits possibility of whole community meeting in Nympha's house); Scott, 1958, p. 93; cf. also Klauck, 1981a, p. 46 who argues for different uses of the term ἐκκλησία in Colossians.

91 Malherbe, 1983, pp. 111-12, argues that the household setting probably assumed by the writer of 3 John, a letter roughly contemporary with Colossians and Ephesians, may also have been constituted by relatively informal house-church cells; also in favour of a more fluid, informal conception of house churches in this period is Wagner, 1949.

92 MacDonald, 1986, pp. 172ff.

93 MacDonald borrows the phrase from Brown and Meier's (1983, p. 72), description of Matthew's community.

94 Ibid., pp. 181f. This seems to be the result of allowing Brown and Meier's description of Matthew's community to shape her treatment of leadership in Ephesians unduly. She also overlooks the possibility of the reference to "pastors" and "teachers" referring to the same function (thus, Bruce, 1984, p. 348); the functions of bishop and teacher are combined in 1 Tim. 3:2.

95 Elliott, 1981, pp. 272f. arrives at a similar conclusion with respect to Silvanus (1 Pet. 5:12), whom he argues was a co-worker or delegate of Peter.

96 I am inclined to the former; MacDonald, 1986, pp. 175f., to the latter; decisions on this point rest on whether the similarities between Colossians and the greeting list in Philemon are purely the result of borrowing (thus, Lohse, 1971, pp. 176-77).

97 This is, in our opinion, the most one can claim for the position of delegates. The theory of Dix, 1946, pp. 255-74, that the office of apostle was subsumed by the episcopate, exceeds the constraints of the evidence. The strongest evidence which he puts forward for this is the reference to Timothy and Titus in the Pastorals, whom he asserts (p. 263) formed a "regional apostolate." But it is more likely that these two delegates, along with the rest of the persons mentioned in the greetings, are referred to as part of the pseudonymous fiction. This is a better interpretation than that which suggests that the references to Timothy and Titus represent a living recollection of arrangements in the seventies; Paul calls Timothy and Titus, together with other fellow-workers, to join him (2 Tim. 4:11, 13, 21; Tit. 3:12) — how "regional" could they have been? See also n. 105 below.

98 Cf. Ezekiel 34:7ff. For further discussion see Schnackenburg, 1977, pp. 418-41; Nauck, 1957, pp. 201-9.

99 Mitton, 1976, pp. 15-17 notes parallels between Eph. and Acts 20.

100 For house-church hosts as administrators in 1 Peter, see Elliott, 1981, pp. 189f., passim. For the origins of the term ἐπίσκοπος and connotations of patronage and oversight in the Graeco-Roman world see Porter, 1939, pp. 103-12, esp. p. 105.

101 For presentations of these arguments see von Campenhausen, 1969, pp. 107ff.; Easton, 1948; Gealy and Noyer, 1955; Grayston and Herdan, 1959-1960; Hanson, 1982; Harrison, 1921; idem., 1956; Karris, 1979; Kertelge, 1972; Kümmel, 1975, pp. 370ff.; Metzger, 1958; Schweizer, 1961, pp. 77f.; Scott, 1957. Kelly, 1963, presents an unconvincing amanuensis hypothesis to defend Pauline authorship. Guthrie, 1957, and Michaelis, 1930, also argue for Pauline authorship.

102 Von Campenhausen, 1951; Hoffmann, 1984, pp. 281f.

103 For parallels see Schoedel, 1967, passim.

104 Thus, e.g., Harrison, 1936; von Campenhausen, 1951, p. 5; Hoffmann, 1984, p. 284; for criticism see Kümmel, 1975, p. 370.

105 For dating around 150 A.D. see von Campenhausen, 1951, p. 12; Gealy and Noyer, 1955, p. 349. These scholars argue that Timothy and Titus are reflections of monarchical bishops or metropolitans, but the fact that Timothy is spoken of as returning to Paul (2 Tim. 4:13) makes this interpretation unlikely; it is better to see references to them as fulfilling a more general function in the fiction of the writings; see Stenger, 1974, pp. 253f. for Timothy and Titus as literary symbols of the transmission of the tradition from the apostle to the contemporary community.

106 Easton, 1948, p. 20 (95-105); Hanson, 1982, p. 13 (100-105); Harrison, 1921, p. 81 (between 95 and 145); Kertelge, 1972, p. 141 (100); MacDonald, 1983, p. 54 (100-140); Scott, 1957, p. xxiv (100-25).

107 Verner, 1983, pp. 91ff.

108 MacDonald, 1983, pp. 59f., puts forward a good case for a connection between the opponents described in the Pastorals and the oral traditions which the author of the Acts of Peter may have used; in the latter document the household is central to the identity and practice of the community. (Passages are listed in the chapter on Ignatius.)

109 A precise description of the organization of and interrelationship between overseers, deacons, and presbyters falls outside the scope of our discussion of this material. We shall address these issues in subsequent chapters. We are assuming that this community was organized along lines similar to that presented in the Shepherd and 1 Clement. This is consonant with Dibelius' and Conzelmann's (1972, pp. 54f.) description of the community as led by a number of presbyter-bishops with deacons as assistants — all drawn from a pool of presbyters who were of higher status within the community, but not necessarily "official" leaders. We disagree with them, however, in their contention that the title πρεσβύτερος is derived primarily from contemporary Judaism. In our view, the presbyter-bishops were the hosts of the various house churches which constituted the local Christian community.

110 Verner, 1983, p. 151.

111 Ibid., p. 133.

112 MacDonald, 1983, pp. 71f.

113 Countryman, 1980, p. 181, n. 42.

114 Ibid., p. 167.

115 Dibelius and Conzelmann, 1972, pp. 8f., 39f.

116 Ibid., pp. 40-41.
117 Ibid., p. 141.
118 For further discussion see Elliott, 1981, pp. 145f.
119 Hatch, 1888, pp. 42-48 notes with reference to 1 Tim. 3:2 and Tit. 1:8 that the term "hospitality" refers to care for the homeless such as orphans, widows, and the poor with common funds, but he generalizes too much from later evidence to the earlier situation and he does not recognize the evidence which suggests that bishops were the church's more prosperous members. We agree that hospitality probably included these more particular acts of care, but we would add that it also involved the more general welcoming of the community into the home — a virtue which the wealthier householders were in a position to practise.
120 For wealthy women as patrons who invited members of the community into their homes see Padgett, 1987, pp. 19ff.; MacDonald, 1983, pp. 50f., 73f. argues convincingly for conventicles of widows residing in the homes of well-to-do women.
121 MacDonald, 1986, pp. 290f. comes to similar conclusions.

Chapter Three
The Shepherd of Hermas

Date

The dating of the *Shepherd of Hermas* is important not only for understanding the purpose of the writing but also the social situation which it describes. However, this issue is clouded because of an apparent inconsistency between internal and external evidence. The *Muratorian Canon* states, "*Pastorem vero nuperrime temporibus nostris in urbe Roma Hermas conscripsit sedente cathedra urbis Romae ecclesiae Pio episcopo fratre eius*" (ll. 73-77).[1] If this is correct, the *Shepherd* was composed sometime between A.D. 139 and 154, the dates of Pius' episcopate. The internal evidence, however, seems to suggest an earlier date of composition. In *Vision* 2:4.3 Hermas is instructed to send a copy of the words that the old lady tells him to Clement, who "then shall send it to the cities abroad, for that is his duty. . . ." Most scholars identify this Clement with the author of the first letter to the Corinthians, which was composed in the last decade of the first century.[2] In addition, there is no evidence in the document that monarchical episcopacy existed in Hermas' church. Hermas, indeed, seems to assume a presbyteral organization of the community (*Vis.* 2:4.3; 3:1.8), which is consistent with an earlier date. Finally, *Vis.* 3:5.1, with its reference to apostles, bishops, teachers and deacons, some of whom "have fallen asleep," but some of whom are still alive, suggests an earlier date than the mid-second century.

Recognizing this conflict of data, scholars have attempted to harmonize the evidence in two ways. Lightfoot suggested a pseudonymity theory and argued that "Hermas" was a *nom de plume* used by Pius' brother for the sake of an apology against Montanism.[3] Nowhere, however, does pseudonymity emerge as an apologetic motif in this work. If the writer had been attempting to ground his composition in the apostolic past, one would have expected him to make far greater and clearer claims to the period he sought to evoke, rather than a single cryptic remark to Clement with no explicit reference to the persecutions in that period. The fact that Hermas alludes to persecutions without feeling the need to explain himself suggests that what he knows regarding past events is common living knowledge in the community. Furthermore, a theory which attempts to find in Hermas' writing an anti-rigorist polemic formulated against Montanism ignores the relationship of the writer's notions of penance and repentance with the social conditions presented in the writing and their connection with what

Notes to this chapter appear on pp. 78-86.

appear to be Hermas' more pressing concerns.

The second and more frequent attempt to solve the dating problem is to postulate a long period of composition during which a series of authors composed
different units of the received work.[4] This has been suggested since the middle
of the last century.[5] Harnack argued for six periods of composition but stated
that it is impossible to determine if the same author wrote the different sections.[6] Joly states that Harnack's theory is "une de ces acrobaties gratuites dont
est si friande l'érudition allemande."[7] But there can be little doubt that the
Shepherd is composed of a number of smaller units written over a period of
time. It is clear that *Vis.* 1 to 4 is a unit, and that *Vis.* 5 (see esp. 5:5) is an introduction to the Mandates. In *Vis.* 1 to 4 it is a woman who explains the meaning
of Hermas' visions, but in *Vis.* 5 it is the Shepherd. Also, the similarity of *Similitude* 9:1.1 with *Vis.* 5:5 as introductions presenting new characters in Hermas'
prophetic experience, the development in *Sim.* 9 of themes in *Vis.* 3, and the
length of *Sim.* 9 compared with *Sim.* 8 and 10 suggest that *Sim.* 9 is a later addition to the parable section, a point which is further supported by manuscript
evidence.[8] This evidence has led several scholars to postulate multiple authorship,[9] one writer suggesting as many as six different authors.[10] The variety of
theological notions present in the work has also suggested multiple authorship.
Giet argues not only on the basis of supposed linguistic and stylistic differences,
but also on the basis of internal theological inconsistencies, that the *Shepherd*
represents the work of three writers.[11] Hilhorst, however, in a monograph
devoted to Hermas' literary style, rejects an argument for multiple authorship
made on literary grounds and argues, "Cette solution soulève plus de questions
qu'elle n'en résout."[12] Furthermore, Giet's argument that *Sim.* 9 represents the
"orthodox" theology of the mid-second century, while the *Mandates* and *Sim.* 1
to 8 present a heterodox adoptionist Christology, poses the question of the
appropriateness of speaking in terms of "orthodoxy" and "heresy" in this
period. As Barnard suggests, it is entirely possible that what appear to be opposing Christological views in the twentieth century could have stood side by side
in the second century. "[T]he *Shepherd*" he argues,

> is a rambling prophetic work which cannot easily be systematized. It may be
> that we should not expect to find a coherent theology running through it. . . .
> Thus a Jewish-Christian Christology of an adoptionist tendency could be
> held side by side with a theologically more advanced Christology which
> asserted that the Son of God was older than creation. What to us seems a con-
> tradiction was not so thought of in an age when much fluidity in doctrine and
> practice prevailed.[13]

If this is true, the warrants for multiple authorship on the basis of internal theological diversity disappear.

But the issue of the purpose of the work, to be addressed in the following discussion, raises in a special way the unsatisfactory nature of solving the dating
problem by reference to multiple authorship. Common to all the sections of the
Shepherd regarded by scholars as units composed by different authors, is the
concern with wealth and the problems it presents to Hermas' community.
Osiek admits that "no consistent patterns in the material about rich and poor
can be correlated with any theory of composite authorship."[14] It will be seen

that the references to wealth and its problems, together with the solution to the difficulties riches present, can be more readily understood if one author was writing over a shorter period of time, rather than several authors over a span of some sixty years. With the exception of Osiek, the scholars who have argued for multiple authorship have been united in their interpretation of the document as a writing primarily concerned to produce theories of penitence. As we shall see, a better interpretation of the document is to argue that Hermas' statements about penitence arise from his primary concern with the purity of his church. The references Hermas makes to penitence are motivated by specific social concerns arising from the misuse of wealth and property.

Since theories dealing with internal evidence do not offer convincing solutions to the dating problem, the evidence of the *Muratorian Canon* calls for closer attention. Any argument regarding the date of this document is hypothetical because of the fragmentary nature of the evidence.[15] It is traditionally assumed that it was composed in Rome sometime between A.D. 150 and ca. A.D. 200 to 220.[16] Koch, however, was an early scholar to question the Roman provenance of the writing by noting that the expressions *"in urbe Roma"* and *"cathedra urbis Romae ecclesiae"* in ll. 73-77 are different from the typical Roman expression of the period *"hic in urbe Roma."* Similarly, he questioned the assumption that the several instances of the term *"catholica"* in the fragment refer to Rome since other writers, such as Cyprian, also used the term to denote the church in places not necessarily confined to Rome.[17]

But the strongest linguistic argument for an early dating of the text rests on the proper interpretation of the superlative construction *"nuperrime."* Usually taken as a diminished superlative, the term is then interpreted as evidence that the *Shepherd* was written within the lifetime of the author of the fragment. Sundberg, however, has correctly stated that this is not the only possible interpretation. If the superlative is translated "most recently" the term may not be a reference to the lifetime of the author, but it "may relate the time-comparison for the writing of the *Shepherd of Hermas* to the previously listed apostolic books. . . ."[18]

Similarly, the expression *"temporibus nostris,"* usually taken to mean "within our lifetime" since it is thought to be connected with Pius, may also be interpreted as a differentiation between the apostolic and post-apostolic period.[19] A passage found in Irenaeus (*A.H.* 5:30.3; cf. Eusebius *H.E.* 5:8.6) suggests that the expression may refer to a period longer than a lifetime. There he uses the phrase ἐπὶ τῆς ἡμέτερας γενεᾶς (*"pene sub nostro saeculo"*) to denote a period of 100 years. Noting this usage in Irenaeus, Streeter argued that the phrase *"in nostris temporibus"* in the Muratorian fragment "cannot be pressed, as has been often done, to imply that the author lived near enough to the time of Pius to be well informed in the matter. In any case such language in early Christian usage allowed considerable elbowroom."[20]

Thus, the phrase *"in nostris temporibus"* and the term *"nuperrime"* may refer not to the lifetime of the author of the fragment, but to the post-apostolic period. This would allow a much later date for the composition of the fragment than is traditionally assumed. Sundberg has shown that a later date of composition makes better sense of the references to the *Wisdom of Solomon* and the *Apocalypse of Peter* as canonical, as well as the concern of the author not to allow the *Shepherd* to be included "among the prophets," that is, the Old Testament. This reflects a fourth-century, eastern concern over the canon more than it does a second century Roman one.[21]

Since it appears that the fragment is in part apologetic, the placement by the author of the *Shepherd* in the reign of Pius may be a polemical effort to argue that Hermas falls outside the apostolic era and therefore must be noncanonical.

If this was a second-century writer's concern it is in opposition to the view of the majority of other second century and even early third-century writers. Irenaeus, Clement of Alexandria, Tertullian, and Origen cited the *Shepherd* as authoritative.[22] Eusebius, writing in the early fourth century, places the *Shepherd* in the category of rejected writings (*H.E.* 3:25.4), but admits that its authority is disputed (*H.E.* 3:3.6-7).[23] These features suggest that the anti-canonical references to the *Shepherd* in the *Muratorian Canon* are more consonant with a later than an earlier date. A later date and the writer's apologetic concern seriously impugn the accuracy of the *Muratorian Canon* composer's remark concerning the date of the *Shepherd*.

In this chapter, therefore, we will assume that the *Shepherd* was composed by a single author some time near the end of the first century. The manuscript differences which suggest a number of separate units need only mean that Hermas did not set out to write a tightly constructed treatise, but that he wrote on separate occasions, expanding certain units and perhaps connecting others together which had been apart. These bits may have become separated in the course of transmission or were perhaps united into a whole by a later editor. This makes better sense of the concern over the proper use of wealth and property which recurs consistently throughout the work. Additional support for this position may be seen in a statement Hippolytus makes in *Ref.* 9:8, that in the third year of the emperor Trajan (A.D. 100) a new remission of sins was preached by Elchesai at Rome. Hippolytus argues that Callistus derives his laxism from this character. The similarity with the *Shepherd* may be significant as an indication of certain theological notions present in Rome *c.* A.D. 100. The reference to persecution in the work, either approaching or past (*Vis.* 2:2.7; 4:1.6-9; Sim 8:6.4; 8:8.2), raises the vexed problem of a persecution carried out by Domitian. It is not necessary to come by a solution of this problem here.[24] The impact which even a locally defined persecution or threat of persecution would have had on this community, it will be argued, could have presented Hermas' community with the social problems he described.

Purpose of the Work

As early as Tertullian, Hermas was understood as a Roman concerned with theological problems of penitence. Tertullian's reading of the *Shepherd* is not surprising: as a Montanist concerned with Christian purity, he found in the *Shepherd* the roots of the laxist practice for which he condemned his opponent Zephyrinus. But modern scholars, too, have found in this document a preeminent concern with post-baptismal sin. By focusing on this aspect of the work in isolation from other problems which Hermas describes, investigators have overlooked the relationship within this writing between notions of repentance and difficulties which wealth and its misuse created for the Christian community. "Sünde und Busse ist ja das Hauptthema" writes Hoh.[25] In a similar way, Vielhauser comments:

> Hermas is set apart from the earlier Christian conceptions which knew only of a repentance at conversion. . . . The sins of Christians had not assumed the proportions of a theological problem — though the actual presence of sins in Christians made any theory of sinlessness impossible — and so neither had the repentance of Christians. This was a result of the eschatalogical expectation. With the weakening of this expectation which resulted from the continuing existence of the world, the sins and the repentance of Christians became a problem.[26]

It cannot, of course, be denied that the *Shepherd* concerns itself with repentance or that there are notions of penance in this writing. And it is also true that Hermas is concerned about the opinion of certain "teachers" who argue that there can be no second repentance after baptism (*Mandate* 4:3.1). But to make these ideas the focus of one's attempts to understand Hermas is to tear him from his social context and place him in a theology seminar or tutorial in the hope that as he sits across from us and reads his essay we will have sufficient insight to question him on the finer points of his composition. Riddle and Osiek are the only scholars to raise serious objections to this way of understanding the *Shepherd*.[27] Riddle writes:

> [T]hat which vitiates the value of most of the discussion of the teaching of Hermas about these matters [i.e. ideas regarding repentance and penance] is that it is altogether doctrinaire, and Hermas is taken as the source for a highly theoretical teaching about abstract subjects. But his lessons are always practical. His problems came to him from an objective or even common sense observation of people, and the crux of the matter for him was by no means the nature of sin and repentance, but the actual difficulties occasioned the churches' by the behavior of their members, namely, the task of the exercise of discipline by the churches in the interest of control.[28]

Rather than demonstrating a concern over post-baptismal sin, the frequent references to wealth and property and their misuse by members in Hermas' community suggest that the primary concern of this author is to maintain the purity of the Christian sect through proper attitudes toward and uses of wealth. For Hermas, problems in the community have arisen because of inappropriate social attitudes. The proclamation of repentance is presented primarily to exert a form of social control on the group, in order to stem a tide which Hermas regards as divisive and destructive.

Wealth and House Churches

The passages in this writing which deal with wealth or related topics are so numerous that it is odd that scholars have not paid more attention to them. Hermas' revelations repeatedly deal with the use and abuse of wealth.[29] These passages deserve brief discussion because they help to establish the general social setting of this Christian community in Rome, and, as will be argued below, they provide a plausible context within which to understand the problems surrounding what appears to be house-church leadership in this community.[30]

The references to wealth in the *Shepherd* occur where Hermas refers directly to members of the community who concern themselves with the pursuit of riches (πλοῦτος), or who glory in their wealth in a way which is damaging to community life. In other passages Hermas instructs wealthier members how to use their wealth properly (*Vis.* 1:1.8-9; 3:3.5-6; 3:9.2-10; *Man.* 6:2.5; 8:3,10; 10:1.4; 12:2.1-2; *Sim.* 1:1-11; 2:1-10; 5:2.9-11; 9:19.3; 9:20.1-4; 9:30.4-5; 9:31.2; 10:4.2). In several of these and in other passages (*Sim.* 4:5-7; 8:8.1-2), Hermas uses the terms πρᾶξις and πραγματεία, which have the general meaning "action" and "occupation" but are usually rendered as "business."[31] This is a justifiable translation because in the majority of these passages Hermas is writing about riches or wealth. It seems likely, then, that the "activities" to which he is referring are of an economic nature. The translation of πραγματεία and πρᾶξις as "business" in the two passages which do not provide an immediate context for references to wealth (viz., *Sim.* 4:5-7; 8:8.1-2) is justified both by the sense that the term usually bears in the rest of the writing and by other contemporary usage.[32] As will be seen below, all these references have important implications for the church's relation to the world. But they also provide some important clues concerning the relation between wealth and power within this community.

Hermas not only expects the wealthier members of the community to care for the poorer members through the contribution of alms (especially *Man.* 10:4.2-3; *Vis.* 3:9.4-6; *Man.* 2:4-6; 8:10; *Sim.*1:8-11; 5:2.9-10; 5:3.7-8), but he also intends that the poor who are cared for pray for their benefactors (*Sim.* 2:1-10; 5:2.9-10). In *Sim.* 1:8, the shepherd commands the rich:

> instead of lands, purchase afflicted souls, as each is able, and look after widows and orphans, and do not despise them, and spend your wealth and all your establishments for such fields and houses as you have received from God. For, for this reason did the Master make you rich, that you should fulfil these services (διακονίας) for him.[33]

It is by this means that the wealthy gain salvation for themselves. Again, in a cleverly formulated analogy, Hermas compares the rich man to a living vine which rests upon an elm tree and bears more fruit because of the support which the elm provides for it. The elm tree is a type for the poor Christian. "The rich person has much wealth," states the shepherd in *Sim.* 2:5-6,

> but is poor in relation to things of the lord (τὰ δὲ πρὸς τὸν κύριον πτωχεύει), being distracted by his riches, and his intercession and confession to the lord is very small, and what he does have is feeble, small and impotent. Whenever, therefore, the rich person rests upon the poor person and gives to him the things he needs, he believes that what he does to the poor person shall be able to find reward with God; because the poor person is rich in intercession and confession and his intercession has great power with God. The rich person, then, supplies all things without doubting to the poor person. But the poor person, because he is helped by the rich intercedes to God by giving thanks to him, on account of the one who gave to him; and the rich person is zealous all the more for the poor one, that his life be continuously

sustained; for he knows that the intercession of the poor person is acceptable and rich toward the lord. (my translation)

By the adoption of this ethic of love patriarchalism Hermas shows that he does not regard wealth *per se* as wicked, but only its improper use. These passages show that there is an important place in the community for the rich Christian as a member who makes his or her wealth available for the common good. That wealth can contribute positively to Hermas' church is also suggested by *Sim.* 4:5-7 where the shepherd states that while those who are involved with much business (τὰ πολλὰ πράσσοντες) sin much, the person who is involved in only one business (μία πρᾶξις) is able to serve the Lord. Again in *Sim.* 9:30.4-5 the shepherd states that it is the Lord's will not to take all the wealth of the rich away from them so that they may be able to do some good in the community with what remains. The presence of wealth and the social inequalities which accompany it are not questioned by Hermas. He does not want to change the social structures that make some Christians wealthier than others, only to reform those structures so that they may contribute to the strength of the community. He is concerned with wealth and social inequalities only when they stand in the way of community cohesion. In *Vis.* 3:9.3, for example, Hermas chastises those who gorge themselves with luxurious food while poor members of the community starve.[34] But the exhortation which follows to share their food with the poor does not mean an abandonment of wealth, only a recognition that with social position comes the responsibility of patronage. The economic structures in the community are in fact maintained intact as a means of community cohesion and as a result are legitimated by the potential good fruits they may bear.

In addition to relying upon the charitable good will of the relatively wealthy for alms, the community also relies upon the good will of wealthier members to open their homes to "the slaves of God," a phrase Hermas uses for the wider community (e.g. *Sim.* 1:1.1). In the parable of the sticks in *Sim.* 8:10.3, Hermas learns of those who "did the deeds of wickedness" — becoming too involved in worldly business (this is implied from the context established by *Sim.* 8:9.3)[35] — but still "received into their homes the slaves of God."[36] Again, in *Man.* 8:10 the shepherd gives a long exhortation to the well-to-do which includes an exhortation to be hospitable and not oppress poor debtors.[37] While such exhortations may not refer exclusively to the well-to-do, the exhortation to be hospitable would have had its most pertinent reference to wealthy persons, who had an important role in providing meeting places for the worshipping community.[38] The rich person not only makes material goods available to the community, but he is also expected to open the doors of his house to the members of the church and to practise hospitality.

The exhortations to care for the poor and to be hospitable suggest that the wealthy member is the person who has the greatest responsibility in creating an environment conducive to harmonious community life. Consonant with this general pattern is the evidence in the document which describes the leadership of the community.

Hermas' concerns about problems in his community become more sharply focused where he describes the abuses of certain leaders of the church. In *Sim.*

9:31.6 the shepherd warns that wrath is in store for the shepherds (ποιμένες) who have fallen away from innocence. This passage occurs in the context of a more general description of members who are in need of reform because of "the vanities of their riches" (*vanitates opum suarum* – 9:31.2) and who have caused schisms within the community (9:31.4). Abuse of wealth and schism among leaders are problems which Hermas describes in several passages. In *Sim.* 9:26.2 he describes ministers (διάκονοι)[39] who "ministered amiss" (κακῶς διακονήσαντες) by using the money which they received, presumably from alms, for the ministry of widows and orphans for their own gain. But it is not only common funds which they abuse; Hermas also chastises them for using their own wealth inappropriately. In *Vis.* 3:9.2-10 the ancient woman describes those who make themselves ill by overeating. She states in 3:9.4f.:

> So this lack of sharing (ἀσυνκρασία) is harmful to you who are rich (τοῖς ἔχουσι – thus Lake), and do not share with the poor. Consider the judgment which is coming. Seek out you rich (ὑπερέχοντες) those who are hungry. . . . Take care, then, you who rejoice in your wealth, that those who are in want (ὑστερούμενοι) may not groan, and their groans go up to the Lord and you be thrown with your goods outside the door of the tower. Now, therefore (οὖν), I am speaking to you who are leaders (προηγουμένοις; cf. Heb. 13:24) of the church and to the ones who hold the first seats (τοῖς πρωτοκαθεδρίταις). . . . You are hardened and you do not want to cleanse your hearts and to mix your pride together with a pure heart, so that you might find mercy coming from the great king. (my translation)

Hermas then goes on to warn the leaders and those in the first seats regarding their disagreements (vs. 9-10). In this passage the leaders of the community are spoken of as wealthy persons who, as those mentioned in the more general descriptions of abuse of riches, do not use their wealth in a way which benefits the community. While in *Sim.* 9:26.2 Hermas describes the misuse of alms given to leaders for distribution, in *Vis.* 3:9.4f. it appears to be their own wealth which they abuse, and so the greed of leaders does not imply the squandering of public funds alone. Private wealth as a criterion for the management of corporate wealth was normative in the ancient world. Analogies exist both in Judaism and in Graeco-Roman clubs. Financial patronage placed members of these groups in special positions of either leadership or honour.[40] Again, Hands has shown how in both Greek and Roman clubs wealthier members donated sums of money in return for honour, and that where an official was elected to an administrative post in the club, such as the oversight of the common purse, his office would have involved him in some personal expenditure on behalf of the association.[41] We find in ancient society, therefore, a pattern which suggests that those members who were most suited for the administration of funds, namely the well-to-do of the group, were chosen for this task. The evidence in the *Shepherd* points in the same direction.

But it is not only when Hermas chastises the leaders for their neglect that evidence of their wealth emerges. He also assumes a degree of wealth on the part of leaders when he presents an ideal picture of bishops as a foil for the negligent ones. In *Sim.* 9:27.2 the shepherd explains that one of the revelations Hermas saw represents, hospitable bishops (ἐπίσκοποι φιλόξενοι),[42] who at all times welcomed the servants of God into their homes (οἴκους) without hypocrisy; and bishops who always and without ceasing sheltered the needy and the widows by their ministry (διακονία) and always behaved with holiness (my translation).

We have already seen how Hermas usually employs the phrase δοῦλοι τοῦ θεοῦ to refer to the entire Christian community. The reference to widows, set alongside a reference to general hospitality offered to the wider community, refers to another duty of the bishops,[43] and functions as a direct contrast to the squandering of public funds by leaders described in *Sim.* 9:26.2. If we read the phrasing of this passage in this way, we find evidence that it was not only the bishops' wealth but also their homes which were expected to be used on behalf of the wider community.[44] Since the passage states that it is overseers who are welcoming members into their homes there is a case for arguing that this is a reference to various house churches and their patrons.[45]

The references to schism which we have noted in Hermas' statements about leaders support the assumption that a series of house cells met in wealthier members' homes. A possible setting for community division may be reconstructed from the general shape of leadership in this church. The plural ἐπίσκοποι in 9:27.2 suggests that there were several bishops in this community. Other references also indicate a plurality of leaders. A plurality of leaders is also suggested by *Vis.* 2:2.6 and 3:9.7 (προηγούμενοι) and *Vis.* 2:4.2 and 3:1.8 (πρεσβύτεροι). Similarly, the plural πρεσβύτεροι προϊστάμενοι in *Vis.* 2:4.3 implies several leaders. Finally, if Clement's references to a plurality of leaders in Corinth, a church closely connected with Rome, is any indication of the structure of his own church, this also indicates a number of leaders.[46] Πρεσβύτεροι and ἐπίσκοποι are the primary terms used both by Hermas and the contemporary Christian literature to describe leadership in the church.

It is difficult to establish the relation between these two terms because Hermas is not concerned to defend a particular form of ministry. He assumes that his readers know what form of leadership they have. Any attempt, therefore, to reconstruct such a relationship is tentative. Given Clement's usage which treats ἐπίσκοποι and πρεσβύτεροι as synonymous (e.g. *1 Clem.* 44:4-5; 47:6), it is unlikely that these terms refer to two distinct orders within the church. But in *Vis.* 2:4.3 Hermas is exhorted to read his revelation "with the elders who are governing the church" (μετὰ τῶν πρεσβυτέρων τῶν προϊσταμένων τῆς ἐκκλησίας). Either this means that there are certain elders who are προϊστάμενοι or that all elders fulfil this function. While the text does not state directly which is the case, a clue is provided in *Sim.* 9:27.1-2 where ἐπίσκοποι φιλόξενοι[47] are described. If our view that these represent a series of bishops, each representing a house church, is correct, given the usage of the term to describe ἐπίσκοποι in roughly contemporary New Testament literature (cf. 1 Tim. 3:1,5; cf. 5:17[48]), there is a case for arguing that these leaders may also be described as προϊστάμενοι. We are warranted in speculating that the πρεσβύτεροι προϊστάμενοι, as distinct from πρεσβύτεροι (*Vis.* 3:1.8), are the same leaders as the ἐπίσκοποι. We suggest, therefore, that certain elders of a larger presbyteral body acted as bishops in the Roman church. There is not yet a full distinction between ἐπίσκοποι and πρεσβύτεροι, nor are all πρεσβύτεροι also ἐπίσκοποι. In the *Shepherd of Hermas* we have to do with presbyter-bishops who are responsible for the superintendence of the church. The other πρεσβύτεροι may be senior (cf. *Man.* 8:10) or honoured members of the community. The references in the *Shepherd* to elders who hold the first seats (*Vis.* 3:1.8; 3:9.7 – πρωτοκαθεδρίται [49]) suggest that there are members who are honoured in the community by a special seating arrangement.

Hermas states that there are divisions among these members. In *Sim.* 8.7.4 the shepherd informs Hermas of members who "were always faithful and good, but they had some jealousy among themselves over the first position (περὶ πρωτείων)[50] and some question of reputation." According to the shepherd these members have turned to schism. We have already seen that in *Vis.* 3:9.2,9-10 and *Sim.* 9:31.4 there is a description of divisions among leaders and prominent members of the community. Schism, either implied or stated directly, is a charge which is repeated against the community (*Vis.* 3:6.3; 3:12.3; *Sim.* 8:7.2; 8:9.4; 8:10.1-2; 9:23.2-3).[51] Many of these passages describe minor quarrels between members. But in a few instances the divisions appear to be more serious than small arguments between fellow believers. *Vis.* 3:9.9-10 and *Sim.* 9:31.6 describe divisions between leaders; in the latter passage "shepherds" (probably a synonym for ἐπίσκοποι)[52] are presented as the cause of the falling away of members. A picture of harmony among the leaders of the apostolic past is presented in *Vis.* 3:5.1 as a contrast to the divisions among the contemporary community's leaders. In *Sim.* 8:10.2 he states that after Hermas' revelation the majority of members repented of their schisms, but some made even a greater schism. Finally, in *Sim.* 9:23.2-3 the shepherd describes members "who are persistent in their evil-speaking, and are become malicious in their rage against one another."

A clue to the impact that quarrelling overseers could have had on the community is in *Sim.* 8:10.3 where, in the context of the description of schism, members are described who repent of their sins and welcome members of the community into their homes. In the instance of such contentious leaders, it is possible that they did not welcome members of other house cells into their homes. And where wealthier elders coveted the first position, one option open to them would have been to separate themselves from the house church which did not accord them the honour they felt fitting, and invite sympathetic members to worship in their own households.[53] In a society in which wealthier members offered patronage to groups with a view to receiving honours proportional to their gifts, it is not difficult to imagine wealthy members of the church feeling dissatisfied with honours given them as not befitting the financial services they were offering.[54] We are not suggesting that this is the only possible interpretation of the evidence, but that the church meeting in the household of wealthy patrons provides a plausible explanation of the nature of the more serious schisms facing Hermas' community.

Summary

Hermas' discussion of wealth assumes a degree of relative wealth on the part of some in the community, including especially its leaders. The references to inviting the members of the church into bishops' homes imply that Hermas' church shared the same social setting as recent New Testament scholars have suggested for the earliest church. House-church patronage was probably a central feature of Hermas' community. While the precise form of the schisms is uncertain, a house-church setting provides a plausible backdrop for the more serious divisions which are described.

Relation Between the Church and the World

In the preceding discussion we have attempted to show that Hermas' references to the abuses of wealth in his community and his exhortations concerning its proper use point to a situation in which wealthier patrons of Hermas' church, often acting as its leaders, invited members into their homes for church activities. If, however, in the course of discussion, we have been able to isolate certain elements of the text which relate to the use and abuse of riches, this should not blind us to the fact that Hermas was not engaged in a theoretical discussion concerning the wealth of certain members of his community. A treatment which rejects the notion that Hermas' predominant concern is with post-baptismal sin must not put in its place one which finds in his writing a theoretical concern with riches.

Hermas' worries regarding the use and abuse of wealth may be more fully understood when placed in the wider social context of his concern with the purity of his community. Both his teachings on repentance and his exhortations concerning the proper use of wealth have as their goal the purification of the Christian community. The fact that Hermas continually employs descriptions of group and personal impurity, defilement, and even disease as metaphors suggests that his community's purity is one of his major concerns.[55] The issue of purity raises for Hermas the problem of his community's relation to the world, a problem particularly acute because, as we have seen above, it seems likely that the leaders of his community were well-to-do and, as we will see below, may have relied for their economic prosperity on "worldly" connections. In this section we will provide a general discussion of Hermas' references to purity and impurity in order to place Hermas' concerns concerning wealth in their proper context. We will concentrate primarily on the causes which have resulted in group impurity, and on the ways Hermas describes the relation of the church to the world. An understanding of these concerns for purity will help us to comprehend in a better way the relationship which existed between what we will call "the response to the world" of Hermas' community and the problems which were undermining its group identity.

The references in this document concerning purity are too numerous to discuss separately. We shall concentrate primarily on a representative portion of the text (*Sim.* 9) which is illustrative of Hermas' concerns. This will help us to see the nature of the impurity which Hermas thinks is contaminating his church.

In *Sim.* 9 Hermas expands the material composed in *Vis.* 3 (*Sim.* 9:1.2). In his vision he is taken to a great plain surrounded by twelve mountains (9:1.4) which represent the nations of the earth (9:17.1). Different stones, with distinctive qualities representative of types of people (9:19.1ff.), are brought from each of the mountains to the centre of the plain for the construction of a tower

(9:3.1ff.), which represents the church (9:13.1). Before the completion of the tower construction is halted and the Lord of the tower comes to test the suitability of the stones for the construction of the building (9:5.2). He strikes each of the stones of the tower with his staff. As a result, several stones turn black or rotten or reveal other flaws (9:6.3f.). These stones are then removed and cleaned or replaced by better stones (9:6.5ff.). After these renovations, Hermas states (9:9.7) that the tower appeared "as if it were all one stone, without a single joint in it, and the stone appeared as if it had been hewn out of a rock, for it seemed to me to be a single stone." The tower is swept by virgins, who represent holy spirits (9:13.2), and water is sprinkled on it (9:10.3). The significance of this cleansing is revealed in 9:18.2-4, where the shepherd explains:

> Thus therefore the Church of God shall be cleansed (καθαρισθήσεται). But just as you saw that the stones were taken from the tower and handed over to the evil spirits and cast out from it (and there shall be one body of those who are purified, just as also the tower became as if it were made of a single stone, after it was purified [καθαρισθῆναι]), so the Church of God shall be, after it has been purified (καθαρισθῆναι), and the wicked and hypocrites and blasphemers and double-minded, and doers of various wickedness, have been rejected from it. After these have been rejected the Church of God shall be one body, one mind, one spirit, one faith, one love, and then the Son of God shall rejoice and be glad in them, when he has received his people in purity (καθαρός).

This whole similitude is an image for the purification of Hermas' community.

It becomes clear who are the persons need purification when the meaning of the various stones which are rejected from the tower is revealed. Hermas' references to the "wicked and hypocrites and blasphemers and double-minded, and doers of various wickedness" in the passage cited above are repeated throughout his writing. While they often function as general descriptions of unfaithful members,[56] in certain instances Hermas provides a more precise description of members who are guilty of these charges. This is particularly the case in descriptions of apostasy. Hermas returns repeatedly to the charges of blasphemy and apostasy as examples of his community's most heinous sins. In *Sim.* 9:19.1 the shepherd states that the stones taken from the black mountain, symbolic of absolute impurity, represent "such believers as these: apostates and blasphemers against the Lord, and betrayers of the servants of God." That these are not mere rhetorical flourishes is suggested by the fact that Hermas singles out Maximus in *Vis.* 2:3.4 as a member who had denied his faith once before. While there is no evidence that wealth was related to Maximus' apostasy, Hermas often links apostasy and blasphemy with riches (*Vis.* 1:4.2 [cf. 1:1.8-9]; 2:2.6-8 [assuming that leaders are well-to-do]; 3:6.5; *Sim.* 1:4-6; 6:2.3-4; 8:8.2; 8:9.1-3; 9:19.3; cf. 9:20.2). In Hermas' view there is a direct relationship between undue regard for riches and lack of allegiance to the church. Because of their riches wealthier members do not "cleave to the saints" (*Sim.* 8:8.1; 9:20.2) but involve themselves instead in "heathen" friendships (*Man.* 10:1.4-5; *Sim.* 8:9.1-3). The result is that the wealthy members, who perhaps rely on their worldly connections for the success of their businesses,[57] find it difficult to separate themselves from their economic interests when it is necessary to show their solidarity with the wider community, as for example in times of persecution,[58] and end in denying their faith.

In *Sim.* 9 and throughout the rest of the writing Hermas describes these wealthy members as being guilty of varying degrees of impurity. In *Man.* 10:1.4 and *Sim.* 8:9.3 the shepherd states that they are corrupted (καταφθείρονται; φθειρόμενοι) by their deeds and associations with the "heathen." For Hermas, corruption is equivalent to impurity (cf. *Sim.* 4:7). We have already seen that the apostates and blasphemers are represented by the black stones in *Sim.* 9. Other stones represent similar impure characters: the stones with spots in *Sim.* 9:26.2 symbolize those who have abused their ministry by using the common funds for their own gain. Hermas also uses the image of round white stones for members who have a degree of purity but are not useful for the building of the tower unless their wealth be cut off from them (*Vis.* 3:6.5; *Sim.* 9:31.1-2). In *Sim.* 6:5.5 the shepherd states that among those who live luxuriously are the covetous who give satisfaction to their "disease" (νόσος). Again, in *Sim.* 8:11.3 Hermas learns that when those who have been described in the preceding parable of the sticks purify themselves "from the wickednesses which have been mentioned before," they shall "receive healing from the Lord for their former sins." While the parable refers to several categories of people, two important examples of members in need of purification, represented by sticks partly alive and partly dead, are those who concern themselves with business activity and "do not cleave to the saints" (*Sim.* 8:8.1) and those who have become "rich and in honour among the heathen" and do not "cleave to the righteous" (*Sim.* 8:9.1). Given these references it appears that the exhortation to be purified from the "vanities of this world" (*Man.* 9:4; cf. 12:6.5; *Sim.* 6:2.2-3) was of particular significance to the community's wealthy members.

We have found in the *Shepherd* a concern regarding the impurity of wealthy members of the group. The impurity which results when wealthy members form allegiances too close to the world has implications for the whole group. Members who become too attached to their wealth cause disorder in the community, both in the sense that they separate themselves from other members and in the sense that they contribute to the erosion of the group's ethical identity. We will return to this latter point in our final section. Here we are interested in the relation between impurity and disorder within the group.

The cultural anthropologist Mary Douglas has argued convincingly that notions of pollution and impurity in both primitive and advanced societies and in ancient and contemporary cultures[59] have to do with the maintenance of order and internal and external group boundaries. She has noted that the concept of "dirt" is a relative notion which implies disorder.[60] "Dirt" according to Douglas is "matter out of place" and its presence implies two conditions: "a set of ordered relations and a contravention of that order." Furthermore, "Dirt . . . is never a unique isolated event. Where there is dirt there is system."[61] Dirtiness and its opposite, cleanliness, apply not only to inanimate objects but also to persons and places.

Rules which are formulated to maintain cleanliness or purity are attempts to preserve personal and group boundaries so that what is regarded as proper order is not upset. As Malina suggests, purity is specifically about the general cultural map of social time and space, about arrangements within the space thus defined, and especially about their boundaries separating the inside from the outside. The unclean or impure is something that does not fit the space in which it is found, that belongs else-where, that causes confusion in the arrangement of the generally accepted social map because it overruns boundaries, and the like.[62]

In the case of the *Shepherd*, Hermas describes wealthier members preoccupied with their business interests who are impure because they have stepped beyond the boundaries of the group to form allegiances with the wider society — result-ing in a withdrawal of their loyalty to the church. To call them impure is to state that they are "dirty," that they have caused social disorder by trespassing certain social lines which are meant to separate members of the group from outside influences.

The presence of riches in the community results in a certain ambiguity in the boundaries separating the group from the world because while it is the case that the misuse of and inordinate attachment to wealth leads wealthier members astray, it also enables the well-to-do to care for the poor and to provide the resources necessary for the functioning of the community, i.e. feasts, alms, a place to worship, and other facilities. Hermas' response to this ambiguity is to establish a purity rule.[63] In *Sim.* 4:5-7 the exhortation to abstain from much business (πρᾶξις) is qualified so that a member is permitted to be occupied with one business. This is one attempt to deal with the anomaly wealth pres-ents. Hermas states that one who follows this rule will not have his understand-ing "corrupted from the Lord," "but he will serve him with a pure mind." A similar point is made by the reference to the white round stones in *Sim.* 9:30.4-5, which represent the wealthy members of the community who become useful to the construction of the tower only after their excess matter (i.e., their excess wealth) is cut off.

Douglas has suggested that it is especially where boundaries are ambiguous that purity and pollution rules are used to reinforce group boundaries and maintain social order.[64] So too, Hermas' concerns about the business preoccu-pations of the wealthier members of his community and the references he makes to their impurity together with a rule for the correct amount of involve-ment the well-to-do may have with business concerns is an attempt to remove any ambiguity, which might result in impurity, surrounding the use of riches and to establish boundaries which limit the wealthier members' economic activ-ities.

The establishment of a purity rule is not the only way that Hermas attempts to establish the purity and order of his group. The proclamation of a second repentance is central to Hermas' references to purity. We have seen that in *Sim.* 9 the Lord of the tower comes to test the edifice and discards stones which are not fit for the building. These stones, however, are able to be returned to the building if they are cleaned (*Sim.* 9:7.2).[65] By this cleaning process Hermas refers to repentance (9:33.1; cf. 9:23.2). In *Sim.* 9:14.3, Hermas, after reflecting on the graciousness of the Lord for providing a period of repentance, states:

I thanked the Lord for all these things, that he had mercy on all who call upon his name, and sent the angel of repentance to us who have sinned against him, and renewed our spirit, even when we were already corrupted, and restored our life, when we had no hope of living.

The proclamation of a second forgiveness of sins which scholars have traditionally seen as an attempt of Hermas primarily to come to terms with post-baptismal sin should rather be seen as an effort to re-establish the boundaries of his church by the removal of impurity. At the end of *Sim.* 8, healing is offered to those who "repent with all their hearts, and purify themselves from the wickednesses which have been mentioned before, and no longer add anything to their sins." But those who do not repent "and live in the lusts of this world" shall be condemned (8:11.3-4). Again, in *Sim.* 6:3.2-5 the angel of punishment is described as a figure who corrects those who "have wandered away from God, and walked in the lusts and deceits of this world." Their punishment is the unsettlement they experience in the conduct of their worldly affairs, and the result of this punishment is repentance. The shepherd explains:

And if they repent, then it enters into their hearts, that the deeds which they did were evil, and then they glorify God saying that he is a righteous judge, and that they suffered righteously, each according to his deeds, and for the future they serve the Lord with a pure heart, and they prosper in all their deeds. . . . (6:3.6)

Exhortations to repentance, especially when connected to a certain urgency that members repent before the construction of the tower is completed (*Vis.* 3:5.5; 3:8.9; cf. *Sim.* 9:19.2), are attempts to re-establish the purity of the group and the church's boundaries.

As a symbol of group identity, the vision of the tower constructed as if it were made from one stone (*Sim.* 9:9.7) is a vision of group solidarity and cohesion. But Hermas also uses images which present the ambiguity of group boundaries. In *Sim.* 3:1-3 Hermas is shown several leafless trees, that appear to be alike. The shepherd explains to him that these represent

those who dwell in this world. . . . Because . . . in this world, neither righteous nor sinners are apparent, but all are alike. For this world is winter for the righteous and they are not apparent, though they are living with sinners. For just as in the winter the trees which have shed their leaves are alike, and it is not apparent which are dry and which are alive, so in this world neither the righteous nor the sinners are apparent, but all are alike.

We have seen that one of the ways the community experienced this ambiguity was when wealthier members rejected closer contact with the church in favour of associations with outsiders.

But there is a more general level on which the world-church or, more precisely, world-sect dichotomy may be discussed. Bryan Wilson's sect-type, used heuristically as a tool to make distant comparisons between contemporary sects and Hermas' church, helps us to identify some of the sources of problems facing this first-century community. Wilson has noted the pressures which are exerted upon contemporary sects by their necessary existence within wider society and, more importantly, the ideological characteristics, special to certain types of sect, which make those pressures particularly acute. He argues that contemporary sects attempt to preserve their separation from the rest of society.

> If the sect is to persist as an organization it must not only separate its members from the world, but must also maintain the dissimilarity of its own values from those of the secular society. Its members must not normally be allowed to accept the values of the status system of the external world.[66]

He states further,

> The sect's desire to be separate from the world and its concerns — and the values which express that separateness — results in certain distinct tensions for the organization and for its members. For each sect there must be a position of optimal tension, where any greater degree of hostility against the world portends direct conflict, and any less suggests accommodation to worldly values.[67]

But the difficulties of maintaining a separate identity from the rest of society is increased by the typical sectarian effort to win recruits.[68] Again, he comments

> The principal tension between the demand for separateness and other sect values arises in the injunction, accepted by many sects, to go out and preach the gospel. Evangelism means exposure to the world and the risk of alienation of the evangelizing agents. It means also the willingness to accept into the sect new members. This throws a particular weight on the standards of admission if, through the impact of recruitment, the sect itself is not to feel the effect of members who are incompletely socialized from the sect's point of view.[69]

When we turn to a discussion of baptismal thought and imagery in the *Shepherd* we will notice how behavioural values are associated by Hermas with entry into the group through baptism, and the importance of this ritual as a group-defining symbol of separation.

A further challenge to sectarian identity occurs through the passage of time. Wilson and other sociologists note that as certain sects continue to exist they often undergo an attenuation of their separatism and increasingly accommodate themselves to the values of the society around them. In some sects this is occasioned by the problem of recruiting the second generation, or children of the original converts, and socializing them into the group.[70] In the case of the *Shepherd* there is evidence that seems to suggest that an attenuation of sectarian response was probably occurring within his community. When we turn to a discussion of *1 Clement* we will identify organizational factors which may have contributed to this accommodation to the world. Hermas' preservation of the social distinctions prevalent in his contemporary society in his solution to the problems of maintaining group boundaries may be interpreted as evidence of a sectarian group adopting worldly structures and a movement away from the pure sect type.

The major question which Wilson's discussion of sectarianism raises for us is the relation which existed in Hermas' community between certain expressions of belief and community boundaries. Here we are interested primarily in attitudes toward the world which may have resulted in weaker community boundaries in this group. We will argue, tentatively, that the impulse in the group toward the winning of outsiders reveals certain patterns of openness toward the outside world and that this response to the world may have allowed contact with outsiders in a way damaging to the cohesion of the group.

It should be stated at the outset that Hermas is not concerned to provide any direct information on the topic of conversion. But there are some clues that ideologically his group responded to the world in an open way by viewing persons outside the group as potential members. In *Sim.* 8:3.2 Hermas hears the explanation of a great tree he saw in his vision. "Listen," says the shepherd,

> this great tree, which covers plains and mountains and all the earth, is God's law which was given to all the world. And this law is God's son preached to all the ends of the earth. And those who are under its shade are nations which have heard the preaching and have believed in it.

Again, in *Sim.* 9:17.1 Hermas is informed that the twelve mountains he sees represent all "the tribes which inhabit the whole world" to whom the apostles preached about "the Son of God." The stones from these mountains which come together to form the tower, i.e. the church, appear bright because, according to the shepherd,

> all the nations which dwell under heaven, when they heard and believed were called after the name of the Son of God. So when they received the seal (i.e.baptism) they had one understanding and one mind, and their faith became one, and their love one . . . (9:17.4).

While the context of this passage refers to present members of the church, in *Sim.* 9:30.3 the shepherd explains that the stones brought from the white mountain represent "both past and future" pure believers. Finally, the image of the tower which is almost but not entirely completed suggests that there are still believers to be converted. And Hermas learns in *Vis.* 2:2.5 that although there is another chance of repentance for the saints within the community but none after the time for renewal has passed, "for the heathen repentance is open until the last day." These images suggest that there was in Hermas' community a degree of openness to the world as a source for potential believers.

A community which regarded the world with a degree of positiveness as a place of potential believers may have been less concerned to control the activities of members involved in secular activities. We suggest this as a tentative connection between an ideology of openness to the world and problems arising from the involvement of members in it. Because of an openness to outsiders, the restraints which otherwise would have functioned to control contacts with the world may have been relaxed, in a way which allowed wealthier members to involve themselves in secular activities with an enthusiasm damaging to the exclusive identity of the church. We can be more certain that as long as the community looked to wealthy members to provide the patronage necessary for the functioning of the community, there had to exist a certain openness to members involving themselves in wider social structures, since the community benefited from such involvement. It is only by contact with the world that resources will be gained for the functioning of the common life and new members will come into the community. A community that relies on these structures and sees itself involved in the salvation of members of the society outside the community will find itself in a tenuous position when it attempts to maintain the purity of its group by lessening the power of the world's influence on its daily life. Any contact with the outside world, which is seen as a place of impurity, will challenge the purity, that is the boundaries, of a group attempting, at least ideally, to maintain an identity separate from it. Similarly, any outside member coming into the group bears the seeds of impurity. As we will see below, baptism functions as a means of removing the threat of impurity.

Summary

We have focused on Hermas' concerns regarding the purity of his community. We argued that the anxiety he has about the purity of members of his group is a worry concerning community boundaries. Particular attention was given to the references to the impurity of wealthier members. Hermas attempts to control their activities by the establishment of a purity rule, which, if successfully enforced, limits the activity of the well-to-do in secular affairs, thereby reinforcing the boundaries separating the church from the world. We have suggested a tentative connection between an openness to the world as a positive place containing future believers and a relaxation of group restraints. This led to wider access by the wealthy to secular affairs, thus damaging the group's identity. There is an inherent tension between the group's attempts to separate itself from the world and its attitude to outsiders as potential insiders, as well as its dependence on the involvement of wealthier members in the wider society for certain resources necessary for the church's common life.

Ethics and Separation from the World

We have argued that the language in the *Shepherd* which describes purity is indicative of Hermas' concerns regarding the community's separation from the world. How is such a separation established and maintained? It was suggested, following Wilson, that there is a tension which confronts the sectarian identity of a group whose response to the outside world is characterized by openness, but which attempts to maintain an identity separate from it. The totalitarian hold which sects typically have on members tends to be undermined by openness to the world. The typical way some contemporary sects attempt to maintain their hold on members can help us to understand how Hermas hoped to maintain the separation of his church from the world. Once again we are using Wilson's concepts heuristically: just as certain tensions confronting modern sects help to show how weak sectarian boundaries in Hermas' church resulted in its wealthier members' engagement in business activities detrimental to the sect's identity, so the form of sectarian control typical of certain contemporary sects can give us insight concerning Hermas' ethical injunctions.

Wilson suggests two ways in which a sect can keep itself from contamination by the world: "isolation" and "insulation."[71] While the isolation tactic avoids contact with the world, insulation permits contact with the world but employs behavioural rules calculated to protect the sect's values by reducing the influence of the external world. In some types of sects Wilson identifies, such as the conversionist type, doctrine and moral commitment are important variables in the maintenance of sectarian identity.[72] The role of ethics as a means of nurturing a common identity which shields the sect from influence by the outside world is a helpful way to understand the significance of Hermas' ethical paraenesis. Even if Hermas' moral exhortation is often general, its significance is that through it Hermas hopes to encourage the growth of an environment representative of what he regards as the church's fundamental nature.

Before we turn to an investigation of Hermas' paraenesis, we shall briefly discuss the role religious beliefs about transcendent reality play in shaping behaviour. The anthropologist Clifford Geertz provides a useful understanding of religion as composed of sacred symbols[73] which have ethical implications. Geertz argues that the importance of a religious symbol is that it serves as a "model of" reality, representing in another medium structures and relationships of transcendent reality, and a "model for" mundane reality, shaping behaviour so that it is consistent with the transcendent view which the symbol communicates.[74] "Religious symbols" he argues, "formulate a basic congruence between a particular style of life and a specific (if, most often, implicit) metaphysic. . . ."[75] Geertz writes,

> sacred symbols function to synthesize a people's ethos — the tone, character, and quality of their life, its moral and aesthetic style and mood — and their world view — the picture they have of the way things in sheer actuality are, their most comprehensive ideas of order.[76]

This implies that a group's ethos

> is rendered intellectually reasonable by being shown to represent a way of life ideally adapted to the actual state of affairs the world view describes, while the world view is rendered emotionally convincing by being presented as an image of and actual state of affairs peculiarly well-arranged to accommodate such a way of life.[77]

Where this occurs a symbol at once induces certain moods, motivations, and dispositions in the individual to whom the symbol has meaning and places them in a cosmic framework in some sense congruent with those personal characteristics.[78] The important point is that it is the same symbol which does both. Reflecting upon the simultaneous metaphysical and ethical nature of religious symbols Geertz writes

> Religion is never merely metaphysics. For all peoples the forms, vehicles, and objects of worship are suffused with an aura of deep moral seriousness. The holy bears within it everywhere a sense of intrinsic obligation: it not only encourages devotion, it demands it; it not only induces intellectual assent it enforces emotional commitment. . . . [T]hat which is set apart as more than mundane is inevitably considered to have far-reaching implications for the direction of human conduct. Never merely metaphysics, religion is never merely ethics either. The source of its moral vitality is conceived to lie in the fidelity with which it expresses the fundamental nature of reality. The powerfully coercive "ought" is felt to grow out of a comprehensive factual "is," and in such a way religion grounds the most specific requirements of human action in the most general contexts of human existence.[79]

Especially in religious ritual, where sacred symbols are explicit often in the form of activity rather than words, a particular sense of the divine is communicated and certain devotional moods are evoked.[80] "In sacred rituals and myths values are portrayed not as subjective human preferences but as the imposed conditions for life implicit in a world with a particular structure."[81]

One of the most potent symbols for the early church is baptism: it symbolizes in a profound way the nature of a new life in a community created by God and set radically apart from the world. With that new life comes an ethical imperative which reflects the nature of the transcendent reality which has called the church into existence and sustains it. The notions surrounding baptism in the Shepherd are no exception.

For Hermas the images of death and life describe in a powerful way the significance of baptism. In *Sim.* 9:16.1 Hermas inquires after the meaning of part of the vision of the tower where he saw stones brought up from a deep place (*Sim.* 9:3.3-4). The shepherd describes these stones as representative of the faithful first generations of Christians (*Sim.* 9:15.4-6), and then (9:16.2-4) explains the significance of "the deep":

> They had need to come up through the water, in order that they might be made alive; for they could not enter into the kingdom of God in another way, unless they laid aside the mortality of their former life. Even these, then, who had fallen asleep received the seal of the son of God and entered into the kingdom of God. For before, said he, a man bears the name of the son of God, he is dead; but when he receives the seal he lays aside mortality and he receives (ἀναλαμβάνειν) life. The seal then is the water; they go down therefore into the water dead and come up alive (Lake with some modification).[82]

In *Vis.* 3:3.5 a similar image is presented where the Lady states that the tower, i.e. the church, is built on water "because your life was saved and shall be saved through water." She goes on to add, probably recalling the baptismal ritual,[83] "and the tower has been founded by the utterance of the almighty and glorious Name, and is maintained by the unseen power of the Master."

Baptism initiates the member into a new life which demands a consequent purity of life. For Hermas, such a life means to live to God (ζῆν τῳ θεῳ).[84] In *Sim.* 9:17.4-5, Hermas learns that impurity results in rejection from the church.

> [A]ll the nations which dwell under heaven, when they heard and believed were called after the name of the Son of God. So then when they received the seal they had one understanding and one mind, and their faith became one, and their love one.... For this cause the building of the tower became bright with one colour like the sun. But after they entered in together and became one body, some of them defiled (ἐμίαναν) themselves and were cast out from the family (γένους) of the righteous, and became again what they had been before, or even worse.

The implication of the language of defilement and the image of the tower "bright ... like the sun" is that to enter the community through baptism is to become pure, in distinction from the outside world. It is to enter the kingdom of God (*Sim.* 9:16.2).[85]

Along with this purity is a characteristic ethical standard by which the individual initiated into the church is expected to abide. Baptism as a symbol of casting off mortality and putting on new life brings with it an ethical demand. But entry into this new life, into "the family of the righteous," is also entry into a new realization of the glory of God in his nature as creator and sustainer. It is this "symbol," using the term in Geertz's sense, which permits the faithful to fulfil the requirements of the new life.

The standards of the new life of the baptized are presented in the *Mandates*. These represent a series of exhortations and behavioural rules which are to guide the activities of the members of the church. The particular rules found in this section will not concern us here. Rather we shall focus our attention on *Mandate* 12:4.2-5 where the shepherd, after hearing Hermas' doubts about the ability to keep all the commandments revealed to him (*Man.* 12:3.4), states that Hermas does not understand the glory of God, "how great and wonderful it is, because he created the world for humanity's sake, and subdued all his creation to humankind, and gave humans all power, to master all things under heaven." (*Man.* 12.4.2). He further explains

> If, then, humankind is the Lord of all the creatures of God, and masters them, is it not possible to master these commandments also? The person . . . who has the Lord in his or her heart, is able to master all things and all these commandments. But those who have the Lord on their lips, but their heart is hardened, and they are far from the Lord, for them these commandments are hard, and difficult to walk in. Do you, therefore, who are empty and light in the faith, put the Lord into your heart, and you shall know that nothing is easier or sweeter or more gentle than these commandments.

The "person who has the Lord in his or her heart" is able to keep God's commandments.

The description of the Christian as a creature of God with the Lord in his or her heart at once states something about absolute reality, namely that God is sovereign Creator, and makes an ethical demand which is designed to express that reality. Thus, the *Mandates* begin with the exhortation to believe that God is one, "who made all things and perfected them, and made all things to be out of that which was not, and contains all things, and is himself uncontained" (*Man.* 1:1). The word οὖν in *Man.* 1:2 connects the accompanying ethical exhortation with this transcendent reality:

> Believe then in him, and fear him, and in your fear be continent. Keep these things, and you shall cast away from yourself all wickedness, and shall put on every virtue of righteousness, and shall live to God, if you keep this commandment.

In *Sim.* 9:14.5-6, Hermas learns that if the whole creation is supported by the Son of God, those who "bear the name of the Son of God" and walk in his commandments are supported all the more. Again, in *Vis.* 1:3.4 the symbol of God as sovereign creator of the world and the church is related to the promise of reward given to those "who keep the ordinances of God, which they received with great faith." In *Vis.* 3:3.5, a baptismal passage cited above, it is stated that the tower "is maintained by the unseen power of the Master." The implication of this language, taken together with Hermas' descriptions of baptism, is that entry into the church is an initiation into a reality created especially by God (*Vis.*

2:4.1; 1:1.6), and that reality obliges those who live within it to embark on a new life of purity. In *Sim.* 4:4 Hermas learns that the "heathen" (τὰ ἔθνη) shall be destroyed because they did not know their creator. Knowledge of the creator brings with it an obligation to obey him; those who know him without obedience are condemned (4:3-4).

Hermas' ethical exhortations, as well as the rules he establishes for contact with the world through business, are not distinct from the identity of his sect; rather, they are formulated as an expression of its identity as the focus of God's redeeming activity. Looking from the outside into the sect, Hermas' paraenesis often appears general and unfocused. But once it is placed into the wider cosmological context he presents, we can see how those exhortations would have taken on a greater significance for the individual within the sect looking at the world outside. For the outside world is impure and dead. Inside the sect is, or at least is meant to be, purity and life.

We turn now to a discussion of the role of ethics in the conversionist sect. Behavioural rules and exhortation help to create an identity which sect members believe to be ethically distinctive. The importance of Hermas' paraenesis is that it is designed to shape the behaviour of members who are participants in the transcendent reality of the church. To be baptized into the kingdom of God, that is the church (*Sim.* 9:13.1-2), brings an obligation to don the apparel of the virgins (παρθένοι) who surround the tower (*Sim.* 9:13.2-5; 9:15.1-2; *Vis.* 3:8.2-8) and whose clothing of linen represents distinctive virtues and purity (*Vis.* 3:8.7). At one point in Hermas' vision (*Sim.* 9:3.4) these maidens carry the stones through the gate and into the tower for its construction. That is, those who would enter the kingdom of God must also have their virtues (*Sim.* 9:13.3-5). But those who are baptized and do not clothe themselves with the maidens' raiment, are rejected from the tower and carried away by the women (γυναῖκες) clothed in black (*Sim.* 9:9.5). These women, with their bare shoulders and loose hair, are presented as beautiful temptresses who lead those who bear "the name of the Son of God" (*Sim.* 9:13.7) astray, so that once-faithful members are "rejected from the house of God (τοῦ οἴκου τοῦ θεοῦ)" and delivered to these women. These seducers represent vices roughly opposite to the virtues represented by the pure virgins (*Sim.* 9:15.3, cf. v.2). Members who are guilty of these vices "shall see the Kingdom of God, but shall not enter into it" (*Sim.* 9:15.3).

From his discussion of members who were once faithful but are later rejected from church, it seems clear that baptism is no guarantee that the member who enters the new community will remain in it. The images we have discussed which describe the impurity of rejected members suggest the same notion. This is not surprising given Hermas' anthropology. In *Man.* 6:2 Hermas learns that there are two angels with man, one of righteousness and one of wickedness (*Man.* 6:2.1). Each of these attempts to influence the actions of individuals; when virtue comes into one's heart the angel of righteousness is present (v. 3), but when the angel of wickedness is at work vices are present (vs. 4-8).[86] Whatever the source of this anthropology, its implication for the community attempting to separate itself from the influence of the world is important. For it implies that members may be in the community yet stray from the sect or act in

ways which do not express their identity as members of the church. It is possible to be "double-minded," which, in the parable of the sticks (*Sim.* 8:7.1),
describes a state in which a believer is neither dead nor alive. Included among
those with this characteristic are those who, because of their business concerns,
do not "cleave to the saints" (*Sim.* 8:8.1; see also 8:9.1-4).[87] This image forms a
striking contrast to the language used of the new life attending baptism. The
unambiguous new life with its fervent obedience to the Creator's commands
can become vague, lukewarm, half-dead.

The use of injunction and the establishment of regulations, such as those limiting the amount of business one may involve oneself in, are important means
of ensuring that the sect maintains a distinctive identity separate from the outside world. The effects of openness to the world are limited by rules and exhortations designed to ensure that a member's primary allegiance remain with the
group. The city of God (see the description in *Sim.* 1:1) has its own law, which
distinguishes it from the earthly city, and those who wish to live in it must abide
by its regulations or risk exclusion (*Sim.* 1:5). One who lives by its laws recognizes that he or she is a stranger in a strange land, that he or she should pattern
his or her lifestyle in accordance with that alien existence. "Rather than lands,"
Hermas writes in v. 8, "purchase afflicted souls, as each is able. . . ." Widows
and orphans are the true costly establishments of this city: it is here where a real
profit is made. The ethic of love patriarchalism is an attempt to create a distinctive group identity which is able to capitalize on the economic benefits involvement with the world brings to individuals.

But the admonitions to be subject to the law of the Lord's city are not purely
an individualistic affair. In *Sim.* 10:3.1-2 (cf. *Man.* 4:4.3), Hermas is informed
that the holy maidens will dwell with him in his house only if he keeps his
house pure. "If then they find your house pure they will remain with you. But,"
explains the shepherd, "if ever so little corruption come to it they will at once
depart from your home, for these maidens love no sort of impurity" (v. 2). Hermas is often chastised for the sins of his family. In *Vis.* 1:3.1 he learns that God
is angry with him for their sins; he is indulgent, he has allowed them to become
corrupt. Hermas is admonished for having disobedient children and a nattering
wife (*Vis.* 2:2.2-3), and the problems which he once had, perhaps arising from
his old economic activities (*Vis.* 3:6.7; see also *Man.* 3:5), the shepherd connects
with his neglect of his family and their transgressions (*Vis.* 2:3.1). Again, in *Sim.*
7:2 Hermas learns that the angel of punishment dwells in his house because of
the sins of his family. Dibelius doubts whether these statements are references
to Hermas' real family, and takes them, together with Hermas' other references
to his household, as a fictional model constructed to convey theological notions
of sin and repentance.[88] He is correct that Hermas' references constitute a
model for instruction, but their primary purpose is not to provide a theoretical
lesson about sin and repentance, but to teach something about the responsibility
of the Christian householder to keep his house in order.

Whether his statements about his family are fictional or not, their role is to
exhort householders to ensure that members of their families refrain from sin-
ning. And included among these sins is the insubordination of wives and children (*Vis.* 2:2.2-4). So, in *Sim.* 7 the shepherd's lesson concerning the punish-

ment of heads of households for their families' sin is generalized as a lesson for
the whole community (v.7). The *paterfamilias* who keeps himself and his household from sin gains salvation for both him and his family (*Vis.* 1:3.2; 2:3.1; *Man.*
2:7; 4:4.3; 5:1.7; 12:3.6; *Sim.* 5:3.9). It is not only on an individual level, but also
on that of the household that the church is to preserve its identity as the locus of
the Creator's redeeming activity. The well-ordered household, regulated by the
faithful householder, contributes to the maintenance of the sect's boundaries.

Summary

Following Geertz' analysis of the role of religious symbols as "models of" and
"models for" reality, we have shown that there is a connection between Hermas' ethical paraenesis and the belief in God as sovereign Creator. Belief in God
brings with it the duty of obedience to his commands, and since humanity is
created by God there is a belief that one can, and therefore must, keep his commands. Baptism signifies entry into a new life of faith in and obedience to God.
This life is marked by virtues which are meant to express the distinctive character of the Church as the particular object of God's action. We argued, borrowing
insights contained in Wilson's sect-type, that Hermas hopes to lessen the influence of the outside world on his church by a series of ethical exhortations.
Among these is an ethic of love patriarchalism, which is designed to turn the
efforts of the rich, who have strong ties with the world, to the care of the poor,
as an expression of their membership in the community. Hermas is also concerned that households be well-ordered. The *paterfamilias* is responsible for the
actions of the members of his household, and the well-ordered household is
one which is subject to his authority. Such traditional authority contributes to
the maintenance of the sect's boundaries and helps to preserve the identity of a
community which regards itself as separate from the world.

Notes

1 The latin text is provided by Dibelius, 1923, p. 421 together with the latin text of
   the *Liber Pontificalis* which follows the *Muratorian Canon*.
2 E.g. Lightfoot, 1890, Vol. 1, Pt. 1, pp. 359-60; Snyder, 1968, p. 22. For the dating of
   1 Clement see Chapter Four.
3 Lightfoot, 1890, p. 360.
4 See Osiek, 1983, pp. 6f.; Hilhorst, 1976, pp. 20f., for a discussion of the most
   recent scholarship.
5 See Dibelius, 1923, p. 420; Hilhorst, 1976, pp. 19-20, for the earlier literature.
6 Harnack, 1897, pp. 257-67.
7 Joly, 1968, p.15.
8 See Snyder, 1968, p. 6 for further discussion of the manuscript evidence.
9 Thus, e.g., Dibelius, 1923, pp. 420-21; Wilson, 1927, pp. 20-21, 50-54; Snyder,
   1968, pp. 3-7; Barnard, 1966.
10 Coleborne, 1969, pp. 133-42; 1970, pp. 65-70 (arguing on the basis of statistical evidence); for criticism of his statistical attempts see Hilhorst, 1976, pp. 21-23.
11 Giet, 1963; for discussion and criticism see Barnard, 1968, pp. 30-33; Hilhorst,
   1976, pp. 21-22.

12 Hilhorst, 1976, p. 186; he argues (pp. 25-31) on statistical grounds for single authorship; similarly, Morton, 1964, pp. 31, 84-85.

13 Barnard, 1968, p.32.

14 Osiek, 1983, p. 7. Osiek goes on to comment, however, that "taking an absolute stand on this complicated question would serve no purpose" (loc. cit.), but in this she has already begun to undermine her thesis that Hermas' primary concern in this document is with socio-economic realities (p. 14). Her thesis is weakened by her failure to provide an explanation of how socio-economic concerns may be harmonized with a theory of multiple authorship.

15 Sundberg, 1973, p. 1 discusses the manuscript evidence.

16 See Sundberg, 1973, pp. 3f. for the arguments of Harnack and Zahn and for further references.

17 See Koch, 1926, pp. 154-60; Koch's argument is summarized in Sundberg, pp. 65-66.

18 Ibid., p. 9.

19 In the early literature there is a conscious differentiation between the apostolic period and that which followed, cf. Ignatius *Ephesians* 12:2; Polycarp *Philippians* 3:2; Hegesippus in Eus. *H.E.* 4:22.4; 3:32.6; Eusebius divides his work into the period of the apostles and that following it, see *H.E.* 3:32.8. For discussion of these references see Sundberg, p. 9.

20 Streeter, 1929, p. 207; he still, however, argued for a second century date (ibid., p. 211). See also Sundberg, p. 9 for further discussion of the Irenaean passage.

21 Sundberg, pp.16f.; recent doctoral research at Oxford University undertaken by J. Heinemann supports this view.

22 *A.H.* 4:20.2; cf. *H.E.* 5:8.7; *Stromata* 1:17,29; 2:1,9,12; Tertullian first accepted it (*De Orat.* 16) but in his Montanist period rejected it as laxist (*De Pud.* 10,20), a shift explicable on theological grounds; Origen in his earlier writings regarded it as scripture (*De Prin.* 1:3.3; 2:1.5; 3:2.4) although he was aware that some were opposed to the work (*De Prin.* 4:1.11 — composed A.D. 230-240), increasingly in a later writing (*Comm. in Rom.* 10:31 — composed before *c.* A.D. 244).

23 For further discussion of the later evidence see Sundberg, pp. 12f.

24 See Workman, 1980, p. 83 for a traditional account of the persecution. While Eusebius assumed that a persecution of Christians had been carried out by Domitian (*H.E.* 3:17; 3:18.4-5; 4:26.9), the secular evidence which apparently led to his belief is ambiguous. Apart from a no longer extant reference which Eusebius claims in the *Chronicon* (Helm, p. 192; cf. Barnes' [1981, p. 31 n. 31] comment) to have found in a senator's account of the fates of the Flavians, Eusebius relied on Suetonius, *Domitian* 15 and Dio Cassius 67:14 for his information about T. Flavians Clemens and Flavia Domitilla. But it is not clear that Flavia Domitilla was charged with Christianity. Clemens' ἀθεότης (Dio Cassius 67.14; *contemtissimae inertiae*- *Dom.* 15) may rather have been Judaism (*Dom.* 17; Suetonius notes that Nerva restored the privileges of exiled Jews after Domitian's death, a point which Barnard, 1966, p. 14, who accepts Eusebius' report, overlooks). Eusebius makes Domitilla the niece rather than the wife of Clemens. This has led Keresztes, 1973, pp. 15f. to argue for the existence of two Domitillas. The only other external evidence, however, that Domitilla was a Christian is the Domitilla catacomb. But the name of this burial spot only proves that Christians came to buried on land which once belonged to the Flavians (thus, e.g., Stevenson, 1978, pp. 27-28; Osiek, p. 94). Moreover, because Eusebius is concerned to show that respectable and prosperous persons were members of the early Christian church (Barnes, 1981, pp. 131-32) his comments about Domitilla are suspect in the face of ambiguous evidence. The postulation of two Domitillas

begs the question of the reliability of Eusebius' account (see Osiek, pp. 93-94 for further discussion). It was, however, a tradition from an early date that Domitian persecuted the Christian church at the end of his reign (see Melito's comment in Eus. *H.E.* 4:26.9; Hegesippus in Eus. *H.E.* 3:20.1; Tertullian *Apol.* 5; New Testament Rev. 13:1; 17:9, cf. Irenaeus *A.H.* 5:30.3 and Kümmel's, 1973, pp. 466ff. discussion). The references in Revelation are problematic and the other references may be derived from Hermas taken together with *Clement* 1:1 which to a writer looking at the text 50 to 100 years later may have suggested an imperial persecution. Suetonius (*Dom.* 3:2), too, implies that Domitian indiscriminately persecuted individuals and it is possible that some Christians became his victims, but not necessarily because they belonged to a specially targeted group. To the Christian community, of course, his actions would have been interpreted in a more sinister way (cf. Barnard, 1966, pp. 8f.)

25 Hoh, 1932, p. 10.

26 Vielhauser in Hennecke, II, p. 639.

27 Riddle, 1927, 561-77; Osiek, 1983, pp. 4, 14. Osiek has attempted to establish some foundations for further work by scholars approaching the *Shepherd* with sociological models and theories (p. 3).

28 Riddle, 1927, p. 572.

29 References to wealth throughout the *Shepherd* imply that there were relatively well-to-do Christians at Rome. In fact, scholars at one time or another have argued for the presence of Roman aristocrats in the Roman church at this time. Pomponia Graecina (*c.* A.D. 57; cf. Tacitus *Ann.* 13.32), Titus Flavius Clemens (d. A.D. 96), Flavia Domitilla (exiled ca. A.D. 96; cf. Dio Cassius 67.14; Suetonius *Dom.* 10, 15, 17) and M. Acilius Glabrio (*c.* A.D. 96; cf. Dio Cassius 67:14) are all Romans supposed to have been members of the church. But in all these instances the evidence is insufficient to support the assertion that they were Christians. See Osiek, 1983, pp. 92f. for full discussion. On the other hand, Justin (*Apol.* 1:67), writing in Rome, states the wealthier Christians help the poor. So it seems that the presence of wealth in the Roman church was not a fantasy on the part of Hermas (cf. also Minucius Felix *Oct.* 31:6; similarly Dibelius, 1923, p. 528; Joly, 1958, p. 36). The well-to-do at Hermas' church were probably comprised of prosperous freedpersons (such as Hermas probably had once been — cf. *Vis.* 1:1.1; 3:6.7) who, as was possible for enterprising former slaves in this period, earned their riches through business and trade (similarly, Osiek, 1983, pp. 134-5; for examples of wealthy freedmen from whom the emperor Claudius was advised by the Senate to borrow money when he complained of his poverty see the references to Narcissus and Pallas in Suetonius *Claud.* 28; also Trimalchio in Petronius' *Satyricon* 48). For further discussion of the wealth of freedmen see Dill, 1904, pp. 100-37; Duff, 1958, pp. 114-28.

30 See Chapter Two for a discussion of house churches in Rome at the time of Paul; the existence of a number of cells loosely connected with each other (as seems to be implied in New Testament Rom. 16), probably continued for some time and may have been similar in this respect to synagogues, which, according to Leon, 1960, pp. 135-70 (similarly, La Piana, 1927, pp. 351ff.), formed a loosely knit community divided according to geographical origin, social condition, and practice. Brown (Brown and Meier, 1983, p. 108), argues that some Roman Jews met in private house synagogues; this may be true since there is no archaeological evidence of synagogue buildings in Rome, but this rests on an argument from silence. La Piana, 1925, pp. 201ff. also speculates that there was in this period a variety of Christian groups differing from one another in various degrees (cf. Eus. *H.E.* 5:24.14). Could not the house church have contributed significantly to this diversity? The other

New Testament literature often associated with Rome (1 Peter and Hebrews) provides little information for our concerns here; the writer of 1 Peter was probably a Christian intimately acquainted with the churches in Asia Minor, and his epistle is best interpreted as reflecting common practice there (cf. 1 Peter 1:1). Brown, op cit., attempts to place these documents, together with the *Shepherd* and *1 Clement*, in a "trajectory" of moderate Jewish-Christianity allied closely with Jerusalem, but his theory that the Roman church retained close connections with Jerusalem and that such ties affected its development of the ministry is unconvincing.

31 Thus, e.g., Lake in the Loeb translation; Lightfoot in *The Apostolic Fathers*; Dibelius in *Der Hirt des Hermas* (Geschäft); Joly in the Sources Chretiennes edition sometimes translates πρᾶξις and πραγματεία respectively with the more general *activité* and *occupations* (e.g. *Man.* 10:1.5; *Sim.* 4:5). But he also chooses the translation *affaire*, a rendering which has economic connotations (e.g., *Man.* 10:1.4). The passages where he chooses *affaire* over occupations are those with references to wealth in them, except in *Sim.* 8:8.1-2, where there is no direct reference to riches and he translates πραγματεία with *affaire*.

32 See especially the second century A.D. astrologer Vettius Valens (ed. Kroll, see index under πρᾶξις = *negotium*), also rabbinic literature which uses the terms as loan-words for business activity (see Jastrow, *A Dictionary of the Targumim, the Talmud Babli and Yerushalmi, and the Midrashic Literature,* פרגמטיה; פרקסים [= "business"]; פרקבון [= "public life"]; for references to πραγματεία and the article on πραγματεία, πρᾶξις by Maurer in *TWNT*, Vol 6, p. 641.) In the *LXX* see Sir. 11:10ff. where the context suggests that the πράξεις referred to are economic (esp. vv. 12, 14, 21f.), Jerome renders the term with *actus*, but the context of the word in his translation suggests the activities he is thinking of are economic (he translates: "*Fili ne in multis sint actus tui: et si dives fueris, non eris immunis a delicto…*"). Πραγματεία also occurs in 2 Tim. 2:4, where it may have an economic sense (see Maurer, p. 641) who translates it as Erwerbsgeschäfte. Most of the translations render it as "affairs" or something equivalent, but the J.B. Philips translation "business" seems to get closer to the cultural metaphor used in the passage. For earlier usage of the terms with an economic connotation see Liddel and Scott, Vol. 2, loc. cit. Lampe does not include references to Hermas' use of these terms. Bauer's lexicon of the New Testament and other early Christian literature provides a variety of translations of the terms as they appear in the *Shepherd*. Osiek, 1983, p. 40, comes to a similar conclusion concerning Sim. 8:8.2; she provides a similar translation of Sim. 4:5-7, but without comment.

33 Unless otherwise stated all translations in this and in following chapters are from Kirsopp Lake, *The Apostolic Fathers* (2 vols.) Loeb Classical Library (London: William Heinemann Ltd., 1977).

34 Such a description reveals the presence of status-specific behaviour often displayed at pagan banquets of the time: Martial complains (3:49) that his host eats oysters while he is given only a mussel to suck on (cf. also Martial 1:20; 3:49,60; 4:68, 85; 6:11; Juvenal *Sat.* 5:24ff.; Lucian *Saturnalia* 17f.; *On Salaried Posts* 26; Luke 14:7-11). The ideal feast was one in which all were equals (Athenaeus *Deipnosophistae* I:3-4,12; cf. Pliny *Ep.* 2:6). For further discussion see Theissen, 1982, pp. 155ff.; Pervo, 1985, pp. 307-29.

35 *Sim.* 8:9.3 does not state directly that the persons described have been involved in business activity, but the description of these members of the community as those who "became rich and in honour among the heathen" (8:9.1) implies that like others who in the course of the writing are described as being misled by their business concerns, so these members abandon the Christian community in favour of worldly

connections and as a result of misuse of wealth. Similarly, the reference to apostasy in 8:9.3 is consistent with references in the writing which connect business activity with lack of allegiance to the church and denial of God.

36 I.e., in contrast to those who did not (cf. 8.9.1).

37 The exhortation to be "poorer than all people" is to be taken in a moral rather than economic sense. Hermas describes in several passages the haughtiness or high-mindedness of the wealthy (e.g. *Sim.* 8:9.1), who separate themselves from the community. In *Man.* 8:10 the reference to poverty occurs in a list of virtues which contribute to the common good of the community. This suggests that the reference to poverty is best understood metaphorically.

38 A century later. Hippolytus (*Apos. Trad.* 26:6ff.) describes a house meeting where a common meal, presumably an agape celebration but not necessarily so (cf. v. 12), occurs in the house of a host. The need for hospitality provided by patrons for such meetings to occur is evident, and Hippolytus emphasizes the respect due to those who offer their homes for the community's use. Again, while such action may not necessarily have been limited to wealthy members of the community, larger meetings would have only been possible if wealthier members used their resources to organize them, especially since the implication is that the "offering" is provided by the host (26:1,6,8-9).

39 Perhaps deacons (thus, e.g. Dibelius, 1923, pp. 632-33) although it is difficult to be certain.

40 Harvey, 1974, pp. 324f discusses ἀρχισυνάγωγοι and the evidence of πρεσβύτεροι and ἄρχοντες, noting that ἀρχισυνάγωγοι were highly respected and responsible positions; see the discussion in the Introduction above.

41 Hands, 1968, p.52. Wealth as a necessary criterion for election to office was especially common in the higher offices of the club. The number of offices in these clubs was not always the same. The office of treasurer, the position in the club which most closely resembles the Christian overseer, was usually named *quaestor*. In those clubs which did not have *quaestores*, the officials named *curatores* took over this function. In the latter case these members where usually rich and influential members. *Quaestores* stood half way between the upper and subordinate ranks of the *collegia* officials (thus, Kornemann, 1901, p. 422).

42 This is the reading of L^2, a Latin MS originating around the fifth century. It omits the καί and reads "*episcopi hospitales.*" E, an Ethiopic and sometimes free translation (thus, Whittaker, 1967, pp. xvii-xviii) of the sixth century, also contains this reading. The strongest support for including the καί comes from the only Greek reading preserved for us — Codex *Athous* (A), a fourteenth or fifteenth century Greek MS (viz ἐπίσκοποι καὶ πηιλόξενοι). L^1, the translation which according to Turner, 1920, pp. 205f, is closer to the Greek original, is adduced by Dibelius, 1923, pp. 407-9, in support of *A's* reading. L^2, however, is corrupt and itself departs from *A* ("*quidam episcopi id est praesides ecclesiarum, alii vero hos* [Dibelius suggests "*hi*"] *lapides* [Dibelius suggests "*hospites*"]). Turner, op. cit., p. 204, notes that "in the relative absence of good Greek authority" [such as in *Sim.* 9:27.2], L^2 has "some importance of its own wherever differences from the Vulgate [i.e. L^1] indicate a different underlying text." And he argues (pp. 204-5) that L^2, though later than L^1, represents a textual tradition independent of the Vulgate MS and was presumably executed when Greek MSS were still available in the West. The weight of the MSS evidence, therefore, falls evenly on both sides. Whatever reading one chooses, the movement of thought in v.2 is clumsy, but the intention of the passage, even if one adopts the reading of *A*, is probably best expressed by L^2. Moreover, if we adopt L^2's

reading, the contrast between the corrupt ministers presented in *Sim.* 9:26.2 and the virtuous ones in 9:27.2 is stronger.

43 The duty of inviting widows into the bishop's home is more fully developed in the *Didascalia*, passim; cf. also the third-century *Acts of Peter* (*Actus Vercellenses* 8; cf. 25) where Marcellus, a rich member of the Roman church whose "house was called the house of strangers and of the poor," is described as casting the church in disarray for ceasing to invite the poor into his home. In 29f. the whole community meets in his home.

44 There is intriguing archaeological evidence which dates from this early period for the remains of house churches in Rome. Peterson, 1969, p. 266 concludes from the evidence of *tituli* churches in Rome (i.e. churches alleged to originate in the homes of wealthy or famous benefactors) that the Roman church worshiped in households until the late second or early third century. But of the twenty-five *tituli* listed in the *Liber Pontificalis* (for further discussion see Snyder, 1985, pp. 75-82), thirteen can be shown to have been created after the peace of Constantine and of the remaining number, generalization from archaeological remains to house churches is tenuous. The oldest and, in the case of Hermas, only germane evidence is San Clemente, which was dedicated to Clement at the end of the fourth century and is alleged to be the house of the first-century bishop, or of T. Flavius Clemens (thus *Liber Pontificalis* 1.1233 — ed. Duchesne, 1886). Kraeling, 1967, p. 29 is highly sceptical of this tradition on the grounds that pre-Constantinian structural remains found under Rome's oldest churches do not necessarily imply the presence of house churches; it would not be unusual in a crowded city for Christians to build on the foundations of pre-existing buildings. Peterson and Lightfoot (1890, Vol. 1, Pt. 1, pp. 91ff.) are less sceptical, but it is now generally agreed that the earliest residential remains are Mithraic, not Christian (Snyder, 1985, p. 76).

45 Riddle, 1938, pp. 141-54 and Chadwick, 1961, pp. 281-85 have rightly pointed out the importance of hospitality given by bishops or other members of the church to travellers in the spread of early Christianity and communication between churches. The notion of "standing hospitality," where an individual can rely upon the good graces of an associate, even a relatively unknown one, was an ancient Greek practice (cf. Homer *Od.* 9.18; cf.3.69; 4.60 — see Stählin, *TDNT*, vol. 5, p.17 for further references) which arose as a result of trade requirements. Standing hospitality is also found in the New Testament (e.g., Acts 21:4; 3 John 5, 10). But together with this form of hospitality is a more general form which involves the invitation of the worshiping community into a member's home. Paul states in Rom. 16:23 that Gaius is the "host (ξένος) to me and to the whole church" and Prisca and Aquila are presented as *de facto* hosts of the church (1 Cor. 16:10). It appears from these references that hospitality can mean the welcoming of individuals in one's home as well as a larger group such as a worshipping community.

46 Cf. *I Clem.* 44:4-5 (plural); 47:6; 54:2; 57:1 (πρεσβύτεροι).

47 See note 42 for this reading.

48 It is generally agreed that 5:17 refers to ἐπίσκοποι.

49 Cf. *Man.* 11:12 where a prophet is described as coveting the first seat (πρωτοκαθεδρία).

This raises the question of the role and place of prophets in this community. Both Harnack's (1884) picture of an itinerant order of prophets and Greeven's (1952/53, pp. 3-15) conception of a local order which governs the church tend to over-simplify, distort, or make too broad generalizations from often complex evidence. As the early church developed there were probably many expressions and forms of authority even within the same community, which were not necessarily consistent with each other. The authority of a house holder over activities in his own home in some cases would have co-existed with the authority of a prophet to instruct or declaim. On the basis of *Vis.* 3:1.8, scholars have debated concerning Hermas' relationship to the presbyters, some arguing that this is evidence that he regarded himself as subject to them, others contending that it shows that he placed himself on the same level as they were (see Reiling, 1973, pp. 151ff. for various positions). The choice is probably an anachronistic one; the relationship between the church leadership excercised by a house-church patron and that wielded by a prophet (assuming that Hermas was a prophet) may not always have been clear-cut. It is just as possible that the ambiguity of *Vis.* 3:1.8 reflects a real one in the community. Hermas may not have possessed explicit criteria to define the limits of his authority with respect to presbyters. And even though Hermas describes both the false prophet (*Man.* 11:12) and elders (*Vis.* 3:9.7; cf. *Sim.* 8:7) with reference to the first seat, it is not necessarily the case that he is referring to identical phenomena. The discussion here and in subsequent chapters focuses on one manifestation of leadership, while at the same time recognizing that there were probably several currents of authority in these communities. In the case of the *Shepherd*, there is no evidence that these were in conflict or competition with each other.

50 Lampe, loc. cit., states that πρωτεῖος refers to ecclesiastical offices.

51 *Sim.* 9:22.2-4 describes teachers who exalt themselves, which may describe *de facto* schism.

52 The association of these terms appears in contemporary New Testament literature (see 1 Pet. 5:2 with the MSS. evidence; Acts 20:28).

53 If there were cases where dependants, such as slaves and freedmen, had converted, the contemporary norms of showing dutifulness by supporting the master's religious practices would have placed an obligation on them to separate as well.

54 Similarly, Countryman, 1980, pp. 157ff., although he does not recognize fully enough the role of wealth in the choice of leadership. For the wealthy calculating honours given for patronage to groups, see Hands, pp. 37f. This was especially prominent in the imperial period and in clubs.

55 On almost every page of the document there is some reference to purity. Hermas is accused of impure desires (*Vis.* 1:1.7) or his family or fellow members are accused of being corrupt(ed) (*Vis.* 1:3.1; *Man.* 10:1.4; *Sim.* 6:2.2-3,4; 8:9.3; 9:14.3 — [κατα] φθείρειν]) or of having an impure heart (*Sim.* 6:5.2). Language of defilement or pollution (*Man.* 3:2; 4:1.9; 5:1.3; *Sim.* 6:7.2,3; 9:17.5 — μιαίνειν) or uncleanness (*Vis.* 3:9.7) or even disease (*Sim.* 6:5.5) often occurs. The woman or shepherd also speak of Hermas, his family, and the church being cleansed or purified (*Vis.* 3:2.2; 3:8.11; 4:2.5; 4:3.4; *Sim.* 9:18.2,3-4 καθαρίζειν; *Vis.* 4:3.5). Christians are exhorted to act with a pure heart or to be pure (*Vis.* 5:7; *Man.* 2:7; 4:1.1; 4:3.2; 4:4.3; 5:1.2; 6:2.2; 9:4,7; 10:3.4; 12:3.2; 12:6.5; *Sim.* 4:7 [cf. διαφθείρειν]; 5:1.5; 5:3.6; 5:7.1; 6:3.6; 7:2,6; 8:3.8; 8:6.2; 8:7.5; 8:11.3; 10:3.2,4). Images with specific colours such as white and black or qualities such as brightness or spottiness are also used in the visions and parables to convey both notions of purity and impurity (purity: *Vis.* 3:1.4; 3:5.1; 3:6.5; 4:2.1-2; 4:3.4-5; 5:1; *Sim.* 6:2.5; 9:1.10; 9:2.1,2; 9:2.4; 9:4.5; 9:9.1; 9:10.2-4; 9:15.2; 9:17.4; 9:29.1; 9:30.3; 9:33.3; impurity: *Vis.* 3:2.8; 4:3.2; 3:6.2; *Sim.* 9:1.5; 9:4.6-7,8; 9:5.2; 9:6.4; 9:8.1,7; 9:15.3; 9:19.1; 9:26.2). Or a divine agent is described as an agent of purification (*Sim.* 5:2.4 [cf. 5:5.3]; 5:6.2,3,5-7; 8:1.2; 9:6.5; 9:7.2; 9:8.1,2,5,7). Divine phenomena are described in terms of purity (*Vis.* 3:7.3; 3:8.7).

56 The references to double-mindedness (δίψυχος) appear numerous times throughout the work. It is used consistently to denote instability in the Christian life or a

cause of difficulty to the community (e.g., *Vis.* 2:2.7; 3:7.1; 4:1.4,7; 4:2.4,6; *Man.* 5:2.1; 9:7; 10:2.2; *Sim.* 1:3; 6:1.2; 8:8.3; 8:9.4; 8:10.2). Seitz, 1947, outlines the use of the term in rabbinic literature as well as James and *1* and *2 Clement.*

57 The role of friendships in business in the ancient world is discussed by Theissen, 1982, pp. 129-32.

58 It is not necessary to postulate a general persecution under Domitian to account for the problems of apostasy which are described in the *Shepherd.* Trajan informs Pliny in *c.* A.D. 111-113 that if Christians are denounced they are to be judged guilty (Pliny *Ep.* 10:96) unless they renounce their faith. If a hostile outside observer brought Hermas' Christian assembly to the attention of a local authority, this could have provided the setting for the problems of apostasy which Hermas describes in his writing.

59 See, for example, her discussion of Levitical purity laws in the Old Testament, 1966, pp.49ff.

60 Ibid., p. 2; cf. also Malina, 1981, pp. 122ff., who has applied her notion of dirt and purity to New Testament texts.

61 Douglas, 1966, p. 35.

62 Malina, 1981, p. 125.

63 Douglas and Malina note that every group suffers from certain ambiguities or anomalies, i.e., realities that do not fit the cues of a culture. Douglas, 1966, pp. 39-40, argues that there are five different ways of a group to remove anomalies. One way is by elites or opinion leaders settling on one interpretation of life, thus reducing ambiguities. This corresponds roughly to Hermas' argument that riches exist solely for the sake of the care of the poor and the building up of the church.

64 Douglas, 1966, p. 138.

65 A similar theme is found in *Sim.* 8 where, after the willow branches are cut from the tree, they are planted for a time to see if they shall live (8:2.6). As a result of this many live and the shepherd explains that these are representative of those who have repented and have been saved (8:6.1f.).

66 Wilson, 1967, p. 41.

67 Ibid., p. 39.

68 Wilson writes (Ibid., p. 43) that the conversionist sect typically "accepts individuals more lightly, socialises them less intensely, and loses them more easily — all of which disturbs the strong sense of community;" see Chapter Two for further discussion.

69 Idem., 1959, p. 11.

70 Niebuhr, 1972, argues that this is a phenomenon common to all sects, but Wilson has successfully challenged this view.

71 Ibid., p. 36.

72 Ibid., p. 43.

73 Geertz, op. cit., defines a symbol as "any object, event, quality, or relation which serves as a vehicle for a conception — the conception is the symbol's 'meaning'."

74 Ibid., pp. 7-8.

75 Ibid., p. 4.

76 Ibid., p. 3. Geertz, 1958, pp. 421 f., presents a fuller discussion of "ethos" and "world-view."

77 Geertz, 1966, p. 3.

78 Ibid., p. 12.

79 Geertz, 1958, p. 421.

80 Geertz, 1964, p. 62.

81 Geertz, 1958, p. 427.

82 In *Sim.* 8.6.3 "seal" (σφραγίς) is used to describe repentance. The implication is that repentance functions, as baptism does, as entry into transcendent reality, but this time the penitent enters with a renewed spirit.

83 Cf. Hippolytus *Apos. Trad.* 22-23 (ed. Easton).

84 This is a favourite formula used by Hermas to describe the redeemed life (*Man.* 1:2; 2:6; 3:5; 4:2.4; 4:4.3; 6:2.10; 7:4,5; 8:4,6,11,12; 9:12; 10:3.4; 12:2.2; 12:3.1; 12:6.3,5; *Sim.* 5:1.5; 5:7.4; 6:1.4; 8:11.1,4; 9:20.4; 9:22.4; 9:28.8; 9:29.3; 9:30.5; 9:33.1). While the formula has been taken for most part eschatalogically, Snyder, 1968, p. 64, is correct in suggesting that the definition of life with God, that is a life lived in obedience to God's commands, is a present reality (*Man.* 7:5). Thus in the parable of the sticks every believer is in some state of life or death (*Sim.* 8:2.9), except the double-minded who are neither — and as we will see below this has important implications for the identity of the church. Snyder is correct when he argues that "the primary nature of 'living to God' is adherence to the community of life. Life is life in the church, and death to God . . ." (*Sim.* 8:6.4; 9:28.5,6; perhaps also *Man.* 12:2.3; *Sim.* 8:7.3; 8:8.1; 8:10.2; 9:18.2; 9:26.2,8) ". . . is alienation from the community" (*Sim.* 8:6.4; 8:8.1; 8:9.1-4; 9:20.2; 9:26.3) "and existence outside the tower" (*Sim.* 8:7.3; 9:13.9 — loc. cit.).

85 In *Sim.* 9:12.3f. the description of reception into the tower as entry into the kingdom of God only if one "takes his [i.e. the Son's] holy name" probably refers to baptism (cf. *Sim.* 9:16.7). Other passages describe entry into the kingdom in a way not directly associated with baptism (*Sim.* 9:13.2; 9:29.2; 9:31.2), but even here the blessed faithful are those who have been baptized. The future tense in these verses implies an eschatalogical reality, but the state it describes has implications for the identity of the individual living in the present. Thus, *Sim.* 9:16.3-4 describes a present as well as a future reality; the kingdom of God is "now but not yet." It is not only the future church but also the present one which is built on the foundation of the first generations (*Sim.* 9:15.4).

86 See also *Man.* 5:2.1-8 for a similar notion.

87 Double-mindedness is often used as an expression to describe lack of allegiance to the community (*Vis.* 2:2.7-8; 3:7.1; *Sim.* 1:3).

88 Dibelius, 1923, pp. 445-46.

Chapter Four

1 Clement

The Setting of the Corinthian Dispute

A satisfactory solution to the vexed problem of the precise nature of the dispute described by Clement in his letter to the Corinthians[1] has eluded scholars for over a century.[2] Most problematic, perhaps, in any attempt to determine the character of the Corinthian dispute is the correct interpretation of Clement's use of rhetorical examples and Pauline language to describe the Corinthian situation.[3] While there has been a debate concerning how much Clement utilizes classical sources and ideas in his letter, and the degree to which his writing has parallels in Jewish and biblical writings,[4] the consensus is that Clement has woven together hellenistic and biblical themes throughout his letter.[5]

But because of this interweaving it is especially difficult to determine the precise character of those who "removed some from the ministry" (44:6) of the Corinthian church. Some have suggested that Clement's use of traditional classical and biblical themes makes it impossible to gain an accurate picture of the Corinthian problem. Wrede argued that most of the passages in *1 Clement*, which had been interpreted by nineteenth-century scholars as descriptions of the Corinthian upstarts, were chosen by Clement more for their rhetorical and exhortatory effect than because they constituted an accurate description of the schismatics.[6] Clement had only an indirect account of the problems plaguing the community and the document therefore is more important as evidence of the state of Christianity in Rome at the end of the first century than in Corinth. Indeed, according to Wrede, so caught up in his rhetoric was Clement that he often forgot the reason why he set out to write the letter.[7] Knopf agreed that Clement had only a hazy picture of the Corinthian dispute, but he argued that Clement's writing is a paraenetic homily, typical of Roman preaching at the end of the first century, which he developed into a letter, rather than an example of Clement's inability to keep to his topic.[8]

Knopf concluded that the letter is largely a sermon and that it is impossible to determine the character of the rebels from passages found within it.

Wrede and Knopf did not take full enough account of the references in *1 Clement* where the writer complains about the report he has heard from Corinth and the danger it presents (47:6-7).[9] In 7:1, Clement states that the "same struggle," i.e. "jealousy and strife" (cf. chapters 3-6), challenges his community,

Notes to this chapter appear on pp. 135-46.

which may suggest that Clement knew enough about the dispute to draw analogies with divisions in his own church. We discovered references to schism in the *Shepherd* and it is possible that Clement is here referring to similar problems. This would explain the reference to mutual admonition better than Knopf's argument that the exhortation is a purely homiletic device without any necessary relation to the communities' problems.[10] Finally, Ziegler has noted that the use of the middle voice of the verb πεποιῆσθαι in 1:1 implies that Clement had a personal concern regarding the Corinthian dispute,[11] and that the perfect form taken together with the report mentioned in 47:6 suggests that the letter has a pre-history of correspondence: it was preceded by some other form of correspondence from Corinth. Clement had begun to respond to the Corinthian church but was delayed because of "a series of misfortunes and accidents" (Grant's translation), and he now turns his attention again to complete what he had earlier started.[12] These passages taken together provide reason to suspect that Clement had more than an indirect acquaintance with the Corinthian dispute. An alternative explanation to Wrede and Knopf's hypothesis is that *1 Clement* does not provide a later reader with precise information concerning the problems in Corinth because the substance of it was already common knowledge. As we shall see there are clues concerning the nature of the dispute in the community. The problem has been more that most scholars have not looked in the right place in the epistle for the dispute, than that Clement provides no substantial information about it.

But other scholars have been more sanguine regarding the possibility of reconstructing the nature of the Corinthian dispute from Clement's letter. Bauer rejected Knopf's hypothesis that Clement was ignorant of the Corinthian dispute and contended that the inclusion "of so much that is quite unexpected" in *1 Clement* means that it is imperative that "one proceed with special care in attempting to determine the letter's purpose, and not limit himself to considering only what appears on the surface."[13] Thus, rather than focusing on the contents of the letter alone, Bauer attempted to place it in the context of the development of orthodoxy in the early church. He argued that the division described in *1 Clement* followed the lines seen in 1 Cor. 3:4f. By the beginning of the second century, according to Bauer, there were two types of Christianity in Corinth, one represented by Paul and Cephas, the other by Apollos. The latter form was a "gnosticizing" kind of Christianity which came to oppose the "orthodox" Pauline party.[14] The Roman correspondence represents the attempt of "orthodox" Rome to extend her sphere of influence over the Corinthian church, important to the Roman church because it was the gateway to Asia Minor and therefore necessary for her expansion of influence into the eastern empire.[15]

Bauer's creative attempt to place *1 Clement* in a wider ecclesiastical setting fails because there is no clear evidence of gnosticism in Corinth at this date. Aside from the problem of determining whether Paul addressed Christians with gnostic tendencies in 1 Corinthians, it is impossible to reconstruct the Christianity of Apollos or the group presumably allied with him. Clement's language in 47:3-5 which distinguishes the present schismatics from those described in 1 Cor. 3:4 implies that the latter-day upstarts have little to do with those described by Paul. Again, Bauer's citation of Irenaeus' reference to Clement's letter and his argument that Irenaeus found in Clement's use of the Old Testament and praise of the creator God evidence against his gnostic opponents (*A.H.* 3:3.3) does not show that Clement was writing against gnostics, only that Irenaeus was able to use *1 Clement* as evidence for the "orthodox" character of what he argued was pre-gnostic Christianity. In fact, if Clement was writing against a gnostic faction it is odd that he does not cite passages in Paul's correspondence with the Corinthians which have been interpreted by scholars as being directed against supposed gnostic tendencies.[16] Bauer's argument that the omission of specific traits of gnosis are passed over in silence by *1 Clement* because Rome was "in the extreme Christian West"[17] (where he argues gnosticism had not yet spread) raises the question whether his interpretation of Clement's references to γνῶσις in fact refer to an incipient form of gnosticism causing problems in Corinth. Also, the correspondence of the Roman with the Corinthian church is better explained by the close ties which existed between Rome and its colony,[18] or, alternatively, by a continuing relation between communities founded by Paul, than it is by an appeal to the attempts of the Roman church to expand its sphere of influence.

But if Bauer's attempt to incorporate *1 Clement* into a larger scheme of emerging orthodoxy in the early church proves too ambitious, other scholars have been no less adventuresome in their attempts to reconstruct the character of the Corinthian problem. In a vein similar to Bauer, Meinhold argued that the conflict was between officials and "pneumatic" Christians, and was a continuation of the problems described in 1 Cor. 12 and 14.[19] "Die spirituale Kirchenbegriff des Paulus steht letzlich hinter dem Vorgehen gegen das Amt in Korinth. . . ."[20] But if Clement was writing against those who were appealing to ecstatic manifestations to support their revolt against authority of a more official nature, it is odd that he did not appeal to Paul's directions concerning the use of spiritual gifts in 1 Cor. 14:6f. or his teaching concerning their relative importance in 1 Cor. 13:8f., especially when he does appeal to 1 Cor. 13 in 49:1ff. Telfer also argued that problems arose in the community because of pneumatic Christians, this time, on the basis of 54:2, persons who had invaded the community from without.[21] But Clement also seems to imply that the trouble-makers are to repent and remain in the community (57:1-2), and 54:2 may simply follow the logic of the theme of self-exile drawn from classical sources.[22] If the rebels were wandering charismatics,[23] it is odd that Clement does not exhort the Corinthians to withdraw hospitality from them and send them on their way.

Lietzmann argued in a different way when he suggested that the revolt was a movement of the young against the old.[24] The motive of the rebellion was "simply the desire for a new distribution of the positions of authority."[25]

Lietzmann found an analogy in the Roman *collegia*, where overseers were elected only for short periods of time. Certain elected leaders, he suggests, had refused to give up their offices and this resulted in a rebellion. But aside from certain terminological similarities, there is no evidence to suggest that, in this sphere, the early church patterned itself after the Roman club. While the *collegia* were ideally democratic institutions,[26] there is no evidence that elected officials in the early church held their office for only a short period of time. The evidence in Paul's writings points to appointed leaders in Paul's absence whose authority rests in part on their patronage, and there is no reason to suspect from the evidence found in the pseudonymous Pauline writings, roughly contemporary with *1 Clement*, that officials were elected for short periods of time. By the middle of the second century there is a tradition of bishops who held office for life (*H.E.* 4:22). It is better to interpret the description and exhortation concerning obedience to "elders" (1:3; 21:6), to which Lietzmann appeals as evidence for a dispute between young and old, as general exhortations consonant with Clement's overall purpose in the composition of his epistle than to see them as specific descriptions of the rebellion. In Clement's view lack of respect for elders has helped to undermine the community's unity, but this is no more the cause of the split in the community than are the women's "factious preferences" (21:7, Lightfoot); they both point, in Clement's opinion, to the general causes of the church's problems, but not to the precise difficulty.

These attempts to identify the nature of the Corinthian dispute illustrate the difficulty of determining the correct interpretation of Clement's references to the division. The scholars discussed above have tended either to see in Clement's letter an exercise in rhetoric almost completely divorced from the Corinthian situation, or they have isolated certain passages which then connect the document to the problems described in 1 Corinthians. (Lietzmann avoids the difficulties which arise from these explanations by attempting to place certain passages in the letter in a more general social setting, but he also isolates passages which in our estimation do not point to the reason for the dispute.)

Those scholars who have argued that the division in Corinth was caused by gnostic or "pneumatic" Christians who, in their view, are similar to those described in 1 Corinthians, do not take sufficiently into account the way in which Clement used both themes he drew from the Old Testament and passages contained in Paul's letter to end the Corinthian schism. Proponents of this view have found their most direct support for a gnostic-inspired revolt in 48:5-6, where Clement writes,

> Let a man be faithful, let him have power to utter "knowledge" (γνῶσις), let him be wise in the discernment of arguments, let him be pure in his deeds; for the more he seems to be great, the more ought he to be humble-minded (ταπεινοφρονεῖν), and to seek the common good of all and not his own benefit.

There is general agreement that Clement based his composition of this passage on 1 Cor. 12:8,9. Although the phraseology is different, the grouping together of the same qualities or gifts[27] leads naturally to this conclusion.[28] But it does not necessarily follow from this similarity that Clement is describing gnostic or pneumatic opponents. This passage must be placed in the broader context of Clement's argument in order to be interpreted properly. A clue concerning the connection between this section and Clement's more general case is provided in 48:6 where he describes humble-mindedness (ταπεινοφροσύνη) as an ideal virtue. Humble-mindedness is a central theme Clement develops to define the proper community ethos and he repeatedly uses the term ταπεινοφροσύνη and its cognates (e.g., 2:1; 13:1,3; 16:1,17; 19:1; 30:3; 38:2; 62:2) to describe the virtues necessary for a harmonious church. As we shall see in final section of this chapter, the theme of humble-mindedness belongs, in turn, to a still more general argument concerning the ordering power of God in the world and in the church: the humble-minded Christian is the one who lives in obedience to the established rule of God. If we place 48:5-6 in this wider context, it is better to interpret Clement's use of 1 Cor. 12:8,9 as supportive of his more general argument than as a precise description of the Corinthian ringleaders. Further, the ending of 48:4, where Clement states that those who are in Christ accomplish all things "without disorder" (ἀταράχως) provides an interpretive framework for the passages borrowed from Paul in v. 5. Clement probably found in the apostle's argument in 1 Cor. 12 a concern that the community remain well-ordered and therefore used it to support his own general case of the necessity of a well-ordered church. 37:5-38:1 is further evidence that Clement drew this conclusion from Paul's teaching in 1 Cor. 12. In this passage he develops the Pauline themes of χάρισμα and σῶμα (cf. 1 Cor. 12:4f., 12f., 21) to exhort the Corinthians to be subject to one another. These examples illustrate both Clement's use of Paul as an authority for his teaching, and the importance of placing what appear to be direct descriptions of the opponents in the context of the whole letter. In the remaining part of this section we shall present our own account of the problem which arose in Corinth.

After rejecting Wrede's hypothesis that Clement's letter had little application to the Corinthian dispute, Chadwick contends that "Clement's letter is ... drafted with the utmost subtlety. Every word is selected with care and with an eye to the maximum of effect."[29] If Clement's examples and language drawn from the Old Testament and classical literature seem to us beside the point, this is because we have not fully understood the social setting of the writing nor have we appreciated the document as evidence of the institutionalizing forces within the Corinthian and Roman communities in the generation after Paul's death. While scholars have directed their attention to the fact that *1 Clement* is a rhetorical letter, they have not concentrated fully enough on the nature of Clement's examples and their probable social effect. The misconceived attempts to find in Clement's writings references to "pneumatics," or "gnostics," or recalcitrant "charismatics" raise an important methodological issue in the interpretation of this letter. In the case of Paul's Corinthian correspondence, where the modern interpreter is provided with relatively straightforward polemical and descriptive statements, a scholar is in a better position to discover more direct correspondence between the apostle's descriptions of his opponents and the real problems facing the community. But *1 Clement* is a document woven into the form of a highly stylized treatise, filled with apparent digressions and conflicting accounts concerning the character of the Corinthian rebels. The nature of this writing means that we must approach the text in a different manner. Ziegler correctly argues that not every reference which *prima facie* appears to describe those who upset the Corinthian church necessarily presents or was intended to present in a strict sense an accurate account of them.[30]

1 Clement does provide some less indirect references concerning the nature of the Corinthian dispute. By putting these into a tentative framework we are able to provide a more satisfactory explanation for the Corinthian problem than those so far offered. Clement states that division in the community has arisen because "one or two persons" (47:6) of the Corinthian church have "removed some from the ministry which they fulfilled blamelessly" (44:6). In 44:1 he argues that the apostles foresaw that there would be strife for the title of bishop, which implies that this is the problem which has arisen in the Corinthian church.[31] These references allow us to infer that the problems Clement refers to originated from within the common life of the church. This interpretation is consonant with Clement's theme of repentance which recurs throughout the letter (7:4-7; 8:1-5; 9:1; 18:2-17; 57:1).

Chadwick has noted the significance of Clement's references to hospitality in 10:7, 11:1, and 12:1. Wrede similarly found in Clement's singling out of faith and hospitality in these Old Testament examples some important clues concerning the nature of the Corinthian dispute. "Das Auftreten dieses Begriffpaares ist für den Leser immer wieder überraschend. . . . Man begreift nicht was für ein Interesse den Schreiber gerade auf jene spezialle Tugend bringt."[32] Wrede argued that Clement highlights this virtue because he is following the Old Testament example. But this is not a virtue emphasized in the passages in question, nor does Wrede's explanation acknowledge the importance of hospitality in the early church. In addition to these passages which Chadwick singles out for comment, it is perhaps significant that in 35:5 inhospitality (ἀφιλοξενία)[33] is added to the list of vices Clement recalls from Rom. 1:29-32.[34] Again, Clement commends the hospitality of the past Corinthian church in 1:2. Chadwick provides a tentative explanation for the reason of Clement's letter by arguing that the references to hospitality should be placed against a background of inhospitality toward Christian visitors, who would have relied upon the hospitality of the Corinthian Christians while they stayed in the great port city of Corinth. As a result of two rival groups of "clergy" within the Corinthian church visitors were confused about which group to associate with. Chadwick goes on to argue,

> [S]ome visiting Christians at Corinth accepted hospitality from the old clergy rather than the new; . . . the old clergy had seen in this act of communion on the part of other churches a golden opportunity of reaffirming their position; . . . the visitors would have become the object of hostile comment from the rest of the church and therefore come away from Corinth with unfavourable impressions.[35]

Chadwick is correct to emphasize the importance of Clement's references to hospitality as clues to understanding the nature of the dispute in the Corinthian community. But his explanation is unsatisfactory because, aside perhaps from the reference in 1:2, there is no internal evidence to suggest that the hospitality described is to outsiders who lodge temporarily with the community. If the problems in the church included inhospitality to visitors, it is surprising that Clement does not develop this theme more fully in the context of his exhortations to repent. Further, he ignores an important opportunity to exhort the Corinthians to be hospitable when he recommends Claudius Ephebus, Valerius Vito, and Fortunatus to their care (65:1; 63:3). Also, Chadwick's hypothesis that the division in the community was between two groups of clergy requires a more precise account than he has provided, because Clement does not write that all the older leaders were deposed, only that "some" (ἔνιοι – 44:6) were.

A simpler explanation for the significance of Clement's references to hospitality in the passages cited above is to place them in the general setting of the church gathered in wealthier persons' homes.[36] There is good warrant for looking in this direction, because we know from Paul's letters that the earlier Corinthian church met in the homes of wealthier members who acted as leaders (Rom. 16:23; 1 Cor. 16:15) and we have argued that divisions in the earlier household communities may have followed household boundaries (Gal. 2:1; less certain 1 Cor. 1:12, cf. v. 16[37]). Also, we have found evidence in the *Shepherd of Hermas*, roughly contemporary with *1 Clement*, which suggests that the Roman church, of which Clement was a member, met in the homes of wealthier Christians who acted as the community's leaders. We argued in the last chapter that the ministry described in *1 Clement* is similar to that described in the *Shepherd*,[38] and this may also imply a similar social setting. Thus it is plausible to assume a situation in *1 Clement* in which Christians meet in the homes of well-to-do leaders.[39] A house church setting helps us to understand the setting of the dispute more fully. In 41.2 Clement argues, "Not everywhere, brethren, but in Jerusalem only are the perpetual sacrifices offered. . . ." Again, in 40:1-2 he states

> we ought to do in order all those things the Master ordered us to perform at the appointed times. He has commanded sacrifices and services to be performed, not in a careless and haphazard way but at the designated seasons and hours. He himself has determined where and through whom he wishes them performed, to the intent that everything should be done religiously to his good pleasure and acceptably to his will. (Grant's translation)

Grant concludes correctly from these references that Clement here argues that "Christian worship cannot be conducted in private assemblies apart from the bishops, presbyters, and deacons whom he is about to discuss."[40] Similarly, Clarke, who notes the importance of well-to-do householders as the early church's possible candidates for leadership, argues that chapters 40-41 refer to an appointed house church.[41] While these references do not show that it was wealthy members of the community who were the church's presbyter-bishops, this is not an unreasonable inference once the Corinthian church setting is placed in what we have seen to be the wider social setting of the early church.

What, then, was the nature of the Corinthian schism? We argued in the last chapter that divisions among patrons of house churches provide a plausible setting for the community divisions Hermas describes and that attempts to find in Clement's descriptions of the divisions within the Corinthian church a continuation of problems described in 1 Cor. are not satisfactory. We suggest, then, that the dispute which Clement describes as arising over the title of bishop is best understood as referring to a division within one or two of the Corinthian house churches which has resulted in the creation of an alternative meeting place, the exodus of members who are sympathetic with these persons and, presumably, the exclusion of members who are opposed to them. The precise reason why this dispute arose is not given. It is possible that the dispute arose independently of any particular theological dispute and that, as Harnack suggested, the division was merely between "personal cliques" ("persönliche Cliquenwirtschaft").[42] We suggest that these groups collected around relatively wealthy householders who then began to hold their own celebrations. As stated above, this is a tentative claim. Still, this setting allows one to place the importance on Clement's references to hospitality which Chadwick has pointed out, but without having to appeal to a pre-history of inhospitality with respect to visitors, for which there is no evidence in the text. It also explains why the division involved only a section of the presbyter-bishops (44:6), for not all the house churches were directly involved in the schism.

1 Clement and Sect Development

We have suggested that a conflict between house churches is a plausible setting for the Corinthian dispute. We now turn to an analysis of institutional development in this community. *1 Clement* has often been placed in a schema of ideological or theological development in the early church. But we hope to show that while it is true that there is evidence of development in the Corinthian church, to analyse it strictly as the outcome of the application of theological ideas is misleading. We shall attempt to show in this section that the house-church setting of the early church provides some important clues concerning sources of institutional development in the Corinthian church. It will be shown further how analysis of contemporary sect development focuses our attention on some of the social forces (overlooked by scholars using other methodologies to assess development in the Corinthian community) which may have been at work in the formation of its leadership institutions.

Some Previous Attempts to Account for Development in the Corinthian Church

Since the appearance of Rudolph Sohm's monumental *Kirchenrecht*, first published in 1892, many scholars have argued that Clement's epistle to the Corinthians represents in differing degrees a departure from the theology of Paul and is evidence of a new stage of theological development in early Christian thought.[43] Sohm argued that *1 Clement* represents a shift from a purely charismatic church order typical of the ancient church and, as a result of the Corinthian dispute over the leadership of the community, the introduction of a legal organization to the church.[44] Clement's letter brought the charismatic structure of the primitive church, which rested solely on the election of God, to an end. Through Clement's argument, as interpreted by Sohm, that a bishop's installation bestowed on him a lasting right to exercise the functions of his office, the Holy Spirit was bound to legal forms. Clement's epistle gave birth to Catholicism, where the presence of the Holy Spirit is guaranteed to every individual church only by means of fixed forms which it is bound to adopt.[45]

It is not necessary here to chronicle the famous debate between Harnack and Sohm.[46] But while Harnack disagreed with Sohm's analysis that spirit and law were mutually exclusive phenomena in the early church, he went some way towards agreeing with Sohm that *1 Clement* represents a theological shift from a genuinely Pauline theology of church order toward a Catholic one.[47] According to Harnack it was under Tertullian that Catholicism entered the church. But *1 Clement* is evidence that developments in that direction were taking place a century earlier. Clement's letter was a fateful first step from a "pneumatic democracy"[48] (the universal "ecclesia" with its charismatic organization present in the local community and characteristic of the ancient church) toward the later "Rechtskirche" (an organization based upon permanent and legally binding institutions). *1 Clement* struck a first blow against the church's pneumatic democracy from which it was never to recover.[49]

The interpretations of Sohm and Harnack concerning *1 Clement* continued to be echoed in subsequent scholarship. Thus Gerke, a proponent of Harnack's position, argued that while it cannot be stated that Clement replaced Paul's concept of the church as a body (*Somasinn*) with a legal understanding (*Rechtsinn*),[50] it is none the less the case that the writing represents an "allmähliche Umwandlung der Demokratie in eine oligarchische Aristokratie von Amtsträgern."[51] But if Harnack had his disciples, so too, if qualifiedly, did Sohm. Hence Bultmann, while critical of Sohm in certain respects,[52] agreed that Clement's letter represents a decisive step toward a legal conception of the church.[53] And *1 Clement*, together with the *Shepherd*, the Pastoral Epistles, and Ignatius' letters, represents "ultimately *a transformation in the Church's understanding of itself.*"[54] The church's self-conception as the eschatalogical people of God, alien to the world and living in anticipation of the imminent eschaton, became transformed as time passed into "*a new religion*"[55] among imperial religions as a result of waning eschatalogical expectation and an increasing emphasis on sacraments.[56]

Bultmann's analysis has been taken up in the work of Käsemann, who, if differing from Sohm in details, agrees that *1 Clement* is indicative of "early Catholicism," "that transition from earliest Christianity to the so-called ancient Church, which is completed with the disappearance of the imminent expectation."[57] This first appears in Luke, the first writer to propagate theories of tradition and legitimate succession.[58]

But the differentiation between officials and laity which is present in *1 Clement* and the Ignatian correspondence is an important milestone along the way toward fully developed Catholicism.[59]

In these letters, as in Luke-Acts and the Pastorals, the institutional office, which stands over against the rest of the community, is the bearer of the Spirit. This distinction between clergy and laity is a departure from the genuine Pauline conception where every Christian receives the Spirit at baptism.[60]

The shift which Käsemann describes is accounted for by the influence of "the Jewish Christian traditions," which, with its non-Pauline notion of ordination, transforms the Pauline heritage.[61] A similar influence is posited by Campenhausen to account for what he regards as a fundamental shift in the theological understanding of the ministry of the early church. Campenhausen, like Käsemann, argues that the genuine Pauline notion of the ministry is purely charismatic.[62] This idea is contrasted with the Jewish-Christian conception which is based on tradition. In the communities which were governed by the latter concept, elders preserved the tradition and acted as the community's leaders.[63]

Consonant with Käsemann, Campenhausen argues that Jewish-Christian conceptions gradually entered Pauline churches and finally overtook the theological notions governing them. The Pastorals, written after Clement's letter, weld together Pauline and Jewish-Christian ideas and represent a new stage in the development toward official authority.[64] But *1 Clement* takes a significant step along the way. The Roman letter for the first time accounts for the presbyteral system "as a datum of tradition."[65] By placing the system of elders under the protection of an apostolic injunction it becomes part of the apostolic tradition. "To this extent" comments Campenhausen, "it may be said that here for the first time the structures of canon law are included in the category of doctrines and dogma, and given the same sacral and immutable character."[66]

A Critique of Previous Accounts of Development in 1 Clement

We have rehearsed these arguments because they show the role *1 Clement* is made to play in the attempt of scholars to account for development in the early church. These writers have not escaped criticism. Sohm was challenged for allowing his interpretation of Paul to be determined by the leading philosophical and religious ideas of his time,[67] as was Harnack.[68] And the reconstruction of Sohm, Käsemann, and Campenhausen, representative of what has come to be regarded as a consensus point of view,[69] has been attacked for an uncritical use of 1 Cor. to describe what is a genuinely Pauline concept of ministry[70] and for its contrast between a Pauline and a Jewish-Christian model of ministry.[71]

But there is a more fundamental criticism which may be made of all of the reconstructions described above. Methodologically these scholars, while differing in details, all begin with what they consider to be Paul's theology of ministry and then attempt to trace a development of thought which, they argue, represents a departure from the original position. Hence Bultmann, in the passage quoted above, can speak of a shift in the church's self-understanding. If there are developments in the early church, these are conceptual transformations which act upon social structures and shape them into new embodiments of theological ideas. For Bultmann the shift is from a self-understanding of the church as the eschatalogical people of God to a self-conception as an institution of salvation.[72] The methodology underlying this understanding of early church development is presented by Schweizer, another scholar who finds in Paul's notion of charisma a theological concept of ministry which distinguishes it as a church order from later conceptions.[73] In the opening pages of his *Church Order in the New Testament* Schweizer, describing his method of investigation, explains

> My concern is not mainly the historical investigation of the church's development, but rather the theological problem of how the New Testament church understood itself, and how it expressed that understanding in its order. The purely historical question, therefore, about the form of the Church at different times and places, while admittedly necessary, need be asked only insofar as *the actual shaping of the Church is always evidence of the concept of its own nature to which it testifies.*

Again he writes:

> In the following pages . . . we are not concerned only with the purely histori-
> cal question of events recorded in the New Testament. . . . We are concerned
> with the much more difficult question of recognizing in the actual ordering
> of the New Testament Church, and in what is said about it, *the theological con-*
> *cerns that caused it to take that form and no other. So when we ask about the Church's*
> *order, we must also try to understand the Church's essential nature.*[74]

The ordering of early Christian communities is accounted for by an appeal to
the theological concepts which are found in writings associated with them and
which shape them.

It is indeed true that self-conceptions pattern behaviour and are an element in
the development of institutions. But to grant concepts, whether they be theological or otherwise, a preeminent and crucial significance at the expense or to
the virtual exclusion of other factors is to forget that ideas are thought by
people: they have their significance in the interactions of persons who belong to
communities which have social interests and concerns. It is to forget that the
Church's so-called "essential nature" is always *in situ* and cannot be understood
apart from its social context without fundamental distortion or the intrusion of
interests which may be theologically profound but force texts or even ideas to
do work which goes beyond their proper role. The blood and sweat of history is
left behind as we rise to an ideal plane where ideas, presented as the realities
infusing the shadows which constitute historical existence, combine, collide,
and compete. In order to understand more fully concepts of church structure
and the development of institutional forms in the early Christian church we
must come down again from the bright heights of theological abstraction and
try to understand what social forces were at work in the development of the
early church. If we do this we shall have a more accurate appraisal of the role of
ideas in shaping early Christian communities and we shall better understand the
genesis of certain theories of leadership in the early church.

As the first passage from Schweizer quoted above shows, it would be an exag-
geration to argue that he, and indeed those scholars listed above who follow a
similar methodology, focus solely on ideas to explain early Christian development. The delay of the Parousia, contact with diverse forms of Christianity, and
human nature are presented as forces at work in the shaping of the early church.
But their emphasis on ideas makes it possible to charge them with what Holmberg has called the "fallacy of idealism."[75] Holmberg notes that while Sohm,
Bultmann, Käsemann, Campenhausen, and Schweizer analyse historical phenomena and pay close attention to them

> the methodologically fateful step comes with the next stage of the work,
> where the historical phenomena are often interpreted as being directly
> formed by underlying theological structures.[76]

He argues correctly that what is missing in this methodology is a recognition that
ideas and social structures exist in a dialectic relationship: "Social life is determined
by social factors, including the opinions and consequently the theology of the
actors."[77] Ideas and social structures interact with each other to form the social
world. If an analysis of the early church is to be accurate it is necessary that it view
phenomena occurring within it from an "interactionist perspective."[78]

The "purely historical question of events" which Schweizer leaves behind too quickly is therefore central to an understanding of the role and formation of theological ideas in the early church. In order to avoid the "methodological docetism"[79] of the approach presented by Schweizer, it is necessary to evaluate the social setting in which the development of notions of ministry occurred. In our discussion of the *Shepherd of Hermas* we found evidence that wealthy household owners of the Roman community played an important role in the leadership of the community to which Hermas belonged. We have tentatively suggested a similar setting for the Corinthian community addressed by the Roman church. If we may adopt this suggested social setting as a plausible description of the Corinthian community at the end of the first century and compare it with the one addressed and referred to by Paul some forty years before, what social developments can we discern? Can we reconstruct the changes that took place in the Corinthian community after Paul's final departure and death? It is the nature of the case that any attempted reconstruction can represent only a possible course of development. But if we are to avoid the methodological shortcomings of the scholars listed above, who regard social development as largely the result of the straightforward application of ideas, then it is necessary to make an attempt to discern possible sources of social development where, in some cases, there are only hints.

Sectarian Development and the Corinthian Church

The topic of social development has been given much attention by sociologists in their investigations of sectarianism.[80] This literature is valuable for our present investigation because it provides some heuristic tools with which to analyse organizational development in the early church. On the basis of his research into various contemporary sectarian groups Wilson states, "It would seem that, when sects do persist, they always undergo processes of mutation. . . . Because sects cannot cut themselves off completely from the world they are influenced by external factors."[81] Wilson's observation helps us to focus our attention on factors which have been overlooked by other scholars in their attempts to describe the development of the Corinthian church.

> Sects tend to be more influenced than they know or care to acknowledge by the prevailing secular facilities of the period of their emergence. Some sects quickly stabilize their life-practices in conformity with these prevailing techniques, and sanctify them to the point of refusing to permit any further change even in styles and arrangements that clearly have no specific religious significance, but which were simply secular styles at the time of the sect's formation.[82]

Wilson is referring in particular here to the adoption of old-fashioned dress and farming techniques of Amish Mennonites and, to a degree, Hutterites. But as we shall suggest below, an important prevailing secular facility of the nascent church was the wealth and ability of the well-to-do householder who invited the church to meet in his home. This had a great impact on later institutional developments.

The emphasis which Clement places on structures of leadership in the Corinthian community also has a significant parallel in contemporary sect mutation. For Wilson has noted that contemporary sects, when they persist, tend to develop some form of centralized organization and a local elite.[83] In a similar vein Stark argues

> In time sects develop a definite class of ministers who are not, it is true, distinguished in a denomination, as they are in a church from the rank and file by a special grace conveyed through ordination, but who *are* distinguished from it by a special function through appointment. These ministers may not be priests, but they are assuredly more than mere laymen, however much this may be denied. This fact leads us, significantly, again back to the very inception of the sect. If the sect is to have any coherence at all, it needs some kind of office-bearers; some infringement of the principle of democracy is therefore unavoidable, if the group is to last.[84]

The reference to denominations in the passage just cited raises a further issue in the contemporary sociological discussion concerning the development of some sects toward centralized organizational structures. Sociologists who investigate sectarianism have noticed that certain sects become denominations over a period of time.[85]

Like Stark, both Wilson and Yinger have noted that the movement toward a professional ministry, where "functions become institutionally differentiated and specialization of roles occurs" is a significant step toward denominationalism, or in Yinger's case, the church type.[86] This development has been applied to the early church. It was Troeltsch who first argued that the development of a specialized organ of ministers in the early church was a movement away from the sect-type toward the church-type.[87] And Yinger, following Troeltsch, noted that the seeds for this development were already contained in Paul's teaching.

> The first organization of Christianity, largely under the leadership of the Apostle Paul, moved rather rapidly toward the church type. Paul, a Roman citizen, prized the state which preserved order and justice. Although there were no rankings within the early church, the group did not fight slavery.... Out of the duality of the Christian ethic (i.e. the universalism of love and radical religious individualism), those aspects which harmonized with the prevailing politico-economic system were emphasized, and received the expression in the institutionalized form of the religious life — the church.[88]

But it is precisely at this point, where it is necessary to suggest elements within the Pauline community that gave rise to the particular ministerial structures which arose in the generations after Paul's death, that both Troeltsch and Yinger are disappointingly silent. Instead, the rise of the church from the sectarian origins of the Jesus movement is explained as the logical outcome of the Christian gospel with its dualistic ethical elements referred to in the passage cited above. Universalism, the desire to win the world for God and make the Church co-extensive with civilization, may have had a profound effect on the development of the Christian sect into a Church, but if it is abstracted from the setting in which the characteristics of a universalist ethic were developed, we shall again find ourselves attempting to understand the development of the early church as the result of the straightforward application of ideas. It is necessary to ask, therefore, what elements in the communities established by Paul helped to give rise to the emergence of a formal body of leaders.

Household Leadership and Sect Development in the Corinthian Church

The importance of the wealthy household owners who invited the church into their homes has been overlooked by the majority of scholars as a possible source of centralized leadership in the generations succeeding the apostle Paul. Indeed, many scholars, in order to explain the rise of centralized authority in the period after Paul, have emphasized notions such as the delay of the Parousia and the transformation of self-understanding so much that they have ignored simple factors such as the impact of the apostle's death and the need to fill the gap of authority which it presented to communities dependent upon his instruction and direction.[89] But Weingarten, writing in 1881, suggested the importance of household leadership in the development of the early church toward so-called Catholicism.[90]

Filson also noticed the possible importance of household leaders after Paul's death when he wrote:

> The house church was the training ground for the Christian leaders who were to build the church after the loss of 'apostolic' guidance, and everything in such a situation favoured the emergence of the host as the most prominent and influential member of the group.[91]

Again he noted:

> The development of church polity can never be understood without reference to the house churches. The host of such a group was almost inevitably a man of some education, with a fairly broad background and at least some administrative ability.[92]

If the role of such household members had an important impact on the shape of community life when the apostle was alive, it is reasonable to suggest that the influence of such members as Gaius, Stephanas, Philemon and Prisca and Aquila would have continued after Paul's death. We argued above that while Paul was still alive, their roles were largely over shadowed by him.[93] For even when he was not physically near, his letters bear testimony to the authority he enjoyed while absent and to the fact that he remained the primary source of direction. As long as the founder was on the scene a fully fledged official structure did not develop.[94] But once he had died it is reasonable to suggest that these members quickly gained preeminence as authorities within local communities. While several types of authority probably continued to be exercised for some time – Hermas, himself perhaps a prophet,[95] writes both of a false prophet and of true prophets who exercise some role of instruction in the church (*Man.* 11:1-2, 9) – the evidence regarding the Roman church contemporary with Clement's epistle[96] is that wealthy household owners played a pre-eminent role in the leadership of the community.

A Comparison Between the Corinthian Church
at the Time of Paul and of Clement

By comparing the level of organization of the Corinthian church while Paul was still alive with that evinced by Clement's letter we shall be better able to recognize evidence of further developments from the original structures. In our discussion of the genuine Pauline epistles[97] we argued that communities such as Corinth possessed relatively fluid authority structures while Paul was still alive. As Paul travelled from community to community, local churches were encouraged to govern themselves. We discussed evidence that suggests that in this situation the well-to-do householder who invited the church to meet in his or her home provided a focal point of stability in a period of institutional adaptation. Such householders provided the leadership and economic resources necessary for the group's survival. We argued that their leadership probably arose "from below," i.e. it was based upon their voluntary service, but that Paul recognized their importance for the survival of the group and exhorted members to be subject to such members. We concluded from this that factors such as the absence of the apostle and the repeated action of members such as house-church patrons (and patronesses) encouraged the development of organizational forms even in Paul's lifetime. The role of the householder in this development was central and, as we shall see, it had far-reaching implications.

Meeks, commenting on the impact of household organization on the church, states:

> The adaptation of the Christian groups to the household had certain implications both for the internal structure of the groups and for their relationship to the larger society. The new group was thus inserted into or superimposed upon an existing network of relationships, both internal — kinship, *clientela*, and subordination — and external — ties of friendship and perhaps of occupation. . . . The household context also set the stage for some conflicts in the allocation of power and in the understanding of the roles in the community. The head of the household, by normal expectations of the society, would exercise some authority over the group and would have some legal responsibility for it. The structure of the *oikos* was hierarchical, and contemporary political and moral thought regarded the structure of the superior and inferior roles as basic to the well-being of the whole society. Yet . . . there were certain countervailing modes and centers of authority in the Christian movement that ran contrary to the power of the paterfamilias, and certain egalitarian beliefs and attitudes that conflicted with the hierarchical structure.[98]

This lengthy quotation, which highlights the consequences of the adoption of household leadership on the growth of the early Christian sect, echoes the passage cited from Stark above in which it is stated that the development of a class of leaders is an infringement of the democratic ideals of sects, but is unavoidable if the group is to survive. Also of significance is Wilson's comment that sects are influenced by external factors and prevailing secular facilities in their genesis and that they quickly stabilize their practices in conformity with these phenomena.

With this picture of incipient institutionalization before us we are now is a position to assess more precisely the degree of organizational development in

Corinth at the end of the first century. An immediate difficulty arises when one attempts to distinguish where Clement is accurately reflecting an already exist-ing reality and where he is using rhetorical tactics to establish what he regards as a proper state of affairs in the Corinthian church. Bauer is an example of a scho-lar who argues that there may have been important differences between the pic-ture of the Corinthian dispute as portrayed by Clement and the actual historical events. But on this point he is ambiguous in a way which has certain conse-quences for his understanding of the conflict in Corinth and which raises important issues for the proper interpretation of *1 Clement*. In one passage he argues, "To some extent ... *1 Clement* describes the situation satisfactorily, as seen from Rome's perspective."[99] In another, however, he states

> We do not hear what the *altera pars* has to say ... ; and yet, in the interests of fairness, we really need to know what the members of the Corinthian com-munity who were so severely attacked could adduce, and no doubt did present, in support of their position. However, the picture that faces us of the conditions in Corinth is sketched from the perspective of Rome, which was doubtless one-sided and based on self-interest — to say the very least, a biased picture.[100]

Now it is certainly possible that one may present a picture fair to one's own interests and interpretations but biased from the perspective of another's. But it seems that Bauer intends more than this in his treatment of Clement's descrip-tion of the Corinthian dispute and that his understanding of Rome's bias takes on force which a proper understanding of the text shows unsustainable. For after the quotation immediately cited he goes on to argue that Clement's letter was a propagandizing treatise designed to bring the Corinthian church under the aegis of Roman ecclesiastical control.[101] This line of argument seems to sug-gest that Clement's letter does not accurately describe the true nature of the dis-pute in Corinth. In fact, according to Bauer, the true facts of the conflict are passed over in silence by Clement.[102] Bauer reconstructs the Corinthian schism as arising from the successful revolt of a gnostic-minded majority against a Pau-line and Petrine minority, who "brought about a fundamental change and insti-tuted a unified take-over of the church offices in accord with their own point of view."[103] Bauer is probably right to note that Clement's letter puts forward a case which distorts to some degree the aims, motivations, and interests of those causing the schism. But it is more reasonable to assume that even if Clement was improvising themes to achieve a desired end, in order for his goal to be real-ized his theorizing would have to have had a greater degree of contact with the reality experienced by the Corinthian community than that implied in Bauer's statements quoted above if it were not to be met with puzzlement or even resentment.[104] Bauer's argument that Clement's letter was motivated by a con-cern to gain influence in and assert control over the Corinthian ecclesiastical orbit leads him to exaggerate any distortion in which Clement may have engaged and to lose sight of the true aims of his letter. Clement's intention is put forward most clearly in 57:1-2 where he urges those causing the schism to repent. The motivation of Clement's letter is not to dominate, still less to offend or further to divide members already contending with one another (which would seem a likely consequence if Bauer's thesis of a majority of gnostics in control of Corinth were correct).[105] He hopes rather to convince the Corinthians to end their dispute. Part of the desired end of the letter is to bring about the repentance of those who have, in Clement's terms, initiated sedition.[106] For this to occur he had to present the case convincingly, and if convincingly also reasonably accurately lest he incur a charge of intransigence.

Alternatively, one could argue in a slightly different way that Clement read the Corinthian dispute with Roman eyes, interpreting the divisions in Corinth from a perspective in harmony with the ideals and institutional structures of his own church, but not necessarily in keeping with those of the Achaean community.[107] Again, as we shall see, Clement may well have contributed to the construction of institutions in the Corinthian community. But the cultural proximity between Rome and Corinth, a city closely allied with Rome, at least makes it possible that there was close contact between these two churches.[108] Further, the connection of these two churches with Paul permits one to infer that they followed similar lines of development.[109] These arguments are of necessity tentative and speculative, but they gain a small measure of further support from references to the contact with the Corinthian church implied in 1:1-2 and 47:7.[110] Even if there were some minor differences between the organization at Corinth and that in Rome it is reasonable to suppose that Clement could have become intimately acquainted with the structures of leadership in his sister church and that references to them in *1 Clement* accurately represent prevailing institutions in that community.[111]

This last point provides us with our first clue regarding the level of general institutional development at this period. For where there was once a relative fluidity of terminology to describe positions of leadership, as may be seen by Paul's use of general nouns in 1 Cor. 12:28, there is now more standardization and precision. Terms such as ἐπίσκοποι, πρεσβύτεροι, and διάκονοι are used by Clement to refer to distinct groups whom he assumes the Corinthians recognize (42:4; 44:4; 47:6; 54:2; 57:1; cf. *Herm. Vis.* 3:5.1). Together with this more formal terminology is evidence that there are particular places which are designated for common worship (40:3; cf. 41:2). We argued above that house churches formed the probable setting of this dispute and it is reasonable to infer from 40:3 that the particular places refer to certain households where the eucharist was celebrated.[112] This is in contrast with the Pauline period during which worship arrangements were probably more diverse. There is no evidence in the Roman letter concerning a place set apart for presbyter-bishops in the worship service itself, but if the suggested similarity of organization at Rome and Corinth is a sound conjecture then the reference in *Herm. Vis.* 3:9.7 (cf. 3:1.8) may lead us to envisage that in the Corinthian church there also had emerged by this period a special seating arrangement distinguishing "laity" and more official functionaries.[113]

One may infer further from Clement's letter that there was a distinct group of members set apart from the rest of the community as its formal leaders (40:3; 41:1; 42:4; 43:1; 44:3,4,5; 54:2; 57:1; cf. 37:3; 38:1). Indeed, Clement's use of the order of Levitical sacrifices (40-41) depends on this fact in order to form a coherent analogy. It is because a certain group of persons are set apart as leaders that a parallel may be drawn between them and Levites. The fact that strife has arisen over the "title" (ὄνομα) of bishop (44:1) is evidence that not everyone may possess it and that it is an object of competition. The parallel drawn by Clement from Numbers 17 (43:2) illustrates the same point. Also indicative of more highly developed organizational structures is the language of appointment (καθιστάναι – 42:4; 43:1; 44:3; 54:2; ἰδρύεσθαι – 44:5). When this is taken together with the reference to what appears to be some form of popular election or ratification (44:3),[114] it seems likely that there was at this date some formal act of investiture which permitted certain members to lead the community. Further, it is possible to suggest that the reference to the deposed presbyter-bishops being appointed by their predecessors (44:3) is a reference to a form of investiture.

The degree of circumscription of functions is difficult to determine from *1 Clement* alone. A relatively clear reference to a distinct liturgical role is 44:4.[115] Similarly, the use of the terms λειτουργεῖν, λειτουργία, and λειτουργός when referring to the services of the Christian church and those who lead it (40:2; 44:2,3,6), parallel with the usage of the same terms to describe the sacral functions of leaders in the Jewish community (32:2; 40:5; 41:2; 43:4), is also suggestive of a formal role in the leadership of worship.[116] Dix's contention, however, that the reference to the High-priest, priests, and Levites in 40:5 corresponds directly to the celebrant-bishop, presbyters, and deacons probably reads more into the text than is intended.[117] The use of the analogy is to show that there are appointed positions for certain functions of leadership, not to demonstrate a one-to-one correspondence between Jewish and Christian orders of ministry.

Hermas states that it is Clement's task to write to cities abroad (*Vis.* 2:4.3) and this may describe another task reserved for overseers. Ignatius is aware that the Roman church has "taught others" (Rom. 3:1) and we learn from Dionysius of Corinth that the Roman church sent another letter besides *1 Clement* to Corinth (*H.E.* 4:23.10-11). Turner notes that one factor which contributed to the rise of centralized leadership in the early church was the need for communication between churches.[118] This observation has a parallel in contemporary sect studies. Wilson has noted that the need for communication between dispersed communities is a significant factor contributing to the growth of centralized authority in contemporary sects.[119] While we have only the reference in the *Shepherd* to the duty of one bishop of the Roman community, it is none the less significant that it is an overseer who has this task. This reference supports a view which sees a distinct group of leaders taking on increasingly defined functions.

Apart from the likelihood that the celebrant overseer, in our estimation the patron of the house church, exercised authority over other presbyters and deacons gathered together with him, there is no information regarding a hierarchy of leadership or the precise relationships between these members. But the reference to extortion of funds by διάκονοι in *Herm. Sim.* 9:26.2 is evidence that there was perhaps a formal duty of deacons to distribute common funds to the needy.[120]

The relation of bishops and deacons to presbyters is more difficult to determine from the Roman letter, as indeed it is from the *Shepherd*. But this difficulty is compounded by the current tendency, particularly in German scholarship, to argue that the references to presbyters refer to a fusion between synagogal and Pauline forms of church organization.[121] As we shall see below, the appearance of presbyters may be accounted for more naturally by a proper understanding of institutionalization in the early church. It is enough to state here that the difficulty presented by the term πρεσβύτεροι in 1:3 and 21:6, as in *Herm. Vis.* 3:1.8, where it is not clear whether to render it "elder men" or "presbyters," is resolved more satisfactorily if one argues that presbyters were in fact elder men.[122] This interpretation has some further support in other contemporary literature. In 1 Pet. 5:5 the term πρεσβύτεροι is used simultaneously to describe an age-group and class of leaders.[123]

Clement may have intended a similar usage in 1:3 and 21:6, and if we interpret the passages from Clement's letter and the *Shepherd* in this way, we will avoid reliance upon the tenuous hypothesis that synagogues possessed a formal group of official presbyters, whose organizational structure was imposed upon Pauline communities from without, in order to account for their sudden appearance in independent contemporary churches (cf. Acts 14:23; 20:17; Tit. 1:5).[124] Further, we will no longer need to refer to a somewhat artificial "fusion" theory in order to explain the development of ministerial structures in the generations immediately succeeding the death of the apostle Paul.[125] If, instead, we rely for our explanation on the observation that age would have conferred authority in these communities (cf. *1 Clem.* 63:3), if for no other reason than because of contact with the founder of the community or his contemporaries, we will have a more natural explanation of an apparently uniform development in many churches across the Roman Empire, and one which is consonant with widely observed processes of institutionalization. The view which regards presbyters as the elder members of the community is also more consistent with the emergence of authority structures from below in the community, a process which we argued began while the apostle was still alive.

A cautious speculation concerning the relationship between bishops and presbyters is to suggest a similar situation to the one we discovered in the *Shepherd.* As in Rome, so in Corinth πρεσβύτεροι were probably a group of members from whose number were selected overseers and perhaps even deacons. Whatever the precise relationship, it is likely that these members were distinguished in some cases by certain functions and in all instances by the degree of respect owed them.[126]

Certain presbyters have a distinctive role of leadership as is evinced by references to obedience in 1:3 and 21:6 (cf. *Vis.* 3:9.7 for the use of προηγούμενοι to describe church leaders). Harnack argues that through these references, together with 40:5, the so-called pneumatic democracy of the Corinthian church was broken through and suppressed.[127] But an appraisal more consonant with our suggested role for household leaders in the early years of the Corinthian church, is to state that these passages are indicative of a process of development toward centralized authority which had begun with the appropriation of household forms for communal needs. It seems likely that in Corinth, as in the Roman community,[128] not all presbyters were in a position of household church leadership. But the exhortations to be obedient to the community's leaders, the liturgical role which they are assigned, and the evidence that there is a

form of popular election of leaders are indicative of a state of affairs in which
there is a degree of separation between a group of formal leaders, or clergy, and
lay persons.[129] In 40:4-5 Clement argues that priests and laity have their
appointed positions and it is significant that this is the first appearance in Christian literature of the term λαϊκός to describe members of a Christian community. The priestly language Clement uses is in part determined by the theme
which he wishes to develop in 41:1-2, but the description in 40:5 assumes that
there is an analogous division in the Corinthian church.[130]

The Corinthian Church as an Established Sect

The evidence in both *1 Clement* and the *Shepherd* suggests a state of affairs in the
early church in which authority has become centralized and functions of leadership have become formalized in such a way that leaders and followers behave
toward one another according to a set of established norms. These documents
are testimony to a stage of sect development toward the official structures of
leadership which we saw already forming in Paul's lifetime. But what was still
relatively fluid in Paul's day has become a more formal division of the community. In Corinth the Christian sect has become similar to what Yinger calls an
"established sect,"[131] that is, during the second and third generation of its existence it has undergone a process of transformation in which it has gradually
taken on some of the characteristics of the church-type while maintaining sectarian characteristics. In particular, the emergence of a power group, still
overshadowed by Paul while he was alive, has resulted in a series of formal distinctions between leaders (who resemble clergy) and laity. As a sect, which still
dominates a large part of the life of its members and continues to offer its members a consciousness of being set apart from the rest of the world as an elect
group,[132] it still shares the characteristic sectarian identity of the first generation.
But as a more highly organized group, probably led by well-to-do patrons, it has
become more fully adjusted to its societal situation — not without challenge as
the *Shepherd* attests, but none the less as a consequence of its social needs.

The passage of time and the process of institutionalization, as we will see
below, contributed to the sect's accommodation to the world. Wilson notes that
the response to the world which the sect founder initiates is difficult for contemporary sects to maintain for successive generations.[133] Paul's teaching, when
compared to that of Jesus, already represents a movement toward accommodation to the wider society. His recognition of household structures as valid (1
Cor. 7:20-21; 11:2-15), his support for the government, (Rom. 13:1-7), and his
validation of economic pursuits (1 Thes. 2:9; 4:11; 5:14) are indications of the
beginning of a process whereby the sect is "settling in." And themes which Paul
develops as he hands on Christ's teaching are taken up and developed further by
successive writers. For Paul these arrangements are still overshadowed by concerns of a more sectarian nature. Household relationships and economic interests have only a secondary importance when compared to the soon expected
second advent of Christ (1 Cor. 7:29-31).

But these themes are conspicuously absent in certain later writers. It is true
that Hermas exhorts his community and warns them of the relative unimpor-
tance of economic gain when compared with God's judgment, but the fact that

economic considerations can have become so out of hand in Hermas' church indicates accommodation to the world and the relaxation of sectarian ideals. Even Hermas, for all his admonition, is unwilling to upset the household and economic structures legitimated by Paul. There is some evidence in the Roman epistle too to suggest that Clement was unwilling to upset secular social arrangements in favour of a democratic community of goods (38:2-3), and, as in Rome, so in Corinth the preservation of the wider socio-economic order probably contributed to the sect's further accommodation to its social situation.

Like Paul, Clement believes that all secular authority is instituted by God (61:1; cf. Rom. 13:1-7) and he feels obliged to pray for its representatives (60:4). But for Clement there is an emphasis that the hierarchical world order follows from the action of the Creator God (60:1; 61:1-2) and that the divine action which has established the secular order is also responsible for the church order (37:1-38:3). This is a motif only germinally present in Paul's letters.[134] It is significant that Clement shifts the emphasis of the motif of the body, used as a paraenetic device by Paul in 1 Cor. 12:21 to emphasize the interdependence of the "pneumatikoi" with those who possess less dramatic gifts, in a way designed to legitimate the institutional order of the third generation Corinthian community (37:5-38:1).

Whereas Paul simply accepted certain conventional norms as a matter of convenience or incidentally, these became for Clement central and indispensable characteristics of the group. This may be seen in the concerns of Clement (and of Hermas) to uphold as a matter of central significance certain patriarchal structures within the church. As Ogletree has noted, whereas existing household arrangements are adopted by Paul as suitable (and we may add only relatively important) spheres for acting out one's Christian life, these same structures are incorporated by Clement into the fundamental framework of the Christian life.[135] When he describes the "golden age" of the Corinthian church, the correctly ordered household is presented as a motif central to its well-ordered past (1:3), and in 21:6-9 reverence for Jesus is associated with respect for patriarchal authority and, by implication, a well-ordered household. Further, we noted in the previous chapter the importance of the well-ordered household for the sectarian identity of the Roman community as represented by the *Shepherd*.

The wider social norms concerning household relationships, first accepted by Paul but overshadowed for him by other realities (cf. Gal. 3:27-28) which in turn gave them a lesser significance for the sect's identity, gain an importance in *1 Clement* and the *Shepherd* which is absent in the apostle's writings. The increased importance of these norms represents a more complete adjustment to the sect's social situation as certain values of the wider society become, to an increasing degree, its own. The emergence in the church of a patriarchal authority structure, a central feature of secular power structures surrounding the sect and embodied in the church in its presbyteral system and adoption of the household code to shape behaviour and relationships, represents a transformation toward a sectarian identity more accommodated to the world. Since it is God who establishes the proper order in both church (37:1f.) and state (61:1), one should expect that formal social arrangements will resemble each other in both arenas.

Summary

In this section we have attempted to show that by focusing on household leadership we are able to account for some directions of sectarian development in the Corinthian Church. By adopting household forms for the ordering of the community Paul prepared the way for formal leadership divisions within the church. As in contemporary sects, the secular arrangements surrounding the Pauline church during its period of emergence had an impact on the shaping of community life. We have attempted to show how house church arrangements may have contributed to the development of leadership structures after Paul's death. We have further noted a development toward "established" sectarianism, begun while the apostle was alive and continued after his death. There is evidence in *1 Clement* that the Corinthian, as indeed the Roman, community was in the process of settling into existence in the world. Finally, we suggested that household forms contributed to the shaping of group ideals and norms.

Institutionalization

In the preceding section we focused on a general process of development in the Corinthian community. In this section we shall attempt to define this process more closely by the use of Berger and Luckmann's model of institutionalization.

Terms such as "institution" and "institutionalization" were frequently employed in the preceding discussion to describe developments in *1 Clement*. Interpreters of this Roman epistle who attempt to understand early church development as the result of the straightforward application of ideas also employ these terms in their analyses of *1 Clement*. Their studies, however, reveal a superficial understanding of the processes of institutionalization which results in distorted interpretations of evidence of development in Clement's epistle. Thus Campenhausen writes that in contrast to the period when the apostle was alive, Clement's letter represents a new institutional stage in which official elders are given formal leadership.

> It is no longer a question of individuals, chosen on a particular occasion, and entrusted by the apostles with a function or task within the Church, but of an institution, which has to be preserved as such, and which must be respected in the persons of its representatives.[136]

Similarly, in a more recent study Brunner argues that *1 Clement* represents a shift toward an institutionalized church which was necessary if the Christian church was to survive.

> Die Gemeinden müssten über einen engen, familiären Rahmen hinauswachsen. Das Christentum musste eine rechtlich verfasste Körperschaft werden, wenn es nicht zerfallen wollte, sondern zur Kirche werden, die doch auch und gerade als Reichskirche die Kraft hatte, dem Staat und staatlicher Willkür die Stirn zu bieten.

> Damit hat sich aber die Ausrichtung auf die organisierte Kirche mit institu-
> tion-alisierter Autorität als die theologische Grundthematik des ersten
> Klemensbriefes ergeben.[137]

While these references are in a certain sense valid, they are ultimately misleading. These scholars are correct when they state that *1 Clement* is evidence of new
developments in the Corinthian church, but they fail to identify evidence of
institutionalization in the period when Paul was alive. Campenhausen is a good
example of a scholar who applies a two-stage model of church development to
the period stretching from Paul to Clement's letter. He contrasts the later
period with the earlier one by analysing ideas thought to be the determining
sources of social development. Thus, in the case of the period when the apostle
was alive he argues

> Paul develops the idea of the Spirit as the organizing principle of the Chris-
> tian congregation. There is no need for any fixed system with its rules and
> regulations and prohibitions. Paul's writings do as little to provide such
> things for the individual congregation as for the Church at large. The com-
> munity is not viewed or understood as a sociological entity, and the Spirit
> which governs it does not act within the framework of a particular church
> order or constitution. . . . It is love which is the true organizing and unifying
> force within the Church, and which creates in her a paradoxical form of order
> diametrically opposed to all natural systems of organization.[138]

Having established these concepts as the ideas governing leadership in the community he goes on to assert

> Paul mentions helpers, controllers and administrators, whose activity he
> includes among the 'spiritual gifts'; and he is plainly concerned that these
> people should not be despised, and that nothing should be done to make their
> work more difficult. . . . Nevertheless, the imprecise terminology which Paul
> uses can hardly be taken to imply a fixed 'office'. Paul has in mind anyone
> who comes forward in one way or another within the congregation to take on
> its problems and to provide material or spiritual help.[139]

Even in the case of the titles of bishops and deacons presented by Paul in Phil. 1:1
Campenhausen argues, "[T]here is . . . no question of offices in the strict sense,
and absolutely none of sacral offices on the lines of the later 'hierarchy'."[140] For
Campenhausen offices "in the strict sense" belong to a second stage of church
development. In *1 Clement* (as in other roughly contemporary documents)
"'bishop' is an official designation. It refers to a particular position and function, in
fact that 'episcopal office' which is permanently undertaken by specific members of
the congregation."[141] In *1 Clement* ". . . the patriarchal element has taken prece-
dence over the pneumatic."[142] Thus stage one (when Paul was alive) is characterized by a church governed by pneumatic ideas; stage two is ruled by patriarchal
ones; the first stage is office-free, the second marks the advent of officialdom.

We suggest that this model of church development is too crude. The idea of
an office-free stage of Christian origins is inaccurate and it leads Campenhausen
to a miscalculated estimation of the evidence of institutionalization in *1 Clement*
and what he regards as a lack of institutions during Paul's lifetime. Campenhausen's theory does not successfully explain how the church passed from

this early stage to officialdom. This occurs, in our view, because he does not have a proper understanding of institutionalization. Campenhausen's dichotomy between an office-free or institution-free period of Christian origins and an official institutionalized one has the effect of obscuring the processes which resulted in the developments outlined in the previous sections. Such a dichotomy arises because he regards theologies as the primary determining factors of the social structures of the early church. He does isolate certain social factors to account for the development of centralized authority such as distance from the church's beginnings, the emergence of heretical ideas, the growth in numbers, and a lessening of Christian zeal.[143] But his general treatment reveals that he perceives the more determinative factor to be a shift in the early Christian concept of the church.[144] He thus uses Paul's idea of Spirit as put forward in 1 Cor. 12-14 and Rom. 12 as an interpretive category to determine which social structures existed when Paul was alive; because the idea of office, in his view, is opposed to this concept of Spirit he argues that offices did not exist. But in arguing this way he misinterprets data which are better understood as evidence of the existence of offices during Paul's lifetime.[145]

In order to understand more fully the development of institutions of leadership and of offices in the Corinthian church it is necessary to have a more accurate understanding of institutionalization and a clearer perception of the focuses of institutional development in the early church. Berger and Luckmann's model of institutionalization provides us with a clearer understanding of this process. Rather than treating institutions as static phenomena, their model presents institutionalization as a dynamic process inherent in human interaction.[146] Their model helps us to see that the development of institutions cannot be relegated to a second generation of Christianity; as a process inherent in community life, it was present from the start.

Berger and Luckmann's Model of Institutionalization

Institutionalization, according to Berger and Luckmann, is a dialectical process in which humans and their social world interact with each other. Humans externalize patterns of action which are then regarded as being independent objective realities. In the course of socialization, this social world is internalized and humans again interact with the institutional order.[147] Thus the process is brought full circle. Berger and Luckmann describe various levels of objectified meaning which are created by this process. The final level forms what they call a "symbolic universe."

> The symbolic universe is conceived of as the matrix of *all* socially objectivated and subjectively real meanings; the entire historic society and the entire biography of the individual are seen as events taking place *within* this universe.[148]

The symbolic universe is created in the course of institutionalization, a process which "occurs whenever there is a reciprocal typification of habitualized actions by types of actors. Put differently, any such typification is an institution."[149] This is a broad model of institution building, but it is justified by its usefulness in the analysis of basic human processes.[150] "Habitualization" occurs when a frequently repeated action becomes cast into a pattern recognizable to both the performer and an observer and which can be repeated in the future in the same way.[151] Typifications of habitualized actions occur when a pattern is imposed on an individual on the basis of his or her recurring behaviour.[152] Reciprocal typifications arise when two parties act toward each other on the basis of performed typifications and modify their behaviour accordingly. The most basic social interactions are governed by such "typifactory schemes";[153] they create "types of actors," i.e., roles which individuals occupy and which are regarded as being separate from themselves.[154] Berger and Luckmann state, "We can properly begin to speak of roles when this kind of typification occurs in the context of an objectified stock of knowledge common to a collectivity of actors."[155] In institutional typifications not only actions but also actors or roles are typified.[156] "The institution posits that actions of type X will be performed by actors of type X."[157] "Institutions are embodied in individual experience by means of roles."[158] While it is the case that on the level of habitualization actors enjoy a flexibility which allows them to modify their behaviour in accordance with new experiences, institutions create predefined, or "crystallized,"[159] patterns of conduct which channel human activity and are thereby instances of social control.

Role expectations take on a new significance with the appearance of a third party, or the equivalent to a second generation.

> Only at this point does it become possible to speak of a social world at all, in the sense of a comprehensive and given reality confronting the individual in a manner analogous to the reality of the natural world.[160]

As long as routine or institutionalized activity remains confined to the interaction of two individuals the routine, although persistent once established, is relatively susceptible to alteration by the actors. With the appearance of a third party or new generation the necessity arises to communicate and pass on the institution to another. "The objectivity of the institutional world 'thickens' and 'hardens'";[161] by communicating and passing on the institution to a third party it acquires an opaque quality which confronts both the initiators and the recipients as something "out there" — an objective "social world" which is normative both for the initiators and the recipients. "A world so regarded attains a firmness in consciousness; it becomes real in an ever more massive way and it can no longer be changed so readily."[162] By the act of transmission the patterns of interaction or institutions become more solid for the creators themselves, a part of the binding normative order by which their own actions are patterned.

But the appearance of a third party or new generation means that the institutional world requires legitimation. Because the recipient has not shared in the formulation of the institution it is not understood or accepted in the same way as it was comprehended by its creators and is therefore in need of legitimation, that is, a process by which the institutional world "can be 'explained' and justified."[163] Legitimation is a means of explaining and justifying the prominent elements of the institutional tradition.[164] Since the original meaning of the institution is not available to the recipient by means of memory it is necessary to interpret its meaning by various legitimating formulas. In order to be convincing these formulas must be consistent with the institutional order. Berger and Luckmann argue

It follows that the expanding institutional order develops a corresponding canopy of legitimations, stretching over it a protective cover of both cognitive and normative interpretation. These legitimations are learned by the new generation during the same process that socializes them into the institutional order.[165]

As groups grow and the institutional order becomes segmented with a corresponding series of types of actors, it becomes crucial that the order provide an integration of the meanings which encompass the society and that the institutional activities of one type of actor *vis-à-vis* other types are legitimated.[166]

The Death of Paul and the Desire to Preserve Sect Ideals

If the model of institutionalization described above is accurate, it is imprecise to speak of the advent of the institutionalized church one or two generations after the death of Paul. Clement was indeed involved in a process of institution building, but he did not invent institutionalization nor did he introduce institutionalization to the early church. Institutionalized authority was not the creation of an early Christian author but a process which was inherent in social interaction in the early church from its inception.

What gave rise to the patriarchal structure described in the preceding discussion? Bultmann argues that *"the incipient regulation of the local congregations* is determined by the congregation's understanding of itself as an eschatalogical community ruled by the Spirit."[167] And he agrees, with Käsemann, that "nascent catholicism was the historically necessary outcome of an original Christianity whose apocalyptic expectation had not been fulfilled."[168] Does not Clement, when putting the hope of the future resurrection before his readers, cite scripture which quotes the sceptic as saying, "We have heard these things even in the days of our fathers, and behold we have grown old, and none of these things has happened to us" (23:3)? It is indeed true that the continuation of a sect is an important element which contributes toward the development of centralized organization. But it is not the only one. Nor is it sufficient to refer to a continuation unanticipated by the original founder. There are more specific reasons for this development.

A factor which these scholars overlook is the impact on communities as a result of the absence of the apostolic community founder, Paul. We noted above that while Paul was still alive community life was overshadowed by his presence. Holmberg, commenting on the reason for lack of development in Paul's churches, argues

> The decisive reason is . . . the personage of Paul himself. The founder has not left the scene, but is fully and energetically active in his churches (especially in Corinth). His letters show that he had full control over the life and development of his churches and regarded himself as having a permanent responsibility for them. Even if he aimed at fostering maturity and independence in his churches the letters do not give the impression that he gave them the reins. And it is just this 'potential accessibility' of the apostle, the fact that he

is still actively present and his authority fully accessible, that prevents the full (social legal and theological) development of those beginnings of an office structure we observe in the Pauline letters. This aspect of local church life does not really start to develop until after the apostle's death.[169]

What impact would the death of such a person have had on the community? What kept the community from disintegrating? For not all sects persist; they sometimes perish with the death or discrediting of their leader. Was there a relationship between the death of the apostle and the increased importance of patriarchal structures? These are questions which are rarely raised by scholars who attempt to account for the development of early church structure and, as far as this writer is aware, have never been asked by interpreters of *1 Clement*. So far we have argued that it was the wealthy householder who became the focus of leadership in the absence and finally after the death of the apostle. We have placed the emergence of a formal group of leaders in a framework of sect development in order to highlight important social developments in the early church. But we have not yet fully answered the more important question of the social reasons for this particular direction of development.

Bengt Holmberg in his work cited above employs Berger and Luckmann's model of institutionalization to describe the whole process of interaction between Paul and his followers and the forms and structures which arose from it. Holmberg's discussion helps to shed light on institutional developments subsequent to Paul's death and places *1 Clement* in a social matrix which is better defined than that proposed by scholars such as Campenhausen and Brunner.

Holmberg identifies Paul sociologically as a charismatic leader. Here he employs Weber's ideal type of charismatic authority. And Stark brings out Paul's unique charismatic position when he calls the apostle a "minor founder," who succeeds "the Founder" Jesus.[170] We shall discuss Weber's notion of charisma in greater detail when we discuss Ignatius of Antioch.[171] It is enough to state here that Weber conceived of charismatic authority as a type of leadership arising from personal devotion to an individual believed to possess extraordinary, heroic, or divinely conferred qualities. Holmberg correctly identifies Paul as a charismatic authority by arguing that the apostle mediated "a closer contact with the vital, sacred center of existence through his articulation of their needs and aspirations, of the new goals and norms, and through his guidance to a new order and a new life."[172] Weber's ideal type belongs to a model which he describes as the "routinization of charisma."[173] He argued that routinization is a process which arises after the death of a charismatic leader as a result of the attempts of the leader's followers, especially his staff, to preserve the benefits which accrued to them while he was alive. They do this by creating and perpetuating agencies and institutions designed to continue the order which their leader established. Weber was perhaps unduly influenced by Rudolph Sohm, from whom he borrowed the term "charisma," for he is justly criticized for distinguishing too sharply between charisma and routinization. He did not adequately treat processes of institutionalization inherent in both phases.[174] In short, by contrasting too sharply between charisma and routinization he overlooked the possible state of affairs in which a charismatic leader contributes to institution building in the community gathered around him.[175] This final criti-

cism has important implications for an accurate assessment of institutionalization and the routinization process during Paul's lifetime.

Holmberg modifies Weber's model by applying to it Berger and Luckmann's
model of institutionalization. He distinguishes between institutionalization and
"cumulative institutionalization." This latter phrase describes the process by
which institutionalization and legitimation work together on already existing
institutions to produce increasingly complex and more developed social
orders.[176] Within this cumulative category he distinguishes between two kinds
of institutionalization. The first (primary institutionalization) refers to the process by which the authority thought to reside in a charismatic leader's person
spills over into his instructions, characteristic ethos, and the institutions formed
by interaction with him. This occurs while the leader is still alive. The second
kind (secondary institutionalization) arises after a charismatic leader's death. It is
the latter form which we shall use to analyse the development of centralized
authority structures after Paul's death. In this period the institutional structures
which developed while the leader was still alive acquire an independent authority of their own.

> The leader's words, his message and example, the rituals and institutions he
> created now enjoy more authority than before, as he is not there to complete,
> interpret or change them. But all these authoritative parts of the charismatic
> group life need to be unified and placed in relation to one another so as to be
> accessible to the group. This is done by means of a secondary institutionaliza-
> tion which transforms unconsolidated verbal tradition into a body of norma-
> tive texts, ways of living and a typical ethical 'atmosphere' into a formulated
> code of behaviour and a paraenetical teaching tradition, community rites into
> organized forms of worship. The most important change is that the former
> staff of assistants become new leaders of the group, responsible for teaching,
> decision-making and development.[177]

The staff does not consciously introduce fundamentally new goals and norms or
invent new forms of group life, but attempts to preserve the original group
through the conservation, exposition, development, and systematization of what
is provided by the order established by the leader. Holmberg notes that this
institutionalization of charismatic authority results in the mediation of charisma
through such representatives as offices, holy traditions, and rituals.[178] This process of cumulative institutionalization is necessary if the group is to survive.

What picture do we discover if we analyse the development of the Corinthian
community toward formal centralized authority with the model of institutionalization described above? A useful way to understand the developments in this
church is to analyse them as examples of cumulative institutionalization. Holmberg places Paul's churches in a schema of secondary institutionalization. Paul is
actively engaged in or oversees the process of institution building in the
churches he founded; while there are a variety of options open to the communities for development, the formulation of structures is guided by and placed in
the context of a corporate tradition. Paul fits them into the framework of the
common stock of knowledge of the Christian group and by doing so he legiti-
mates them. If need arises, he also corrects institutional developments which he
thinks are inappropriate, such as the assertion of preeminence by pneumatic

Christians (1 Cor. 12-14), again by reference to the knowledge of the community. By means of these institutional developments and their legitimations the symbolic universe is formed, expanded, solidified and transformed.

But if Paul was part of a process in which the message, example, rituals, and institutions given by Jesus were integrated into a more systematic code for community life, this is not to deny that Paul also was a charismatic leader. As a charismatic "minor founder," Paul was believed by his churches to be in vital contact with the sacred centre of the Christian movement. Just as the communal benefits surrounding the disciples' relationship with Jesus were perpetuated through the verbal tradition of his teachings, ethos, and customs, so too with Paul, the benefits which were present when he was still alive continued after his death by the preservation of the institutional order, teaching, code of conduct, and rituals which the apostle either initiated himself or passed on. As after the founder's death the staff assumed positions of leadership, so after the minor founder's disappearance his staff assumed similar positions. The character of such institutionalization was probably different after the death of a figure like Paul than it was after that of someone like Clement. Both were involved in processes of progressive institutionalization, but they did not have the same impact on the movement. Stark illustrates this distinction well when he differentiates between those whom he calls "the second" and the minor founder. The second's primary role is to conserve what the founder or minor founder initiates.[179] He is primarily an administrator and his activity is crucial if the community is to survive.[180] This distinction will be useful in our attempt to understand the authority structures which arose after Paul's death.

How did institutionalization arise in Paul's churches? The model outlined above cannot fill in gaps where we lack information, but it can suggest a possible course of development which allows us to place the evidence of institutions in *1 Clement* in a wider context. What follows is put forward as one possible way of placing the evidence contained within *1 Clement* in a developmental scheme of institutionalization. If we are correct in our estimation of the apostle as a charismatic leader, then it seems probable that as different institutions began to arise from interaction with the apostle and take shape in the community, his authority flowed into them. Examples of this include the exhortation to be subject to Stephanas and his household (1 Cor. 16:15) as well as the προιστάμενοι of Thessalonica (1 Thes. 5:12), Paul's recognition of Prisca and Aquila's co-workmanship, which probably included the oversight of the church which met in their house (Rom. 16:3-5), his regard for Philemon (Phlm. v. 2) and Gaius (Rom. 16:23) who probably oversaw house churches, and his recommendation of the minister Phoebe, patroness of Paul and perhaps the church at Cenchreae (Rom. 16:1).[181] And by connecting the activities which these individuals carried out for the community (1 Cor. 12; Rom. 12: 4-8) with his spiritual instruction, Paul established for them a legitimate place in the symbolic universe of the group.

Such members as these formed a recognized body of co-workers sharing in the apostle's mission. They formed part of his staff and inasmuch as they occupied roles which were regarded by Paul and fellow members as furthering the aims of the apostle's mission they were "enveloped in the vague and powerful nimbus of the authority of the entire institution."[182] Or, differently stated, because the roles they occupied as house-church patrons and leaders ensured the smooth operation of the community and encouraged the growth of the church, they were placed in a privileged point of contact with the "serious" — God's will in the establishment and expansion of the church. Their roles were enhanced because of the important contributions they made to the common life of the church.

It is reasonable to suppose that with the death of the apostle this staff took on a position similar to that of the staff surrounding a charismatic leader. The authority which the apostle and the community conferred on them while the minor founder was still alive probably did not evaporate; instead it continued to assert itself in the institutions which local staff such as house-church patrons embodied. In Clement's letter, the institutional order includes not only certain individual roles, but also the places of worship. The advantages which the community enjoyed while Paul was alive were perpetuated through the institutions which formed while he was still available to the community. One may infer that the relatively wide variety of institutional expressions open to communities while the apostle was alive, subject to modifications as the apostle and those acting out certain roles interacted with one another, became more rigidly channelled when those structures were challenged or adaptation was required to carry out new tasks. We shall argue that *1 Clement* provides evidence of precisely this type of channelling. As institutionalization continued after the apostle's death and new institutional needs arose in the community, the order established by the apostle and implied in his writings required the kind of further reflection found in *1 Clement*.[183] But the further institution building which may be adduced from Clement's letter was a variation on a theme rather than the creation of something radically new. In our view *1 Clement* is evidence of a "thickening" and "hardening" of the institutional order after the death of Paul; it is evidence of a social world handed on to succeeding generations and confronting them as a normative order.

Clement's argument in 42:1-4 and 44:1f. shows that the order which developed around the apostle has become part of the normative state of affairs. He was probably not inventing anything new when he stated that the apostles appointed bishops and deacons in the churches they founded (42:4; 44:2). Evidence in roughly contemporary literature (Acts 14:23; Tit. 1:5) suggests that the belief may have been relatively widespread. The common judgment that these descriptions are purely fictional must be treated with caution.[184] If our argument concerning the emergence of local authority structures "from below" when Paul was alive is correct, then Clement's description (as that of his contemporaries) is better interpreted as ascribing to the apostle structures which had developed through the course of one or two generations, but which were continuous with the community's initial pattern of organization.[185] This is a more satisfactory explanation than Campenhausen's "fusion theory" of a welding together of Jewish-Christian and Pauline forms.[186] Placed within the model of cumulative institutionalization described above, we may state that the normative order which confronted the Corinthian community was an instance of the expansion of institutions which arose around Paul and which took on a new significance after his death.

Elders and Institutionalization

The rise of the importance of elder Christians or presbyters to which both Hermas and Clement give testimony is further evidence of a cumulative institutionalization. We noted above that household relationships were imported by Paul into the group when he baptized households. While it is true that passages such as 1 Cor. 7:29-31 reveal that Paul attached only a relative importance to household arrangements, other passages such as I Cor. 11:3-16 shows that he did regard them as valid structures. Patriarchal arrangements were part of the apostle's teaching and, as in other structural arrangements which were recognized by Paul, they gained importance after the apostle's death.

There is a slight difficulty in determining to which members of the community the term πρεσβύτερος refers. It may be interpreted to refer either to seniority in age or seniority in the faith. While reverence for age was a norm in the Graeco-Roman world, the possible importance of the length of time one had been a Christian should not be ignored, especially in a period of institutional consolidation. Ernst von Dobschütz notes the importance of these members for the protection and preservation of the group's values in the period directly following Paul's death.[187]

It is reasonable to assume that acquaintance with these values and experience in the Christian life conferred authority on these members. In some cases there may also have been members who had had some connection with the apostle's founding work or the period when he was alive.

The respect accorded to elder members is seen in 63:3 where a qualification of the Roman church's emissaries is their seniority in the Christian faith. This, together with their moral purity, puts them in positions of authority. While Clement does not state directly that the other elders of the community have authority conferred upon them for the same reason, this is a reasonable inference. Seniority in the faith was probably one criterion for distinguishing Christians in Pauline churches from the start. Paul includes in his exhortation to be subject to Stephanas and his household the fact that they were the first converts of Achaia (1 Cor. 16:15) and it may be that this conferred upon them a special place in the community. In Rom. 16:5 he also singles out for special greeting Epaenetus, the first convert in Asia. When Clement states in 42:4, therefore, that the apostles appointed their first converts (ἀπαρχαί — the same term used in 1 Cor. 16:15 and Rom. 16:5) to be bishops and deacons, there is probably a kernel of historical truth present. The importance attached to the criterion of seniority suggests a degree of development toward more formal leadership over the period of time between Paul's presence in Corinth and the composition of *1 Clement*. Still, it is a reasonable but obviously tentative conclusion to draw from these facts that seniority in the faith continued to distinguish members as suitable candidates for leadership in the community after the death of the apostle.

Clement's Contribution to the Institutionalization of the Corinthian Church

So far we have attempted to determine what were some of the focal points of institutionalization in the first generations of the church; we have argued that the leadership provided by house-church patrons was an important one in the Corinthian church. In the quotation taken from Brunner above it is stated that the creation of institutions was necessary if the church was to survive. We have tried to show that, stated in this way, Brunner's observation is misleading. Institutionalization cannot be treated adequately as the application of an idea or concept without fundamental distortion. But Brunner's argument is correct in a sense perhaps unintended by him: Clement was engaged in a form of institution building. To understand this properly it is necessary to place the process of institution building in the early church in a context more precise than Brunner presents. It is to Clement's contribution to the institutionalization of the church that we now turn.

The Role of Conflict in Institution Building

Obviously Clement's letter was written to end the conflict in the Corinthian community. But less obvious is the role conflict played in the process of institution building in this church. A number of sociologists and anthropologists have focused their attention on the phenomenon of conflict in order to determine how disagreement between and within groups contributes positively to the development of community structures. We shall concern ourselves primarily with Coser's reflections on Georg Simmel's seminal work, entitled *Conflict*.[188] Coser defines conflict as "a struggle over values or claims to status, power, and scarce resources, in which the aims of the conflicting parties are not only to gain the desired values but also to neutralize, injure, or eliminate their rivals."[189] But in the attempt to be rid of one's opponents or the threat they present, Coser argues, conflict contributes in a positive way to society by giving rise to new norms and rules for new situations, or by bringing into awareness certain norms and rules that were dormant before the particular conflict arose.[190]

These are called the "law-creating aspects" of conflict,[191] and Coser notes further that the application of new rules which arise out of conflicts leads to the growth of new institutional structures centring on the enforcement of the rules and norms which are created or discovered as a result of conflict.[192]

But solutions to conflicts do not always occur of their own accord. The role of specialists in the creation of solutions in intra-group conflicts has been noted by Hoebel, who has conducted several anthropological studies into the processes at work in the creation of law among so-called primitive peoples.[193] Hoebel has observed that in the case of intra-group conflict where there are no explicit laws determining the rights of individuals or punitive measures, specialists, that is certain authoritative members of the group, are called upon to determine what the appropriate norms are which govern given situations of discord and to show how these norms fit into what he calls the culture's "basic postulates" — what we have chosen to call the symbolic universe.[194]

Obviously legal problems represent a highly sophisticated and formal instance of conflict resulting in increased group structure. But specialists are no less important on more basic levels. And it is here that we begin to come closer to the significance of conflict for institution building in the early church. Eisenstadt notes that any institutional differentiation which arises through the process of institutionalization can become the object of conflict.[195] Unless these conflicts are solved through further differentiation or the creation of facilities to deal with them, the group or institution may collapse.[196] For example, the differentiation introduced and legitimated by Paul when he encouraged members to be subject to the heads of certain households created the possibility that other households might separate themselves and create a schism. This perhaps painfully obvious observation has been completely overlooked by most scholars who wish to see in *1 Clement* a purely ideological struggle between gnostic, pneumatic or some other form of deviant group and "orthodox" Christians. Eisenstadt notes the importance of those whom he calls "elites" or "*entrepreneurs*," "who are able to articulate new goals, set up new organization, and mobilize the resources necessary for their continuous functioning" in the creation of institutions.[197] By implication, we add that such elites are also important when conflicts arise within the institutional framework and that they have a central role to play in further institution building when existing structures are threatened.

Institution Building and the Corinthian Conflict

These observations help us to assess more accurately than in previous studies Clement's intervening role in the Corinthian conflict. If we see him as an "*entrepreneur*" who was engaged in institution building in the Corinthian community we shall see how the conflict in this church contributed to the process of institutional development. By presenting the rejection of the authority of the deposed leaders as a rejection of divinely established community structures, Clement made those structures explicit and by showing how the group's beliefs committed them to support for the leaders, he strengthened the normative character of those structures. We may describe Clement as involved in institution building, or better, institution strengthening activity. In 7:2-3 Clement urges, "Let us put aside empty and vain cares, and let us come to the glorious and venerable rule of our tradition, and let us see what is good and pleasing and acceptable in the sight of our Maker." While this exhortation has perhaps a limited reference in the context of this chapter, in the rest of the letter Clement's efforts may be described as an attempt to identify the proper norms and values of the group, to show how they fit in with the community's tradition, and to apply them to the conflict in an effort to bring division within the group to an end.

The Corinthian conflict focused the attention of the group on existing institutional arrangements and Clement's role as a mediator in the conflict was to show how those structures were expressions of the group's beliefs and how certain values held by the group implied a commitment to its organization. In chapters 40-44, where Clement is less indirect in his description of the conflict, the Roman writer attempts to place the community's leadership structures in a sacred context by presenting the various roles associated with it as analogies of other sacral arrangements. In this section he connects the church's practices and arrangements with the will of God (40:1; 41:1; 44:1-2). By drawing on themes associated with the sacral arrangements in Jerusalem, which also issued from the will of God (40:5; 41:2-4), and by casting church practices in a similar light (40:2-5), leadership structures are connected with the group's vital and inspiring symbols and are thereby given inviolability. Thus by developing certain themes of the group's beliefs, Clement integrated existing social arrangements into the group's symbolic universe and thereby contributed to the strength and perma-nence of the established institutional order.

The segmentation of the institutional order in the Corinthian community led to the problem which arises in the process of institutional differentiation, of providing integrative meanings that encompass society and place each member of society in his or her proper context *vis-à-vis* differing roles and responsibili-ties. The conflict within the institutional order of the church at Corinth brought this problem into greater relief and by demanding solution, through the creation of legitimations which related institutions to one another and located them in a proper context, the group's structural arrangements were fur-ther strengthened. The Corinthian conflict therefore served to enhance the institutional order by focusing energies on its maintenance. A result of the con-flict was to identify the values and historical events or interpretations of them which were normative for the proper functioning of community life.

Clement's Contribution as a Legitimator of Institutions

How did Clement contribute to the process of the institutionalization of leader-ship in the Corinthian church? Campenhausen, following Sohm, argues that in *1 Clement* "for the first time the structures of canon law are included in the cate-gory of doctrines and dogma, and given a sacral and immutable character."[198] He interprets 44:1-5 as "the famous passage in which he (Clement) lays down the legal status of the episcopate as an order and institution of the Church created by the apostles and valid for all time."[199]

Is this in fact the case? In our view, Clement's theory, put forward in 44:1-3, that the apostles appointed bishops and later added a "codicil" that appointed leaders should be succeeded in due course, does not signal the birth of canon law. It is more precise to state that Clement's contribution to institutionalization in the early church was to provide a formal legitimation of certain leadership structures. Clement's interest does not appear to be the establishment of a uni-versal regulation of succession, although this may have been an unintended consequence of his argument, especially in so far as his letter itself became a more widely distributed authoritative writing. The focus of the argument is not on the so-called "codicil,"[200] but rather on the apostles' foreknowledge that there would be strife over institutional arrangements established by them (44:1-2). Clement's introduction of this theme of foreknowledge echoes and belongs to themes which he develops in earlier parts of his letter and to which he returns again at its conclusion. All order is established by God (20:1-12; 33:2-3; cf. 61:1-2) and demands obedience because of its sacred origin (37:1-38.4; 40:3; 41:1,3).

This is no less true of the order of church leadership established by the apos-tles. The notion of foreknowledge "through the Lord Jesus" (44:1) is introduced to show that all structural arrangements have their origin with God (in 44:2 he writes that Christ is "from God" – ἀπὸ τοῦ θεοῦ). In particular, the "codicil" that appropriate successors be appointed after the death of the first appointees is a direct consequence of God's ordering activity in the community. The significance of Clement's argument for the situation to which he is addressing himself is that the Corinthian dispute was foreseen by the apostles. By appealing to the apostles' foreknowledge, what Clement is engaged in is the legitimation of the authority of those who have been deposed, not the construction of certain formal structures of leadership as the Sohmian interpretation would have it. Campenhausen's assertion that in 44:1-4 we have the birth of canon law misinterprets what is a secondary reaction (Clement's theory of apostolic regulation as a legitimation of the contemporary order) to certain social phenomena in the Corinthian community (the exclusion of established leaders and the creation of alternative places of worship) as the primary structuring principle of the group.[201] This is not to deny that when the need for further successions arose Clement's theory may have provided an already existing justification for a certain process of selection. But if we focus our attention on the institutional setting of the conflict we will notice that Clement is primarily concerned with an end to a particular dispute.

Similarly, Brunner's argument that *1 Clement* is addressed not only to the individual needs of the Corinthian community but to the whole church,[202] misrepresents the primary purpose of Clement to bring an end to a particular social conflict. Although Clement hints that there is some social unrest in the Roman church also (7:1), one cannot generalize that Clement attempts to solve institutional problems present in the empire-wide church. This is to draw more from the text than is appropriate and to engage in unwarranted speculation.

Clement's contribution must therefore be assessed primarily on the local level. His letter does not signal a new stage of institutional development in the so-called universal church; he is engaged rather in the legitimation of an already existing order in a particular community which has been upset by certain individuals. In the process of this attempt he makes explicit the institutional order and shows how it is integrated in the group's symbolic universe. By integrating and connecting institutions with beliefs in an explicit way, Clement contributes to the process of cumulative institutionalization. In our estimation, von Campenhausen is probably correct in saying that Clement worked out more precisely and systematically beliefs regarding the origins of the institutional order that were already present in the Corinthian community;[203] even the theory that the apostles made arrangements for succession after their first appointees (44:2) may have been a common belief in the Corinthian church. Clement's unique contribution is his connection of what seem to have been shared beliefs about the origins of the institutional order with the group's wider beliefs.

Summary

Berger and Luckmann argue that an institution cannot be fully comprehended until the historical process by which it was produced is understood.[204]

By accounting for institutional development by the straightforward application of ideas, we suggest that analysts of *1 Clement* have overlooked the significance of the social processes which led to Clement's efforts to legitimate certain institutions and that this has led to an inaccurate understanding of institutionalization in this community. Instead, we have examined sect development in the Corinthian church by the use of a more precise model of institutionalization. We have attempted to show that the seeds of later institutional development in the Corinthian church may be found in what we have interpreted as evidence of house-church leadership in the Pauline epistles. The role of house-church management became a primary focus of institutional development both because of its usefulness in the functioning and growth of the group and its connection with the apostle Paul. The desire to preserve the benefits of the order established or recognized by the apostle probably resulted in a continuation of that arrangement after his death and encouraged the increasing emergence of the apostle's staff as important leaders within the local community. In the following section we will show more precisely how Clement attempted to legitimate institutionalized leadership in the Corinthian community.

Legitimation

In our discussion of evidence of institutionalization in the Corinthian community we argued that Clement was engaged primarily in an effort to legitimate leadership structures in the Corinthian church. In this section we shall discuss evidence of the process of legitimation in *1 Clement* more fully. By focusing on themes of legitimation it can be shown that *1 Clement* is a relatively unified document, *pace* Wrede and Knopf, and that its writer was engaged in an explication of the group's symbolic universe in order to justify and validate the institutional order to his readers and to demonstrate its normative character.

Berger and Luckmann's Model of Legitimation and the Institutional Setting of the Corinthian Community

As in the case of institutionalization, Berger and Luckmann provide a useful model of legitimation which brings into focus social processes at work in Clement's letter. It was noted in the preceding section that institutions take on a significantly new character when handed on to a third party or second generation. This is an important observation because the conflict in *1 Clement* describes a situation in which conflict has arisen in the Corinthian church in the second or third generation. According to the description of the conflict presented in 44:2-3, after the death of the first leaders appointed by the apostles, conflict arose around those leaders' successors (cf. v. 5). If Clement was writing *c.* A.D. 96 it is likely that several of the original leaders of the community were either dead or very old and that new leaders had already begun to take their place.[205] As we have already noted, Berger and Luckmann argue that because recipients of an institutional order which has been handed down are not involved in its inception, that order needs to be explained and justified to them. The reality of the social world confronts the recipient as an historical one and comes to the new generation not as a memory but as a tradition.[206] Because of this the institutions formed by the initial actors lose their self-evident character and can no longer be maintained by reference to memory.[207] In the context of the Corinthian situation, the leaders who succeeded the actors involved in the development of institutional patterns while Paul was still alive did not have the benefit of memory of a relationship with the apostle which served to legitimate their predecessors' roles of leadership, nor did the later generation of the community enjoy recollection of days past when Paul worked hand in hand with local leaders. What the new generation of leaders and followers alike did possess, however, was a series of institutional arrangements passed on to them. In Berger and Luckmann's terms, this was an objectivated order, i.e., an external socially produced reality which confronted members as normative.

These sociologists also note that as time passes and institutions become more permanent, conflicts may arise which call the transmitted order into question. Not all recipients of the institutional order receive its objectivated meaning in the same way, nor are all socialized into it equally. This fact can result in conflict within the institutional order. Berger and Luckmann note that in the Christian tradition it was heresy which provided an impetus for theoretical development of the symbolic universe.[208]

We have argued that depictions of *1 Clement* as an answer to an heretical challenge are not convincing. We may still see in Clement's letter, however, a response to a form of deviant behaviour. In fact much of his letter is devoted to showing that the leaders of the dissenting groups have departed from the group's beliefs. By identifying these beliefs and locating the institutional order inthe context they provide, Clement made explicit the social meanings contained within the institutional order, and by showing how the group's beliefs relate to the institutions passed on to the community he strengthened the normative character of the group's structures of leadership. This may be described as a theoretical development of the group's symbolic universe.

If, then, the so-called schismatics were not heretics, nevertheless the discord in the Corinthian community functioned in a way analogous to heretical challenges in other situations in the history of the church: to strengthen already existing institutions and to provide an impetus for a theoretical conceptualization of the group's symbolic universe. Any social meaning passed on to individuals who do not have access to a memory which makes that phenomenon meaningful requires some explanation if its normative force is to be preserved. Further, the act of transmission does not guarantee that the meaning will be communicated perfectly or even convincingly. This model of legitimation provides us with a useful heuristic framework in which to place the patterns of institutionalized authority discovered in the last section, and Clement's role in the cumulative institutionalization of the Corinthian church. We may notice from the general nature of the Corinthian dispute that the meanings which were passed on by members associated with Paul evidently were not enough to prevent a denial of the authority of certain presbyters appointed as leaders of the community (cf. 44:3). As a writer attempting to legitimate the authority of those whose positions had been undermined, Clement's task included the necessity of making the institutional order subjectively plausible to members of the Corinthian community.

The Four Levels of Legitimation

Institutions are made plausible to those to whom they are passed on in several ways. Berger and Luckmann distinguish four levels of legitimation.[209] "Incipient legitimation" belongs to the first level — the simple transmission of language to describe institutions. By the act of transmitting kinship language, for example, kinship structures are legitimated. On the next level are contained rudimentary theoretical propositions, such as apophthegms, proverbs, legends and folk tales, which relate sets of objective meanings by means of explanatory schemes. On the third level an institutional segment is legitimated by means of explicit theories which integrate varying sectors of institutionalized conduct through relatively comprehensive frames of reference. It is on this level that we may place Clement's theory of the apostolic establishment of leadership structures (chapters 42; 44) and his paralleling of proper worship arrangements with the Levitical organization of sacrifices (40:5-41:2).

The final and most encompassing and integrating level of legitimation is that of symbolic universes. "These are bodies of theoretical tradition that integrate different provinces of meaning and encompass the institutional order in a symbolic totality. . . ."[210] Here legitimation takes place through symbolic totalities which integrate all segments of the institutional order in an all-encompassing schema. It is called a universe because all human activity and experience is conceived of as taking place within it. We shall focus on this level of legitimation as we discuss the efforts of Clement to promote particular institutional structures in Corinth.

1 Clement as a Unified Document

It may strike the reader as odd that so far we have concentrated so heavily on only a handful of passages in the preceding discussion. Indeed, *1 Clement* is composed of some sixty-five chapters, and to focus our attention on only isolated portions of the text would be methodologically unsound. Our purpose so far has been to attempt to reconstruct the historical and institutional setting of the Corinthian dispute and this has necessitated that we place the weight of our discussion on passages where Clement is less indirect in his description of the Corinthian dispute, namely select verses in chapters 40-44 and a few passages outside this section. But this is not where the discussion can end without fundamental distortion of Clement's aims and method. Failure to understand how the rest of the letter is integrated with these central chapters has led scholars to misrepresent Clement's purposes throughout the document. Thus Bauer, for example, agrees with Knopf that most of *1 Clement* has "little or nothing to do with its clearly defined purpose." "Indeed," he adds, "it is easy to get the impression that by far the greater part of the letter serves only to increase its size, in order thereby to enhance its importance and forcefulness."[211] Bauer is following Knopf here and this viewpoint has been repeatedly asserted in past scholarship of *1 Clement*.[212]

The view that the majority of *1 Clement* is a form of "epistolary stuffing" arises perhaps from a misunderstanding of the role and nature of moral teaching in the letter, for a great portion of Clement's epistle is concerned with appropriate moral behaviour. Harnack, commenting upon the amount of moral teaching in *1 Clement*, writes

> Der stärkste Eindruck, den man aus dem Brief erhält, ist der, dass die neue Religion in der erster Linie keine kultische, auch keine enthusiastische, noch weniger eine gnostische oder spekulative-mysteriöse, sondern eine sittliche Bewegung gewesen ist, eine sittliche Bewegung auf dem Grunde des mit höchstem Ernst und höchster Lebendigkeit empfundenen Monotheismus, oder besser: auf dem Grunde der Wirklichkeit Gottes.[213]

And later in the same work he concludes that *1 Clement* represents "eine geschlossene und feste sittliche Bewegung in dem sicheren Bewusstsein, den lebendigen Gott zu kennen und als die Erlösten in Christus zu leben."[214] But how the morality of this "firm moral movement," on which Clement focuses his attention, relates to the issues he addresses is not satisfactorily answered by Harnack. In the preceding discussion we argued that passages formulated with a view to a more general case have been misinterpreted by scholars as relatively precise descriptions of the Corinthian disputants. In our view such misinterpretations have arisen because scholars have not correctly connected Clement's moral teaching with the broader religious ideas of the letter, i.e., the symbolic universe which Clement shared with his audience. Jaubert gives a valuable warning to those setting out to interpret 1 Clement when she writes, "La diversité des themes est frappante et pourrait déconcerter, surtout lorsque l'on quitte l'optique d'ensemble pour s'attacher aux morceaux particuliers pris en eux-memes."[215] Clement's writing becomes especially confusing if his overall purpose is not accurately assessed.

In order to assess more accurately the role of Clement's moral exhortations it is necessary to understand how moral teaching, especially when it is religious, is connected with more encompassing phenomena. Berger and Luckmann argue, "Legitimation not only tells the individual why he *should* perform one action and not another; it also tells him why things *are* what they are."[216]

On the all-encompassing level of the symbolic universe, roles and certain forms of behaviour are not only presented as normative; the reason why they are normative is also explained. If we apply this observation to *1 Clement*, we may state that Clement not only tells the Corinthians that they should submit to the normative institutional order, but more importantly, why they should. Berger and Luckmann's observation is similar to Geertz's anthropological observation, noted in our discussion of the *Shepherd*, that moral precepts, i.e., an ethos, are not fully understood until they are seen in the context of the transcendent beliefs which encompass them, that is, a world-view. Harnack's observation above, therefore, that *1 Clement* represents a moral movement which exists in the conviction that one knows the living God and lives as a redeemed member in Christ, tells only half the story of the role Clement ascribes to this knowledge in the legitimation of the institutional order. It is necessary to inquire further how the institutional order relates to the morals and beliefs which are presented in the letter. In other words, we want to know, again using Geertz's terms, how ethos and world-view are related in *1 Clement* and how the institutional order fits into them.

The Symbolic Universe Implied in 1 Clement

What world-view did the Corinthian church contemporary with Clement's letter share? According to Campenhausen, *1 Clement* represents a departure from the insights of genuine Paulinism. He expresses this viewpoint forcefully when, commenting on the Roman epistle, he writes

> The abstract concept of order has become completely detached from any specifically Christian meaning — that is to say, one connected with Christ and the Gospel — and thus threatens to lose altogether its concrete and historical actuality. The empty generalities and the lack of any really penetrating human and religious insights, which characterize *1 Clement*, are however by no means devoid of practical implications; for the decision has already been reached in favour of a particular side. The political and social self-awareness, in the widest sense, of the official Church with its natural morality spontaneously thrusts itself forward, and in the place which the Gospel has left vacant sets its own ready-made system. As a result the diffuse, respectable sentiments of the sermon acquire a positive platform, and ecclesiastical organization the needed safeguard and reinforcement of an edifying presentation.

He then continues,

> In this way the elders and church officials win the victory over the slackening energies of the Christian proclamation; and wherever there is a struggle over the rights of ecclesiastical office, again and again it is 1 Clement which the adherents of officialdom like to adduce in support of their position.[217]

Thus Clement is cast in the role of a somewhat insipid *homme de parti* who takes over a stolid church which has moved from the heady days of the Spirit to the phlegmatic period of the routine and uninspiring Institution. *1 Clement* fares little better in the hands of Eduard Schweizer:

> The designations used of the Church are not illuminating, being taken over from the tradition. Favourite ones are the image of the flock ... and 'the elect'. ... How little the taking over of traditional titles means is shown by the fact that, although the Church is still called the body (of Christ) ... only the parabolic meaning in relation to joint membership and the mutual ordering of the members is relevant ... , and not the present union with Christ which it characterizes.[218]

For Schweizer, as for Campenhausen, the concepts Clement borrows from Paul do not possess their original dynamic force. Rather, they become in his hands a wooden expression of tradition. When adopted, their implications are barely comprehended; *1 Clement* reproduces the letter but not the spirit of Pauline theology.

A response to these misinterpretations of *1 Clement* must seek to avoid the opposite error committed by Sanders, who argues that Clement was a thoroughgoing Paulinist.[219] Sanders correctly points to the use of Pauline concepts in the establishment of Clement's case. But Campenhausen, Schweizer, and others[220] rightly argue that *1 Clement* represents, to a certain degree, a reinterpretation or application of Pauline themes for a new situation. Nevertheless, all these scholars overstate their case. Reinterpretation and borrowing do not necessarily imply, on the one hand, misunderstanding or, on the other, wholly faithful appropriation. The ideas which Clement borrowed from Paul operate in this later context in a more accepted, unargued, and assumed way than when the apostle developed and used them. It is more likely that this reflects distance from the founder than it does an uncomprehending aping of tradition. The response of the original community to the founder probably became domesticated over time, but Campenhausen's conclusion that 1 Clement represents "the slackening energies of the Christian proclamation" does not necessarily follow from this. As we shall see, the work and person of Jesus, however much they are presented in an assumed and unargued way, are symbols which are at the very centre of Clement's letter to the Corinthian church and, by implication, the identity of his audience. If we are to understand how the Roman epistle worked to encourage certain kinds of behaviour in the community we must determine how these symbols were related to the Corinthian church's own convictions and how they were used by Clement to secure harmony in this community.

Sectarian Existence in Christ

Clement, like Paul, often uses the expression ἐν Χριστῷ, (21:8; 22:1; 32:4; 38:1; 46:6; 48:4; 49:1; 54:3; cf. 3:4) and he is also fond of the construction διὰ Χριστοῦ or its equivalent (Inscrip.; 12:7; 36:2; 50:7; 58:2; 59:2,3; 61:3; 64:1; 65:2).[221] The preposition ἐν with the dative indicates either a locative sense, or, more rarely, an instrumental one.[222] Where is salvation to be found? In Christ. How is salvation attained? Through Christ. Similarly, διά with the genitive indicates space, time, or agency.[223] In the passages cited above which contain διά with the genitive case we have to do with examples of agency. The prepositional phrases with ἐν, however, are more problematic, as they often are in Paul.[224] Some passages should be interpreted in a locative sense (e.g., 22:1), but others are better understood in either a locative or instrumental sense (e.g., 32:4; 49:1).

Still, these syntactical difficulties should not confound our understanding of the significance of these passages as vehicles of tremendous social meaning. The symbol of Christ in 1 Clement is an example of what Mary Douglas has called a "condensed symbol," that is, a symbol which encompasses a wide range of meanings.[225] Harnack's comment on the formula ἐν Χριστῷ as an expression of a fact which is remembered and, by implication, something less important to the Corinthian community fifty years after Paul, fails to recognize the significance of these passages for the identity of the group.[226] When Clement states that the Corinthian church is "in Christ" he is not repeating "old formulas" as Harnack suggests; he is stating something about the dynamic identity of the group he is addressing. To be in Christ or to be in a certain state of existence through Christ, sociologically understood, is above all a group-defining symbol.

Clement addresses the Corinthians in the opening lines of the letter as "called and sanctified by the will of God through our Lord Jesus Christ" (Inscrip.) and this language of election through Christ is repeated throughout the letter (32:4; 50:1-7; 59:2,3; 64:1). This language implies a consciousness not only of being specially chosen, but also of being separate from the rest of the world. Especially in 59.2, where Clement uses powerful images of contrast (σκότος/φῶς; ἀγνωσία/ἐπίγνωσις), there is striking evidence of awareness of separation.[227] As a result of its consciousness of being called "through Christ" or existing "in Christ" the group is aware of separation from the rest of the world. Similarly, Clement's employment of the participle παροικοῦσα (Inscrip.), a term used in the Graeco-Roman world to describe a certain social status of non-citizenship,[228] suggests a consciousness of feeling set apart from the world; group members are resident aliens in the world, an image similar to those used by Hermas (e.g., *Sim.* 1:1).[229] This may be interpreted as sectarian language; Clement expresses this sectarian identity by the use of such sacred imagery as is found in 29:1-3, where he cites Old Testament passages to describe the group as a holy people chosen out from the nations, and in 30:1, where, expounding this image, he calls the church "a portion of one who is holy."[230]

The sectarian language of being "in Christ" describes a state of contact with the sacred through incorporation into a group closely identified with Christ. Following Paul, Clement expresses the identity of being "in Christ" by the use of the symbol of the body of Christ (37:5-38:1; 46:6-7). Although Clement does not develop this theme to the degree found in Paul's letters, it is none the less significant that, like Paul, Clement uses this symbol to express an intimate connection with the sacred through incorporation into the church. To be a member of the group is, in some sense, to identify oneself with Christ. As in Paul's letters, it is not always clear whether Clement uses this motif metaphorically to portray the community, or to describe the actual body of Christ. In 38:1 the noun σῶμα seems to be used in a more metaphorical sense to describe the group as centered around Christ. But the use of συνπνεῖ in 37:5 to describe the group as a body in which all "breathe together" should caution us not to see in this imagery an attenuated Paulinism which omits deeper or more mystical meanings found in Paul, as Knopf would interpret this passage.[231] The organic theme of the body motif is again presented in 46:7, where the vivid description of the Corinthians as "the members of Christ" (τὰ μέλη τοῦ Χριστοῦ) suggests a close identification of the community with Christ. Schweizer's judgment quoted above that the use of this motif reveals Clement's use of traditional themes, reflecting a concern for mutual ordering rather than present union with Christ, underestimates the role this symbol probably continued to play in defining the identity and self-understanding of the sect. Far from being a non-illuminating designation for the church which has been simply taken over from tradition, as Schweizer would have it, the body of Christ symbol points, as in Paul's letters, to the Christocentric identity of a group conscious of its separation from the world through common belief and union with sacred reality.

Existence in Christ further signifies redemption. The self-understanding of the group as a holy and chosen people and the body of Christ is closely related to the symbol of the atonement of Christ. The mediating work of Christ stands at the centre of Clement's Christology.[232] In the prayer in 59:3 Clement states that Christ has made him and his readers "holy" (ἁγιάζειν) and "honourable" (τιμεῖν). The blood of Christ is a symbol of salvation (7:4; 12:7-8; 21:6; 49:6). Far from being rationalistic or moralistic as Knopf suggests,[233] Clement's emphasis on the blood of Christ communicates the importance of Christ's redeeming work for this sect. Flesh by his flesh, soul by his soul — the sectarian enters a new reality by the death of Christ as he is received by the Master in love (49:6).[234]

This theme of love represents language of belonging which is vital to the sectarian identity. To be "in Christ" is to be "in love" (49:1-6; cf. 50:1-2). The "bond of the love of God," interpreted as a subjective genitive,[235] which Clement mentions in 49:2, flows from existence in Christ (v.1), uniting the believer to God (v.5) as a privileged sign of God's favour (50:2).

The believer also finds in Christ a redeemer who mediates for him special access to transcendent reality. In 36:1-3, Clement (probably drawing on themes from Hebrews)[236] states that believers in Christ possess privileged understanding of "the Master"; through Jesus, Clement states, "the eyes of our hearts were opened, through him our foolish and darkened understanding blossoms toward the light . . . through him the Master willed that we should taste the immortal knowledge" (v. 2). Jesus is presented as the group's high priest, their defender and patron (προστάτης – also 61:3). The image of patron implies that he protects the Christian's interests and pleads his case.[237] And one of Clement's favourite descriptions of the church as "the flock of Christ" implies an understanding of the group as uniquely attached to and protected by Christ, its shepherd (16:1; 54:2; 57:2; cf. 59:4). Harnack's comment that Clement's religion is that of the Old Testament or of late Judaism does not take sufficient account of the importance of the mediation of Christ for this group.[238] "Le Christ n'est pas seulement celui dans lequel s'achevé l'histoire du salut; il est le médiateur *actuel* du salut. . . . ," argues Jaubert.[239] The phrase "in Christ" signifies a privileged position of redemption which identifies the group as holy and separate from the rest of the world.

Existence in Christ and the Institutional Order

At the centre of the Corinthian church's identity, then, was the symbol of Christ. The phrase "in Christ" is a condensed symbol which indicates separation from the world, salvation, and contact with transcendent reality. Christ is the focal point of this group's symbolic universe, and it is from this centre point that Clement's legitimations of the institutional order radiate. We cannot agree with the quotation from Campenhausen cited above which states that the concept of order with which Clement mainly concerns himself is completely detached from Christ and the Gospel. In his attempts to make the institutional order subjectively meaningful to the later generations of the Corinthian community Clement in fact expends much energy to show how the order he recommends is connected with the group's existence in Christ or the benefits granted them through Christ.

The symbol of Christ represents for Clement, as for his readers, not only the central symbol of the group's symbolic universe, or world-view, it also communicates to them a characteristic ethos. Part of Clement's aim is to show how existence in Christ carries with it a moral commitment to the institutional order. In 46:5-7 the unity which Clement recommends follows directly from the group's beliefs in one God, one Christ, and one calling in Christ. This belief commits members to a harmonious co-existence rather than division. Similarly, Clement's exhortation in 33:1 to do good works and to continue in love follows from the redeemed identity of justification in Christ (32:4). This does not represent a conscious attempt on the part of Clement to reconcile the theology of James and Paul as Lightfoot suggests.[240]

Still less can this be described as a departure from Paul's "solafideism" toward "synergism" as Knopf argues.[241] Clement is writing neither as a dogmatizing synthesizer, nor with a view toward anachronistic Reformation models of justification; he is attempting to show how the commitment of the group to a particular world-view carries with it a certain ethical demand consistent with the group's beliefs. And he does this in the context of justifying the institutional order to his readers. Since the Corinthians are a portion of the holy, Clement argues in 30:1-8 (using language which indicates consciousness of special election which in other passages is connected with Christ — e.g. 64:1), they should do the deeds of sanctification. Included among these actions is to live in concord, resisting those who are proud. In a statement probably containing a barb for those who support the schismatics, he urges that the Corinthians should not praise themselves, for such arrogance and boldness belong to those cursed by God (30:7-8). As we shall see below, the terms Clement uses to describe arrogance (ὑπερήφανος / ὑπερηφανία / ἀλαζονεία / αὐθάδεια) are employed repeatedly to describe those who oppose God's appointed order.

Again, in 49:1, Clement writes that he who is in Christ should perform the commandments of Christ. The bond of God's love implies a characteristic ethos which includes, alongside Paul's catalogue of virtues in 1 Cor. 13, an avoidance of schism and sedition and the pursuit of concord (v. 5) — themes, as we shall see below, which Clement reiterates several times in the course of his epistle. The many examples of virtue taken from the Old Testament, on which Clement draws to infuse his epistle with a high moral tone, capture for him the proper ethos which is to flow from the life in Christ. Elijah, Job, Abraham, Moses, David (e.g., chapters 17-18) — these figures tower in the epistle like statues in the Hellenistic style, taking on an extra-human massiveness and becoming symbols which embody the values which Clement thinks the community which has been made alive in Christ should embrace.

Clement presents and develops these values in order to encourage a proper attitude toward what he thinks are the proper structures of leadership. "Christ is of those who are humble-minded and not of those who exalt themselves over His flock," Clement writes in 16:1; he then goes on to describe the greatest moral symbol of all — the Suffering Servant (vv. 2-15). Humble-mindedness was a virtue Christ possessed and the fact that he practised it has a direct implication for the Corinthian community, which defines itself as existing in Christ. "If the Lord was thus humble-minded, what shall we do, who through him have come under the yoke of his grace?" Clement asks in v.17. Again, the theme of humble-mindedness is one which Clement associates with support for the divinely established order (2:1; 56:1; cf. 57:1-2; 58:2). These select examples demonstrate Clement's attempt to join attitudes towards local leadership structures with the group's beliefs and self-understanding, organized around the symbol of Christ. By drawing out ethical themes connected with the group's world-view he was attempting to justify a certain posture toward the institutional structures of the group.

God as Master and the Institutional Order

Clement places arguments such as the ones described above in the framework of another symbol which dominates his epistle. Alongside the condensed symbol of Christ, he places the symbol of God the Master (δεσπότης) of the universe. These two symbols are not distinct in this writing. One of the chief benefits which the individual in Christ enjoys is knowledge. We have already noted passages in which Clement describes the knowledge members possess by being incorporated into Christ (36:2; 40:1; 59:2). Included in this knowledge is the revelation of God, the sovereign ruler of the universe. When Clement urges in 40:1 that the Corinthians should do all things in the order which the Master commanded since they have looked "into the depths of the divine knowledge" (εἰς τὰ βάθη τῆς θείας γνώσεως), he is probably referring generally to the entire preceding discussion.[242] But, more particularly, this passage also echoes what Clement already has stated in 36:2. If the community has any insight into God's nature this is because of enlightenment through Christ. Again, 59:2 speaks of the revelation that Christ has brought as one which makes known the glory of the Creator's name.

With this knowledge comes a recognition of the ordering power of God "the Master" in the cosmos. In 59:3 Clement states that God is the source of all creation and that it is Christ who has opened the believers' eyes to recognize God the Creator's majesty. Clement's invocation of God as Master (δεσπότης) characterizes God as an all-controlling being. Used some twenty-four times in the course of the epistle,[243] alongside the symbol of Christ, God the Master is central to the world-view Clement presents. It is from the concept of God as δεσπότης that Clement's themes of order, harmony, and humble-mindedness follow, as well as his descriptions of the Corinthian upstarts as arrogant, proud, and seditious. This symbol is used to justify the institutional order by portraying the structures of leadership in the Corinthian community as an instance of the Master's ordering power.

In the previous section we stated that Clement's argument in chapters 42 and 44 contains legitimating applications of the idea that all structures in the universe are ordered by God. The theme of the order of the cosmos has been investigated by several scholars who have debated whether Clement's description of order in chapter 20 is Stoic.[244] But the way in which this passage and others like it (33:2-3; 61:1-2) relate to Clement's overall purpose has been inadequately assessed. Clement wants to show that central to the knowledge of the divine will revealed through Christ is that all things should be done according to the will of God. The portrayal of God as a δεσπότης is intended to communicate the all-powerful nature of God as an ordainer of order and harmony.

The institutional order of the Corinthian community is placed by Clement in a symbolic universe of a divinely appointed order. Jaeger shows how Clement weaves together rhetorical, philosophical, and Christian themes to present God as a sovereign master of order and harmony. But this weaving together does not represent, as Jaeger argues, the transposition of Christianity into a philosophical key which is then transmitted as "a new concept of Christian paideia."[245] The fact that Clement borrowed themes from his environment does not necessarily imply that he had a definite idea that Christian culture was analogous to Greek, nor that he was consciously attempting to transform his religion into hellenistic ideals.[246] It is more likely that Clement found in contemporary philosophical and rhetorical expressions a meaningful way to draw out the implications of the beliefs of the community which he wanted to emphasize in order to legitimate the authority of its deposed leaders.

Jaeger points out that Greek paideia, by deriving the norms of social behaviour from the divine norms of the universe, connected cosmology and social ethics with each other.[247] Similarly, when Clement explicated the community's beliefs about God the Master of the universe, he was very probably attempting to show how the group's world-view carried with it a certain ethos. In 19:2 Clement exhorts the Corinthians to meditate upon the Creator and his gracious character. This is seen in the order he has established in the universe (20:1f.). The ideals of "harmony" (ὁμόνοια) and "peace" (εἰρήνη), themes drawn from the wider philosophical milieu, which the Roman presents to the Corinthians are illustrated for them by the order of the cosmos (20:1,3,9,10). This cosmic order is an example for Clement's readers to be in peace and harmony, especially since they have received mercy from the Father and Creator of the cosmos through Christ (v. 11). It is this same structuring God who has established the order of the Corinthian church.

Subjection, Harmony, and Humility – The Community Ethos and the Institutional Order

The prayer for the governing authorities which Clement presents in 60:4-61:2 may be interpreted as a cleverly devised expression of the theme which he has developed throughout the preceding epistle: all authority is from God and since it is divinely established members should be subject (ὑποτάσσεσθαι) to those to whom it is given (61:1). This is not, as Eggenberger argues,[248] an apologetic message for the governing authorities, assuring them that the Christians pray for them. It is better understood as a reiteration of the theme of the sovereign ordering power of God. The message is probably more for those whom Clement regards as questioning divinely appointed authorities than it is an appeal for imperial benevolence.

Subjection to Leaders and Subjection to God

The theme of subjection is developed in a more pointed way earlier in the epistle where Clement, weaving together Paul's body motif in 1 Cor. 12:12-31 with other non-biblical Greek themes,[249] exhorts the Corinthians to obey God, who has established different ranks in the Corinthian church, in the same way as an army obeys its leader (37:1-3). It is God who distributes each spiritual gift (χάρισμα – 38:1) and this implies a certain order in which members subject (ὑποτάσσεσθαι) themselves to one another according to their particular gifts. As we noted earlier in this chapter, in the process of borrowing Paul's motif of the body in 1 Cor. 12 Clement emphasizes God's sovereign dispensation of various gifts to support his argument that there is a certain order to be preserved in the community.

The presentation of themes such as this in the course of the epistle means that Clement's exhortations concerning the order of the Corinthian community in chapters 40-44 are placed within the context of beliefs concerning the more general cosmic order. In 42:2-4 Clement emphasizes that the structures of leadership in the Corinthian church originated with the ordering power of God. And when he cites in v. 5 the prophecy that God would do this, he is further highlighting the belief that behind the institutional order in Corinth, as behind all order, there is an all-powerful and all-knowing God who has established it.

Clement's theory that the apostles established the church's leadership structures belongs to a larger symbolic universe which envelopes and penetrates the institutional order with subjectively meaningful beliefs. By concentrating on themes which are developed from the group's beliefs in a Creator God, Clement puts forward an ethos which is both consistent with the Corinthian's worldview and demands an end to the schism in the community. The belief, for example, in myriad heavenly angels subject (ὑποτάσσεσθαι) to God's will implies (cf. οὖν, v. 7) that the Corinthians are also to exist in concord (34:5-7). Concord is a favourite theme which Clement employs to describe the characteristic ethos that flows from obedient submission to the Master God. Clement repeatedly uses the term ὁμόνοια to express the ideal of obedience to God (21:1; 34:7, cf. v. 5; 49:5, cf. v. 1; 50:5; 63:2; cf. 60:4) and the orderly community life which flows forth from it (30:3). The ὁμόνοια which Clement describes in chapter 20 is presented as an instance of God's graciousness (19:3), given especially to the redeemed Corinthian community (19:2; 20:11).[250] In other passages, following the Greek classical tradition before him, Clement also uses the term to describe a state of ideal citizenship worthy of God (21:1; cf. 54:4). In a similar way in 2:8, although not using the term ὁμόνοια, Clement associates good citizenship under God's rule with obedience to his commandments and ordinances (τὰ προστάγματα καὶ τὰ δικαιώματα – cf. 3:4) – a virtue evinced according to the context of these passages by harmonious community life.

A second theme which in one passage is associated with ὁμόνοια (30:3) is humility or humble-mindedness. The root ταπεινο- occurs twenty-eight times in the epistle as a favourite expression used to describe varying states of humility. Among the occurrences of this root, the most significant are passages in which the verb ταπεινοφρονεῖν (2:1; 13:1,3; 16:1,17; 30:3; 48:6; 62:2; cf. 38:2) and the noun ταπεινοφροσύνη (21:8; 30:8; 44:3; 56:1; 58:2) and related forms appear: in these passages the term describes a state of humble submission to the will of God or a virtue of meekness which contributes to the common good of community life. Concord and humble-mindedness flow directly from submission to the will of God. The themes of concord and humility arise ultimately from belief in a Master God who has established all cosmic and social order.

Strife, Sedition, and Arrogance: The Ethos of the Disobedient

If all order comes from God, then the community's institutional structures are also divinely established and not to subject oneself to them is therefore a transgression of what is willed by God. Clement not only presents the virtues which are consonant with belief in an ordering God, he also puts forward the vices which follow from disobedience to his will. His characterization of the Corinthian dispute as strife or sedition (στάσις – 1:1; 2:6; 3:2; 14:2; 46:9; 51:1; 54:2; 57:1; 63:1) is another instance of his use of rhetorical themes borrowed from the Hellenistic tradition.[251] This theme follows well from Clement's presentation of Christianity as a politeia (2:8; 54:4).

But Clement's development of these concepts is not merely an exercise in rhetoric. The portrayal of the schismatics as seditious fits in with the belief that all order is established by God. Sedition, according to Clement, is disobedience to God (3:2-4; 14:1-2; 51:1-3; 57:1-2; 63:1-2; cf. 2.6). Further, Clement's exhortations to be obedient to God (9:1; 14:1; 58:1; 59:1; 63:1) are not evidence, as Harnack argues, that Clement's letter represents "enthüllte alttestamentliche Religion," i.e, a "Gesetzreligion."[252] This interpretation of the references to obedience and disobedience in 1 Clement obscures Clement's social concern in his attempt to portray an ethos which follows from the group's symbolic universe. Harnack overlooks the role these ideas are made to play in the justification of the community's institutional structures and instead treats the Roman epistle as though it were a treatise devoted to topics of salvation. Of course, Clement does possess a certain soteriology, but his interest in putting it forth is connected with the Corinthian situation; it is not simply an exercise in dogmatics. When he writes in 44:4 that those who have ejected the presbyters from the place established for them (v. 5) are guilty of no small sin, behind this contention stands a belief in a sacred, inviolable, and divinely-willed order. He connects dis-obedience and obedience to God with respect for properly established structures of leadership, thus giving them a holy status.

Arrogance is a theme which Clement associates with strife and sedition. His portrayal of arrogance as an undesirable quality (30:1; 35:5; 49:5; 57:2; cf. 30:8), a pointed judgment of the leaders of the Corinthian rebellion, stands in opposition to his ideals of humility and meekness. In 35:5, pride and arrogance, vainglory (κενοδοξία), and inhospitality are associated with a character opposed to God's will. Just as those who follow God's will demonstrate certain ethical ideals, so the consequences of disobedience is a corresponding negative ethos (see the catalogue of vices in 30:1; also, 35:5-11; 57:2-7).

The Institutional Order as the Will of God and the Call to Repentance

Strife, sedition, arrogance – these are themes connected in Clement's mind with rejection of God's will. Since it is God who has established the institutional order of the Corinthian church, the upstart Corinthians have opposed His purposes by upsetting it. Clement places the Corinthian church's leadership structures in an inviolable sacred order which demands respect. To oppose those institutions which have been divinely established is not only to engage, according to Clement, in division, it is to call the group's symbolic universe or worldview into question. The theme of the will of God appears repeatedly in 1 Clement (Inscrip.; 20:4; 21:4; 32:4; 34:5; 36:6; 40:3; 42:2; 49:6; 56:1,2; 61:1) and by means of it Clement places the Corinthian dispute in a sacred context. In 40:3, Clement argues that God has established "by his supreme will" the order of leadership in the Corinthian church. The Corinthian church's organization is presented as part of a universal order that originates with God's will. Clement states that the proper cosmic (20:4; cf. 33:3) and the more general social order (61.1) are divinely established. He further connects the themes of both concord (20:3-4; 21:1,4; 34:5,7) and humble-mindedness (56:1-2) to union with the will of God. When he states in 56:1 that "those who have fallen into any transgression," i.e., the ringleaders of the so-called revolt (see chapters 54-55), are to submit themselves to the will of God, he has already established in 40:3 that God's will includes submission to the leaders these individuals have rejected. It is implicit in this way of treating the Corinthian dispute that the opposition to the established leaders in the community is presented not only as violation of a sacred order established by God, but also as opposition to God's will.

Clement's call to repentance, then, is an exhortation to live in accordance with reality — to act in ways consistent with the general beliefs of the group. Clement's urging that the sedition come to an end is also a call for repentance (57:1). The catalogue of the great characters of the Old Testament who preached repentance (7:5-7), together with the recollection of the forgiveness of God (7:3-4; 8:1-5), help to enhance the themes of the rejection of the authority of the deposed presbyters as a violation of a sacred order.

Summary

We have attempted in this section to show that Clement's epistle may be described sociologically as an attempt to legitimate a certain pattern of institutionalized leadership in the Corinthian church. Clement places the institutional structures of leadership in Corinth, together with what may have been widely held beliefs concerning their origin, in the context of the Corinthians' wider religious beliefs and thereby attempts to show how the group is committed to the support of these structures. The central ethical themes in this epistle of concord and sedition, humble-mindedness and arrogance, and obedience and disobedience are developed within the context of the group's world-view in order to show how a certain ethos follows from the group's beliefs. Clement makes support for institutionalized structures of leadership in Corinth part of the group's ethos and attempts to show how respect for those patterns is implied in their beliefs — their identity in Christ and their faith in a sovereign God. In this way he presents the institutions of leadership in Corinth as normative and subjectively plausible to his readers.

Notes

1 His epistle is dated by most scholars around A.D. 96, and we shall assume this date in the following discussion. Robinson, 1976, pp. 327-34, dates it *c.* A.D. 70. Here he follows Edmundson, 1913. (For criticism see Sturdy, 1979, pp. 255ff.) On the other side are scholars like Merrill, 1924, pp. 217ff., and Eggenberger, 1951, who date it *c.* A.D. 150. An earlier date seems to be excluded by the distinction Clement makes between the persecution at the time of the apostles (5:1-6:2) and the present struggle described in 7:1. The period of time described in 44:1-3 is most naturally interpreted as stretching over thirty to forty years.

2 Some earlier attempts are discussed in Knopf, 1899, pp. 156 ff.

3 For the use of rhetorical and classical devices in *1 Clement* see Sanders, 1943; Jaeger, 1961, pp. 12ff.; Bardy, 1922, pp. 73ff.

4 Harnack, 1929, pp. 52ff.; Van Unnik, 1950, pp. 181ff.; Jaubert, 1971, pp 35ff.

5 Ibid., p. 39; Grant and Graham, 1965, pp. 10ff., passim.

6 Wrede, 1891, pp. 54 f.

7 Ibid., p. 2.

8 Knopf, pp. 174 f.

9 Grant, op. cit., p. 79 follows Lightfoot, 1890, p. 145 and Knopf, 1920, p. 124 in arguing that the danger referred to is damnation, but the context of v. 7 suggests more than a spiritual danger. This interpretation is supported by the emphasis on στάσις and ἀπόνοια in the writing. Mikat, 1969, pp. 23ff., argues on the basis of these terms that Clement is afraid that the communities in Corinth and Rome will be charged with *seditio, turba,* or *tumultus* — charges brought against other feuding organizations of the period.

10 Knopf, 1899, p. 187.

11 Ziegler, 1958, pp. 125f. Ziegler argues that the middle voice may be interpreted as a dynamic middle in which case the verb has a meaning which implies personal interest in the matter (see also Blass and Debrunner, 1961, p. 166).

12 Ziegler, p. 127. But his argument (p. 129) that 39:1 refers to derision of Clement because of an earlier letter is unconvincing; this passage was probably intended in a more general sense than this.

13 Bauer, 1971, pp. 95-96.

14 Ibid., p. 99.

15 Ibid., pp. 101-2.

16 See Kümmel, 1975, p. 274 for further discussion and literature.

17 Bauer, p. 102.

18 For the political relationship between Rome and Corinth in the early empire see van Cauwelaert, 1935, pp. 267-306.

19 Meinhold, 1939, pp. 100f.; similarly, Campenhausen, 1969, pp. 86f.; Gerke, 1931, pp. 34f. Beyschlag, 1966, p. 348, argues that the dispute arose from a continuation of the conflict described in 1 Cor. 1:10f. between those associated with Paul and those allied with Peter.

20 Meinhold, p. 100.

21 Telfer, 1962, pp. 57ff.

22 See Mikat, p. 32; Sanders, 1943, pp. 42-47; Knopf, 1929, pp. 131-32 for examples.

23 For discussion of this phenomenon in early Christianity see Theissen, 1978, pp. 8ff.

24 Lietzmann, 1961, Vol. 1, pp. 192f.

25 Ibid., p. 192.

26 Lietzmann does not sufficiently take into account that officials of both *collegia* and synagogues were often re-elected and sometimes held appointments for life.

27 I.e., πιστός – πίστις; γνῶσις – λόγος γνώσεως; σοφὸς ἐν διακρίσει λόγων – λόγος σοφίας.

28 For further discussion see*f. The New Testament in the Apostolic Fathers*, p. 42.

29 Chadwick, 1961, p. 285.

30 Ziegler, pp. 1ff.

31 Cullmann, 1930, pp. 294ff., comes to similar conclusions but he presents an unconvincing line of argument when he draws them on the basis of the examples in chapters 4-6.

32 Op. cit., p. 2.

33 There are textual difficulties connected with this reading. The earliest reading (*Alexandrinus* – φιλοξενία) seems unlikely given the context. The reading of the Latin version, inhumilitatem (trans. φιλοδοξίαν – Knopf, 1899, p. 123) preserves

the parallelism in the passage, but if the reading in *Alexandrinus* represents a simple emendation (thus, Lightfoot, Part 1 Vol. 1, p. 109), the weight of the manuscript evidence favours the reading ἀφιλοξενία.

34 *The New Testament in the Apostolic Fathers*, 1905, pp. 37-38.

35 Op. cit., p. 284.

36 Similarly Lipsius, writing over a century ago, suggested this as a setting for the dispute, but he made too strong a case by reading too much into certain passages.

37 P. 63. n. 28.

38 For further discussion, contra Dix, 1946, pp. 253ff., see Jay, 1981, pp. 99, 133f.

39 Countryman, 1980, pp. 154f. and notes, arrives at similar conclusions, but *1 Clem.* 3:1-3, part of the basis for his argument, cannot be used to support his case. There Clement quotes Deuteronomy 32:15 ("My beloved ate and drank, and he was enlarged and waxed fat and kicked"). Countryman concludes that the difficulties in Corinth arose as a result of well-to-do householders asserting their rights of recognition over against local officials. He is correct to draw parallels between the situation which we are arguing is assumed in *1 Clement* and the *Shepherd* and to point to the earlier Corinthian church for evidence of leadership by the relatively prosperous. But he overstates his argument by referring to *1 Clem.* 3:1-3 for support. It is impossible to determine whether Clement's use of this Old Testament passage was intended as a reference to economically motivated unrest, and Countryman too quickly discounts the possibility of its use to describe spiritual prosperity and growth. In chapters 1-2 it is precisely such a state of spiritual well-being which is described. Countryman's argument that Clement "would hardly have considered an increase in spiritual well-being to be the prelude to spiritual disaster" ignores the possibility that Clement may have been linking confidence arising from spiritual blessing with self-reliance, arrogance, and competition.

40 Grant, op. cit., p. 70.

41 Clarke, 1937, pp. 25-26. He argues further that the emphasis on the appointment of places by the Lord for worship shows that the Corinthians needed one place of assembly governed by one bishop to ensure unity. There is a case for this especially in the light of Rom. 16:23 where Gaius is described as host of the whole church, but it is not necessarily the case that a single community eucharist continued, especially as the community grew in size. There is no evidence that there was one bishop at the head of the Corinthian church when Clement wrote his epistle. In our view, the references to a plurality of presbyter-bishops imply a plurality of house churches celebrating their own eucharists. See also Brown and Meier, 1983, pp.173f. for a discussion of house churches in Corinth and Rome in this period.

42 Harnack, 1929, p. 92; thus, also, Lightfoot, Part 1 Vol. 1, 1890, p. 82. Lightfoot suggests that a dispute arose over the resurrection, but the point of the references to the resurrection in chapters 23-27 occurs in 27:1 where the certainty of the resurrection is connected with God's coming judgment. Clement's purpose, then, is to admonish the schismatics to repent rather than to persuade them that there will be a resurrection. The quotation from an unknown source which describes those who doubt that the prophesied events will occur may be interpreted as a purely rhetorical caricature of the rebels as doubters in God's promises.

43 For a discussion of treatments of *1 Clement* since Sohm, too numerous to include here, which place the Roman epistle in a schema of theological development, see Fuellenbach, 1980.

44 Sohm, 1892, pp. 157ff.; for a shortened version of the argument see Sohm, 1895, pp. 31-43.

45 Sohm, 1892, p. 164.

46 For further references see introduction above.

47 Harnack's conception of the development of the early church's organization is summarized succinctly in *History of Dogma*, Vol. 1, pp. 209-20.

48 Harnack, 1929, p. 88.

49 Ibid., pp. 89-90.

50 Gerke, 1931, p. 59.

51 Ibid., p. 61.

52 Bultmann, 1951, Vol. 2, pp. 95ff. Bultmann sides with Harnack against Sohm because, he argues, Sohm is not justified in his opposition of the development of church order and office with the work of the Spirit. (p. 99) But he agrees with Sohm's famous dictum that *"legal regulation contradicts the Church's nature"* (p. 97 — his emphasis).

53 Ibid., p. 107.

54 Ibid., p. 111; Bultmann's emphasis.

55 Ibid., p. 116; Bultmann's emphasis.

56 Ibid., pp. 111-18.

57 Käsemann, 1969, pp. 237, 236ff.

58 Idem., 1964, p. 91.

59 Idem., 1969, p. 247.

60 Idem., 1964, p. 87.

61 Ibid., pp. 86-87.

62 Campenhausen, 1969, pp. 55ff.

63 Ibid., pp. 76ff.

64 Ibid., pp. 107ff.

65 Ibid., p. 86.

66 Ibid., p. 92.

67 Fuellenbach, p. 28.

68 Kee, 1980, pp. 14-15, notes the influence of liberal idealism on Harnack's understanding of the development of early Christianity. See especially Harnack, 1904, pp. 90-127.

69 Brockhaus, 1975, p. 89, states that the idea of a charismatic church order or charismatic period of origin in Pauline communities is so commonly accepted among German-speaking scholars that one may speak of a consensus in this respect.

70 The relevant literature is cited by Holmberg, 1980b, pp. 192f. The formulation of the ministry in Pauline communities on the basis of Paul's epistles to the Corinthians is methodologically unsound because it appears that the problems described in these letters arising from some form of enthusiasm were endemic to Corinth. We know about the organization in this community because Paul had to intervene there. There is no evidence from Paul's other letters that ecstatic spiritual manifestations threatened to divide the church and the Corinthian community may therefore have been atypical of Pauline churches. As Holmberg notes, "The very fact that the apostle a whole five years after the founding of this church has to intervene so emphatically against such a number of bad practices and deficiencies in the church's maturity makes it precarious to consider the church order in Corinth as a model one" (ibid., p. 192). Paul's theology of charisma is formulated not as the basis of a church order, as Sohm, Käsemann, and von Campenhausen argue, but as a theologically grounded "interpretive category" (ibid., p. 194) to be applied against the claims of enthusiastic or, to use Paul's language (cf. e.g. 1 Cor. 2:15; 3:1; 12:1; 14:37), "pneumatic" Christians in order to correct a development in the Corinthian community. It functions as "a theological-paraenetical creation, a uto-

pian model for Christian life in any congregation" (Holmberg, 1980a, p. 121), particularly in Corinth where a special and atypical structure of interaction is in need of correction.

71 Käsemann and von Campenhausen draw too firm conclusions from relatively scanty evidence for a Jewish presbyteral system; their distinction between a Pauline and a supposed Jewish-Christian organization is therefore unconvincing. As we saw above (p. 4, n. 21) it is not clear that πρεσβύτερος was a common designation for officials in Judaism of the early Christian era. We shall present an alternative account for the existence of presbyters below.

72 Bultmann, op. cit., pp. 111-12.

73 Schweizer, 1961, p. 7m.

74 Ibid., preface, p. 7 and p. 1a; my emphasis.

75 Holmberg, 1980a, pp. 201-3.

76 Ibid., pp. 201-2.

77 Ibid., p. 202.

78 See Gill, 1977, pp. 24, 129f. for this phrase.

79 The phrase is taken from Scroggs, 1980, pp. 165-6.

80 Thus, e.g., Troeltsch, 1931, Vol. 1, pp. 62ff., 331ff.; Niebuhr, 1972, pp. 19-20; Yinger, 1961, pp.16ff.; Clark, 1947, pp. 16f.; Stark, 1967, Vol. 2, pp. 301f.; Wilson, 1959; 1961, pp. 2-3; 1967, pp. 22ff.; 1970, pp. 233f.; 1973, pp. 35f.; 1982, pp. 96f.; 1984, pp. 371f.

81 Idem., 1984, p. 371.

82 Idem., 1982, p. 106.

83 Idem., 1967, pp. 33-35.

84 Stark, op. cit., pp. 306-7.

85 The sect-denomination dichotomy, while making some important distinctions for the analysis of contemporary sects, is roughly parallel to Troeltsch's sect-church typology (see Troeltsch, op. cit., pp. 331f.). Niebuhr, op. cit., argued that all sects become denominations, but Wilson has shown that this is true in only certain instances (e.g., 1967, pp. 22f). For a full presentation of the type see Wilson, 1959, pp. 4-5.

86 Wilson, 1967, pp. 33-34; Yinger, 1961, p. 22; also, Stark, op. cit., pp. 306-7.

87 Op. cit., pp. 89ff.

88 Yinger, op. cit., p. 38; cf. Troeltsch, op. cit., pp. 335-36. Yinger's church type is borrowed from Troeltsch and is similar to Wilson's denomination type.

89 This is particularly true of German scholarship. Recent French scholarship, however, has attempted to outline social factors which contributed to the rise of institutionalized authority (thus, e.g., Grelot, 1974, p. 45; Pesch, 1971, pp. 446f.; Budillon, 1971, p. 486).

90 Weingarten, 1881, pp. 444f.

91 Filson, 1939, p. 112; Brown and Meier, 1983, pp. 174-75; also, with reservations, Hainz, 1972, pp. 202f.

92 Op. cit., p. 111.

93 See pp. 36f. above.

94 Holmberg, 1980a, p. 116; Pesch, op. cit., p. 446; Martin, 1972, pp. 29f.; Schürmann, 1968, p. 331, f.n. 120; Goppelt, 1970, p. 92.

95 Wilson, 1927, pp. 21ff.; cf. *Vis.* 3:8.9-11.

96 See above, pp. 54ff.

97 See p. 37 above.

98 Meeks, 1983, p. 76.

99 Bauer, 1971, p. 102.

100 Ibid., 1971, p. 96.
101 Ibid., p. 97.
102 Ibid., p. 102.
103 Ibid., p. 101.
104 Campenhausen, 1969, p. 91, agrees that Clement was not creating theories unknown either to the Corinthian or the Roman church.
105 It may be inferred from the letter of Dionysius of Corinth (fl. ca. A.D. 170) to Rome that Clement's letter accurately identified the ideals of a section of the community, for Dionysius' description of the letter seems to imply that it was an authoritative writing in the Corinthian church (Eus. *H.E.* 4:23.11). Bauer cites this as evidence of a Roman victory in Corinth, but he leaves unexplained how it came to be that a majority of gnostics were won over into the "catholic" camp. A better explanation of this evidence is that Clement's letter accurately represented the interests and beliefs of the majority of the Corinthians and so quickly gained prominence as an authoritative writing in the Corinthian community.
106 True, there is a tension between this passage (assuming that the reference to being found honourable "in the flock of Christ" in 57:2 refers to the Corinthian community) and his advice in Chapters 54-55, where he exhorts those who have caused the unrest to practise self-exile from the Corinthian church. But in our view the intention of this exhortation is rhetorical rather than prescriptive and, when read in the context of what follows, has the effect of an *a fortiori* argument: Clement's desire is that the trouble-makers repent, his advice that they leave helps to underscore that primary objective; i.e. repent and go, but if you must stay, it behoves you all the more to repent. The inclusion of a theme of self-exile is best explained by Clement's desire to utilize examples (cf. 55:1-6; again, a common rhetorical ploy) to underscore and illustrate his more general ends.
107 This seems to be assumed in Schweizer's (1961, p. 16a) argument that the dispute in Corinth was between an older pneumatic and more recent institutional form of Christianity. Similarities between descriptions of leadership structures in the *Shepherd* and *1 Clement* permit us to assume that Clement's descriptions of leadership accurately reflect prevailing patterns in Rome.
108 It may be adduced from the movement of Prisca and Aquila from Rome to Corinth and back again (Rom. 16:3; Acts 18:2) that there were close links between these two churches forty to fifty years before Clement's letter.
109 The use of 1 Cor. in Clement's exhortations to Corinth indicates that Paul is an authority for both communities. Parallels between *1 Clement* and 1 Cor. and other Pauline letters are listed in *The New Testament in the Apostolic Fathers*, pp. 37f.
110 For further discussion of these passages and a possible pre-history of correspondence, see above, pp. 79ff.
111 We thus agree with those scholars who argue that the organization of Rome and Corinth was the same: Lightfoot, 1890, Vol. 1, Part 1, pp. 82-83; Clarke, 1937, p. 24; Streeter, 1929, p. 213; Harnack, 1929, p. 88; Jaubert, 1971, pp. 75f.
112 See above, pp. 79ff..
113 Campenhausen, 1969, pp. 84-85. Cf. *Didascalia* 57:1-58:6 which presents seating arrangements in a house church for laity, perhaps composed before A.D. 200 (Gamber, 1967, pp. 343-44). Ignatius *Mag.* 13:1 may describe a similar arrangement and Rev. 4:4 may also reflect liturgical organization. Streeter, 1929, p. 219 argues that *Man.* 11:1, which describes men seated on a bench, refers to the board of Elders. But vv. 13-14 is suggestive of a different setting. Dix, 1978, p. 33, argues that the reference to "places" *1 Clem.* 40:3 and 41:2 indicates "the semi-circle of seats around the throne" of the bishop, but it seems unlikely from the context of

the passage that Clement is here referring to seating arrangements.

114 Gerke, 1931, p. 133.

115 See *Didache* 14 where there is mention of a liturgical function and which in 15:1 is, according to the context of the passage, carried out by bishops and deacons. The phrase προσενεγκόντας τὰ δῶρα in 44:4 has loose parallels in other passages which indicate a cultic function (40:2; 41:2) and Hippolytus uses the same phrase to describe a eucharist (*Apostolic Tradition* 3:4 ed. Dix). Dix, 1978, p. 102 finds MS support for a cultic reference at 41:1 where *Codex Alexandrinus* reads εὐχαριστείτω instead of εὐαρεστείτω (cf. Lightfoot, 1890, Part 1, Vol. 2, p. 124, n. 4), but even if one adopts this reading, it is not clear that the verb εὐξαριστεῖν is employed here in a liturgical sense.

116 For further discussion of the use of these terms in other contexts in Clement's letter, see Gerke, 1931, pp. 117-22; Strathmann, 1967, pp. 228-29.

117 Dix, 1978, p. 1.

118 Turner, in Swete, 1921, p. 87.

119 Wilson, 1967, p. 33.

120 The term διάκονοι may be a general description of "ministers" and this translation has some support from Justin who comments that the president of the eucharist supervises the distribution of funds (*Apol.* 1:67) without mention of deacons, but in Hippolytus *Apos. Trad.* 9:3 and 30 (ed. Dix) deacons have the role of carrying out the bishop's commands and informing him of the needs of the community. These references together with Justin's description of the deacons' role of distribution of the eucharistic elements in *Apol.* 1:65 make it reasonable to suggest that deacons had certain sacral and administrative functions from an early date.

121 A classic treatment is found in Campenhausen, 1969, pp. 76ff., esp. p. 107 (German edition pp. 82f.); British scholars as early as Lightfoot, 1888, have suggested a similar source for the early Christian presbyterate, some arguing that it was a later addition, others arguing that a presbyteral system borrowed from the synagogue was present from the start; see Introduction above.

122 Scholars who follow this interpretation are Grant and Graham, 1965, pp. 18, 46; Gerke, 1931, pp. 33-34; cf. also Weingarten, 1881, p. 450; Campenhausen, 1969, p. 84 agrees that presbyters were elder members.

123 For πρεσβύτερος as a senior Christian in 1 Peter see Elliott, 1981, pp. 190f.; for a similar interpretation of the relevant passages in the Pastorals see MacDonald, 1986, pp. 300f.

124 Campenhausen, 1969, pp. 84-85f.; Schweizer, 1961, p. 16c; Käsemann, 1969, pp. 246-47; Bultmann, 1951, Vol. 2, pp. 101f.

125 Campenhausen, 1969, p. 84, writes of the appearance of the titles of bishops and presbyters in the *Shepherd* and *1 Clement*, "The fusion [Verschmelzung] of the two titles, of which we have so far seen strong hints, is in Rome already an accomplished fact; and the presbyteral constitution has completely intermingled with elements of an episcopal system, which in Rome probably preceded it." He does not, however, provide an explanation of how it came to be that communities incorporated such structures, or how this "fusion" arose in apparently similar ways in communities across the Roman Empire (for example, in the communities represented by the Pastorals). This is a criticism which may be levelled more generally at those scholars who argue that writings such as *1 Clement* represent a welding of a Jewish-Christian and Pauline form of church government.

126 Thus also Campenhausen, 1969, p. 84, but with conclusions which are unconvincing.

127 Harnack, 1929, pp. 89-90.

128 For further discussion see chapter 4 above.

129 Jaubert, 1971, p. 81; Clarke, 1937, p. 26; Gerke, 1931, p. 74.

130 Grant and Graham, 1965, pp. 69-70.

131 Yinger, 1961, p. 22.

132 *1 Clem.* 1-2 and 21:6-9, especially the household rules in these passages, present
     ideals which emphasize devotion to the moral ideals of the sect and obedience to
     its leaders — rules indicative of the social control the sect exercises on the personal
     life of each member. The consciousness of being an elite group is evident espe-
     cially from Clement's language of election (30:1; 36:1-4; 59:2,4; 64:1).

133 Wilson, 1984, p. 371.

134 Wengst, 1987, p. 107, notes that for Clement "obedience to God and obedience to
     rulers correspond. That means . . . that the latter is the specific form of the former
     in the political sphere." Again, he notes that Clement's prayer "closely reflects the
     structures of Pax Romana as subjection to Roman authority." But he overstates the
     point when he states that Clement's perception of and solution to the Corinthian
     conflict "are determined completely by his political attitude" (p. 113). As we will
     see, just the opposite is the case.

135 Ogletree, 1984, p. 166.

136 Campenhausen, 1969, p. 92; cf. similarly Schweizer, 1961, p. 16a, who states that 1
     Clement is evidence of a "more far-reaching dispute in which the defenders of an
     older and freer order opposed the consolidation of the institutional Church."

137 Brunner, 1972, p. 158.

138 Campenhausen, 1969, p. 58.

139 Ibid., pp. 64-65.

140 Ibid., p. 69.

141 Ibid., p. 84.

142 Ibid., p. 85.

143 Ibid., pp. 79-80.

144 This is evident from the broader context of the passage cited in the previous note.
     On p. 76 Campenhausen writes, "With the system of elders we move into the
     sphere of *a fundamentally different way of thinking about the Church*, which can only
     with difficulty be combined with the Pauline picture of the congregation, and cer-
     tainly cannot be derived from it" (my emphasis). Where elders are mentioned,
     Campenhausen writes on p. 78, "we may attempt to grasp *the distinctive character of
     the concept of authority* in the setting of the new 'patriarchal' overall vision of the
     Church" (my emphasis).

145 For example, the evidence of house-church leadership and Paul's concerns that
     members of the local community submit themselves to certain local leaders (e.g. 1
     Cor. 16.15-16; 1 Thes. 5.12-13) who have important roles of governance while he
     is absent. For the misuse of 1 Cor. 12-14 and Rom. 12 as a "church order" see n.
     70 above. Brockhaus, 1975, p. 24 n. 106, identifies five characteristics of "office"
     which helps us to determine to what degree we may speak of officials in the period
     of the apostle Paul. These are: 1) permanency; 2) recognition by the church; 3) a
     position of being set apart from the rest of the church; 4) a regular commission
     such as by the laying on of hands; 5) a legal element. Holmberg, 1980a, p. 110
     argues convincingly that there is evidence of characteristics 1-3 in Paul's letters;
     characteristic 4 may be adduced from Acts 13:1-3; only characteristic 5 seems to be
     lacking in Paul's lifetime. Campenhausen's use of the term "office" seems to
     assume that only where characteristic number 5 is present can one legitimately
     speak of "office." But this is an unduly rigid conception of office and Brockhaus'
     analysis helps to bring out subtleties which Campenhausen ignores. The legal cat-

egory is an important one for a proper interpretation of *1 Clement*; Campenhausen, 1969, p. 86 argues that Sohm was correct to see *1 Clement* as "the beginning of canon law in the Church." We shall argue that it is better to interpret *1 Clement* as evidence of legitimation of institutions which arose when Paul was alive.

146 See also Eisenstadt, 1965a, pp. 32f.; 1968, p. 414, who prefers to speak of "the process of institutionalization" rather than of institutions as static phenomena.

147 Berger and Luckmann, 1971, p. 83.

148 Ibid., p. 114.

149 Ibid., p. 72.

150 Ibid., p. 221, n. 21.

151 Ibid., pp. 70-71.

152 Ibid., pp. 44f.

153 Ibid., p. 45.

154 Ibid., p. 90.

155 Ibid., p. 91.

156 Eisenstadt, 1965, pp. 31f. argues that roles are not static phenomena, but are subject in their expression to the interpretation of the occupant.

157 Berger and Luckmann, 1971, p. 72.

158 Ibid., p. 91.

159 Eisenstadt, 1965, p. 17.

160 Berger and Luckmann, 1967, p. 77.

161 Ibid., p. 76.

162 Ibid., p 77.

163 Ibid., p. 79.

164 Ibid., p. 111.

165 Ibid., p. 79.

166 Ibid., p. 102.

167 Bultmann, 1951, Vol. 2, p. 97.

168 Käsemann, 1969, p. 242; Bultmann, op. cit., p. 112.

169 Holmberg, 1980a, p. 116.

170 Stark, 1969, Vol. 4, p. 84.

171 Pp. 300ff.

172 Holmberg, 1980a, p. 187; for further discussion of Paul as a charismatic authority see pp. 154f. In her recent doctoral dissertation Margaret MacDonald also identifies Paul as a charismatic leader; she writes (1986, p. 63), "Paul's authority may be described in the language of Weber as 'charismatic authority'; his powers and qualities are not regarded as accessible to everyone, but are viewed as stemming from divine origins." Paul obviously differs from Jesus, who more closely approximates Weber's ideal type. Holmberg places Paul in a broader context of institutionalization after Jesus' death, but this is not to deny his charismatic qualities.

173 Weber, 1968, pp. 246f., 1121ff.

174 Weber is not always consistent concerning the role of the charismatic leader in routinization; in one passage (1968, p. 1121, also p. 452) he states that the leader has an active role in this transition; in another (ibid., p. 246) he argues that routinization occurs after the leader's death. For further discussion see Eisenstadt, 1968a, pp. xviiiff.

175 Holmberg, 1980a, p. 164.

176 Ibid., p. 170.

177 Ibid., p. 177.

178 Ibid., p. 178.

179 Stark, 1969, p. 86.

180 Ibid., pp. 173-74.

181 This interpretation is supported by the fact that Paul used similar terms to describe his own work and that of local leaders such as householders; see p. 78 n. 72.

182 Shils, 1965, p. 206. This quotation belongs to a general argument concerning Weber's model of routinization. Shils (1965, 1968) argues that Weber contrasted too sharply between charisma and routinization. He argues that charisma exists not only in the pure form described by Weber, but also in those structures, rules, norms, and symbols which contribute to a society's interests and which embody its defining values. According to Shils, these phenomena are treated with reverence by the group which shares them because of their "awe-arousing centrality" (1965, p. 201). He thus redefines charisma as "contact with, or embodiment of, something very 'serious' . . . which is thought to be, and therewith becomes, central or fundamental to man's existence" (ibid., p. 201). We agree with Wilson (1975, pp. 4-13), however, that it is misleading to treat charisma as a phenomenon which pervades or permeates mundane social structures. But, in our opinion, Shils is right to note that those "rules, institutions, symbols and strata or aggregates of persons" (1965, p. 200) which most clearly embody or express what is central to a group's identity are perceived to possess a higher or enhanced status by the members of the society in which such phenomena find their meaning.

183 The pseudonymous Pauline epistles may also be interpreted as more direct evidence of this process, especially the Pastorals where a relatively advanced development of church structure is legitimated by connecting local institutions to the apostle's instructions.

184 Fuellenbach, 1980, shows that the majority of Protestant scholars, and several Roman Catholic ones, regard these descriptions as purely fictional.

185 Similarly, Brown and Meier, 1983, pp. 174-75.

186 Campenhausen, 1969, p. 77-78.

187 Dobschütz, 1904, pp. 174-75; cf. also Gerke, 1931, pp. 33f.

188 Simmel's (1955) theses are presented in point form by Coser, 1965, and then commented upon and further developed.

189 Coser, 1968, p. 232.

190 Coser, 1965, p. 127.

191 Ibid., p. 125.

192 Ibid., p. 126.

193 Hoebel, 1954; 1958.

194 Hoebel, 1954, p. 13; cf. also 1958, pp. 482, 158f.

195 Eisenstadt, 1965, pp. 43f.

196 Ibid., p. 53.

197 Eisenstadt, 1968b, p. 413.

198 Campenhausen, 1969, p. 92; cf. p. 86.

199 Ibid., p. 89.

200 The eleventh century Latin MS *L* reads *legem* where *Codex Alexandrinus* reads ἐπινομὴν and *Codex Constantinopolitanus* reads ἐπιδομὴν; the consensus is to read ἐπινομὴν although this reading is difficult to translate. We follow the majority of scholars who render it "codicil."

201 Schweizer, 1961, p. 16c similarly confuses these issues when he argues, "What we hear about its [the Corinthian church's] order fits in with the concept of the Church." Institutions are regarded as reflections of ideas and this results in obscuring the interaction between social structures and ideas. Holmberg, 1980a, p. 202 notes a similar confusion in the treatment by Campenhausen and others of the New Testament evidence.

202 Brunner, 1972, p. 26, n. 50.
203 Campenhausen, 1969, p. 91.
204 Berger and Luckmann, 1971, p. 72.
205 Gerke, 1931, p. 64, citing evidence in 3.3, argues that the division arose as a result of younger members revolting against the authority of elders, but this passage was probably intended to illustrate the more general character of the division and Gerke's argument is therefore unconvincing.
206 Berger and Luckmann, 1971, p. 79.
207 Ibid., p. 111.
208 Ibid., p. 125.
209 Ibid., pp. 112-13.
210 Ibid., p. 113. Berger and Luckmann understand symbols as phenomena which refer to realities other than those of everyday experience.
211 Bauer, 1971, p. 95.
212 Knopf, 1899, pp. 174-75; 1920, p. 42; Wrede, 1891, pp.1, 53f.; Harnack, 1929, p. 52; cf. Jaubert, 1971, pp. 23, 28.
213 Harnack, 1929, p. 58.
214 Ibid., p. 102.
215 Jaubert, 1971, p. 28.
216 Berger and Luckmann, 1971, p. 111.
217 Campenhausen, 1969, pp. 94-95.
218 Schweizer, 1961, p. 16b.
219 Sanders, 1943, especially pp. 143ff.
220 E.g. Beyschlag, 1966, pp. 16f., 339f.; Harnack, 1909, p. 76.
221 For comparison of Paul and Clement's uses of διά with the genitive, which differ slightly, see Grant and Graham, 1965, p. 58.
222 Blass and Debrunner, 1961, pp. 117-18.
223 Ibid., p. 119.
224 For discussion of Paul's usage see MacDonald, 1986, pp. 97f. The general shape of the following discussion of these phrases is in part derived from her discussion of Paul's usage.
225 Douglas, 1973, p. 11.
226 Harnack, 1909, p. 49.
227 Knopf, 1920, pp. 136f; Jaubert, 1971, pp. 39-40; Clarke, 1937, p. 106 argue that the prayer at the end of 1 Clement is borrowed from the contemporary Roman liturgy but their arguments are unconvincing since there is no means of assessing whether this prayer is liturgical except by the use of documents which post-date this letter.
228 See Elliott, 1981, pp. 24f.; Lightfoot, 1890, Part 1 Vol. 2, pp. 5-6.
229 See also 1 Pet. 1.:7; 2:11; similarly, Heb. 11:13.
230 We are following Codex A which is parallel with the end of 29:2.
231 Knopf, 1920, pp. 109-110; Jaeger, 1961, p. 22 notes the classical origins of the term συμπνεῖν and also notes that the body motif maintains its "mystic" application in Clement's usage (p. 19).
232 Jaubert, 1971, p. 72.
233 Knopf, 1920, p. 56; similarly, Clarke, 1937, p. 27; these writers incorrectly interpret certain passages without keeping Clement's over-all purpose in mind. On the basis of Clement's statement in 7:5, that repentance was offered to all generations, these writers criticize Clement's understanding of the atonement as being too universalistic, but Clement is presenting these themes in order to develop a theme consistent with his portrait of the persons causing problems in the Corinthian community as sinners, in order to show that they are in need of repentance. We

should not try to find a "theology of atonement" in these references, nor an abstract teaching on penance as Jaubert, 1971, pp. 50-52, does.

234 Knopf, 1920, p. 126; Harnack, 1929, pp. 117-18 argue that this verse refers to the eucharist but it is too general to be certain.

235 Knopf, 1920, p. 125.

236 Grant and Graham, 1965, pp. 63-64.

237 Lightfoot, 1890, Part 1, Vol. 2, p. 111.

238 Harnack, 1929, p. 70.

239 Jaubert, 1971, p. 73.

240 Lightfoot, 1890, Part 1, Vol. 2, p. 100; idem., Part 1, Vol. 1, p. 96.

241 Knopf, 1920, p. 98.

242 Grant and Graham, 1965, p. 69.

243 E.g., 20:11; 24:5; 33:1; 36:2; 40:1; 49:6; 61:2.

244 Thus, e.g., van Unnik, 1950, pp. 181ff.; Sanders, 1943, pp. 109-30; Bardy, 1922, pp. 73-85.

245 Jaeger, 1961, pp. 116-18. As Grant and Graham, 1965, p. 97 argue, "Threskeia, at the beginning of the chapter (62:1), is more important than paideia at the end. . . . Like Judaism, Christianity was a cult before it was a philosophy."

246 Grant and Graham, 1965, p. 89.

247 Jaeger, 1961, p. 18.

248 Eggenberger, 1951, p. 183.

249 Jaeger, 1961, pp. 19-23.

250 Ibid., p. 15.

251 Ibid., p. 113, n.2 notes that στάσις is one of the most discussed problems in Greek political thought.

252 Harnack, 1929, p. 70; see also Jaeger, 1961, p. 115, n. 13, who sees in *1 Clement's* concern with obedience a Jewish soteriology.

Chapter Five

Ignatius

The Social Setting of the Ignatian Epistles

In the following discussion we shall focus our attention on the evidence in Ignatius' letters concerning the social setting of the Asia Minor churches with which Ignatius was in contact. Recent attempts to reconstruct the setting of Christianity in Antioch contemporary with Ignatius[1] rest on a high degree of speculation based on a very limited amount of evidence which can be legitimately interpreted in many different ways. In the case of Ignatius' letters, it is not evident that the problems in Asia Minor reflected those which presumably existed in Antioch. Corwin, for example, assumes too quickly that the opponents whom Ignatius addressed in Asia Minor were the same as those whom she supposes that he attacked in Antioch.[2] In this chapter we shall assume that there was a connection between the opponents[3] Ignatius described and the communities he addressed. The more general question of the relationship between these opponents and Ignatius' experiences in Antioch must be left open. Throughout our discussion we shall assume that the modern consensus — first suggested by Lightfoot and Zahn[4] — regarding the letters of Ignatius contained in the so-called middle recension, is correct: namely, that the epistles written to Christians at Ephesus, Magnesia, Tralles, Rome, Philadelphia, and Smyrna as well as the epistle to Polycarp were composed by Ignatius some time between A.D. 100 and 113.[5]

In this section we shall briefly describe the divisions which confronted the Asia Minor churches addressed by Ignatius. Then we shall attempt to place these divisions in a more general social milieu by discussing evidence of the setting of documents before and after Ignatius' letters (2 and 3 John and the Apocryphal Acts of the Apostles). After establishing a probable setting for these communities we shall attempt to fill out more fully the social setting of church divisions and meetings which Ignatius describes. By presenting the argument in this way we hope to show that a house-church setting provides a compelling setting for community division and meetings at the time of Ignatius.[6] Finally, we shall argue that evidence regarding Polycarp supports our contention that wealthy members of the community were candidates for church leadership. It will be seen that this evidence also harmonizes with references to leadership by the

---

Notes to this chapter appear on pp. 187-97.

well-to-do in the Apocryphal Acts and the profile of Diotrephes which certain scholars adduce from 3 John.

The Setting of the Community Divisions

There is no direct mention in Ignatius' letters of household meetings. This is not surprising since both Ignatius and his readers would have taken for granted the prevailing patterns of social organization and their attendant problems. A problem arises when one attempts to establish what it was that both reader and writer assumed about the social context of community life in these churches. Ignatius' comments regarding the divisions he had knowledge of are often epigrammatic or elliptical. Whether this was the result of "great nervous strain,"[7] or, more likely, a distinct rhetorical style,[8] the consequence is that the modern reader must do a substantial amount of "unpacking" in order to determine what social milieu Ignatius was describing when he discussed problems upsetting the communities with which he corresponded. But, notwithstanding the difficulties of Ignatius' style, it is possible to establish the probable social setting of certain aspects of Ignatius' descriptions.

Several passages in Ignatius' letters either describe or assume some form of local division. In *Eph.* 5:2-3 he describes the person who does not join "the common assembly" (ὁ μὴ ἐρχόμενος ἐπὶ τὸ αὐτό) [9] but separates himself. The description in *Mag.* 4:1 of those who "do not meet validly in accordance with the commandment" indicates that such separation included separate meetings.[10] Ignatius is probably also referring to the separate meetings of these individuals when he exhorts his readers not to do anything apart from the bishop (*Mag.* 7:1-2; *Tral.* 2:2; 7:2; *Smyr.* 9:1). The activities which Ignatius has in mind are enumerated in *Smyr.* 8:1-2: any eucharist, baptism, or agape meal not authorized by the bishop is not to be considered valid. It was probably the case, as Lightfoot suggested,[11] that these members had their own form of eucharist. In *Smyr.* 7:1 Ignatius states that these persons keep themselves away from (ἀπέχεσθαι) "eucharist and prayers" because of their beliefs. This passage may also provide a background for the admonition in *Phld.* 4:1 to celebrate one eucharist, which is connected with (cf. οὖν) his warning in 3:3 regarding anyone who follows a schismatic. Some type of separate meeting taking place within the Philadelphian community seems to be assumed in these passages. We may gather from these references, then, that there was a series of rival meetings occurring in all of these churches — excluding Rome, of course, which is not referred to as suffering from division. How should one interpret these references to community divisions? Did Ignatius envisage a single community eucharist celebrated exclusively by one bishop or by an individual appointed by him in his absence (for example, when the bishop was away visiting him)? Are all gatherings in the absence of the bishop schismatic? Or was Ignatius somewhat more flexible: did he envision several smaller local groups meeting together with the approval of the bishop? In either case, where did these meetings (both those approved and those unapproved by Ignatius) occur? By providing an answer to this final question we shall be in a better position to respond to the other ones.

The setting Ignatius assumes for the divisions and meetings he mentions is placed in higher relief by noting the presumed social background of the prob-

lems described in 2 and 3 John (documents which probably antedate the Ignatian corpus)[12] and the setting presented in the Apocryphal Acts of the Apostles
(writings which postdate it). This Johannine literature and many of the Apocryphal Acts are associated with Asia Minor. These documents are important for
our discussion because they provide analogies between communities in some
instances existing in the same geographical area and thereby help us to place the
divisions Ignatius describes in a general social context.

The second and third epistles of John, probably composed in the vicinity of
Ephesus[13] (a city which Ignatius addressed), contain references to household
hospitality which can shed light on Ignatius' letters. It is possible that they
reflect a level of organization in a period shortly before Ignatius' correspondence. The passages in these letters which describe hospitality and inhospitality
toward travellers (2 John 10; 3 John 5-10) are especially fecund for helping us to
determine the setting of divisions within the churches Ignatius addressed.

In 2 John 10 the writer warns that anyone who comes (presumably from
without into the community) and who does not bring the proper teaching is not
to be received "into the house." Such a case of not welcoming travellers into the
household seems to be behind much of 3 John. 3 John 5-10 should be understood in the context of a letter of recommendation for hospitality for Demetrius
(v. 12) (of a kind familiar in the ancient world[14]). We are given valuable clues
regarding the importance of hospitality in the early church as well as hints concerning divisions which could arise from the offering of hospitality to travelling
Christians. The events which preceded the letter may be reconstructed from vs.
9-10 as follows: certain individuals ("the brethren"- v.10) were sent to the
church where Diotrephes, probably a leader of the community, presided.
Diotrephes "himself" (RSV) did not welcome (ἐπιδέχεσθαι) these travellers,
i.e., did not offer them the hospitality of his own house (in letters of recommendation of the period compounds of the verb δέχεσθαι are used to express
requests to extend hospitality).[15] These travellers were then welcomed by other
members of the church which Diotrephes led. The information which follows
is especially significant. As a result of welcoming these travellers, again presumably into their homes (cf. ἐπιδέχεσθαι), Diotrephes "put them out of the
church" (ἐκ τῆς ἐκκλησίας ἐκβάλλει). The term ἐκβάλλειν has been interpreted by scholars as a reference to a formal act of excommunication,[16] but the
arguments put forward for this interpretation are unconvincing. The same
verb, it is true, is a technical term used for banning someone from a synagogue
and on this basis scholars have found in Jn. 9:34f. an instance of the term used
in this sense. But such a usage is not necessarily implied in this passage nor need
the term imply official action against members of the community referred to in
3 John.

What gave Diotrephes the authority to exclude members from the fellowship? Many scholars answer this by stating that he was, or else arrogated to himself, the position of a monarchical bishop.[17] But the participle φιλοπρωτεύων,
used by the "elder" to describe Diotrephes, does not necessarily mean, as it is
often interpreted, that Diotrephes is in fact in a first position: only that he is
ambitious to be.[18] It appears, then, that there is not sufficient evidence to justify
accounting for his authority as based on a position of monarchical episcopacy. A

further clue is provided by the sequence of verbs in vs. 9-10: . . . ἐπιδέχεται . . . ἐπιδέχεται . . . ἐκβάλλει. Throughout this passage the writer is referring to events surrounding the offering or withholding of hospitality. If we interpret the verb ἐκβάλλειν in the light of this context, we may regard it as a further instance of an issue related to hospitality. Because members of the church which Diotrephes led welcomed those to whom he refused to offer hospitality, the leader withdrew his welcome to them also and thereby excluded them from the community. Given the probable household setting of these epistles, it seems likely that members were excluded from a household meeting. The verb ἐπιδέχεσθαι (along with λαμβάνειν – another verb used in contemporary letters to indicate hospitality – cf. 2 John 10) is best interpreted as an antonym for εκβάλλειν. This implies that ἐκβάλλειν here refers to inhospitality. We can account for the power which Diotrephes had in offering and withdrawing hospitality if, together with Malherbe,[19] we see him as inviting the church into his own house.

The writer, therefore, relies upon the continued hospitality of Gaius to provide accommodation for Demetrius. It is possible, but purely a matter for speculation, that Gaius was a relatively wealthy host,[20] and was attached to another house church maybe even meeting in his own home. There is no evidence of any animosity between Diotrephes and Gaius which may suggest that he was not involved in the earlier exclusion; if Gaius belonged to a separate house church (perhaps in a nearby city) contact between Diotrephes and him could have been minimal. This reconstruction can only be put forward as, at best, a plausible interpretation of the evidence. What does seem certain, however, is the adverse effect hospitality offered to travellers could have on a Christian community, and its importance as a factor in the maintenance of a harmonious community life.

The second body of evidence which helps us to shed light on the social setting of the Asia Minor communities Ignatius addressed is the literature known as the Apocryphal Acts of the Apostles and parts of the Clementine Homilies and Recognitions. These documents, composed in the second and early third century, contain some valuable and much ignored information regarding the church in this early period. They also help us to shed some light on practices within the communities addressed by Ignatius. Commenting on the historical value of the Apocryphal Acts, Quasten writes,

> They throw considerable light on the history of Christian worship in the second and third centuries; they describe the earliest forms of religious services in private homes; they contain hymns and prayers which constitute the beginnings of Christian poetry.[21]

Similarly, with respect to the Clementine Homilies and Recognitions, Waitz argues that there is evidence contained within them which provides valuable information concerning the structure of the early church in Syria.[22] Any further reconstruction of the structures in the churches addressed by Ignatius is hypothetical, but these documents help us to see how they may have appeared.

The late second or early third century apocryphal Acts, among which are included the *Acts of John, Peter, Paul (and Thecla),* and *Andrew* share a set of common literary characteristics which have led scholars to group them together. To this list we may add what has been identified by some scholars as a source of the Clementine Homilies and Recognitions, given the title *Periodoi Petrou* or *Praxeis Petrou*, and which is distinct from, although perhaps partially dependent on, the *Acts of Peter*.[23] The complex history of redaction of the Clementine literature falls outside the scope of this discussion,[24] and we shall be concerned with this body of literature only insofar as the so-called *Praxeis Petrou* contained within it includes themes which are relevant.

The audience of most of the Acts probably belonged to Greece or Asia Minor,[25] except for the *Acts of Thomas* which was most likely for a Syrian audience,[26] and the *Praxeis Petrou* which may have been composed for an audience in Antioch.[27] Tertullian (*On Baptism* 17) is the earliest writer to refer to one of these writings and he states that the *Acts of Paul and Thecla* was composed in Asia Minor. Similarly, the *Acts of John*, probably the earliest of those documents to be written (*c.* 150-80) is also likely to have been composed in Asia Minor because it recounts the mission travels of John throughout that area.[28] The apocryphal *Acts of Peter*, dating from the end of the second century, probably build on the *Acts of John*.[29] The *Acts of Andrew* are probably the latest of these Acts, composed *c.* 260.[30] Various attempts have been made to argue for differing combinations of the dependence of these documents on one another, but it is difficult to distinguish between use of a document and utilization of a common tradition.[31]

The household is the primary setting of these Acts. There are numerous passages which describe the hospitality offered by a wealthy householder to the wandering apostle, worship services conducted by the apostle in a wealthy person's home, and even leadership arising from patronage.[32] All of the passages which describe hospitality offered to an apostle present wealthy people who either become Christians or are attracted to the apostle in such a way that they invite him to lodge with them.[33] This invariably results in the establishment of the wealthy person's home as a place of teaching and worship.

The *Acts of John* recounts how John was invited with his companions to stay in the house of Lycomedes, *praetor* of Ephesus(19), and his wife Cleopatra (25). Later in the same work it is in the house of Andronicus, a wealthy Ephesian Christian, that John both instructs Ephesian converts and leads worship (46). James includes in his edition of this document a translation of an eleventh century manuscript which states that upon John's departure from Ephesus to Smyrna he left Bucolis, Polycarp, and Andronicus to preside over the district.[34] Since it appears that the writer of this fragment assumed a high degree of church organization, one must be cautious of regarding it as a part of the original Acts of John. Given the reference to Polycarp, the fragment may date sometime after 155 and the reference to presiding over the district seems to suggest some form of "chorepiscopacy." Also, the fact that this fragment is inconsistent with the reference to Andronicus travelling with John in chapter 59 indicates some other manuscript tradition which may post-date an earlier work.[35] The reference to Andronicus, patron and leader of the church at Ephesus, must be treated with great caution. It is in his house, however, that the church continues to meet throughout the story (62; 86).[36]

The Clementine *Praxeis Petrou* provides some more secure references to patrons of the church who were also its leaders. The stories contained in this document probably included legends about the apostle Peter and his comrades, and his enemy Simon, all of whom relied upon the hospitality of generally well-to-do patrons. In the course of these legends, Peter meets with his converts in the house of his host, teaching and leading worship, and in certain passages he appoints his patron as bishop of the church which continues to meet in his house. In *Rec.* 3:65-67 (cf. *Hom.* 3:60-73), Zacchaeus, Peter's host and the host of those instructed by the apostle, is appointed bishop upon Peter's departure from Caesarea.[37] Again, in *Rec.* 4:1-2 (*Hom.* 8:1), Peter stays with Maro (*Hom.* = Maroones) who had invited him to hold his debate with Simon in the garden of his house (*Rec.* 4:6). In *Rec.* 6:15 (*Hom.* 11:36), the writer states that upon Peter's departure, Maro is ordained bishop along with twelve presbyters and deacons.[38] Finally, in *Rec.* 10:71 the writer portrays Peter as teaching in Antioch and then recounts how Theophilus, "who was more exalted than all the men of power in that city" consecrated "the great palace of his house under the name of a church." It is not clear whether Theophilus is presented as a leader of the church, since the work probably originally ended at 10:72 with Peter in Antioch, but the passage is another instance of the organizational role wealthy patrons are made to play in this writing. The evidence of a single manuscript in 10:72 that Peter ordained one of his followers as bishop is probably a later addition to the text modelled after what seems to be the formulaic construction which occurs in *Rec.* 10:68 (*Hom.* 20:23) and which is similar to the construction which appears in passages in the *Homilies* to complete an episode (*Hom.* 7:5,8,12).

If we look behind the story of the wandering apostle who founds house churches and establishes his hosts as bishops and ask what social experience seems to be assumed by these documents, we may see evidence of a social setting of the second-century church in which an important leadership role is played by the relatively wealthy patron who invites the community to meet in his home. The presentation of this pattern without apology or explanation seems to indicate that the writers' audiences did not regard it as abnormal. In the case of the Theophilus episode in *Rec.* 10:71 we may even possess evidence of a transition to official buildings set aside strictly for meeting places.[39] Any conclusions from this evidence must be drawn cautiously, but the descriptions of household leadership and house meetings may reflect the contemporary setting of the earlier Acts.

Both the Johannine letters and the Apocryphal Acts selected for comment here assume a household setting for the background of community worship, problems, and divisions. The house-church setting of these documents warrants the conclusion drawn by scholars that the household was the general setting of the meetings and divisions described by Ignatius. Commenting on *Smyr.* 7:1, Schoedel notes that separate meetings in different houses were common in this period.[40] Similarly, Corwin's reconstruction of the organization of the Asia Minor churches addressed by Ignatius includes a household setting.[41]

But scholars have not drawn attention to other references which suggest that it may be a house setting which has contributed to division in the community. Ignatius warns his readers not to receive (παραδέχεσθαι) certain persons in *Smyr.* 4:1. He writes in a similar way in *Phld.* 11:1 when he thanks the Philadelphians for "receiving" (δέχεσθαι) Philo and Rheus Agathopous. As we have already seen,[42] the verb δέχεσθαι and its compounds occur in contemporary letters of recommendation to refer to hospitality. It is likely that Ignatius is here referring to hospitality offered to these deacons on their way to meet him and to their reception by certain members of the community. The offering of hospitality to visitors and messengers was a universally recognized duty of presbyters in the early church, especially since inns were few and uncomfortable.[43] Ignatius is probably, therefore, referring in *Smyr.* 4:1 to the reception of certain members into the homes of presbyters. Further hints are provided in his letter to Ephesus. In *Eph.* 9:1 Ignatius states that certain persons, presumably his opponents, "have passed by on their way from there (ἐκεῖθεν) with evil teaching."[44] Precisely where "there" refers to is not clear. But we may adduce from *Eph.* 7:1 (where Ignatius describes those to whom he is opposed as "carrying about the name") that these persons were some kind of travellers. The verb περιφέρειν is used by Ignatius in other passages in connection with travel (*Eph.* 11:2; *Mag.* 1:2; *Tral.* 12:2). These observations, taken together with Ignatius' description in *Eph.* 9:1, indicate that Ignatius wishes to guard against travelling teachers who stay with the community, presumably to teach, draw members away from the common assembly, and establish rival meetings.[45]

Again, 2 and 3 John provide a possible analogy which helps us to understand Ignatius' concerns and strategy for curtailing the influence of his opponents. Brown interprets Diotrephes' action as a caution against receiving those who come with false teaching such as the type referred to in 2 John 10.[46] As in the case of Diotrephes, Ignatius recognized that the withdrawal of hospitality was an effective means of excluding undesirable influences from the community. A household setting provides a probable backdrop for the meetings of Ignatius' opponents.[47]

The Setting of the Common Assembly

Can we be more precise about the assemblies which Ignatius recognized as valid? Ignatius' references to coming together to a common meeting (ἐπὶ τὸ αὐτό – *Eph.* 5:3; cf. 20:2) and his exhortations to "hurry together as to one temple of god, as to one altar, to one Jesus Christ" (*Mag.* 7:2 – trans. Schoedel) lead to the conclusion that there was a common meeting in the community where the eucharist was celebrated. Ignatius is concerned that the Philadelphians should "celebrate one eucharist" (*Phld.* 4:1), an exhortation which may be interpreted as assuming one common meeting. Again, the language of being "within the sanctuary", or "altar" (θυσιαστήριον) in *Eph.* 5:2 and *Tral.* 7:2 (cf. *Mag.* 7:2; *Phld.* 4:1) probably reflects a setting of a common meeting. Further, the link between obedience to the bishop and presbyters and "breaking one bread" (*Eph.* 20:2), the instruction to do nothing apart from the bishops, presbyters, and deacons (*Tral.* 7:2), and the exhortation that wherever the bishop appears the congregation is to meet (*Smyr.* 8:2) all suggest a common meeting. Ignatius' description of docetists as remaining aloof from "eucharist and prayers" (*Smyr.* 7:1) is best interpreted as referring to one common assembly rather than a variety of meetings regarded as valid.[48] These references taken together make the postulation of a common meeting probable.

It seems unlikely that Ignatius viewed *all* other meetings apart from the bishop as schismatic. When he writes in *Smyr.* 8:2 that it is not lawful to baptize or hold an agape without the bishop he is probably not restricting those activities to only one assembly;[49] in 8:1 he states that a eucharist is also valid when celebrated by one appointed by the bishop. This provision makes sense especially if agape meals included a eucharist.[50] Thus, in other meetings Ignatius allows for eucharistic celebrations but he forbids them if they take place without the consent of the bishop, as presumably they did in circles where docetic teachers had gained some influence. The concern in 7:1 and 8:2 is to increase control and solidarity among the groups which constitute the community, rather than to prescribe a single valid meeting. Even if the community met for a common eucharist once a week, of a type described by Justin (*Apology* 1:67), this does not preclude the possibility of other meetings of smaller cells during the week. A morning hymn or common meal such as that described by Pliny (*Ep.* 10:98) need not have occurred in a plenary meeting; a member's household would have sufficed.[51]

It is probably significant, however, that the references to agapes without the knowledge of the bishop appear in the letter to the Smyrnaeans, as does the concern regarding meetings apart from the bishop's permission. For it seems likely that Ignatius' opponents enjoyed the support of some kind of local church leader. In *Smyr.* 6:1 Ignatius urges, "Let position (τόπος – Lake – "office") inflate no one; for faith and love are everything, to which nothing is preferable." The noun τόπος is employed in a technical way in other early Christian literature (*Pol.* 1:2; *Pol. Phil.* 11:1 – *locum*; Acts 1:25) to refer to a position of leadership in the community and it is likely that it is being used in that sense here.[52] Bauer's inference from this passage that Ignatius' opponent was "something like a gnostic anti-bishop of Smyrna" exceeds the constraints of the evidence;[53] if there had been an anti-bishop, Ignatius would probably have protested much more vigorously and clearly than in this one somewhat cryptic passage. It is more likely that the person in question was a presbyter.[54] And it is very possible that he was behind the meetings implied in *Smyr.* 7:1 and 8:2. When Ignatius commands in 8:1 that only he who is appointed by the bishop is permitted to celebrate a eucharist, an instruction contained only in this letter, he may be referring to the practice of a high ranking member of the community who would be in a position to lead a eucharist if he had the bishop's consent.[55] Given the likelihood that there was a person who, according to Ignatius' interpretation, abused his position to bring about meetings in separation from the rest of the community, and Ignatius' warning to the Smyrnaeans not to receive (παραδέχεσθαι) certain persons regarded as opponents (4:1), it is probable that these individuals were connected with each other. One possible reconstruction of the situation at Smyrna is that a presbyter welcomed certain teachers into his home and that this became a location for further meetings – perhaps even a base for activities in other households.[56] This explains Ignatius' somewhat ambiguous presentation of his opponents as being both inside and outside the community (cf. 7:2; 9:1) better than Schoedel's impression from these passages that Ignatius wanted to think that "the docetists were the dupes of outside agitators."[57] Such a tentative reconstruction also helps to make sense of Ignatius' progression of thought from the references to abuse of office at the end of 6:1 to his description of his opponents' lack of love for widows, orphans, prisoners, and similarly needy people in v. 2.[58] Ignatius is probably contrasting the collection which occurs in the general meeting with the absence of it in the smaller gatherings around his opponents. Both Justin (*Apol.* 1:67) and Tertullian (*Apol.* 39) describe such collections for the disadvantaged: Justin states that it occurs during a common meeting on Sunday.

This reference to the abuse of position together with Ignatius' acknowledgement of the permissibility of a eucharist celebrated in the absence of the bishop allows us to speculate that there were a number of household meetings usually led by presbyters alongside the common assembly. Abuse of τόπος for Ignatius probably did not mean merely conducting smaller meetings, but doing so without the permission of the bishop. The "official" support of Ignatius' opponents perhaps only occurred in Smyrna (in the other letters there is no admonition concerning the abuse of positions of leadership), but what Ignatius would have regarded as legitimate household meetings in presbyters' homes of a sort separate from the common eucharist was probably common to all of these communities.

We can only speculate that the setting of the meetings regarded by Ignatius as legitimate was similar to that presented in the apocryphal Acts and the early source(s) behind the Clementine literature. This hypothesis gains a small measure of extra support from the reconstruction presented above of the setting of the conflict described in 3 John. If our interpretation is correct, it is likely that the well-to-do played an important role in the community life of churches in at least one Asia Minor city. Again, in the *Acts of John* there is great concern that the wealthy use their riches to care for the widows of the community (34-36; cf. 30). Although there is a long discourse against wealth contained within a Latin manuscript (14-18 — James, pp. 257-62), the role the wealthy person plays in this writing in caring for the apostle and inviting members into his home probably indicates that wealth remained important in the church's common life. Evidence from the apocryphal source in the Clementine literature leads to a similar conclusion.[59]

Turning again to the evidence in the Ignatian letters, the evidence of Polycarp's social position is consonant with references to the wealth of leaders in this apocryphal literature. He is the only bishop referred to by Ignatius of whom we have information which can shed light on the social rank of leaders in the churches addressed by him. The *Martyrdom of Polycarp* provides some valuable information concerning the Smyrnaean bishop. This data must be interpreted cautiously since the writer of the martyrdom may have patterned his work after Christ's passion (cf. *Mart. Pol.* 1:1), inserting events or shaping his report to conform to this model.[60] But it is significant that not all the historical details of the report are made to mirror the Passion.[61] And it is more likely that certain historical events, such as the betrayal, called attention to Christ's death. There is no reason to doubt the overall accuracy of the document nor to regard it as anything other than it purports to be — a contemporary letter from the Smyrnaean church to Christians at Philomelium intended to describe events surrounding their bishop's martyrdom.[62]

This letter contains sufficient evidence to suggest that Polycarp was relatively affluent. In 6:1-2 we learn that he was betrayed by young "slaves (παιδάρια) of his own house". Again, the implication from the reference to the two farms mentioned as his hiding places (5:1; 6:1) is that they were his own.[63] Also, Ignatius' instruction that Polycarp be not haughty to slaves (*Pol.* 4:3) harmonizes well with this other evidence. We may cautiously conclude from the evidence we have that Polycarp was well-to-do. It is possible that like certain well-to-do individuals described in the apocryphal literature listed above, Polycarp invited the church into his home for the common eucharist. This provides a plausible background for Ignatius' exhortation that Polycarp make the meetings more numerous (cf. also *Eph.* 13:1) and that he seek all by name (ἐξ ὀνόματος *Pol.* 4:2).[64] As in the case of 3 John, where we argued that an explanation for Diotrephes' power to exclude members from the church was connected with his power as a host of the church, so in the case of Polycarp, the ability to convene meetings more often may have arisen from his position as a host of the church meeting in his home. We do not have any evidence of the economic position of the other bishops.

A possible social setting for the meetings regarded by Ignatius as legitimate were the households of local bishops. Just as a Smyrnaean presbyter probably welcomed Ignatius' opponents into his home and allowed meetings to occur in what Ignatius regarded as defiance of the bishop, so bishops of these churches may have led the common meeting in their own homes. This is only one possible reconstruction, but it is consonant with what was probably the case in the setting presented in 2 and 3 John, and it gains a degree of extra support from other early evidence which presents a setting similar to the one suggested here.

Summary

We have attempted to reconstruct the social setting of the communities Ignatius addressed. The house church provides a compelling setting for the activities of these communities and the problems confronting them. 2 and 3 John as well as later apocryphal literature have been explored in our attempt to understand more precisely how these communities operated. We suggested that behind this literature there was a house-church setting in which patrons of the church had a central role of leadership. We saw that evidence concerning the social status of Polycarp helps to confirm this. On this basis we tentatively suggested that house-church patrons had a similar role in the governance of the communities Ignatius addressed. In the case of Smyrna we were able to be more precise concerning divisions arising from the support of a church leader. Perhaps a presbyter invited Ignatius' opponents into his home. Our reconstruction of legitimate meetings included a common eucharist with other smaller meetings such as agapes taking place in the homes of presbyters or other members.

Charisma in the Ignatian Epistles

The personality of Ignatius — the bishop from Syria who marched from his home in Antioch to distant Rome, chained "to ten leopards — which is a company of soldiers" (*Rom.* 5:1) — has fired the imagination of scholars for over a century.

> May I benefit from the wild beasts prepared for me, and I pray that they will
> be found prompt with me, whom I shall even entice to devour me
> promptly — not as with some whom they were too timid to touch; and should
> they not consent voluntarily, I shall force them. Indulge me; I know what is
> to my advantage; now I begin to be a disciple. May nothing of things visible
> and invisible envy me, that I may attain Jesus Christ. Fire and cross, and packs
> of wild beasts, the wrenching of bones, the mangling of limbs, the grinding of
> my whole body, evil punishments of the devil — let these come upon me,
> only that I may attain Jesus Christ (*Rom.* 5:2-3 — trans. Schoedel).

Ignatius' gory imagination has resulted in mixed judgments. According to
Streeter, he suffered from "a psychic over-compensation for an inferiority complex."[65] In short, he was neurotic. Not so, responded Moffatt: he may have
been neurotic but his passion for martyrdom originated in an intense personal
religiosity — his letters "are one of our first items in the psychology of the
saints."[66] Yes, agreed Campenhausen, but his belief that he could attain God
through martyrdom made him the first Catholic saint, and it was not so much a
personal relationship with Jesus that motivated him as a need to win salvation
for himself.[67] And not only was he Catholic, contended Preiss. He was also a
mystic who desired (through his martyrdom) to cast off the dregs of material
flesh and to set his semi-gnostic spirit free through unity with God.[68] Yes, he
was a mystic, responded Tinsley, but his mysticism was not "a kind of yoga of
self-endeavor after God" as Preiss argued; rather it was "profoundly and
penetratingly Christian ... a good early example of Christian 'incarnational'
mysticism in which the historical life of Jesus has a central place."[69] Not so
much a mystic, contended Bultmann, as a Pauline Christian; Ignatius was
"*existentiell*" — the only second-century writer to conceive of Christian existence
in a way close to the "even now — not yet" paradox of primitive Pauline Christian eschatology.[70]

The attempts to reconstruct Ignatius' personality, though valuable in remind-
ing the reader that with Ignatius' epistles we have to do with flesh and blood and
not a theological construct,[71] perhaps reveal more about those who set about the
task, than about the man himself. For if it is true that one age's madman is
another's saint, then the, perhaps insurmountable, difficulty of choosing a
model of personality with which to analyse a historical character which is not
question begging may doom the venture from the start. At the least, one must
be very cautious in reconstructing Ignatius' self-conception if only because we
have a mere seven letters, and most of those written to persuade audiences of
the desirability of a certain course of common action rather than to chronicle
the thoughts of a soul. If it is true that Ignatius was employing rhetoric in his
letters,[72] then the distinction becomes all the more important. For what appear
to the modern reader as expressions of existential *angst*, neurosis, the desire for
the mystical unity, or the winning of salvation may have been intended for a
quite different effect.

Still, we cannot get past Ignatius' personality. It dominates his letters, for it is
not as a bishop or holder of some other official position that he exhorts the Asia
Minor communities to avoid schisms and unite with their bishops — Ignatius

never makes use of this kind of authority — but as an individual who demands (without demanding, Ignatius would add) obedience to his exhortations. If we cannot solve the puzzle of his personality, perhaps we can come to a solution of his ability to command others to follow certain courses of action. We shall be in a better position to assess the authority of Ignatius' person if we step back from the personality and direct our attention to the situation. Ignatius relates to a particular group as an authority and it is by analysing how those around him may have seen him that we can gain a more accurate picture of how he viewed himself.

A point often overlooked in theological accounts of the Ignatian letters is the great effort which was undertaken by Ignatius' comrades to meet with him and to carry out his requests. There is evidence of much travelling in these letters, not only by Ignatius, but also by several others. A messenger was sent ahead of Ignatius to Rome to bring his situation to the attention of others (*Rom.* 10:2); messengers had probably preceded Ignatius' arrival in western Asia Minor to inform the communities that he was coming (*Eph.* 1:2); the Ephesians, Magnesians, and Trallians sent representatives (five from Ephesus and four from Magnesia) to meet with Ignatius; the Ephesians and Smyrnaeans contributed funds to allow a deacon to accompany Ignatius to Troas (*Eph.* 2:1); Philo and Rheus Agathopous followed Ignatius from Cilicia and Syria to Troas to give Ignatius the news of peace at Antioch (*Phld.* 11:1; *Smyr.* 10:1); and Ignatius requested that all the Asia Minor communities send letters and personal messengers to congratulate the Antiochenes on their peace (*Phld.* 10; *Smyr.* 11:2-3; *Pol.* 8:1), which was carried out soon after Ignatius' departure from Philippi (cf. Pol. *Phil.* 13:1). Since travelling in the ancient world involved a good deal of expense, time, and energy, the evidence of travel in these letters is significant.[73]

The evidence of energy exerted to meet with Ignatius or to fulfil his requests is impressive. Schoedel argues that behind all this activity was a good deal of "staging," that is, a carefully planned strategy both to establish boundary division between the Asia Minor communities and to vindicate Ignatius' ministry by sending messengers to Antioch to ensure the success of its new-found peace.[74] But behind all of this activity there is also an authority relation. Ignatius makes great requests of the Asia Minor churches and he expects them to conform with his wishes. Thus, if he often describes himself as unworthy to give orders in his letters (*Eph.* 3:1; *Tral.* 3:3; *Mag.* 12:1), he does also on occasion write with a note of strong authority (*Tral.* 5:1-2). We turn to a closer analysis of this authority relation.

Ignatius' Charismatic Authority

As in the case of Paul,[75] so, too, with Ignatius, Weber's charismatic type helps us to illuminate certain important aspects of his authority. Weber describes charisma as

> a certain quality of an individual personality by virtue of which he is consid-
> ered extraordinary and treated as endowed with supernatural, superhuman, or
> at least specifically exceptional powers or qualities. These are such as are not
> accessible to the ordinary person, but are regarded as of divine origin or as

exemplary, and on the basis of them the individual concerned is treated as a 'leader'.[76]

Unlike legal and traditional types of authority, the exercise of which involves some appeal to an external standard, charismatic authority rests upon a personal quality which testifies to extraordinariness. In its pure form, charismatic leadership is revolutionary: "It is written, but I say to you" is a typical charismatic statement. In contrast to the bureaucratic machinery typical of legal forms of authority,

> charisma knows no formal and regulated appointment or dismissal, no career, advancement or salary, no supervisory or appeals body, no local or purely technical jurisdiction, and no permanent institutions . . . which are independent of the incumbents and their personal charisma. Charisma is self-determined and sets its own limits. Its bearer seizes the task for which he is destined and demands that others obey and follow him by virtue of his mission.[77]

Weber is not interested in the question of whether the charismatic does in fact have these qualities; what is important for him is that the qualities of the charismatic leader are "regarded as of divine origin or as exemplary."[78] For those dominated by the charismatic leader, obedience is a compelling duty. But what it is in the charismatic that makes obedience to him or her compelling was not a problem which Weber successfully addressed.

He sometimes appealed to a pathological state among a charismatic leader's followers, born of various kinds of socio-economic distress, in order to explain their predisposition to follow him or her.[79] More recent sociologists prefer instead to focus on the bond uniting the group to the charismatic leader and to analyse charisma as a distinct form of social action.[80] Weber already hinted at the direction more recent sociologists have developed his type when he noted that a prophet (an example of a "purely individual bearer of charisma"[81]) presents "a unified view of the world" to his or her followers.[82] If the prophetic message is to have any significance, it must be relevant to persons other than the prophet; the perception of the charismatic quality by others is culturally determined. Shils has developed this understanding of charisma more fully by noting how charisma is related to that which is in contact with or embodies something "serious" or "awe-arousing."[83] Weber's pure charismatic is charismatic by virtue of what the group finds awe-inspiring. His or her authority is not fully intelligible without reference to the values, beliefs, and norms of his followers. In Shils' terms, perceived contact with what the group thinks is "sacred" gives the charismatic his or her authority[84]

This revision of the charismatic type provides us with some heuristic tools with which to understand Ignatius' authority. Ignatius was probably perceived as extraordinary. Several passages suggest that he too thought this. In both cases it seems likely that this belief rested on a perceived closeness to what was sacred to these communities. Schoedel notes his extraordinary position when he writes

> Ignatius is . . . far from seeing his journey in sober historical terms. He views it rather as a triumphant march . . . of mythic proportions. . . . He thus invites fellow Christians to see beyond appearances and to grasp the hidden meaning

of his wretched condition. It seems obvious that Christians who had been nurtured on the story of the crucified Lord and who had experienced the rejection of society in their own lives . . . would be prepared to welcome such a figure.[85]

In the following discussion we shall attempt to explicate more fully the social factors which contributed to the perception of Ignatius as an extraordinary authority.

The Asian communities were not only called upon to welcome Ignatius, they were also challenged to obey him. This may be partially accounted for by recognizing that he was probably regarded as possessing prophetic qualities.[86] The most explicit evidence of this appears in *Phld.* 7:1-2, where Ignatius describes a meeting with members of the Philadelphian church. He argues that some of his opponents entered the meeting surreptitiously, and he defends his knowledge of local divisions by an appeal to what may classified as prophetic inspiration:

> For even if some desired to deceive me according to the flesh, still the spirit which is from God is not deceived. For it knows whence it comes and whither it goes, and it exposes the hidden things. I cried out when I was among you, speaking with a great voice, with the voice of God, "Devote yourselves to the bishop and to the presbytery and deacons." But as for those who suspected me of saying these things because I had foreknowledge about the division of some — he is my witness in whom I am bound, I did not know of this from any human being. It was the spirit who proclaimed, saying these words, "Do nothing apart from the bishop, keep your flesh as a temple of God, love unity, flee divisions, be imitators of Jesus Christ, as also he was of his father." (my translation)

Here Ignatius makes direct reference to an inspired utterance.[87] His description of himself as speaking "with a great voice, with the voice of God" is similar to other accounts in early Christian and Hellenistic literature which describe prophetic or inspired pronouncements.[88] In this passage, then, Ignatius claims to have been the vehicle of a prophetic utterance. A less clear instance which may also reveal that he regarded himself as in some sense inspired with a prophetic spirit may be found in *Rom.* 7:2. Here, in a way reminiscent of a Johannine theme,[89] Ignatius refers to "living water" which speaks in him, saying from within, "Come to the Father." In the Hellenistic world, water and prophecy were traditionally linked together, and it is possible that such a connection was intended in this passage.[90]

Alongside the evidence of prophetic characteristics, we may also place Ignatius' conviction that he possessed great spiritual insight. In *Tral.* 4:1, he writes that he has "much knowledge in God." He continues in 5:1-2,

> Am I not able to write heavenly things to you? Yes, but I am afraid that I should do you harm seeing you are infants. Pardon me, for I refrain lest you be choked by what you cannot receive. For I myself, though I am in bonds and can understand heavenly things and the places of the angels and the gatherings of principalities, and the things seen and unseen (ἀόρατα), not for this am I a disciple even now, for much is lacking to us, that we may not lack God. (trans. Lake and Schoedel)

There is no direct reference to prophetic ability in this passage, but there is a claim to extraordinary spiritual knowledge, which may have been associated in Ignatius' mind with prophetic insight. In *Pol.* 2:2, Ignatius exhorts Polycarp to pray for unseen things (ἀόρατα) to be revealed to him, so that he may "abound in every spiritual gift (χάρισμα)." The term ἀόρατα here and in *Tral.* 5:2, where he uses it to describe his ability to comprehend invisible things, probably refers to theological mysteries. Since Polycarp is exhorted to pray for the revelation of invisible things to him, it is likely that Ignatius regarded his own spiritual insights as divinely bestowed. Ignatius was confident of the value of his spiritual knowledge; *Eph.* 19 may be an example of it, and in *Eph.* 20:1-2 he promises that there is more to follow.[91] In *Tral.* 4:1, Ignatius states that he has many thoughts (πολλὰ φρονεῖν) "in God," and he knows that he is in a position to boast about it. This may be taken as a reference to a high degree of spiritual knowledge; πολλὰ φρονεῖν is a phrase used in Greek literature to express this.[92] If the communities Ignatius addressed also saw in him an individual with prophetic gifts and remarkable spiritual knowledge, which is likely given Polycarp's comment concerning the value of Ignatius' letters (Pol. *Phil.* 13:2), this could well have been the main ground for their regarding him as an authority figure.

But alongside the more evident expression of charismatic authority, there is evidence of a more subtle form which may also be described as charismatic. Ignatius was especially indirect when he exhorted his audience to pursue a certain course of action. The complexity of his authority is that he seemed conscious of the prestige that being a potential martyr conferred upon him, while at the same time being diffident when he exhorted or admonished his readers. This is most clearly to be seen in passages where he uses concessive clauses to express his authority. In *Eph.* 3:1, for example, after requesting that Burrhus may stay on with him as an assistant and recommending that the Ephesians be subject to their bishop and presbytery (2:1-2), Ignatius writes, "I do not command you as being someone; for even though (εἰ γὰρ καί) I have been bound in the name, I have not yet begun to be perfected in Jesus Christ" (trans. Schoedel — also, *Mag.* 12:1; cf. *Tral.* 5:2; *Rom.* 9:2; *Smyr.* 11:1). Conscious of the authority he is in a position to wield, Ignatius curiously qualifies it by referring to his unworthiness.

Taking up the positive side first, Ignatius was aware that being bound to Christ conferred a large degree of prestige upon him. The passages in which he uses concessive clauses are an instance of this. The positive content of his self-conception may be seen in *Mag.* 1:2, where he describes himself as "being counted worthy to bear a most godly name." Again, in *Eph.* 21:2 he states that he was "thought worthy to attain honour for God." The references to members of his audience who "puff" him up or praise him (*Tral.* 4:1; *Smyr.* 5:2) indicate that these communities, too, saw Ignatius as in some way set apart from them. His reference to his need for humility in *Tral.* 4:1 and his criticism of those who revere him indicate his consciousness of the high repute his position as a prisoner for Christ conferred upon him. He was probably not exaggerating the high regard accorded to him. Polycarp is witness to the honour given to him as one on his way to be martyred. In Polycarp's view Ignatius was specially elected by God specifically, as in the context of the passage shows, to be a martyr (Pol. *Phil.*

1:1).[93] He has borne the chains fitting for a saint, which are in fact his crown. His endurance is set alongside that of the apostles as an example for the Philippians to follow (Pol. *Phil.* 9:1).

Ignatius' attitude to his chains is similar to that of Polycarp. He is most explicit about the honour he feels himself to be enjoying where he describes his bonds and his journey as a prisoner. If he sometimes portrays himself as a common criminal (*Eph.* 12:1; *Tral.* 3:3; cf. *Smyr.* 10:2), in other passages he refers to his status as a prisoner in a way that suggests he saw in his condition a more honourable significance. He regards himself as a "prisoner for (ἐν) Christ Jesus" (*Tral.* 1:1; also, 12:2; *Eph.* 3:1; *Rom.* 1:1; *Phld.* 5:1). And like Polycarp, he describes his bonds as having a sacred significance. They are "spiritual pearls" (*Eph.* 11:2) or "most God-pleasing bonds" which he has been counted worthy to bear (*Smyr.* 11:1); they exhort his readers (*Tral.* 12:2); and it is in them that Ignatius "sings the praise of the Churches" (*Mag.* 1:2). It is perhaps in this metaphor of bearing the bonds of Jesus that the explanation of Ignatius' second name, Theophorus, is to be found (e.g. *Eph.* Inscr.; *Mag.* Inscr.).[94]

Whatever the explanation of Ignatius' second name, it is probable that he, together with the members of the Asia Minor churches, regarded his martyrdom as bearing a deep significance. "Why have I given myself up to death?" he asks his docetic opponents.

> Because near the sword is near to God; with the wild beasts is with God; in the name of Jesus Christ alone am I enduring all things, that I may suffer with him, and the perfect man himself gives me strength. (Smyr. 4.2)

If Christ did not really suffer, he argues in *Tral.* 10, then he is dying in vain; he is lying about the Lord. Behind these statements is an *a fortiori* argument which relies for its success on a recognition that Ignatius' anticipated death echoes the death of Christ (cf. *Rom.* 6:3). If Christ did not suffer, then why is he going to suffer? Since it is true that Ignatius is or will soon be suffering, the claim that Christ suffered is all the more vindicated. 'Of course, the docetists could have responded that he was begging the question by arguing this way, but for a group centred, as we shall see, on the symbols of Christ's death, it is Ignatius' anticipated martyrdom that provides his most powerful argument for Christ's true passion. Anyway, Ignatius was apparently not very optimistic about convincing his opponents (*Smyr.* 4:1). He expended most of his energy exhorting those relatively unaffected by docetic opinions, in order to ensure that his opponents enjoyed no further successes in these communities. If the members of this group recognized that Ignatius was participating to a large degree in a sacred reenactment of the drama of Christ's passion, this would have made his argument very compelling.

It was probably because of his perceived participation in what, for him, was the sacred symbol of Christ's suffering that Ignatius could portray his experience as a prisoner in sacrificial terms (*Eph.* 8:1; *Tral.* 13:3)[95] and describe "fighting with wild beasts" as a hope (*Eph.* 1:2). In fact, the symbolism of bloody martyrdom was probably associated in Ignatius' mind with supreme identification with Christ. In *Smyr.* 4:2, Ignatius states that he is enduring his tribulations so that he may suffer with Christ, and in *Rom.* 6:3, he states that he wishes to follow the example of Christ's passion.[96] It is in his suffering that he is becoming a true disciple (*Eph.* 3:1).

If the communities Ignatius addressed were convinced by his interpretation of his imprisonment and anticipated suffering — a claim we shall attempt to substantiate in the following section — it seems probable that he would have enjoyed a status which separated him from the rest of the community and earned him reverence. In the context of the group's beliefs, Ignatius was regarded as being in contact with a certain "awe-arousing centrality" which clothed him with a nimbus of authority. When he stated that he carried his bonds for the sake of Jesus Christ (e.g. *Tral.* 12:2), or that his chains were the bonds of Jesus (*Phld.* 5:1), the nearness to the sacred and group-defining symbols of his audience with which these statements endowed him set him apart from local members and conferred upon him an extraordinary quality. Those whom he addressed probably believed that, as a Christian about to be martyred, he was in intense contact with a very central feature of human existence and the cosmos. This enables us to account for his ability to exhort and admonish communities hitherto unconnected with him.

Ignatius' Charismatic Authority and the Sectarian Identity of the Asian Churches

According to Weber, the legitimacy of a charismatic leader's authority arises from the perception among his followers that it is their duty to recognize its authoritativeness and to act accordingly.[97] Such feelings of dutifulness on the part of the leader's followers cannot be comprehended without reference to their social context, beliefs, values, and interests. So too, Ignatius' charismatic appeal cannot be understood apart from his status as a prisoner and potential martyr — a status which was interpreted by him and his audience as echoing the passion of Christ. This way of interpreting his suffering and anticipated martyrdom would have placed him close to those symbols most meaningful to the group.

We are interested here in those general community beliefs, ideals, and norms which were associated with Christ and which contributed to the community's self-definition. An understanding of these phenomena provides the context necessary to make Ignatius' authority more intelligible. The relationship between that authority and the experiences and beliefs of the Asian communities has been overlooked by those who focus exclusively on theological aspects of Ignatius' thought in order to account for his leadership. According to Campenhausen, for example, Ignatius' authority originates in the fact that he "feels himself to be a man of the Spirit," and his position as a "pneumatic" "is simply a case of an exceptional heightening of the general 'spiritual' nature, as this is made known to and bestowed upon Christians as a corporate body. . . ."[98] Campenhausen adds that it was Ignatius' superior knowledge of spiritual matters that gave him superiority over others.[99] While this may be part of the explanation for his authority, it is not a full enough account of it. What is more important in this authority relation than how Ignatius "feels" himself to be, is the way he is perceived. Without reference to the beliefs of the group, the authority Ignatius possessed in the Asia Minor communities, several of which he had never met, is hard to understand.

It is here, however, that we must proceed cautiously. For we do not possess a definitive account of the beliefs of Ignatius' audience. How can we know that Ignatius' conviction of the importance of certain symbols was shared by the Asian churches? Indeed, there were members of that audience who held docetic beliefs. But having stated this, it is important to note that it seems unlikely that these members were in a majority position in these communities.[100] And it was not one unsure of the allegiance to his own beliefs who asked the Philadelphians and Smyrnaeans to send messengers hundreds of miles to congratulate the Antiochene Christians on their restoration of peace (*Phld.* 10:1; *Smyr.* 11:2-3; *Pol.* 7:2-3). Further, Polycarp describes Ignatius' letters as of great benefit (Pol. *Phil.* 13:2), a statement which indicates that he found in Ignatius' teaching and exhortation instruction that was compelling. But more importantly, the symbols of the death and resurrection of Christ were used by Polycarp in ways similar to Ignatius to define Christian existence.[101] If we add to these observations the recognition that Ignatius probably wrote his letters with the intended result of protecting his audiences from false teaching, it seems unlikely that he would have consciously employed imagery which had little significance to his readers. The high regard accorded Ignatius by Polycarp (Pol. *Phil.* 1:1; 9:1-2) probably indicates that Ignatius' use of symbolism and interpretation of the Christian life were consistent with the beliefs of certain portions of his audience.

Placing Ignatius and the Asian churches he addressed in a more general sectarian context facilitates our understanding of what made obedience to him a compelling duty. We recall from Bryan Wilson's sect type that sects emphasize exclusiveness, conceive of themselves as an elect, gathered remnant, and are hostile or indifferent to secular society and the state; their beliefs provide a framework for interpreting life both within and outside the group and for discerning the purposes that are thought to underlie the universe.[102] Wilson's ideal type is a useful heuristic tool to determine the self-defining beliefs of the Asian churches which contributed to their reception of and obedience to Ignatius. In particular, the close identification of the churches with Christ's death and resurrection, creating a framework within which all aspects of human life and experience were placed and interpreted, the self-conception of being an elect group marginal to the rest of society, together with a consciousness of being a privileged minority, provide a sectarian background of beliefs for Ignatius' authority.

The symbols of the suffering and raised Christ were of more than merely theoretical interest to Ignatius' readers — we are probably right to see them as definitive for their self-understanding. It is likely that these were group-defining symbols for most members of these communities.[103] In several passages Ignatius identifies Christians with the cross: he calls true members of the church "branches of the cross" (*Tral.* 11:2); in Smyr. 1.2 he describes them as the fruit of the cross and nailed upon it; Christian life springs up from Christ's death (*Mag.* 9:1; *Tral.* 2:1; cf. *Smyr.* 5:3); Christ is the life of the church (*Eph.* 3:2; 11:1; *Mag.* 1:2). Christians act and live in Christ's suffering, as, indeed, in his resurrection. This may be seen in *Phld.* Inscr., where the preposition ἐv with the dative is employed to describe the Philadelphians as rejoicing "in the passion of our Lord," and being "fully assured . . . in his resurrection."[104] In *Eph.* 1:1, Ignatius employs a phrase similar to "in the blood of Christ" used in the Philadelphian greeting and in *Smyr.* 12:2 to describe the aid offered to him.

If we may cautiously conclude that the symbols of Christ's death and resurrection functioned as group-defining images, in a way similar to that found in Ignatius' letters, then it seems probable that when the Syrian passed through these communities and interpreted his imprisonment with christological language, this would have made a profound impact on most members and marked him as an extraordinary example of devotion. These churches would have seen in Ignatius a supreme embodiment of the sacrally significant events defining their existence. His position as a potential martyr probably embodied in a concentrated or intense form the sectarian identity of a community defined by the symbols of the suffering and raised Christ.

Closely associated with the symbols of the suffering and resurrected Christ are references to special election. Such passages bespeak a privileged position of favour for the Asian communities. Language of election appears repeatedly in the Ignatian corpus and probably indicates a consciousness of separation from the rest of the world. In his salutation to the Ephesians Ignatius recalls images from New Testament Eph. 1:3f.[105] by describing that church as "predestined before the ages, for abiding and unchangeable glory, united and chosen through true suffering by the will of the Father and Jesus Christ our God. . . ." Direct language of election also appears in the opening of Ignatius' letter to the Trallians, where the Syrian prisoner describes this church as "elect and worthy of God, at peace in flesh and spirit by the suffering of Jesus Christ, who is our hope through our resurrection unto him."

But it is not only where Ignatius refers directly to election that there is evidence that he considered the Asia Minor communities as an elect group. Again, in a way which echoes the image employed in New Testament Eph. 2:20-22,[106] he uses the sacred image of a temple in *Eph.* 9:1 to portray the identity of the Ephesian church. He describes the Ephesians as "stones of the temple of the Father, made ready for the building of God our Father, carried up to the heights by the engine of Jesus Christ, that is the cross, and using as a rope the Holy Spirit." They are incorporated into a distinct sacred identity which distinguishes them from the rest of the world. In 9:2 the Ephesians are described as "all companions on the way, God-bearers and temple-bearers, Christ-bearers, bearers of holy things, in every way adorned with the commandments of Jesus Christ" (Schoedel trans.). He again makes use of the temple image in *Eph.* 15:3: "Let us do everything in the conviction that he dwells in us. Thus we shall be his temples and he will be our God within us".[107] The image of the indwelling Christ or God is repeatedly employed (*Mag.* 12:1; *Rom.* 6:3; cf. *Mag.* 14:1). All of these images indirectly testify to separation from the rest of the world, and a consciousness of being a special elect, enjoying the favour of God.

The sectarian language of separation is evidenced in passages which contrast the church with the world. In *Mag.* 5:2, Ignatius, identifying the members who meet apart from the bishop as unbelievers, writes

> just as there are two coinages, the one of God, the other of the world, and
> each has its own stamp impressed on it, so the unbelievers bear the stamp of
> this world, and the believers the stamp of God the Father in love through
> Jesus Christ. . . .

This is an example of a series of statements in which Ignatius speaks of the
world or the rest of society. Not all refer to separation, but there is an undercur-
rent of a sense of distinction from the rest of society. He hopes converts will be
won, but he is also conscious of society's hostility to the church. *Eph.* 10:1-3
contains Ignatius' most positive references to the outside world, but even here
there is a consciousness of being separate. He exhorts the Ephesians to pray for
the repentance of "other men", i.e., non-Christians,[108] but as the imprisonment
of Ignatius indicates, outsiders were not so accommodating. An indication that
these communities also suffered opposition appears in 10:2-3 where Ignatius
appeals to them to respond to the hostility of outsiders with openness. "Yield to
them therefore so that they may become disciples, at least through your deeds."

> Before their wrath be gentle, before their boasting be humble minded, before
> their slanderings offer prayers, before their error be steadfast in the faith;
> before their fierceness be gentle, not being eager to imitate them in return.
> (Trans. Schoedel with some alteration)

Consciousness of opposition from outsiders also appears in *Tral.* 8:2, where
he exhorts the Trallians not to have anything against their neighbours. Ignatius
connects church discord with outside opposition when he continues, "Do not
give any pretext to the gentiles, in order that the congregation in God may not
be slandered because of a few fools" (my translation). These passages imply an
awareness of being separate, alien, and vulnerable to outside persecution. When
Christianity is hated by the world it is characterized by greatness (*Rom.* 3:3).

It is peculiar that, aside from the two appearances of the term in *Mag.* 5:2,
Ignatius' only use of the term κόσμος appears in his Roman epistle (2:2; 3:2,3;
4:2; 6:1,2; 7:1). Among these passages, 3:3 and 7:1 contain the most direct contrasts between the the church and the world. There seems to be more here to
Ignatius' references to the world than a deepening of "negative attitudes toward
Rome shared by many an eastern inhabitant of the empire."[109] To a member of
a group which identified itself as separate from the wider society, it is more
likely that the imperial capital symbolized the world. A better interpretation
than that offered by Schoedel for Ignatius' numerous references to the world in
this epistle is that as the Syrian prisoner contemplated his anticipated martyrdom and the meaning of his identity as a member of a group conscious of being
separate, the world-church dichotomy became most explicit. He probably also
knew the tradition of Peter and Paul's martyrdom in Rome (*Rom.* 4:3),[110] and
this knowledge may have contributed to an association between Rome and the
world and to the identification of the capital as a symbol of opposition. Thus, it
was not primarily eastern hatred of Rome that resulted in the several references
to the world in the Roman epistle, but what Rome symbolized to a member of a
sect already conscious of its separateness.

The mythic imagery which describes "the prince of this age" also indicates
separation from the world. Scholars traditionally focus their attention on *Reli-*

gionsgeschichtliche and *Traditionsgeschichtliche* questions concerning Ignatius' use of such imagery to such a degree that they overlook the role it may have played in self-definition.[111] If we are to understand more fully the social meaning of certain images Ignatius employed, it is necessary to determine the role certain symbols played in his social world.

Wayne Meeks, in an essay on the man from heaven imagery in John's gospel, has shown that mythic language and social identity were related in early Christian groups.[112] Meeks asks what social function myths, such as the descending/ascending redeemer, played in John's community.[113] He recognizes that Johannine symbols were intended for a certain community, and that they reflected and integrated its self-identity, experience, and beliefs. Turning again to Ignatius, it seems possible to deduce a social identity from cosmic and mythic imagery employed by him. We must proceed cautiously, since symbols which were relevant to Ignatius may not have been meaningful to his readers. But Ignatius' direct contact with representatives and, in some cases, with the communities themselves, makes it likely that, even if his themes may have originated in another context, they will have been adapted to their new setting. Further, the position he enjoyed as an inspired instructor (*Eph.* 20:1-2; *Tral.* 5:1-2; cf. Pol. *Phil.* 13:2), allows us to suggest that Ignatius and portions of the communities shared a more or less similar symbolic universe.[114]

One of the "world passages" which appears in a more mythical context is *Rom.* 7:1.

> The prince of this age (ὁ ἄρχων τοῦ αἰῶνος τούτου) wants to abduct me and to corrupt my mind set on God. Let none of you present help him, rather be on my side, that is, God's. Do not profess Jesus Christ, and desire the world (κόσμος). (trans. Schoedel and Grant)

Professing Jesus Christ and desiring the world are contrasted as opposites, and the term κόσμος is apparently associated with the "prince of this age." The Romans are not to assist him — they are not to desire the world — rather they are to be on God's side, that is on the side of Ignatius' desire for martyrdom. References to the "prince of this age" reappear several times throughout Ignatius' correspondence (*Eph.* 17:1; 19:1; *Mag.* 1:2; *Tral.* 4:2; *Rom.* 7:1; *Phld.* 6:2). Grant notes that Ignatius employs the terms "age" (αἰών) and κόσμος synonymously[115] (as is most clearly evident in *Rom.* 6:1).[116] If this is the case, the ascription of "this age" to the rulership of the ἄρχων further defines the separation of the church from the world. Not only are these communities separated from society, their separation is symbolized by a belief concerning the ultimate powers controlling the realm of the church and that of the world.

Ignatius also identifies persecution by society as an attempt of the ruler of this age to destroy the church. In *Mag.* 1.2, Ignatius' persecution at the hand of authorities is interpreted as an act of this power. He writes: ". . . if we endure the whole abuse of the ruler of this age and escape, we shall attain God." The first person plural is ambiguous, since it is not clear from the context whether Ignatius is referring only to himself or to the Magnesians as well. But in *Smyr.* 9.2, he again alludes to endurance, this time clearly applying it generally.[117]

If the groups Ignatius addressed were conscious of being marginal in the way his descriptions of the world and their status as the elect suggest, it is plausible that as a martyr Ignatius would have embodied this marginality in a particularly striking way.[118] Although to the wider society he was a common criminal (*Tral.* 3:3; *Rom.* 4:3; cf. *Eph.* 12:1), to these communities he would have appeared as an embodiment of separation from the world and an extraordinary example of devotion in the face of hostile opposition. Ignatius' vivid and somewhat mythic language in *Rom.* 5:1, perplexing as it is to the modern reader, probably expressed for his contemporaries the struggle facing all Christians.

The basis of Ignatius' charisma can be more fully understood by placing Ignatius in the context of the group's wider beliefs and values. His authority arose out of a more general system of beliefs which were self-defining for the group and of supreme significance to them. Both as a marginal person suffering imprisonment by the world and as an individual who regarded himself, and perhaps was regarded by those to whom he wrote, as being identified with the passion of Christ, Ignatius was seen as an extraordinary embodiment of the group's values. By understanding Ignatius as a charismatic authority and placing him in a sectarian context, the social power he wielded becomes more readily explicable.

The Unworthiness of Ignatius

Ignatius' authority was not clear-cut. *Tral.* 4:1 and *Smyr.* 5:2 are evidence that he was aware of the reverence accorded him as a prisoner and potential martyr for Christ. However, here he is also critical of those who praise and revere him. Consonant with such criticism is his language of self-effacement: he describes himself as less than his audience (*Eph.* 12:1; *Mag.* 11:1), unworthy (*Mag.* 14:1; *Tral.* 4:1-2; 13:1; *Rom.* 9:2; *Smyr.* 11:1) — a self-effacing sacrificial victim (περίψημα, ἀντίψυχον — *Eph.* 8:1; 18:1; *Eph.* 21:1; *Smyr.* 10:2; *Pol.* 2:3; 6:1).[119] Why did Ignatius feel himself so unworthy? What constrained him to decline the honour accorded a potential martyr? Is such self-negation compatible with charismatic authority? It was precisely this ambiguity which led Streeter to suppose that Ignatius was neurotic.[120] Ignatius' references to his unworthiness, while in tension with a charismatic type of authority, are peculiar to his circumstances and analogous to statements of unworthiness employed by Paul, also a charismatic authority.

The complexity of these references to unworthiness originates in the ambiguity connected with contrary claims about his status. Ignatius sometimes interprets his bonds or status as a prisoner in sacral terms; at others times he refers to himself as a convict, even a slave (*Tral.* 3:3; *Eph.* 12:1; *Rom.* 4:3). Even though he describes himself in some places as bearing the bonds of Christ, in *Rom.* 9:2 he calls himself an "abortion" (ἔκτρωμα); he has the honour of suffering for the name, but regards himself as least (ἔσχατος) of the Antiochenes (*Eph.* 21:2; *Tral.* 13:1; *Rom.* 9:2; *Smyr.* 11:1; cf. *Mag.* 14). Schoedel, following Swartley, argues that this ambiguity is a real one, arising from a responsibility Ignatius felt for a lack of church unity in Antioch.[121] In our view, any opinions about what was or was not happening at Antioch during Ignatius' sojourn are highly tentative,[122] and it is not always evident that the freedom from care after the announcement of peace which Schoedel and Swartley adduce is as marked as they suggest. Three of the five instances of the term ἀντίψυχον (sacrificial language which Schoedel argues is indicative of self-effacement) appear *after* he learns of the peace! If Ignatius felt himself responsible for an Antiochene schism, then his self-deprecating language becomes explicable. But, in our opinion, conclusions on this matter are so speculative that the question must remain open.

Still, scepticism about attempts to locate the historical origins of Ignatius' unworthiness does not remove the difficulty of assessing its place in the context of his charismatic authority. Here it is important to remember that ideal types are not definitions. They are heuristic devices designed to isolate phenomena, such as Ignatius' feelings of unworthiness, which are then subjected to further analysis. Our understanding of his self-effacement is facilitated by focusing briefly on similar language used by an earlier charismatic authority, the apostle Paul.

Jacob Jervell captures the paradox of Paul's authority when he calls the apostle "the weak charismatic."[123] Its complexity emerges most clearly in 2 Cor. 10-12: Paul claims that he performed "signs and wonders and mighty works" (12:12), he endured hardships for the sake of Christ (11:23-28) — a heroic wonder-worker, in these passages he ascribes to himself the characteristics of a charismatic authority. But this portrait is obscured by references to his weakness, in which he, characteristically, boasts (11:30; 12:9-10).[124] Paul developed this theme as a strategic counter to criticisms: he knows that some say his personal presence is weak, his speech unimpressive (10:10). Rather than entering into a competition of claims and counter-claims with his opponents, he focuses on the power given him as a servant of Christ (12:9). When Paul is weakest, he is strongest. It is in his weakness that God's power shines forth and compensates for any of his shortcomings.[125] This paradoxical language is explicable sociologically as an instance of what Weber called routinized charisma.[126] Weber argued that Jesus had no successor; he was the only figure in the period of the early church to exercise a pure form of charisma.[127] All others, including Paul, possessed a derived or conferred form of charisma. Paul's separation of his person from his role as apostle is most clearly evidenced where he distinguishes between himself and the source of his authority (1 Cor. 7:10,12,25; 2 Cor. 4:5-7; cf. Gal. 1:8).[128] Paul *qua* Paul is nothing; *qua* apostle he is a heroic wonder-worker. His charisma resides in his role. His argument in 2 Cor. 10-12 rests upon this distinction.

Returning again to Ignatius' self-effacement, we find a similar form of routinized charisma. Ignatius is thrown in the role of a martyr for Christ, but feels himself unworthy of it; the authority he possesses is conferred upon him by virtue of his status as one imprisoned and about to die for the faith. *Smyr.* 11:1 contains the clearest reference to this conferred authority.

> I greet all as one who comes thence [from Syria] in bonds which are most God-pleasing, although I am not worthy to be from there, for I am the least (ἔσχατος) of them; but by the will of God I have been counted worthy, not because of the witness of my own conscience [thus Schoedel], but because of the grace of God. . . .

Ignatius may regard himself as personally unworthy, but he knows that the status of being a prisoner and future martyr for Christ is a worthy one. When he wants to emphasize the former, he can interpret his bonds in self-denigrating terms; but that status itself is sacred. Thus he is "counted worthy" (καταξιωθείς) to occupy it (*Mag.* 1:2). His future martyrdom rests solely in God's hands (*Rom.* 1:1; 9:2). Any authority he enjoys is derived from his circumstances, behind which he perceives God's activity.

Summary

Ignatius' authority is best understood as charismatic. Placing him in a sectarian context helps to explain his authority. In particular, his marginality and his identification with the suffering of Christ placed him in an extraordinary position. The paradoxical references to his worthiness are explicable in terms of a conferred or routinized form of charisma. We shall now show how Ignatius used his charismatic authority to strengthen existing institutions of leadership and protect the Asian churches from divisive influences.

Ignatius and Community-Protecting Charisma

Having classified Ignatius' authority as charismatic, it is necessary to inquire further concerning the role of his charisma in the the Asian communities. What was his contribution to the life of the group? What does that contribution reveal about local institutional needs?

In order to determine Ignatius' particular role it is necessary to describe more precisely the social significance of the conflict within those communities. This provides the context within which to place Ignatius' authority. The divisions between docetists and other members are not clear. In *Mag.* 3:2-4:1 Ignatius provides some significant clues regarding the attitude toward the bishop of those swayed by docetic beliefs. In 3:2 he refers to obedience toward the bishop without hypocrisy and deception: ". . . it is right to obey without hypocrisy; for the point is not that a man deceives this bishop who is visible, but that he tries to cheat him who is unseen; in such a matter the reckoning is not with flesh but with God who knows our secrets" (trans. Schoedel). What precisely he is referring to is indicated at the end of 4:1, where he alludes to members who do not act "in good conscience" because they do not meet "validly". Ignatius states (4:1), "It is right, then, not only to be called Christians but also to be Christians; just as some certainly use the title 'bishop' but do everything apart from him." On the basis of this description it seems that the members influenced by docetic teaching still regarded themselves as community members — they called themselves Christians,[129] they recognized in some sense the bishop, but without participating in the common eucharist.

Ignatius called this "hypocrisy." An alternative interpretation is that the divisions were not as clear as he portrayed them. Possibly those with docetic sympathies did not regard meeting for a separate eucharist as undercutting the authority of the bishop and in other respects they followed local leaders. According to *Smyr.* 7:1, docetists kept away from the common eucharist because of their rejection of the physical suffering of Christ, not because they were opposed to the bishop's authority.

A setting similar to that behind *Mag.* 3-4 is implied in Ignatius' description of deception in *Phld.* 7:1-2. In v.2 he records that some members suspected him of exhorting the community to preserve unity because he had previous knowledge of church division. No, he did not have human knowledge of this: "For even if some desired to deceive me after the flesh the spirit is not deceived, for it is from God." We may infer from this description that, unbeknownst to him, some of his opponents, or at least those sympathetic to them, were present when he delivered his prophetic utterance. His description of an act of deception may reflect a state of affairs in which divisions were not clearly drawn; members who met for separate eucharists were not necessarily separatist in other aspects of community life, and in the case of the meeting with Ignatius fully involved themselves.[130] Further the disrespect with which Philo and Rheus Agathopous were treated at Philadelphia (*Phld.* 11:1) may be interpreted as evidence that there the community was not divided explicitly.[131] This interpretation of the degree of division receives some further support from the fact that the opponents joined with the rest of the community in their reverence of him (*Smyr.* 5:2). In certain aspects the docetists[132] did not separate themselves, e.g., visiting Ignatius and following the bishop and the other ministers in affairs not having to do with the eucharist, but in other respects they did, e.g., celebrating their own eucharists and welcoming docetic teachers.

If this assessment is correct, what does this tell us about the challenges facing these churches? As we saw in Chapter Four, sects typically strive after totalitarian control of the lives of their members. The evidence listed above suggests that the totalitarian control over the actions of group members was being seriously threatened. Instead of maintaining a cohesive commonality of values and activities, the reception of docetic teaching resulted in the avoidance of the common meeting and division. Together with this arose a certain ambiguity among members: some recognized the authority of the bishop, presbyters, and deacons in some things, but not in everything; others followed them in all things.

Coser notes that in sectarian groups where a totalitarian control is exerted on members to conform to established beliefs and practices, any dissent is likely to result in great social turmoil.[133] He distinguishes between the impact made on the internal life of sects by renegades, heretics, and "dissenters."[134] Renegades, or apostates, provide the least problems because by shifting their loyalty to the out-group, their response is easily identifiable as a denial of the in-group's legitimacy. But in the case of heretics and dissenters the challenge is more profound.

> Whereas the [apostate] deserts the group in order to go over to the enemy, the heretic presents a more insidious danger: by upholding the group's central values and goals, he threatens to split it into factions that will differ as to the means for implementing its goal. Unlike the apostate, the heretic claims to uphold the group's values and interests, only proposing different means to this end or variant interpretations of the official creed.... The heretic proposes alternatives where the group wants no alternatives to exist.... In this respect, the heretic calls forth all the more hostility in that he still has much in common with his former fellow-members in sharing their goals.[135]

In the case of dissenters the confusion and threat to the sectarian group are even greater.

the dissenter creates even more confusion than the heretic who has left the group, for he claims belongingness. In small, struggling and close groups, the dissenter who still claims belongingness threatens to break up the group from within, for he does not represent to it the clear-cut danger of the heretic or apostate, against whom the group may find it easier to act concertedly. The dissenter is unpredictable and creates confusion: will he go over to the enemy? Or does he intend to set up a rival group? Or does he intend to change the group's course of action? His fellow-members can be sure only that he is 'up to something'. By attacking the unanimity of group feelings he obtrudes an element of personal choice into a structure which is based on unanimity of choice.[136]

Coser observes that in sectarian groups expression of dissent is not permitted and results usually in either expulsion of or withdrawal by the dissenter.

It is difficult to know whether to classify the activities of Ignatius' opponents as indicative of heresy or dissension. In this period notions of heresy and orthodoxy were in a process of development — a process to which Ignatius was probably a significant contributor. But it is plausible that the conflict had a character similar to "dissent." The situation in the churches was probably more ambiguous than Ignatius was willing to acknowledge. If we are correct that his opponents acknowledged the authority of the bishop, except in the matter of eucharistic practice, and that they were present with the rest of the community when it visited with Ignatius, it is likely that they threatened the well-being of the group in a way similar to the dissenter. If, however, they had entirely broken away, they may more appropriately be designated as heretical. Where there were groups which had not broken off from the community, but remained within it (such as seems to have been the case in Philadelphia), professing similar beliefs and perhaps holding the same values, such members would have represented an even greater challenge to the self-identity of the group.[137] If they met separately for their own eucharist but otherwise involved themselves in the life of the community, their presence would have brought confusion; it would not have been immediately clear whether they were separatist or not, whether their intention was to establish a rival group in competition with the one associated with the bishop's eucharist, or whether they intended to supplant the beliefs of the group with new interpretations.[138]

Berger and Luckmann note that the problem of heresy (and, we may add, dissension) is often "the first impetus for the systematic theoretical conceptualization of symbolic universes."[139] In meeting the challenge which an alternative interpretation presents, community leaders find the need to reflect on the symbolic universe they are defending, and, in doing so, discover new meanings within it, which lead to its expansion and development. Coser remarks similarly where he describes the positive ways in-group conflict contributes to the building of a community threatened by heretics or dissension:

a weakening of the group is not a necessary result of such [in-group] struggles. On the contrary, the perception of this inside 'danger' on the part of the remaining group members makes for their 'pulling together,' for an increase in their awareness of the issues at stake, and for an increase in participation; in short, the danger signal brings about the mobilization of all group

defenses. Just because the struggle concentrates the group's energies for purposes of self-defense, it ties the members more closely to each other and pro-
motes group integration.[140]

In the Asian communities, conflict provided an impetus to identify the
norms, beliefs, and values which helped to ensure harmonious community life.
As we will see below, conflict resulted in institution-building efforts as internal
divisions were made more explicit and as community life was more firmly attached to structures of leadership.

How did Ignatius use his charismatic authority to meet the challenges engendered by dissent? Weber emphasized the revolutionary qualities of the charismatic leader; according to his ideal type, the charismatic is destructive, radical,
and innovatory of the old order.[141] Weber has been criticized for emphasizing
too strongly these aspects of charisma. Friedrich argues that this understanding
of charisma is too general, and that it does not distinguish sufficiently between
various manifestations of charisma. According to Friedrich, not all charismatic
authorities initiate new orders, some use their leadership to preserve and maintain an existing one; not all charismatics are necessarily revolutionaries.

Friedrich introduces helpful distinctions which avoid some of the confusion
entailed by Weber's type. He distinguishes between initiating, maintaining, and
protecting charismatic leadership.[142] His distinctions are perhaps too firm, but
they provide a heuristic set of categories with which to explicate the way charisma can be exercised by leaders in different settings. In particular, his conception of the protecting type of charismatic leadership helps us to clarify Ignatius'
use of authority. Friedrich defines the use of charisma for protection as follows:

> Protecting leadership provides security for the following, more particularly
> security against bodily, physical destruction, but also security for a particular
> way of life, a culture and its values, beliefs and interests.[143]

We are interested here, of course, in the form of protection which involves
security for a group's values and beliefs, since it is on this level that Ignatius
attempted to insulate his audience from alien influences. Friedrich goes on to
argue that in the protecting type of leadership acclaim is elicited by the following who "willingly grant whatever is required to have their leader continue
those activities which provide the desired security."[144]

Now, while it seems to be the case, as we shall see below, that Ignatius is
involved in a community-protecting exercise of leadership, it must also be
recognized that his authority was relatively short-lived. Since, as a prisoner on
his way to execution, he was able to be in contact with the Asia Minor churches
for only a short time, the security arrangements which Ignatius formulated to
protect the community from the influence of harmful beliefs had necessarily to
be connected not with his person, but with more permanent structures. It was
in the already existing leadership that Ignatius found this more permanent
means of community protection. His protecting leadership can be seen most
clearly, therefore, where he exhorts his audience to be obedient to the established leaders in these churches.

But there is also an aspect of initiating to Ignatius' charismatic authority.
Friedrich writes, ". . . initiating leadership transcends the established system of

values as it proposes to conquer or to invent new values."[145] Ignatius was not a figure like Paul, engaged in community-founding activity, but he did provide a justification, which probably did not exist before his arrival in these communities, for established patterns of leadership. Moreover, this justification probably contributed to the emergence of monepiscopacy as a normative institutional form and as the preeminent agency of social control.

Using Friedrich's terminology, we may describe Ignatius' charismatic leadership as protecting and innovating. He used his position to protect the community from docetic influences by identifying norms which limited the likely success of his opponents, and by making explicit the obligations toward existing institutional structures. In these ways he helped to define more precisely local divisions communities and thereby provided a set of criteria by which to assess which activites were permissible.

Ignatius' efforts to solve the problems created by dissenting Christians resulted in the development of norms and the explication of ideals which were calculated to restore harmony and provide protection from those with unacceptable beliefs. His activity was institution building. We may describe him as an *entrepreneur*[146] who was able to offer solutions to local problems through the identification of the values, beliefs, and collective ideals which committed the community to rejection of dissenting opinions and practices.

In the following sub-sections we shall attempt to identify Ignatius' community-protecting strategies by discussing his insulating tactics, his identification of the beliefs of the group, and his exhortations to remain in unity with community leaders.

Insulating Tactics

Ignatius' attempts to lessen the influence of false teaching are easily identifiable. On the most general level, Ignatius was more concerned with the insulation of those potentially in contact with his opponents, than with the refutation of false teachers. We noted in Chapter Four that insulation is a means contemporary sects use to protect themselves from influences deemed dangerous to their identity. We may see a similar tactic employed here.

He exhorts his Smyrnaean readers not to have any contact with the docetists. "It is right to refrain from such men and not even to speak about them in private or in public. . . . Flee from divisions as the beginning of evils." (*Smyr.* 7:2) A similar admonition appears in *Smyr.* 4:1, where he again urges his readers not to receive (παραδέχεσθαι) docetists, probably into their homes,[147] nor to meet with them. In 5:3 his concern that his readers have no contact with his opponents is expressed by his refusal even to mention their names. Thus Ignatius' advice to the Smyrnaeans was to shun those who propagated docetic beliefs. This helped to establish boundaries between groups holding different beliefs, thereby facilitating the removal of ambiguity engendered by dissent in the church. By exhorting members to separate themselves, in effect he expelled his opponents from the group. He exhorts the other communities in similar ways. The Ephesians are to "shun" the docetic teachers "as wild beasts" (*Eph.* 7:1; cf. 9:1; 16:2; 17:1); the Magnesians are urged "not to fall into the snare of vain doctrine" (*Mag.* 11:1); the Trallians are to "guard against" those who "mingle Jesus

Christ with themselves" (*Tral.* 6:2-7:1), they are to be "deaf" when anyone speaks to them "apart from Jesus Christ" (9:1), and he instructs them to "fly from these wicked offshoots" (11:1). He urges the Philadelphians to "flee from division and wrong doctrine" (2:1; cf. 6:2). Further, he repeats the plant imagery used in *Tral.* 11:1 when he instructs, "Abstain from evil plants, which Jesus Christ does not cultivate, because they are not the planting of the Father. . . ." And, like the Trallians, they are not to listen to his opponents (6:1).

This paraenesis is evidence of the mobilization of group resources to limit the effect of false teaching. A probable consequence of the "flight" which he advised would have been that already existing divisions became greater. The endeavour to protect the community probably helped to limit the influence of teachers who held differing beliefs. But where Ignatius' protective measures were enacted, they may also have polarized members. He did not seek to make internal boundaries impenetrable – in some cases he still hoped for the repentance of dissenters (e.g. *Smyr.* 4:1), but it seems probable that if his advice was followed, there must have arisen profound divisions.[148] Increased internal definition of this sort focused the attention of members on potentially divisive activities. This in turn could have resulted in increased unity among those attempting to insulate themselves from false teaching.

Protection Through Definition of Belief

A second means of protecting the group was the definition of beliefs. Charismatic leaders are typically believed to be in close contact with the realities which define and govern human action. As one believed to be in proximity to the group's defining or awe-inspiring symbols it seems probable that Ignatius was regarded as a mediator of sacred truths. Not only when he boasted of his abilities to describe transcendent realities (*Tral.* 5), or presented the cosmic history of salvation (*Eph.* 19) did he demonstrate this ability; he also showed it when he presented basic group beliefs. These statements are more than credal utterances; issuing from a charismatic mediator of divine truth, it may be supposed that their force was great.

Ignatius presents several short statements of belief (*Eph.* 7:2; 18:2; *Mag.* 11; *Tral.* 9; *Smyr.* 1; *Pol.* 3:2). The fullest one appears in *Smyr.* 1:1-2, where he writes that Jesus is

> truly of the family of David according to the flesh, Son of God according to the will and power of God, truly born of a virgin, baptized by John that all righteousness might be fulfilled in him, truly nailed for us in the flesh under Pontius Pilate and Herod the Tetrarch – from the fruit of which are we, from his divinely blessed passion. . . .

Zahn argued that this statement indicates that Ignatius possessed a definitive baptismal creed.[149] Later scholars, calling this interpretation into question, argue for a slower development of credal formulation. Kelly contends against Zahn that credal statements developed slowly in the context of the demands and events of daily church life, such as "the day-to-day polemic of the Church, whether against heretics within or pagan foes without."[150] Campenhausen also states this and argues that Ignatius was the first writer to use semi-credal statements as a means of refutation of opponents. Ignatius' statements represent a transition from simple confession of Christ to formulated statements of belief, encapsulated in short phrases.[151] He, however, does not admit fully enough of the possible influence of traditional elements.[152] Ignatius probably used already existing semi-credal material, but employed it in a novel way for polemical purposes, interpolating it with anti-docetic statements in order to meet challenges facing the Asia Minor churches.

The anti-docetic phraseology in the statements listed above is commonly recognized. Several of these appear in the passage cited from Smyrnaeans. "Truly" (ἀληθῶς) is a favourite anti-docetic adverb which Ignatius uses to emphasize the physical incarnation (cf. also *Mag.* 11; *Tral.* 9); the inclusion of a reference to Pilate, as indeed Herod, also functions ground the incarnation firmly in history (cf. also *Mag.* 11; *Tral.* 9);[153] references to Christ being of the family or seed of David and to Mary have a similar purpose (cf. also *Eph.* 7:2; 18:2; *Tral.* 9:1).[154] But alongside these more obvious examples there are other terms and phrases which he freely used to stress the reality of Jesus' incarnation, such as the reference in *Smyr.* 2 to Jesus' "divinely blessed passion". Similarly, in *Eph.* 7:2 his description of Jesus as "first passible and then impassible" emphasizes the physical passion by appearing as the last in a series of antitheses, as does the order of these adjectives introduced by the word πρῶτος. [155] In *Mag.* 11 there is a reference to the πάθος, as indeed the γέννησις and ἀνάστασις of Jesus. One may find similar concerns in less typical descriptions: Christ as σαρκικός, ἐν ἀνθρώπῳ, ἐν θανάτῳ in *Eph.* 7:2; the reference to Christ as one who "both ate and drank" in *Tral.* 9:1; the statement of Jesus' "blood" in *Smyr.* 1.

The appearance of these statements in often polemical contexts implies that they were intended as regulative statements.[156] In *Tral.* 9:1, for example, Ignatius urges his readers to be "deaf" to anyone who speaks "apart from Jesus Christ" and then proceeds to list a series of beliefs which he regards as true; we may interpret this as a formulation to determine who such persons might be. Through this definition of belief he hopes to curtail the reception of false teaching. In *Eph.* 7:1, Ignatius cautions the Ephesians to be on their guard for his opponents, and then (v.2) includes a statement of belief. This provided a means of following his advice and of limiting the potential "deception" which Ignatius believed his opponents to practise (8:1). Such statements helped to sharpen the boundaries of groups contending for allegiance and thereby served to protect members from the ambiguities which threatened the solidarity of the community.

Ignatius' far-reaching contribution was the initiation of a formal criterion to assess orthodox belief. Through his handling of his disputants, dissension began to be regarded in a more formal sense as heresy.[157] Here for the first time the terms ἑτεροδοξεῖν (*Smyr.* 6:2) and ἑτεροδοξία (*Mag.* 8:1) begin to describe doctrinal error. This is probably true also of the term ἑτεροδιδασκαλεῖν (*Pol.* 3:1), although it finds similar application in the Pastoral Epistles (1 Tim. 1:3; 6:3).[158] Also, Ignatius' letters mark the first appearance in Christian literature of the term αἵρεσις as a pejorative description of a teaching (*Eph.* 6:2; *Tral.* 6:1).[159] Hermas employs this term in a way similar to more primitive Christian usage (cf. *Sim.* 9:23.5); αἵρεσις for him refers pejoratively to factions, but there is no connection to doctrine. For Ignatius, however, αἵρεσις refers to divisions based on points of a doctrinal nature.[160] His semi-credal statements provided a standard with which to measure the acceptability of teaching which was introduced into the community. His protective leadership may be seen here also as innovatory. By weaving together traditions into polemical definitions of belief, he contributed to the creation of formal norms of belief. His investment of the term αἵρεσις with doctrinal meaning as well as his use of the terms ἑτεροδοξία, ἑτεροδοξεῖν, and ἑτεροδιδασκαλεῖν to describe his opponents, provided a second means of neutralizing the danger of dissenting factions.

Protection Through Unity With Leaders

The community-protecting tactic Ignatius employed was to place all aspects of community life under local supervision. Ignatius' emphasis on the authority of the bishop is what he is famous for, but scholars have not adequately addressed the degree to which Ignatius' conception represents a departure from structures which existed before him. In order to understand this more fully, we shall first tentatively reconstruct leadership structures before his arrival. Then we shall portray his picture of community leadership as an innovation derived from the house church.

Opinions have been diverse concerning the form of community leadership which existed before Ignatius' sojourn in Asia Minor. Some have interpreted Ignatius' letters as evidence that he was not introducing anything new: monarchical episcopacy was an already established institution.[161] Others have suggested that Ignatius' description of monarchical bishops reveals more about his ideals than reality; Ignatius was virtually a creator of monepiscopacy.[162] Both of these reconstructions do not take sufficiently into account the evidence of institutional leadership in Asia Minor before Ignatius' arrival there. Ignatius' contribution to local leadership patterns was to mould already existing institutions into tighter organizational units and to make explicit already existent authority relations.

Any reconstruction of patterns of leadership in these churches before Ignatius' arrival is tentative; it requires hypothesizing what may have been true in one situation on the basis of what we know about another. Still, it is useful to make the attempt to measure Ignatius' picture of leadership against earlier patterns because such a comparison facilitates the identification of his contribution to existing institutional structures.

The earliest clue comes from New Testament Ephesians.[163] Our discussion of the New Testament evidence of the ministry showed that the reference to ποιμένες in *Eph.* 4:11 is probably to be taken as a reference to ἐπίσκοποι. Acts 20:17ff. contains another reference to Ephesian leaders — this time presbyter-bishops (vv. 17, 28). Given the association of πρεσβύτεροι and ἐπίσκοποι in other roughly contemporary literature, it seems probable that our earliest reference to the leadership of the Ephesian community reflects a similar pattern. But if there was a common meeting from an early date, it is unlikely that all presbyter-bishops enjoyed the same amount of authority, even if titles were the same. If there was in Ephesus a common meeting from an early date of the kind hinted at in New Testament Rom. 16:23, it is reasonable to suppose that its host would have had a distinctive role in the community and that such a role could have contained the seeds for further institutional growth. Evidence from 3 John supports this supposition.

Other evidence may be gleaned from the Johannine literature. John, the author of the Apocalypse, has been seen as a monarchical bishop, but he describes himself as a prophet, not a bishop (Rev. 1:3; 10:11; 19:10; 22:7,9,10,18,19). Again, the references to the angels of the churches in Rev. 2:1,8,12,18 and 3:1,7,14 have been interpreted as descriptions of monarchical bishops. This, if true, would be significant, since two of the seven churches are Ephesus and Smyrna and because the document probably antedates Ignatius' letters. But there are problems with this interpretation: there is no unambiguous evidence for episcopal authority in Revelation and it may be asked how an individual could be held responsible for the character of a church. Better interpretations are that the angels are either personifications of the churches or their angelic guardians.[164]

3 John sheds more light on one possible pattern of organization before Ignatius. We have already argued that the action of Diotrephes is of a house-church host attempting to protect the church meeting in his home from missionaries whom he feared were bringing false teaching. Scholars have attempted to see in the conflict between Diotrephes and the Elder a dispute between two different types of ministry.[165]

Streeter theorized that the Elder was a metropolitan and Diotrephes was a monarchical bishop.[166] We have already argued against the latter contention.[167] The former is also unconvincing: if such an institution had developed toward the end of the first century, it is very odd that there is no hint of its existence in Ignatius' letters. Ignatius hoped, as we shall see, to insulate certain Asia Minor churches from false teaching by connecting community activities with formal leaders. The absence, therefore, of any mention of a metropolitan (a potential agent of great social control), would be extremely puzzling, especially in his letter to the Ephesians, were Streeter's view correct. The revised view, that the presbyter was a monarchical bishop is also unconvincing.[168] The title πρεσβύτερος is too enigmatic to permit a connection it with any one community. It is better interpreted as a more general title unconnected with any one community.[169] Thus, attempts to find evidence of monarchical episcopacy in this literature fail.

Nonetheless 3 John contains valuable information concerning the potential power of a single leader in the early church. Lieu, attempting to place the dispute between Diotrephes and the Elder in a general social context, interprets Diotrephes' action as representative of a movement toward a single authority similar to that described by Ignatius.[170] If this interpretation is correct, we may see in Diotrephes' attempts to preserve the community from false teaching the kind of action which Ignatius wished bishops to carry out, even though in the former case without a formal monepiscopal position of the type he envisioned.[171]

The case of Diotrephes illustrates that the absence of certain formal distinctions later drawn by Ignatius does not exclude the possibility of such differentiation existing *de facto*. Further, the power of Diotrephes, which probably arose from his position as a host of the church, points to the way the household could have contributed to the emergence of monepiscopacy; such an influence would illustrate once again the way secular facilities affected the development of early Christian sects.[172] We must, therefore, be careful not to assume that Ignatius was the creator of a new system of authority. On the other hand, the earlier evidence does not allow us to make the other claim that monepiscopacy of the formal kind Ignatius describes had always existed in these communities. Ignatius had an uphill struggle in his efforts to ensure the kind of social control he wanted bishops to practise. His letters point to a position somewhere between these two extremes and are best interpreted to support a view which regards monepiscopacy as an emerging phenomenon.

In order to gain a fuller understanding of that emergence, it is necessary to place this development in its proper context. Ignatius' intentions in asserting the authority of the bishop can only be determined by reference to the more general situation. His support of local leaders is a further means of erecting boundaries to protect the community from the influences of his opponents.

He urges his audience to be subject (ὑποτάσσεσθαι) to the community leaders (Eph. 2.2; Mag. 2.1; 13.2; Tral. 2.1-2; 13.2; Pol. 6.1; cf. 2.1); to obey or respect them (Eph. 6.1; 20.2; Mag. 3.1,2; Tral. 3.1; Phld. 7.1); to be in harmony or in union with them (Eph. 4.1; 5.1; Mag. 6.1,2; 7.2; Tral. 12.2; Phld. inscr.; 8.1). A similar pattern appears where Ignatius defines a valid meeting as one in which the community leaders are present. Nothing can be called a church without the bishop, presbyters, and deacons (Tral. 3.1). The connection of the true church with the bishop also occurs where he exhorts members to follow the bishop as sheep their shepherd (Phld. 2.1). He similarly defines the true church where he states that anyone in the sanctuary is pure and connects impurity with acting apart from church leaders (Tral. 7.2; cf. Eph. 5.2-3). More particularly, and in contrast to the earlier evidence, Ignatius draws a distinction between bishops and presbyters. It is primarily the bishop whom he identifies as the person to control all aspects of community life. His emphasis upon the authority of the bishop may be seen where he singles out the bishop alone for special reference (e.g. *Eph.* 3:2-4:1; 6:1; *Phld.* 1:1-2; *Smyr.* 9:1). He is above the presbyters and deacons (*Mag.* 3:1; *Tral.* 12:2; cf. *Eph.* 4:1; *Mag.* 2); he summons councils (*Pol.* 7:2)[173] and has responsibility over funds for widows (*Pol.* 4:1). But more importantly, Ignatius permits no meetings[174] to occur apart from (ἄνευ) the bishop or without (χωρίς) his permission (*Phld.* 7:2; *Smyr.* 8:1-2; *Pol.* 4:1). Similar uses of χωρίς and ἄνευ appear in non-Christian literature to assert political and administrative authority.[175] Ignatius' application of these terms implies that he places all aspects of community life under stricter episcopal supervision. Ignatius wants the bishop to decide where and by whom the eucharist may be celebrated (*Smyr.* 8:1-2); he alone can authorize baptisms and agape meals; he even determines the frequency of meetings (*Pol.* 4:2).

But two qualifications are necessary, for there is evidence that Ignatius' ideals did not always harmonize with the realities of life. First, there is some indication that his portrait of episcopal control gave more authority to bishops than they were accustomed to. A hint that Ignatius was trying to regulate community activities more firmly than normal is where he urges Polycarp, "Become more diligent than you are" (*Pol.* 3:2). The anti-docetic christological antitheses which follow imply that he is to attend to the prevention of divisions.[176] The division in Smyrna probably involved an official who used his position to establish alternative meetings. Ignatius' instruction, therefore, that only a eucharist celebrated by the bishop or his appointee is valid (*Smyr.* 8:1) may be indicative of a situation in which Polycarp did not have the episcopal control implied elsewhere. Schoedel correctly infers that "the office of bishop did not mean as much in Smyrna as Ignatius would like to have thought."[177] Ignatius portrays alternative meetings as a rejection of the bishop's authority, but perhaps he ascribed a degree of community leadership to the bishop which had not hitherto existed.

A further indication appears (again in *Smyr.* 8:2) where he places agape meals under the direct supervision of the bishop. The practical difficulties of controlling the behaviour of hosts who welcomed docetic teachers into their homes and conducted such meetings would have been compounded by the legitimacy of the householder's authority to welcome guests as he wished. If we are correct that presbyters welcomed smaller groups into their homes, even if they did not receive false teachers, the forces contributing to a decentralization of authority must have been great. Ignatius' attempts to enhance a centralized form of control are especially significant in a situation where such stresses and strains could destroy or at least seriously divide local communities organised on this basis. Possibly meetings such as agape meals customarily occurred without the knowledge of the bishop and Ignatius is attempting here to establish stricter regulations concerning activities such as these.

A second qualification centres on the relationship of the ἐπίσκοπος to other leaders. Ignatius increases the control of the bishop over community affairs, but he also associates the bishop very closely with the presbyters and deacons (*Eph.* 2:1,2; 20:2; *Mag.* 6:1,2; 13:1; *Tral.* 3:1; 13:2; *Phld.* inscr.; 4; 7:1; 8:1; *Smyr.* 12:2; *Pol.* 6:1) and thereby treats all leaders as a unified whole. In most of these references Ignatius urges subjection to the leaders generally, not to the bishop alone. Streeter exaggerates when he writes that the importance of the bishop had become an obsession to Ignatius.[178] Ignatius strengthened the authority of the episcopate, but with a view to strengthening the authority of all leaders, not one in isolation from the others. Even in this strengthened position, the bishop is less a "monarchical" bishop, in the later sense of the term,[179] than a president of a body of elders or "monepiskopos" who acts together with them and the deacons in the leadership of the community.[180]

A close connection between the bishop and presbyters is further suggested by the form of Polycarp's greeting to the Philippians, where he writes "Polycarp and the Elders with him to the Church of God sojourning in Philippi" (*Phil.* inscr.).[181] It is sometimes suggested that the ambiguity of this salutation was purposely formulated by Polycarp with a view to a more primitive church order in Philippi, since in his letter there is no mention of a single bishop (Pol. *Phil.* 5:3; 5:2; 6:1).[182] This is possibile, but a better explanation is that his position was very close to that of the presbyters. Although in an important sense distinct from them, he was united so closely as to present himself virtually as a fellow elder.

Still, Ignatius' use of ἐπίσκοπος as a singular term of reference is unique. He could identify an individual around whom the local church was to unite. He would not have connected community activities so closely with such figures had there not already existed such persons identifiable and commonly accepted by members. It is reasonable to suppose that this usage arose from a situation in which a dominant presbyter-bishop led a number of presbyter-bishops. This explains the close connection Ignatius makes between the bishop and his presbyters, as well as the intimations of a less centralized form of leadership than Ignatius' ideal picture might otherwise lead one to suppose. His contribution was not wholly new, but a novel way of naming what was already in existence. In a situation where the common meeting probably took place in the home of the ἐπίσκοπος or leading presbyter-bishop, it is reasonable to suppose that, like Diotrephes, such a figure would have had a dominant role in community life. Ignatius' conception of community leadership in which such a dominant member was at the head is best understood as reinforcing social impulses inherent in a situation in which the hierarchically ordered Graeco-Roman household was adopted as a means of church organization. He used already existing currents within the community for its protection. His understanding of the church led by a single bishop may be seen as both arising from and reinforcing, as well as bringing to more definitive expression, certain social forces already present in house churches governed by hosts.

Interpreted as a means of sect consolidation, the practical effect of Ignatius' support of the bishop was to define local divisions more precisely. By presenting the separation of members from the common assembly as a rejection of the authority of formal institutions of leadership, he was able to show how their behaviour failed to accord with group beliefs and ideals. This enabled him to promote a heightened consciousness of community divisions among his audience. Further, through increasing social control by the bishop, he helped to protect members from the influence of divergent beliefs. Ignatius' conception of the church is not merely where two or three are gathered, but where the bishop or one whom he appoints presides (*Tral.* 3:1; *Smyr.* 8:1-2); by linking the legitimacy of meetings with such more formal agencies, he provided an institutional means to control the reception and propagation of false teaching. Through him institutions of leadership were more formally distinguished within the community and made part of the church's self-definition.

Summary

Ignatius' charismatic authority was protective and innovatory. He exercised his authority to protect these communities from the influence of divergent beliefs and thereby increased community definition and structure. Insulation, the definition of belief, and the circumscription of community activities to the control of the bishop helped to neutralize the danger presented by internal dissent. In the final case, he gave formal expression to structures of authority inherent in the house-church organization of these communities. He thereby helped to make a certain pattern of community life normative and to contribute to the control of belief within the local churches.

Legitimation

In order to increase the control of leaders and thereby insulate the communities from the influences of his opponents, it was necessary for Ignatius to show how the beliefs of the community committed them to support existing or latent authority structures. He focused his attention on the legitimation of institutions of leadership.

Scholars have not assessed accurately the relationship between Ignatius' formulations of beliefs and the development of authority structures in these churches. By directing their attention to ideas alone, many investigators have failed to recognise the function of ideas and beliefs in meeting specific needs. Ernst Dassmann argues that theological conceptions of the monarchy of God were the sole determinants of monarchical episcopacy: belief in one God, the idea that the earthly order reflects the heavenly hierarchy, and beliefs about relations within the heavenly order resulted in monepiscopacy.[183]

One may criticize this position by questioning the degree to which Ignatius believed that earthly structures of leadership were reflections of a heavenly realm. More importantly, it is methodologically unsound because of the insufficiency of accounting for institutions by ideas alone. A fuller understanding of the role of ideas is facilitated by placing them in the context of the community's social structures and needs. Ignatius' letters imply that beliefs may have influenced the shape of institutions by reinforcing social impulses in house churches. Ideas alone cannot account adequately for the emergence of monepiscopacy, nor is their role understood accurately if separated from local social challenges.[184] Neither can social arrangements alone explain it. Only by reference to an interaction between ideas and social structures will a more accurate picture emerge. Inasmuch as Ignatius used specific ideas to reinforce the authority of certain roles and those roles accorded well with local beliefs and ideals, he was engaged in the legitimation and construction of leadership institutions.

Berger and Luckmann's model of legitimation provides us with a useful heuristic device with which to analyse the kind of legitimation found in these letters. Their fourth level of legitimation, that of the symbolic universe, provides a useful way of assessing Ignatius' role in the structural development of the Asian churches and of explaining how he provided the support of the authority of local leaders necessary for protection and insulation from false teaching. According to Berger and Luckmann, the advent of heresy results in the development of a "systematic theoretical conceptualization of symbolic universes"; as a result of this theorizing new implications within the original symbolic universe are discovered and that universe is developed in new directions, both on the level of belief and of practical institutional arrangements.[185] Chief among Ignatius' tactics to protect the churches from deviant belief was connecting community activities more closely to the oversight of a leading bishop. He reinforced episcopal authority by showing how the group's beliefs committed members to support local leaders. By connecting different ranks within the group's structures of leadership with different orders of authority which were contained in its symbolic universe, he helped to make those structures explicit and subjectively plausible. The hierarchical structure of the Graeco-Roman household was an important factor in determining the form that this process of legitimation took. The explication of beliefs about hierarchical relations between the group's defining symbols was relevant in view of certain hierarchical patterns already emerging from house-church structures of leadership.

As a charismatic in privileged contact with the group's awe-inspiring symbols, Ignatius was in a position to explicate the relations between the heavenly and earthly order (esp. *Tral.* 5:2). Since the appearance of Hans Schlier's seminal work it has been repeatedly asserted that Ignatius' conception of church and ministry rests on the belief that the earthly order is a reflection of the heavenly one.[186] In 1938, Theodore Preiss followed Schlier's lead by arguing that at the root of Ignatius' concern to be martyred was a gnostic conception of imitation. Preiss rightly focused on unity as the centre of Ignatius thought; the term "union" (ἕνωσις) and its cognates are a distinctive formulation Ignatius uses to express community ideals.[187] But he argued incorrectly that Ignatius based his exhortations to be unified upon the conviction that the church was an earthly copy of heavenly unity. According to Preiss, "L'union est la qualité essentielle du monde spirituel"; indeed, "... Ignace ne se contente pas de rappeler que Dieu est un, il va jusqu' à identifier l'unité a Dieu. ..."[188] These statements are based on the apparent identification of unity with God in *Tral.* 11:2 and *Eph.* 14:1, and passages in which the root ἕν- with a genitive referring to either God or Christ occurs (e.g. *Mag.* 1:2).

Preiss interpreted the genitives which refer to God or Christ in the "unity" passages listed above as objective genitives. This led him to suggest, that unity in Ignatius' letters is a soteriological concept.[189] Earlier this century Bauer argued that they should be understood as genitives of source – a position put forward most recently by Schoedel.[190] Interpreted in this way, the genitives refer not to a goal to be reached in order to win salvation, but a state of affairs which is created by God; they express an ecclesiological rather than a soteriological concern. This interpretation fits better with Ignatius' general instructions that there be no meetings apart from the bishop. Unity with the bishop reflects a sacred state of affairs which follows from right belief; the divisions which his opponents create do not originate with God, they are the devil's handiwork (*Eph.* 13:1; 17:1; *Tral.* 8:1; *Phld.* 6:2; *Smyr.* 9:1; cf. *Pol. Phil.* 7:1).

If we are correct that terms of unity in these letters do not refer primarily to a mystical theology of union, but rather to church unity, the other evidence which Preiss adduces for his interpretation should be interpreted in another way. The identification of unity with God in *Eph.* 14:1 and *Tral.* 11:2 should be interpreted in the light of the use of the relative pronoun with the verb εἶναι throughout the epistles. Ignatius is fond of these constructions. Many instances are relatively straight forward (*Eph.* 9:1; 14:1; 17:2; 18:1; 20:2; *Mag.* 8:2; 10:2; *Tral.* 11:1,2; *Rom.* 5:1; *Phld.* inscr.; *Smyr.* 5:3), but some are more difficult to construe (*Mag.* 7:1; 15; *Tral.* 6:1; 8:1; *Rom.* 7:3). Among these latter passages we may place *Tral.* 11:2 and *Eph.* 14:1. A real difficulty arises if one attempts to interpret literally the identification apparently expressed in these passages; it is best to see their function not as the equation of two or more diverse realities but as the creation of striking juxtapositions.[191] It is unnecessary to postulate that Ignatius literally identifies unity and God. The striking identification of faith and love together as God in *Eph.* 14:1 is best understood as a highly compressed way of expressing what he states in *Phld.* 8:1: where these virtues are present (especially when in the context of a united community), God is present.

Henry Chadwick argues in a slightly different way that for Ignatius the earthly ministry is a reflection of the heavenly hierarchy.[192] Noting that Ignatius identifies God and silence (*Eph.* 19:1; *Mag.* 8:2; cf. *Eph.* 15) and that he associates the bishop with God (*Eph.* 5:3; *Mag.* 6:1; *Tral.* 3:1; *Smyr.* 8:1-2), Chadwick contends that the bishop's silence (*Eph.* 6:1; *Phld.* 1:1) imitates God's silence; behind these conceptions is a view that "the earthly church is nothing less than a microcosm in which the relationships of the heavenly hierarchy are to be found reflected."[193]

Chadwick is correct to note parallels in Ignatius' letters between earthly and heavenly powers, but there is not enough consistency in these to merit the conclusions which he draws from them. Even where Ignatius draws the most consistent parallels (between the bishop and the Father) he is sometimes inconsistent. In *Tral.* 2:1, Ignatius exhorts his readers to be subject to the bishop "as to Jesus Christ". This could perhaps be explained by Ignatius' high christology, which on occasion identifies God and Jesus, but for the parallelism to be consistent, it would have been necessary to identify the bishop with the Father alone. Yet later in the same section (3:1) he urges the Trallians to respect the deacons "as Jesus Christ", and follows with the more usual comparison between the bishop and presbyters and the Father and the Apostles (*Mag.* 6:1; *Smyr.* 8:1; cf. *Phld.* 5:1). Further, the strict hierarchy which Chadwick and others argue reflects the heavenly state is not consistent on the lower levels of leadership; Ignatius relates both the presbyters and the deacons to the "command of God" or "law of Jesus Christ" (*Smyr.* 8:1; *Mag.* 2). Although deacons are lower than presbyters, they are sometimes linked with a higher metaphysical rank (*Mag.* 6:1; *Tral.* 3:1).

Admittedly, these difficulties should not detract from the significance of the parallelism which does appear between the community leaders and their counterparts. It reinforces the authority of the local authorities and is an instance of justification of authority and ethical behaviour.

There are a number of levels on which this justification occurs. But at the centre is an argument for being submissive to local authorities, rather than an interest in identifying ministers with a heavenly hierarchy. Generally, these parallels link structures of authority with the sacred defining symbols of the group. When Ignatius stated that the local communities were to be subject to the bishop as to God the Father, or to the presbyters as to the apostles, or to the deacons as to Christ, he was increasing their authority by linking local institutions to what was regarded as central to human existence.[194]

This is perhaps clearest in the case of the bishop. Ignatius indicates in several passages that at the head of the community is God. In Pol. inscr. he states that Polycarp (as presumably the Smyrnaean church) "has for his bishop God the Father and the Lord Jesus Christ". A similar conception appears in Rom. 9.1. These references imply that God is the true ordering power of the community and further that those who keep themselves apart from what Ignatius defines as the church (i.e., where the community leaders are present) do not belong to groups ultimately governed by God the Father or, more significantly for a sectarian Christian group, Jesus Christ. As the references to the devil listed above suggest, they are under the power of Satan.[195]

The bishop as head of the legitimate meeting, is God's representative. In *Eph.* 6:1, the image of a master and his representative is used to indicate the divinely conferred authority which the bishop receives. To yield to the bishop, which means primarily not to engage in divisive activities, is to yield to God's purposes. That purpose is primarily expressed in the assembly which believes in the physical incarnation. Thus, when in *Mag.* 3:1, Ignatius states that in yielding to Damas, the presbyters yield "not indeed to him, but to the Father of Jesus Christ, the bishop of all," he is not identifying as metaphysical parallels a heavenly rank with an earthly one. He intends to state that the bishop represents a group which holds fast to correct beliefs and practices, and by submitting to him members are in fact submitting to God. As a representative of the purposes of God, the bishop is in contact with a certain awe-arousing centrality, which confers authority upon him.

In the case of the presbyters and deacons the case is more complex, but ultimately the parallels with sacred symbols function in a similar way. Perhaps most difficult is the connection Ignatius makes between the presbyters and the apostles (*Mag.* 6:1; *Tral.* 2:2; *Phld.* 5:1; *Smyr.* 8:1). A possible interpretation is that the presbyters are reflections of a heavenly council of apostles seated around the throne of God in heaven (cf. Rev. 4:4). But the image in John's Apocalypse is open to other interpretations, and Ignatius probably did not intend this. He generally conceives of the apostles as great heros of the past. In *Rom.* 4:3, he contrasts himself with Peter and Paul; again, in *Phld.* 9:1 the order: Abraham, Isaac, prophets, apostles, church probably indicates the temporal sequence of salvation history. Further, he refers to the historical subjection of the apostles to Christ (*Mag.* 13:2; cf. 7:1).[196] Ignatius' connection of the apostles with the presbyters is best interpreted as designed to strengthen their authority by associating them with awe-inspiring historical figures. Respect for presbyters is to be on the same level as respect for the apostles. The office of deacon is also connected with what is awe-arousing merely by paralleling it with Christ (*Tral.* 3:1), or, perhaps more appropriately to their appointed tasks, with the service (διάκονια) of Christ (*Mag.* 6:1). Like bishops and presbyters, they also are directly associated with the will of God by their association with the "law of Jesus Christ" (*Mag.* 2) or the "command of God" (*Smyr.* 8:1). Ignatius' purpose is not to portray a hierarchy parallel with heavenly authorities, but to strengthen local institutions of leadership. By connecting them with sacred symbols of authority it follows that members must abstain from meeting in their absence. The way in which we have explained these connections is truer to the flexible and not always consistent way in which Ignatius develops them, than accounts like Chadwick's which lay more stress on the church hierarchy as the reflection of a heavenly hierarchy.

As in the case of *1 Clement* and the *Shepherd*, so too in the Ignatian epistles there is a link between the group's symbolic universe or, to use Clifford Geertz' conception, world-view and its ethos.[197] Ignatius shows how the practices he urges them to follow are implied by their beliefs. Here we are interested primarily in the way he justifies submission to local institutions of leadership.

Central to his instructions is the exhortation to be submissive. The argument that Ignatius had a conception of parallel hierarchies between heaven and earth obscures what was his primary intention in associating leaders with the group's defining symbols. The term ὑποτάσσεσθαι (Eph. 2.2; 5.3; Mag. 2.1; 13.2; Tral. 2.1,2; 13.2; Pol. 6.1; cf. Pol. 2.1) captures Ignatius' concern in presenting these associations. An ethos of submission follows directly from his explication of belief. The association of Christ's submission to the Father with that of believers to the bishop clearly shows that Ignatius wished primarily to emphasize submission in creating such parallels.[198] In *Mag.* 13:2 the submission of Christ (and the apostles) to the Father is the pattern to be followed in the church; similarly the Smyrnaeans are exhorted to "follow (ἀκολουθεῖν) the bishop, as Jesus Christ follows the Father" (*Smyr.* 8:1); again, in *Eph.* 5:1 union with the bishop is compared with the union of Christ with the Father.

Geertz' notion of cultural symbols as "models of" and "models for" reality helps us to understand Ignatius' use of Christ's submission as a guide for a proper moral attitude towards leadership.[199] For the majority of members, Christ's life, death, and resurrection were community-defining symbols with tremendous social meaning. It was the symbol of Christ which communicated to them what was "really real." The social relations or patterns of leadership which already existed probably affected the way Ignatius explicated these symbols. His explication, in turn, helped to bring social conditions into accord with the groups' central beliefs.

In response to local challenges, Ignatius showed that particular beliefs associated with Christ and God the Father had certain moral implications; by describing the relationship of Jesus to God the Father in terms of submission or of union, he drew attention to a symbol of obedience and unity which he could then employ as a model to mould behaviour in the institutional realm. An ethos of submission followed from a belief about relations between the group's sacred symbols. Ignatius relates the whole ethos of living "in Christ", a phrase appearing some twenty-five times, or according to the Lord (*Eph.* 8:1; *Tral.* 2:1; *Phld.* 3:2; 4:1) to church unity and submission to the bishop. As a charismatic in close contact with the the "really real," Ignatius explicated the interrelationships which were believed to exist between the group's defining symbols, their relevance for the institutional order, and their consequent ethos. He thus showed how group beliefs committed members to support leadership institutions, and legitimated the authority of leaders. It is plausible that this contributed to making these structures subjectively more meaningful to his readers, thus integrating more firmly group members otherwise disposed to follow diverse beliefs and practices.

Summary

A central aspect of Ignatius' attempts to bring the Asian communities under the control of their leaders was the legitimation of their authority. The need for such legitimation arose from the challenges presented by deviant belief. By relating the institutional hierarchy to the heavenly one Ignatius showed how an ethos of submission to local leaders was a compelling duty. He was able to provide such legitimation because of his perceived position as one in special contact with and possessing extraordinary knowledge of the communities' sacred symbols. The interaction between ideas and social structures provides an adequate means of understanding both Ignatius' explication of local leadership institutions and the emergence of monepiscopacy. Hierarchical social arrangements which arose out of worship in the household helped to shape Ignatius' reflection on the relationship between the heavenly and earthly hierachy. That reflection, in turn, reinforced and gave more formal expression to such arrangements, thereby contributing to the development of institutions of authority.

Notes

1　For example, Barrett, 1976; Donahue, 1978, pp. 81-93; Swartley, 1973, pp. 81-103.

2　1960, p. 29; she postulates the existence of Essene cells in Asia Minor, but is there any evidence for this which is not circular? See also Trevett, 1983, pp. 1ff. who connects Ignatius and the *Didache* to reconstruct a profile of Christianity in Antioch; again the question must be asked: did the situation in Asia Minor reflect that in Antioch? Brown and Meier, 1983, pp. 74-80 connect Matthew and Ignatius' community in a trajectory, but they admit that this raises several problems which they leave unsolved.

3　We shall assume that Ignatius confronted only one group of opponents. A full discussion of this falls outside our immediate scope. Schoedel, 1985, *passim*, is the latest scholar to argue for two groups — one docetic, the other Jewish-Christian (similarly, Corwin, 1960, pp. 52-87; Richardson, 1935, pp. 51-54, 79-85; Bammel, 1982, pp. 83f.). Molland, 1954, pp. 1-6 and Barnard, 1963, pp. 193-206 argue for one group, while Barrett, 1976, pp. 231f., contends that there were two groups but that both were docetic. Chief among the older scholars who argued for one group is Lightfoot, 1885, Pt. 2, Vol. 1, pp. 373-77.

4　Ibid., Pt. 2, Vol. 1, pp. 70-106, 222-66, 315-414; Zahn, 1873.

5　For challenges to the consensus see the discussion in Schoedel, 1985, pp. 5-7. Davies, 1976, pp. 175-180, presents a compelling argument for placing Ignatius' arrest in A.D. 113. This does not accord with the traditional dating of Ignatius' martyrdom (*c.* A.D. 107), but that date is derived from episcopal lists which are not consistent with each other. For further discussion of these lists, see Lightfoot, 1885, Pt. 2 Vol. 1, pp. 29f.; Harnack, 1897, pp. 70f., 208-13; Downey, 1961, pp. 584f., *passim*; Bauer, 1971, pp. 114-19 (his theory that Rome was behind the formulation of an Antiochene succession list is unconvincing).

6　Most scholars argue that the Antiochene church was also composed of various household cells: Corwin, 1960, p. 49; Downey, 1961, p. 277.

7　Streeter, 1929, p. 163.

8　Riesenfeld, 1961, pp. 315f.

9　Lake (Loeb trans.) and Camelot, 1969, translate ἐπὶ τὸ αὐτό this way; cf. the identical usage in 1 Cor. 11:20 and Klauck's (1981a, p. 291) argument that this phrase indicates a common meeting of all Christians together. Corwin, 1960, p. 85 argues that *Mag.* 7:2 may indicate that there was one assembly.

10　Trans. from Schoedel, 1985, p. 108.

11　Lightfoot, 1885, *The Apostolic Fathers*, Part 2, Vol. 2, p. 306.

12　Kümmel, 1975, p. 452, dates them *c.* A.D. 90-110.

13 The Johannine influence on Polycarp falls outside the limits of our discussion, but he was probably acquainted with the Johannine letters (cf. Bammel, 1982, p. 80) and his community may have had contacts with a Johannine circle. Irenaeus also connects Polycarp with John (Eus. *H.E.* 5:20.6), but he probably confused the John Polycarp referred to with a different John since there is no evidence in Polycarp's letter of use of the Gospel. Lieu, 1986, pp. 125f., and Meeks, 1972, pp. 44ff. postulate the existence of a relatively self-contained Johannine group possibly existing alongside other Christian groups. If it was isolated this would not affect our argument, since it depends upon the ability to draw analogies from roughly contemporary documents — not the demonstration of continuity between various traditions.

14 Malherbe, 1983, p. 103; see p. 102 for letters of recommendation in the ancient world. Lieu, 1986, pp. 118f. remains unconvinced that the epistle is a letter of recommendation, but she perhaps has too rigid a view of the elements constituting such letters. Kim, 1972, pp. 9-97, notes a variety of constructions and elements within a general form. In the case of Christian letters of commendation, such as Philemon, he argues (p. 124) that they do not necessarily show the same form and structure of pagan commendations. He states (p. 121) that 3 John 12 is a commendation. Anyway, Lieu agrees (p. 113) that ἐπιδέχεσθαι in 3 John 10 refers to hospitality and her conclusions concerning the hospitality of Diotrephes are similar to Malherbe's. Malherbe (p. 96) cites a study by J.B. Mathews (*Hospitality and the New Testament Church: An Historical and Exegetical Study*, Th.D. Thesis Princeton Theological Seminary, 1965, pp. 166-74 — unavailable to me) for the existence of a technical vocabulary of hospitality in the early church. Included in this terminology are " λαμβάνειν,

δέχεσθαι, and πέμπειν and their cognates" (Malherbe provides Mathews's biblical references in n. 11).

15 Malherbe, p. 103; he further argues (pp. 106-7) that the use of the verb ἐπιδέχεσθαι in v. 9 ("does not acknowledge my authority" RSV) does not refer to the monarchical authority of a bishop over his elders, as several scholars have suggested (cf. p. 93 for references), but to the fact that, in letters of recommendation, request was made that the traveller be received for the sake of the writer. The affront, then, is not to ecclesiastical authority, but to the writer's person; for criticism see Lieu, 1986, p. 119.

16 Thus, e.g., Streeter, 1929, p. 84.

17 For a summary of this interpretation see Kümmel, 1975, p. 448.

18 Malherbe, 1983, p. 108.

19 Ibid., 1983, p. 109; similarly Brown, 1982, pp. 734, 738 and Lieu, 1986, pp. 132, 135.

20 Brown, 1982, pp. 730-32, 738.

21 Quasten, 1983, p. 129.

22 Waitz, 1904, p. 249-250.

23 Waitz, 1904, pp. 188f., was an early scholar to argue for this view (according to Jones, 1982, p. 8 this theory originated *c.* 1844). There is a large body of literature on the sources of the Clementines; most scholars agree that there are earlier documents behind the Homilies and Recognitions. A majority argue that the writers of these two documents used a common source, G (*die Grundschrift*), composed *c.* 200-220 A.D. The passages associated with *Praxeis Petrou* are connected with G by those who argue for only this source behind the Homilies and Recognitions. We are inclined to agree with those who distinguish earlier sources behind G, but even if *Praxeis Petrou* is a fiction of modern exegetes, G may be interpreted as an

early testimony to patterns of organization which existed in this period. See Rehm, 1957, pp. 197-206, and Jones, 1982, pp. 1-33, 63-96, esp. pp. 8-20 for an overview of the discussion regarding this literature.

24 For a full account of the history of the redaction see Jones, 1982, and Powell, 1981, pp. 113-23.

25 Ibid., p. 10

26 James, 1980, p. 364; Bornkamm, *NTA* Vol. II (1965), p. 427.

27 Waitz, 1904, p. 244; Powell, 1981, p. 119. The author was acquainted with the tradition of Peter at Antioch (*Rec.* 10:71; cf. Eus. *H.E.* 3:36.2).

28 Quasten, Vol. 1, 1983, pp. 135-36; Schäferdick, *NTA* Vol. II (1965), p. 214.

29 Schneemelcher, *NTA* Vol. II (1965), p. 259.

30 James, 1980, p. 337.

31 Davies, 1980, p. 10.

32 Instances of household settings are as follows: hospitality: *A. Jn.* 25; 62; *A. Pl.* 2:2,5; *A. Th.* 81; 131; *A. Pt.* 8; 17; 22; *A. And.* 22; Clem. *Hom.* 3:29 (*Rec.* 1:73); 4:1 (*Rec.* 4:1); 4:10; 8:1 (*Rec.* 4:2); Clem. *Rec.* 8:35-38; 9:38; worship or teaching in a household: *A. Jn.* 25; 46; 86; 106-111 (house of Verus?); *A. Pl.* 2:6, 42 (cf. 23!); 6 (in the house of Longinus?); 7; James, 1980, p. 575; p. 577; *A. Th.* 93; 100; 101; *A. Pt.* 7 (at the house of presbyter Narcissus); 19-22; 29; 31; Clem. *Hom.* 3:29 (*Rec.* 2:19); 8:8 (*Rec.* 4:7); *Rec.* 3:50; 4:6; cf. *A Xan. and Pol.* 10; 11; leadership drawn from hospitable householders: James, 1980, p. 239; *A. Th.* 169; Clem. *Hom.* 3:63 (*Rec.* 3:66); 11:36 (*Rec.* 6:15); *Rec.* 10:71.

33 Gregory of Nyssa in his *Life of Gregory the Wonderworker* (*c.* A.D. 213-270) recounts (Migne 46, p. 922C) a scene in which a leading member of a city invites the missionary to stay with him; this suggests that the apocryphal stories probably reflect contemporary practices.

34 James, 1980, p. 239.

35 A later state of affairs seems also to be assumed by the Latin fragment (ch. 21) which describes the construction by Aristodemus, a priest of Artemis, of a church "in the name of Saint John."

36 The (possibly) third century *Life of Polycarp* presents a setting of the origins of the Smyrnaean community similar to that presented in the Apocryphal Acts. In ch. 2 Paul meets with Strataeas and the faithful are gathered together, presumably at his home, for instruction. In ch. 3 we learn that Strataeas "succeeded to his (i.e. Paul's) teaching". The use of this document as a source to reconstruct Christianity in Smyrna is a much debated topic (Lightfoot, Vol. 1, Pt.2, 1885, pp. 419-20; Streeter, 1929, pp. 265-72; Cadoux, 1938, pp. 308f.). The writer claims to have used older documents (ch. 1), but it is impossible to determine the accuracy of his statements and it is most likely that the story of the church's foundation is apocryphal. It is at least possible that both the fragment published by James and the story told by "Pionius" reflect a tradition concerning the earliest practices in these communities but one that is presented in the form of structures of ministry contemporary with the later writers.

37 Waitz, 1904, p. 181 argues that this episode originated with the Clem. *Acts of Peter* but that there has been some reworking of the tradition — namely, the presentation of Zacchaeus as successor of Peter and a modelling after the *Epistle of Clement to James* (esp. sec. 3; cf. *Hom.* 3:60 — Waitz, 1904, pp. 64f.).

38 Waitz, op.cit., pp. 182, 191, argues that the Maro legend together with the other similar accounts of the establishment of hosts as bishops originated with the Clementine *Acts of Peter*.

39 The argument in ibid., p. 247 that the Theophilus mentioned is the second century apologist is unconvincing.

40 Schoedel, 1985, p. 240.

41 Corwin, 1960, p. 65.

42 See note 14 above.

43 Chadwick, 1961, p. 283.

44 Trans. Schoedel, 1985, p. 65; cf. Lightfoot, Vol. 2, Pt.2, 1885, p. 52.

45 The diverse effect entertaining teachers could have on communities is seen in *Acts of Peter* 8, where Marcellus, a wealthy senator, cast the church in turmoil by ceasing to be its patron after he invited Simon to teach in his house.

46 Brown, 1979, p. 98.

47 A good analogy can be found in the synodal letter of Gangra formulated at the time of the Synod of Gangra in Paphlagonia in northern Asia Minor (*c.* 350 A.D.). In section 2 (ed. Hefele, 1876, Vol. 2, p. 326) "Eustathians" (cf. Socrates *H.E.* 12:43; Sozomen 3:14 for description) are condemned for causing "many to forsake the public assemblies for divine service, and to organize private conventicles." Again, in Canon 5 (p. 329) they are anathematized for teaching "that the house of God is to be despised, and likewise the services there held." In Canon 6 the synod condemns "anyone [who], avoiding the churches, holds private meetings, and in contempt of the church performs that which belongs only to her, without the presence of a priest, without authority from the bishop." Finally, in Canon 11 (p. 331) they are condemned for staying away from private agapes offered by orthodox members of the community.

48 There is ample evidence of the practice of early Christians meeting more than once a day (Pliny *Ep.* 10:98; Hip. *Apos. Trad.* cf. 33, 35, — ed. Dix). Justin (*Apol.* 1:67), in his description of a common meeting, seems to distinguish between a period of prayer and the eucharist proper.

49 There is evidence from the Council of Laodicea in Phrygia, probably convened sometime between A.D. 341 and 381, that "bishops" and "presbyters" were accustomed to offer "sacrifices" in houses; Canon 58 (Hefele, Vol. 2, p. 322) condemns this practice. It is possible that this reflects an earlier state of affairs. The general Council of Seleucia-Ctesiphon in A.D. 410 perhaps reflects a development of controls over private meetings, for after it had come within the orbit of Nicene orthodoxy, the Syrian church attempted to standardize ecclesiastical practice. In Canon 13 (Chabot, 1902, pp. 266f.), the synod declares that from thenceforth only one "sacrifice" is to be offered in each town, and the practice of celebrating several eucharists in various local private households is to be stopped. Closer to our period, but this time in Rome, Hippolytus in *Apos. Trad.* 26:11 (ed. Dix) instructs Christians how to conduct a private agape when a presbyter or deacon is present but a bishop is absent.

50 It is a vexed question in contemporary scholarship, one which falls outside the confines of this discussion, whether the two were originally united. In our opinion, there is no compelling reason to suppose that they were not, even at this date. Schoedel, 1985, p. 244, noting that in *Smyr.* 8:2 "baptism and love feasts are juxtaposed as the two cardinal liturgical acts of the church," concludes that the agape included a eucharist. Dix, 1978, pp. 82ff. argues that they were separated by the time of Ignatius, but his case is weakened by generalizing from later evidence. Keating, 1901, pp. 52ff. lists the evidence for agapes in the second century and argues that the eucharist and agape were still united at the time of Ignatius. The dissertations of Williams, 1978, pp. 70f. and Wagner, 1949, pp. 34f., also make strong cases for the inclusion of the eucharist within the agape.

51 Again, Hippolytus *Apos. Trad.* 33 assumes that such smaller meetings were the norm in Rome and the evidence from the canons of councils and synods cited above suggests a similar diversity.

52 Schoedel, 1985, p. 235.

53 Bauer, 1971, p. 71.

54 Grant, 1966, p. 119; Grant wonders if he might have been a deacon; it is impossible to be certain which was the case.

55 Schoedel, 1985, pp. 236-37.

56 There is a loose parallel in Irenaeus *A.H.* 1:13.5 where Marcus is invited into the home of a deacon. No eucharist is mentioned in this section, but in the preceding sections of 1:13 Irenaeus describes the rituals of Marcus and, given Irenaeus' description of him as a wandering teacher, it is likely that he relied chiefly on the hospitality of what seem (from Irenaeus' description) to have been wealthy women to perform them.

57 Schoedel, 1985, p. 231.

58 Schoedel, 1985, p. 238 obscures this connection by creating a division between vs. 1 and 2. The exaltation of office and the practices of his opponents were probably closely connected in Ignatius' mind; without the former, the latter could not have occurred.

59 Rehm, 1957, p. 204.

60 Thus, Campenhausen, 1957. Campenhausen's argument is criticized by Barnes, 1968, pp. 511f., who argues for the historical accuracy of the account (p. 527).

61 For example, 5:1; 6:1; 7:2-3; 8:2,3; 9:2,3; 10:1-2; 12:3; 14:1; 18:1. The parallels and contrasts are further discussed by Reuning, 1917.

62 Barnes, 1968, p. 510.

63 Cadoux, 1938, p. 356. *The Life of Polycarp* records that Polycarp spent time both at home and in the suburbs or environs (προάστειον) of Smyrna (ch. 7), which may reflect property outside the city.

64 This curious phrase probably indicates that Polycarp is to ensure that every member is present at the common eucharist.

65 Streeter, 1929, p. 168.

66 Moffatt, 1930, p. 171.

67 Campenhausen, 1936, pp. 76-78.

68 Preiss, 1938, pp. 198, 234; similarly, Bower, 1974, pp. 1-14.

69 Tinsley, 1957, p. 554.

70 Bultmann, 1961, pp. 267-68.

71 For a wholly theological approach to Ignatius see Meinhold, 1979, p. 1, who accounts for Ignatius' complex character by analysing certain theological conceptions which he argues were at work in his personality.

72 For Ignatius' style as an example of "Asianism" cf. Perler, 1949, pp. 57-61; Riesenfeld, 1961, pp. 315ff. On "Asianism" generally see Norden, 1909, pp. 263ff.

73 See the discussion of travel in Meeks, 1983, pp. 16f.; for a more general discussion see Bouquet, 1959, pp. 95-113; see also Paul's description of hazards of travel in 2 Cor. 11:25-27.

74 Schoedel, 1985, pp. 12-13, 213.

75 See above pp. 102ff.

76 Weber, 1968, p. 241.

77 Ibid., p. 1112. It is important to remember that we are dealing here with an ideal type; not all manifestations of charisma are revolutionary.

78 Ibid., p. 241.

79 Weber, 1947, p. 333.

80 Shils, 1965; Eisenstadt, 1968a, pp. xxivf.
81 Weber, 1968, p. 439.
82 Ibid., p. 450.
83 For further discussion and criticism see p. 131 n. 182 above.
84 Shils, 1965, p. 204.
85 Schoedel, 1985, pp. 11-12.
86 Streeter, 1929, pp. 228-29, was an earlier scholar to note this. Meinhold, 1979, pp. 8f., following the usual categories of German theological scholarship, describes this quality as pneumatic. Behind Meinhold's description is a misleading way of understanding 1 Cor. 12-14, where "pneumatikoi" are described (see above p. 126 n. 70). Meinhold's reduction of Ignatius' personality into component theological categories (bishop, pneumatic, martyr) seems artificial, and also imports misleading distinctions into the historical data; in Ignatius' mind being "pneumatic" (i.e. prophetic) and being a martyr and bishop may not have been distinct phenomena. Also of importance is the question of the appropriateness of using theological categories borrowed from different writings to characterize an historical figure not associated with them; the term "pneumatic" is never used by Ignatius to describe himself.
87 Cf. Aune, 1983, pp. 291-93, for the social background of this utterance as an inspired saying. Aune (p. 293) argues that the admonitions at the end of *Phld.* 7:2 were uttered by several individuals. But there is no reason to suppose that these statements were not his own; as Aune himself notes, the language of these staccato statements is Ignatian.
88 E.g. Luke 1:42; Origen *Contra Celsum* 6:75; see Dölger, 1936, pp. 218f.; Schoedel, 1985, p. 205, n. 6 for further examples.
89 I.e. John 4:10; 7:38; Lightfoot, Pt. 2, Vol. 2, 1885, p. 224, emends the text, but there is not sufficient reason to reject this reading.
90 Schoedel, 1985, p. 185.
91 It is perhaps significant that here also he refers to revelation: Ignatius will send further instruction if the Lord reveals (ἀποκαλύπτειν) to him that the Ephesians join together in the common meeting (20:2). Aune, 1983, p. 294, finds evidence here of divine revelation similar to that described in *Phld.* 7:1-2. Lightfoot, 1885, Pt. 2, Vol. 2, p. 86, following Zahn, rejects the ὅτι and replaces it with τι (viz." . . . if the Lord should reveal anything to me. Assemble. . . ."), but the MSS support for this is weak and such an emendation seems unnecessary once the passage is understood in a wider prophetic context. His interpretation of συνέρχεσθε as an imperative because it fits in with a dependent εἰς clause (cf. e.g. *Tral.* 12:3) ignores Ignatius' various uses of εἰς with the articular infinitive (e.g. *Mag.* 8:2; 14:1; *Pol.* 7:1).
92 Schoedel, 1985, p. 144.
93 Bauer, 1923, p. 233, notes that praise for martyrs is a common theme in early Christian literature (cf. Rev. 7:9-10, 13-14; 2:7-10,17, 26-28; 3:21 — [note that this is a document connected in some sense with Ephesus, Smyrna, and Philadelphia: 2:1,8; 3,7]; Eus. *H.E.* 5:2.2-3; *1 Clem.* 6:1; Herm. *Sim.* 8:1.18; 8:2.1; 8:3.6. *Mart. Pol.*, a writing composed in Smyrna, also describes the superior position of a martyr (2:1-4; 49:1).
94 Grant, 1966, p. 57; there is evidence in later literature that martyrs were named Χριστοφόροι or something similar (cf. Bauer, 1923, p. 191, for further discussion). Campenhausen's (1936, p. 76) interpretation of this title as indicative of a shift from christocentric Paulinism to Catholicism reads too much into the text. What Ignatius means by Theophorus is most likely synonymous with his descrip-

tion of the Ephesians as χριστοφόροι (see *Eph.* 9:2 where both nouns appear together).

95 We shall discuss this terminology more fully when we turn to a discussion of Ignatius' references to his unworthiness.

96 *Rom.* 6:3 and, to a limited degree, *Eph.* 10:3, indicate the presence of an imitatio Christi motif, but as Swartley, 1973, pp. 81f. notes, other allusions to imitation do not apply strictly to the passion (*Eph.* 1:1; *Mag.* 10:1; *Tral.* 1:2; *Phld.* 7:2) and this leads him to argue correctly that Ignatius possessed a broad concept of the imitation of Christ, which included but went beyond imitation of his passion.

97 Weber, 1968, p. 241.

98 Campenhausen, 1969, p. 104; similarly, Meinhold, 1979, pp. 8f.

99 Campenhausen, loc. cit.

100 Bauer, 1971, pp. 61-76 is puzzlingly ambiguous on this point. In some places he argues that the bishops who met with Ignatius represented larger or smaller majorities (e.g., p. 69). In other places he states that they constituted a minority (e.g., pp. 62-63). There is not sufficient reason to doubt that the docetists comprised a minority, although their separation from the common eucharist may have had an impact on the life of the community not consistent with their numbers. If it is true that the divisions were not explicit in each community (see the discussion below), then the picture of majorities and minorities fiercely contending with each other seems misleading.

101 See n. 103 below for references.

102 For further discussion see pp 28f. above.

103 Again, we must be cautious not to make the argument circular. Images in New Testament Eph. support the contention that the suffering and resurrection of Christ were powerful symbols to the Ephesians (1:.7; 2:6, 16); Revelation provides similar testimony for communities in Smyrna, Philadelphia, and Ephesus (e.g. 1:5,7,17-18; 2:8; 5:6-14; 7:10-17; 12:11; 13:8; 19:13). Pol. *Phil.* also contains references to the suffering of Christ which seem to indicate that this was an important symbol for many in his community (8:1; 9:2; cf. 7:1, in a polemical context); cf. *Mart. Pol.* 1:1-2.

104 A locative interpretation of these phrases follows from the opening phrase which contains ἐν, where Ignatius writes that the Philadelphian church is "established in the harmony (ἐν ὁμόνοια) of God."

105 For parallels see Schoedel, 1985, p. 37; a more cautious assessment is given by von der Goltz, 1894, pp. 103-105.

106 Bauer, 1920, p. 208; Grant, 1966, p. 40 suggests the influence of 1 Pet. 2:5 but this is unconvincing.

107 We are here following Kleist's 1961, translation, which correctly captures the force of ὡς with the participle.

108 Thus, Bauer, 1923, pp. 209-10; Grant, 1966, p. 41; Schoedel, 1985, p. 69. The context and degree of openness to these persons suggests that Ignatius is probably not referring here to the false teachers.

109 Schoedel, 1985, p. 15.

110 Scholars agree that *Rom.* 3:1 probably contains a reference to *1 Clement* (cf. *1 Clem.* 5:3-5). For further discussion see Schoedel, 1985, p. 172; Grant, 1966, p. 88; Bauer, 1923, p. 246; Lightfoot, 1885, Vol. 2 Pt. 2, p. 203.

111 For example, the work of Schlier, 1929, and Bartsch, 1940 for the history of religions, and Maurer, 1949, and Berghardt, 1940 for the history of traditions. For criticism of the history of religions method as not addressing the life-world of early Christian groups see Kee, 1982, pp. 42-60.

112 Meeks, 1972, pp.44-72, esp. pp. 66-72.

113 Ibid., pp. 49, 68.

114 In the case of the Ephesians, Ignatius might have found a group which shared some similar convictions. For example, the Ignatian notion of the "prince of this age" has some parallel in New Testament Eph. (cf. esp. 6:12; also, 2:1-3 — note the connection between "the prince of the power of the air" and his work in the "sons of disobedience").

115 Grant, 1966, p. 47; Corwin, 1960, p. 156 notes that when Ignatius uses the term κόσμος, "he means by it the aspect of things that contrasts with the things of God".

116 Richardson, 1967, p. 69 notes that the expression ὁ ἄρχων τοῦ αἰῶνος τούτου is Pauline in form (1 Cor. 2:6,8; cf. 2 Cor. 4:4; Eph. 2:2), but we agree with Grant, 1966, p. 47, that the expression seems to be more Johannine in content (Jn. 12:31; 14:30; 16:11). If this is the case, Meeks' observation behind concerning the sectarian identity of Johannine imagery forms an interesting parallel with our conclusions here.

117 Endurance is also a virtue Polycarp puts forward (Pol. Phil. 8:2); similarly Schoedel, 1985, p. 106.

118 Ibid., p. 264.

119 Περίψημα and ἀντίψυξον were connected as sacrificial terms in Hellenistic usage; cf. Schoedel, 1985, pp. 63-64. At the time of Ignatius the former term was used as a polite expression (e.g. Bar. 4:9; 6:5; cf. Lightfoot, 1885, Vol. 2, Pt. 2, pp. 50-51), but its appearance with other stronger themes of self-effacement indicates that it is to be taken in a stronger sense. Cf. Schoedel, 1985, pp. 63-64.

120 Streeter, 1929, pp. 169f.

121 Schoedel, 1985, pp. 13f.; 1980, pp. 36ff.; Swartley, 1973, pp. 81ff.; cf. Harrison, 1936, pp. 84f.

122 The references to the restoration of peace in Antioch (Phld. 10:1; Smyr. 11:2) was interpreted by Lightfoot, 1885, Vol. 2, Pt. 2, p. 277, as referring to the end of persecution. Harrison, 1936, p. 84; Grant, 1966, pp. 107-8; Schoedel, 1985, p. 213 argue they refer to the restoration of unity.

123 Jervell, 1976, pp. 185ff. He applies the term "charismatic" theologically, but the phrase also has a more sociological application. For more detailed discussion see Schütz, 1975, pp. 238-49.

124 Cf. 1 Cor. 2:3-5; 4:9-13 where similar themes are developed. Jervell, 1976, p. 193 argues that Paul's references to weakness were to physical ailments (cf. Gal. 4:12-14; 2 Cor. 12:7-9).

125 Meeks, 1983, p. 183; Jervell, 1976, pp. 195-98.

126 Cf. Chapter Four for this concept.

127 Weber, 1968, p. 1123.

128 For further discussion see Holmberg, 1980a, pp. 154-58.

129 References to his opponents as possessing Jesus Christ (Mag. 10:3), carrying about "the name with wicked cunning" (Eph. 7:1), and mingling "Jesus Christ with themselves" (Tral. 6:2) also imply this. The allusion in Mag. 10:1 to those who are called by another name, probably does note refer to anything more than a reference to alleged Judaizing characteristics.

130 In Mag. 8:2 he describes a conversation he had, presumably, with some of his opponents. It is quite probable that such a debate occurred during such a meeting with the wider community.

131 Schoedel, 1980, p. 36; if this interpretation is correct then Ignatius' reference to his opponents being filtered out in Phld. 3:1 should be read cum grano salis — in actual-

ity community divisions appear to have been much more ambiguous than Ignatius' statement would suggest.

132 We are using this term broadly to describe both travelling teachers and local members sympathetic in varying degrees to them. Bauer, 1971, pp. 67f., distinguishes too strongly between local docetists and non-docetists and thus incorrectly posits the existence of two distinct groups opposed to one another. The lines were probably much more blurred than he supposes.

133 Coser, 1965, pp. 67f.

134 Ibid., pp. 69f., 101f.

135 Ibid., pp. 70-71.

136 Ibid., p. 101.

137 Corwin, 1960, pp. 53-54 argues on the basis of *Smyr.* 7:1 that Ignatius' opponents had fully withdrawn from the rest of the community, but it is difficult to know whether such a break had occurred before Ignatius' writing and Corwin admits that an alternative interpretation of the passage is that they had until recently still involved themselves in other aspects of community life. It is difficult to systematize events in all the communities to discover one picture of community division; one may speculate that divisions were in various stages of development – in Philadelphia, for example, divisions were probably less explicit than in Smyrna; in Tralles the separation may have been complete since in this letter Ignatius nowhere hints at reconciliation through repentance. Corwin argues that in Smyrna the docetists were part of the community until a crisis precipitated a split. Is it not possible that Ignatius represents that crisis, through his explicit teaching on church unity and the illegitimacy of eucharistic celebrations apart from the bishop? The Smyrnaean docetists were united with the rest of the community in their reverence for Ignatius (*Smyr.* 5:2); it seems probable that it is Ignatius, as Schoedel, 1980, p. 32, suggests, "who polarizes the situation."

138 Norris, 1976, p. 28, observes that as groups pressured by the larger culture, even very limited internal opposition may have been interpreted as a threat to their survival. This, according to Coser, 1965, pp. 100f., is common among sectarian groups.

139 Berger and Luckmann, 1971, p. 125.

140 Coser, 1965, p. 71.

141 Weber, 1968, pp. 243-44, 1115-17.

142 Friedrich, 1961, p. 21.

143 Loc. cit.

144 Loc. cit.

145 Loc. cit.

146 For this term see pp. 108f. above.

147 See the discussion of this term see pp. 136f.

148 Similarly, Norris, 1976, p. 34.

149 Zahn, 1899, pp. 67, 87-91; similarly, von der Goltz, 1894, pp. 93-98; Camelot, 1969, pp. 25, 100-101.

150 Kelly, 1983, p. 14; against Zahn see p. 69; for opinions similar to Kelly cf. Grant, 1966, p. 114; Corwin, 1960, p. 80.

151 Campenhausen, 1972, pp. 241ff.

152 Schoedel, 1985, loc. cit., provides a useful discussion of the possible influence of traditional materials on Ignatius' formulations.

153 Lightfoot, 1885, Vol. 2 Pt. 2, p. 136.

154 Schoedel, 1985, p. 153.

155 Ibid., p. 61; Lightfoot, op. cit., p. 48. In Pol. 3:2 the order is reversed, but there is evidence that, in this passage, Ignatius was being guided by the use of traditional philosophical categories (cf. Schoedel, op. cit., pp. 266-67 for further discussion). Nevertheless, it is significant that he ends this passage with a reference to the passion, which in its context functions as parae nesis for Polycarp (note the use of the same verb ὑπομένειν in 3:1).

156 *Pol.* 3:2 is probably an exception to this since the statement is addressed to Polycarp, but here too there are anti-docetic themes.

157 Bauer's, 1971, pp. xxii-xxiii use of the terms "heresy" and "orthodoxy" as "what one customarily and usually understands them to mean," by which he presumably means the full-blown understanding of heresy which developed in the fourth and fifth centuries, hides the significant contribution Ignatius makes in the creation of orthodoxy and the definition of heresy in this early period. By using these terms in this sense Bauer neglects to ask the important question of how the "customary" usage of them developed, and as a result he imports an anachronistic understanding of the term into the early evidence.

158 For discussion of non-Christian usage of the former terms see Simon, 1979, pp. 111f.; for the latter term see Rengstorf, *TDNT*, loc. cit.

159 For a summary of non-Christian usage see Simon, 1979, pp. 104f.

160 Ignatius uses the term μερισμός to describe factions (*Phld.* 3:1; 7:2; 8:1; *Smyr.* 7:2), although in one passage (*Phld.* 2:1) this term, too, is associated with false doctrine (κακοδιδασκαλία).

161 Thus, e.g., Camelot, 1969, p. 40; Lietzmann, 1961, Vol. 1, p. 248.

162 Thus, Bauer, 1971, pp. 61-76.

163 There is an account of the earlier history of Smyrna in the *Life of Polycarp*, in which the writer states that he is following information as found in "ancient copies" (1). But it is difficult to determine whether the narrative of earlier events is reliable (see Lightfoot, 1885, Vol. 2, Pt. 2, pp. 1012-13). The description of the monarchical bishop Strataeas, who "succeeded to his (Paul's) teaching" seems to imply that the later author was imposing a later organizational pattern onto earlier events.

164 See Hemer, 1986, pp. 32-34 for a discussion of the various theories.

165 The discussion of these theories falls outside the scope of this thesis. For discussion of the various interpretations and relevant literature see Brown, 1982, pp. 733f.; Lieu, 1986, pp. 153f.

166 Streeter, 1929, pp. 85f.

167 See pp. 136f. above.

168 For relevant literature see Lieu, 1986, pp. 54f.

169 Ibid., p. 54; Brown, 1982, p. 649.

170 Lieu, 1986, pp. 125-65, esp. pp. 156ff.

171 Lieu argues that Diotrephes and the Elder, representatives of different types of authority, lacked common criteria to assess one another's claims to legitimacy. The Johannine case was probably a unique instance, but it is possible that the authority claims of wandering teachers and of house-church hosts, when they came into conflict, could have presented a similar difficulty. Ignatius' attempt to provide criteria to assess beliefs and practices can be seen as an important step in the clarification of different claims to authority and the development of leadership institutions.

172 See pp. 89f. for a discussion of this phenomenon in contemporary sects.

173 The noun συμβούλιον is an official term and may refer either to a summoning of presbyters or the whole church; cf. Schoedel, 1985, p. 278.

174 This is evident in *Mag.* 7:1 where Ignatius links ἴδια with the plural ὑμῖν ("by yourselves"); cf. Schoedel, 1985, p. 116.
175 See ibid., p. 109 for references.
176 This interpretation is supported by the use of the term καιροί (i.e. critical or difficult times) here and in *Pol.* 2:3; in the latter passage Ignatius employs καιρός to refer to the situation brought about by docetic teaching; ibid., p. 264.
177 Ibid., p. 237.
178 Streeter, 1929, p. 173.
179 Compare, for example, the third century *Didascalia* (4; 19 [Connolly pp. 28, 86, 96]) and the fourth century *Apostolic Constitutions* (2:25; 3:19-20) where the bishop is more sharply distinguished.
180 For further discussion of this distinction see Schöllgen, 1986, pp. 146-51; Staats, 1986, pp. 134f.
181 Bauer's, 1971, p. 70, interpretation of this as a reference to those presbyters allied with Polycarp as opposed to those who are not is unconvincing.
182 Bauer and Paulsen, 1985, p. 113; cf. Schoedel, 1985, p. 237.
183 Dassmann, 1974, p. 77.
184 Idem, 1984, pp. 90f. recognises the influence of the household in the creation of monepiscopacy in these communities but does not sufficiently explain the role of ideas in helping to shape their leadership institutions.
185 Berger and Luckmann, 1971, pp. 110ff.
186 Schlier, 1929, pp. 82-124.
187 These terms appear as follows: ἕνωσις — *Mag.* 1:2; 13:2; *Tral.* 11:2; *Phld.* 4:1; 7:2; 8:1; *Pol.* 1:2; 5:2; ἑνόω — *Eph.* inscr.; *Mag.* 6:2; 7:1; 14:1; *Rom.* inscr.; *Smyr.* 3:3; ἑνότης — *Eph.* 4:2; 5:1; 14:1; *Phld.* 2:2; 3:2; 5:2; 8:1; 9:1; *Smyr.* 12:2; *Pol.* 8:3.
188 Preiss, 1938, p. 229.
189 See Corwin, 1960, pp. 247f.
190 Bauer, 1923, p. 257, commenting on *Phld.* 4:1; Schoedel, 1985, *passim*, esp. p. 105.
191 Schoedel, 1985, p. 98.
192 Chadwick, 1950, pp. 169-72.
193 Ibid., p. 170; similarly, Moffatt, 1936, p. 35; Preiss, 1938, pp. 230f.; Bartsch, 1940; Bieder, 1956, pp. 38-43; von der Goltz, 1895, pp. 62-66.
194 See pp. 104f. above.
195 Consonant with this conception is the description of those who are not "in the sanctuary" (θυσιαστήριον) as impure, (*Tral.* 7:2), or lacking "the bread of God" (*Eph.* 5:2).
196 See also Pol. *Phil.* 6:3, where the apostles are referred to as historical figures.
197 See pp. 66f. above.
198 Similarly. Corwin, 1960, p. 195; for a systematic discussion which agree with what is argued for here see Schoedel, 1985, pp. 113-14, n.7.
199 See pp. 66f. above.

Chapter Six
Epilogue

"Christianity was from the beginning not a mere doctrine but also a church." This statement, written by George La Piana[1] some sixty years ago can be read as both a reminder and a warning to scholars who embark upon the precarious and often elusive task of reconstructing from the fragments which have been preserved for them the social shape and setting of the early Christian ministry. It is a reminder that the early church was situated in a certain society, in a particular time and place, and that the expectations, beliefs, and values of those who populated it were in varying degrees shaped by such factors. Some, like Ignatius, were remarkable; others, like the businesspeople against whom Hermas railed, were more commonplace; but all alike shared a world different in many respects from our own.

Few scholars would deny this. Yet in our evaluation of the theories concerning the origins and development of structures of leadership in the early church we have found that while much of the scholarship devoted to this topic often explicitly states the necessity of recognizing the social and historical factors which contributed to the shape of the early ministry, its practical effect is to minimize their importance in favour of more theological concerns. Whether it be the more extreme form of the "early Catholicism" thesis as propounded by Rudolf Sohm, or its more moderate expression as represented by Eduard Schweizer, the result is to leave behind too quickly the flesh and blood of history and focus on ideas as the true determinants in the development of the early church.

Our treatment of early Christian structures of leadership has not attempted to supplant the role of ideas played in the development of the early church with social explanation. To assert the opposite version of a history of ideas approach — perhaps a modified materialist view — would be equally unsatisfactory. We have instead sought a middle ground which at once seeks to take account of ideas and social structures together, the one affecting the other, neither necessarily in all instances being primary.

More particularly, we have argued that the development of the early ministry in the communities chosen for investigation cannot be understood fully without reference to the power wielded by relatively wealthy household owners who invited the church to worship in their homes; and that a set of beliefs or a way

---

Notes to this chapter appear on p. 201.

of stating Christian belief also made such a setting possible. We have not questioned the legitimacy of attempts by contemporary scholars to evaluate those beliefs, only their one-sided emphasis on ideas as the sole determinants of early ecclesiastical structure (or at least the only ones worth comment).

This is why we have argued that method is so important. By making explicit the ideal types and models employed to recover and interpret historical phenomena, the historian is able to control his or her own interests in the interpolation of data. Of course, no historical reconstruction is "value-free," but some are more value-laden or value-conscious than others. In a topic such as the early ministry, where, since the Reformation scholars have fiercely and forcefully put forward radically differing theses, often to justify broader more contemporary theological concerns, the need to recognize one's own prejudice is especially acute — if only to assess the multitude of early church portraits which scholars of the last five hundred years have painted.

The way common people viewed the church is usually different from the way its theologians do — that is probably as true for the early church as it is for the contemporary one. But such a factor becomes especially important in attempting to determine the form of the early ministry, because what common people thought about their leaders and leadership probably affected to a great degree the development of governing institutions. Ideal types and models have helped us to identify the kinds of beliefs and values the early Christians possessed. Of course, Ignatius' letters, like Paul's, may have been judged as containing "some things hard to understand" (2 Pet. 3:16), but there must have been some point of contact between such writers and their audience. That overlap has not always been easy to identify; it is often implied in what is or is not stated explicitly, and sometimes we have been able to offer no more than an educated guess. But not to attempt to identify the common ground between writer and reader has led to scholarship which sometimes oversimplifies the role of theological conceptions of the church in the shaping of early Christian institutions.

As well as a reminder, the statement by La Piana with which we began can also be interpreted as a warning. The early Christian movement presents to the historian all the ambiguity, complexity, and subtlety of any historical phenomena. And so it should, for the early Christians were neither the embodiment of successfully applied ideas, nor were they cogs in a social machine, moving along a predetermined course. Again, few scholars would adhere to either of these positions as stated in this extreme form, but the effect of much scholarship is to oversimplify the early church and impose upon it a homogeneity which it probably did not possess. The claims of the preceding pages are specific to the communities chosen for investigation. In some cases we have assumed that similar or analogous structures of leadership existed in communities not represented by the documents chosen for investigation. But this should not be mistaken for a broad or generalizing claim. The problem with reconstructions which attempt to reconstruct the rise of the early ministry from the work of apostles or their delegates, or the extension of synagogue structure, or the fusion of presumed Jewish and Pauline structures, or the decree of Jerusalem Christians is not only that the evidence is often fragmentary and spread across a vast Empire, but that it is open to many differing interpretations. The reconstruction of the church's early ministry and its social setting may be likened to a puzzle with several of its pieces missing. Some of the pieces stand alone without anything to connect them to the rest of the picture, others join with one or two other pieces to provide clues of how they might fit into the whole, but one's final estimation can only be a matter of probability. In such a situation we have found it best to make cautious and often tentative claims about a few selected communities rather than the Christian movement as a whole. We have argued that the church meeting in the homes of wealthier Christians provides a means for imagining how some of the missing pieces may have looked; we have claimed, further, that our reconstruction is better than others which have been proposed; but over any such reconstruction there must always be placed a question mark.

Any historical construction is a matter of probability and a chief task of the historian is to state accurately the weight of his or her claims and conclusions. The novelist Margaret Atwood describes the challenge of the historian well when she has one of her characters say

> we may call Eurydice forth from the world of the dead, but we cannot make her answer [questions we ask her]; and when we turn to look at her we glimpse her only for a moment before she slips from our grasp and flees. As all historians know, the past is a great darkness, and filled with echoes. Voices may reach us from it; but what they say to us is imbued with the obscurity of the matrix out of which they come; and, try as we may, we cannot always decipher them precisely in the clearer light of our own day.[2]

The echoes of Christian communities in Rome, Corinth, and Asia Minor come to us in the voices of Clement, Hermas, and Ignatius, sometimes clearly, often only distantly. Imbued with the obscurity of their matrix they come to us. The task of the historian is to listen patiently and attentively and to discern their meaning, even if only tentatively.

Notes

1 1925, p. 202.
2 *The Handmaid's Tale* (Toronto: McClelland and Stewart-Bantam Limited, 1985), p. 293.

Abbreviations

CIG	Corpus Inscriptionum Graecarum
CIL	Corpus Inscriptionum Latinarum
CIJ	Corpus Inscriptionum Judaicorum
ECH	Early Church History (eds. Stephen Benko, John J. O'Rourke)
HThR	Harvard Theological Review
JBL	Journal of Biblical Literature
JCSD I	Jewish and Christian Self-Definition Vol I. (Ed. E.P. Sanders)
JTS	Journal of Theological Studies
NovT	Novum Testamentum
NTA I & II	New Testament Apocrypha. Vol I & II (Ed. W. Schneemelcher)
NTS	New Testament Studies
RAC	Reallexikon für Antike und Christentum
RGG3	Die Religion in Geschichte und Gegenwart
PW	Pauly's Real-Enzyclopädie der classischen Altertumswissenschaft
SIG3	Sylloge Inscriptionum Graecarum
TDNT	Theological Dictionary of the New Testament
TU	Texte und Untersuchungen zur Geschichte der altchristlichen Literatur
TWNT	Theologisches Wörterbuch zum Neuen Testament
VC	Vigiliae Christianae
ZKG	Zeitschrift für Kirchengeschichte
ZNW	Zeitschrift für die neutestamentliche Wissenschaft
ZThK	Zeitschrift für Theologie und Kirche

Bibliography

Edition of Primary Sources

Lake, Kirsopp. 1977. *The Apostolic Fathers*. 2 vols. Loeb Classical Library (ed. G. P. Gould). London: William Heinemann.

Secondary Sources

Afanassieff, Nicolas. 1974. "L'assemblée eucharistique unique dans l'Église ancienne." *Kleronomia*. 6:1-34.

Aland, K. "Clemen I." RGG³ 1830-31.

Alexander, L.C.A. 1972. "Luke-Acts in its Contemporary Setting with special reference to the Prefaces (Luke 1:1-4 and Acts 1:1)." D.Phil. thesis, Oxford.

Alföldy, Géza. 1985. *The Social History of Rome*. (Trans. David Braund and Frank Pollock) London: Croom Helm.

Altaner, Berthold von. 1949. "Neues zum Verständnis von I Klemens 5,1-6,2." *Görresgesellschaft Historisches Jahrbuch* 62:25-30.

Audet, Jean Paul. 1967. *Structures of Christian Priesthood. Home, Marriage and Celibacy in the Pastoral Service of the Church*. London: Sheed and Ward.

Aune, David E. 1983. *Prophecy in Early Christianity and the Ancient Mediterranean World*. Grand Rapids: William B. Eerdmans.

Balch, David L. 1981. *Let Wives Be Submissive. The Domestic Code in I Peter*. Chico: Scholars Press.

Bammel, C.P. Hammond. 1982. "Ignatian Problems" *JTS* 33:62-97.

Banfield, Edward C. 1958. *The Moral Basis of a Backward Society*. Illinois: The Free Press.

Banks, Robert. 1980. *Paul's Idea of Community. The Early House Churches in their Historical Setting*. Exeter: The Paternoster Press.

Bannenbauer, H. 1932. "Die römische Petruslegende." *Historische Zietschrift* 146:239-62.

Bardsley, H.J. 1913. "The Testimony of Ignatius and Polycarp to the Apostleship of 'St. John'." *JTS* 14:489-99.

———. 1913. "The Testimony of Ignatius and Polycarp to the Writings of 'St. John'." *JTS* 14:207-20.

Bardy, Gustav. 1922. "Expressions stoiciennes dans la 1e Clementis." *Recherches de Science Religieuse*. 12:73-85.

Barnard, L.W. 1963. "The Background of St. Ignatius of Antioch." *VC* 17:193-206.

———. 1968. "The Shepherd of Hermas in Recent Study." *Heythrope Journal* 9:29-36.

———. 1966. *Studies in the Apostolic Fathers and their Background*. Oxford: Basil Blackwell.

———. 1978. *Studies in Church History and Patristics*. Thessalonika.

Barnes, Arthur S. 1938. *Christianity at Rome in the Apostolic Age*. London: Methuen.

Barnes, Timothy D. 1981. *Constantine and Eusebius*. London: Harvard University Press.

———. 1967. "A Note on Polycarp." *JTS* 18:433-7.

———. 1968. "Pre-Decian Acta Martyrum" *JTS* 19: 509-31.

———. 1971. *Tertullian. A Historical and Literary Study*. Oxford: Clarendon Press.

Barrett, C.K. 1968. *A Commentary on the First Epistle to the Corinthians*. London: Adam and Charles Black.

———. 1976. "Jews and Judaizers in the Epistles of Ignatius." In *Jews, Greeks, and Christians. Essays in Honor of William David Davies*. Leiden, pp. 220-44.

———. 1961. *Luke the Historian in Recent Study*. London: The Epworth Press.

Bartchy, S. Scott. 1973. *Mallon Chresai: First Century Slavery and the Interpretation of I Corinthians 7:21*. Missoula: The Society of Biblical Literature.

Barth, Markus. 1974. *Ephesians*. 2 vols. Garden City: Doubleday.

Bartsch, Hans Werner. 1940. *Gnostisches Gut und Gemeindetradition bei Ignatius von Antiochien*. Gütersloh: Bertelsmann.

——— "Ignatius von Antiochen." RGG³ 665-67.

Battifol, P. 1918. "Polycarp." *Hastings Dictionary of the Apostolic Church*, Vol. 2 (ed. James Hastings et al.) Edinburgh: T. & T. Clark, pp. 242-47.

Bauer, W. 1920. *Die Briefe des Ignatius von Antiochia und der Polykarpbrief*. Tübingen: J.C.B. Mohr.

Bauer, W., and Paulsen, H. 1985. *Die Briefe des Ignatius von Antiocha und der Polykarpbrief*. Tübingen: J.C.B. Mohr.

Bauer, W. 1979. *A Greek English Lexicon of the New Testament and other Early Christian Literature*. (trans. by William F. Arndt and F. Wilbur Gingrich). Chicago and London: University of Chicago Press.

———. 1923. "Die Briefe des Ignatius von Autiochia." In *Handbuch zum Neuen Testament Ergänzungsband die Apostolischen Väter*. Tübingen: J.C.B. Mohr.

———. 1971. *Orthodoxy and Heresy in Earliest Christianity*. (trans. Robert A. Kraft et al.) London: SCM Press.

Baur, Ferdinand Christian. 1835. *Die sogenannten Pastoralbriefe des Apostel Paulus*. Tübingen: Gotta.

———. 1879. *The Church History of the First Three Centuries³*.(trans. by Allan Menzies). 2 vols. London: Williams and Norgate.

———. 1838. *Über den Ursprung des Episcopats Prüfung der neuestens von Hrn. Dr. Rothe Aufgestellten Ansicht*. Tübingen: Fues.

Baur, P. V. C., and Rostovtzeff, M. I. 1931. *The Excavation at Dura-Europas*. Preliminary Report of Second Season of Work Oct. 1928-April 1929. Conducted by Yale University and the French Academy of Inscriptions & Letters. New Haven: Yale University Press.

Bendix, Reinhardt. 1977. *Max Weber. An Intellectual Portrait*. London: University of California Press.

Benko, Stephen, and O'Rourke, John J. (eds.). 1972. *Early Church History. The Roman Empire as the Setting of Primitive Christianity*. London: Lowe & Brydone.

Berger, A. "Lex Iuliae." *PW* 12² 2362-65.

Berger, Peter L. 1966. *Invitation to Sociology. A Humanistic Perspective*. Middlesex: Penguin.

Berger, Peter L. and Luckmann, Thomas. 1971. *The Social Construction of Reality*. London: Penguin.

———. 1967. *The Social Reality of Religion*. London: Faber and Faber, 1967.

Berger, Peter L., and Kellner, Hansfried. 1981. *Sociology Reinterpreted. An Essay on Method and Vocation*. Middlesex: Penguin.

Berghardt, Walter J. 1940. "Did Saint Ignatius of Antioch Know the Fourth Gospel?" *Theological Studies* I:1-26.

Betti, Emilio. 1954. "Wesen des altrömischen Familienverbands (Hausgemeinschatt und Agnatesgenossenschaft)." *Zeitschrift der Savigney-Stiftung für Rechtsgeschichte.* Rom. Abt. 71:1-24.

Bevan, G. M. 1927. *Early Christians of Rome.* London: SPCK.

Beyschlag, Karlmann. 1966. *Clemens Romanus und der Frühkatholizismus.* Tübingen.

Bieder, M. 1956. "Zür Deutung des kirchlichen Schweigens bei Ignatius von Antiocha." *Theologische Zeitschrift.* 12:28-43.

Bigg, Charles. 1890. "The Clementine Homilies." *Studia Biblica et Ecclesiastica.* II:157-193.

––––––. 1909. *The Origins of Christianity.* Oxford: The Clarendon Press.

Bingham, Joseph. 1708. *Origenes Ecclesiasticae or, The Antiquities of the Christian Church.* London.

Bisbee, Gary A. 1983. "The Acts of Justin Martyr: A Form-Critical Study." *The Second Century.* 3:129-157.

Blass, F. and Debrunner, A. 1961. *A Greek Grammar of the New Testament.* Chicago: Chicago University Press.

Blondel, David. 1646. *Apologia pro Sententia Hieronymi de Episcopis et Presbyteris.* Amsterdam.

Bocock, Robert., and Thompson, Kenneth (eds.). 1955. *Religion and Ideology.* Manchester: Manchester University Press.

Boeft, Jan den, and Bremmer, Jan. 1981. "Notiunculae Martyrologicae." *VC* 35:43-56.

Boeft, Jan den, and Bremmer, Jan. 1982. "Notiunculae Martyrologicae II." *VC* 36:383-402.

Böhmer, J.H. 1711. *Dissertationes Iuris Ecclesiastici Antiqui ad Plinium Secundum et Tertullianum.* Lipsiae.

Bornkamm, G. 1965. "Acts of Thomas." *NTA* II:425-42.

Bouquet, A.C. 1959. *Everyday Life in New Testament Times.* London: B.T. Batsford.

Bower, Richard A. 1974. "The Meaning of 'epitugchano' in the Epistles of St. Ignatius of Antioch." *VC* 28:1-14.

Braun, O. 1900. *Das Buch der Synhados.* Stuttgart.

Brockhaus, Ulrich. 1975. *Charisma und Amt. Die paulinische charismen Lehre auf dem Hintergrund der früchristlichen Gemeindefunktionen.* Wuppertal.

Brooten, J. 1982. *Women Leaders in the Ancient Synagogue.* Chico: Scholar's Press.

Brown, Peter. 1972. *Religion and Society in the Age of Augustine.* London: Faber and Faber.

Brown, Raymond E., and Meier, John P. 1983. *Antioch and Rome. New Testament Cradles of Catholic Christianity.* London: Geoffrey Chapman.

Brown, Raymond E. 1979. *The Community of the Beloved Disciple.* London: Geoffrey Chapman.

––––––. 1982. *The Epistles of John.* New York: Doubleday.

Brown, Raymond, Donfried, Karl P., and Revmann, John (eds). . 1973. *Peter in the New Testament.* Minneapolis: Augsburg Publishing House.

Bruce, F.F. 1953. *The Acts of the Apostles.* London: Tyndale.

––––––. 1984. *The Epistles to the Colossians, to Philemon, and to the Ephesians.* Grand Rapids: William B. Eerdmans.

Bruders, Heinrich. 1904. *Die Verfassung der Kirche von den ersten Jahrzehnten der apostolischen Wirksamkeit an bis zum Jahre 175 n. Chr.* Mainz.

Brunner, Gerbert. 1972. *Die theologische Mitte des ersten Klemensbriefs. Ein Beitrag zur Hermeneutik frühchristlicher Texte.* Frankfurt.

Budillon, Jean. 1971. "La Première Épitre aux Corinthiens et la controverse sur les ministères." *Istina* 16:471-88.

Bultmann, Rudolf. 1961. "Ignatius and Paul" in *Existence and Faith* (trans. Schubert M. Ogden). London: Hodder and Stoughton, pp. 267-77.

———. 1951. *Theology of the New Testament*. 2 vols. New York: Scribner's.

Bunsen, C.C.J. 1847. *Ignatius von Antiochien und seine Zeit*. Hamburg: Brockhaus.

Buren, A.W. van. 1937. "Oikos." *PW¹* 72 pp. 2119-23.

Burke, Patrick. 1970. "The Monarchical Episcopate at the End of the First Century." *Journal of Ecumenical Studies* 7:499-518.

Burke, Peter. 1980. *Sociology and History*. London: George Allen and Unwin.

Burkert, Walter. 1982. "Craft Versus Sect: The Problem of Orphics and Pythagoreans." In *Jewish and Christian Self-Definition. (Self-Definition in the Graeco-Roman World)* (ed. Ben F. Meyer and E.P. Sanders). London: SCM Press, pp. 1-22.

Cadbury, Henry J. 1931. "Erastus of Corinth." *JBL* 50:42-58.

Cadoux, Cecil John. 1938. *Ancient Smyrna. A History of the City from the Earliest Times to 324 A.D.* Oxford: Basil Blackwell.

———. 1955. *The Early Church and the World. A History of the Christian Attitude to Pagan Society and the State Down to the Time of Constantine*. Edinburgh: T. & T. Clark.

Camelot, P. T. 1969. *Ignace d'Antioche Polycarpe de Smyrne Lettres Martyre de Polycarpe*. Paris: Editions du Cerf.

Campenhausen, H. F. von. 1972. "Das Bekenntnis im Urchristentum." *ZNW* 63:210-53.

———. 1957. *Bearbeitungen und Interpolationen des Polykarp Martyriums*. (Sitzungsberichte der Heidelberger Akademie der Wissenschaften: Philosophisch-historische Klasse). Heidelberg.

———. 1969. *Ecclesiastical Authority and Spiritual Power in the Church of the First Three Centuries* (trans. J. A. Baker). London: Adam & Charles Black.

———. 1936. *Die Idee des Martyriums in der alten Kirche*. Göttingen.

———. 1951. *Polykarp von Smyrna und die Pastoralbriefe*. Sitzungsberichte der Heidelberger Akademie der Wissenschaften. Heidelberg.

——— "Polykarp, Polykarpbrief." *RGG³* 448-49.

Cannon, George E. 1983. *The Use of Traditional Materials in Colossians*. Macon: Mercer University Press.

Carney, T.F. 1975. *The Shape of the Past: Models and Antiquity*. Lawrence: Coronado Press.

Carcopino, Jérôme. 1981. *Daily Life in Ancient Rome* (trans. E.O. Lorimer). London: Penguin.

Case, S. J. 1934. *The Social Triumph of the Ancient Church*. London: George Allen & Unwin.

Cauwelaert, R. van. 1935. "L'intervention de l'Église de Rome à Corinthe vers l'an 96." *Revue d'Histoire Ecclésiatique* 31:267-306.

Chadwick, Henry. "Florilegium" (trans. J. Engemann). *RAC* 1131-59.

———. 1961. "Justification by Faith and Hospitality." *Studia Patristica* 4 *TU* 79:281-85.

———. 1950. "The Silence of Bishops in Ignatius." *HThR* 43:169-72.

Chabot, J.B. 1902. *Synodicon Orientale*. Paris.

Chapman, John. 1911. *John the Presbyter and the Fourth Gospel*. Oxford: Clarendon Press.

———. 1908. "On the Date of the Clementines." *ZNW* 21-34, 147-59.

Claereboets, Ch. 1945. "In Quo Vos Spiritus Sanctus Posuit Episcopos Regere Ecclesiam Dei (Apg. 20, 28)." *Biblica* 24:370-87.

Clark, Elmer T. 1947. *The Small Sects in America (Revised Edition)*. New York: Abingdon-Cokesbury Press.

Clarke, W.K. Lowther. 1937. *The First Epistle of Clement to the Corinthians.* London: SPCK.

Cochrane, Charles Norris. 1957. *Christianity and Classical Culture. A Study of Thought and Action from Augustus to Augustine.* New York: Oxford University Press.

Colborne, John J. 1970. "The Shepherd of Hermas: A Case for Multiple Authorship and Some Implications." *Studia Patristica* 10.1 (*TU* 107).

Connolly, R.H. 1937. "Agape and Eucharist in the Didache." *Downside Review* 55:477-89.

————. 1929. *Didaskalia Apostolorum. The Syriac Version Translated and Accompanied by the Verona Latin Fragments.* Oxford: Clarendon Press.

Corwin, Virginia. 1960. *St. Ignatius and Christianity in Antioch.* New Haven: Yale University Press.

Coser, Lewis A. 1968. "Conflict: Social Aspects." *International Encyclopedia of the Social Sciences.* Vol. 3 (ed. David L.Sills). New York: Macmillan and The Free Press, pp. 232-36.

————. 1965. *The Functions of Social Conflict.* London: Routledge and Kegan Paul.

Countryman, William. 1977. "Patrons and Officers in Club and Church." *SBL Seminar Papers* (ed. P. Achtemeier). Missoula: Scholars Press.

————. 1980. *The Rich Christian in the Church of the Early Empire: Contradictions and Accomodations.* New York, Toronto: The Edwin Mellon Press.

Crouch, James E. 1972. *The Origin and Intention of the Colossian Haustafel.* Göttingen.

Cullmann, O.. 1930. "Les Causes de la mort de Pierre et de Paul d'après le témoignage de Clément Romain." *Revue d'Histoire et de Philosophie Religieuses* 10:294-300.

————. 1962. *Peter Disciple–Apostle–Martyr* (trans. Floyd Filson). London: SCM Press.

————. 1930. *Le problème littéraire et historique du roman pseudo-clémentin.* Paris: Delachaux et Niestlé.

————. 1925. "Les récentes études sur la formation de la tradition évangélique." *Revue d'Histoire et de Philosophie Religieuses* 5:564-79.

Daillé, Jean. 1661. "Exposition de la Premiere Épitre de l'Apotre Saint Paul a Timothée." *En Quarante-Huit Sermons.* Geneva.

Daniélou, Jean. 1977. *The Origins of Latin Christianity.* London: Darton, Longman, and Todd.

————. 1961. *Primitive Christian Symbols* (trans. Donald Attwater). London: Burns and Oates.

Dassmann, Ernst. 1984. "Hausgemeinde und Bischofsamt." *Jahrbüch für Antike und Christentum* Ergänzungsband 11:82-97.

————. 1985. "Haus." *RAC* 13:802-905.

————. 1974. "Zur Entstehung des Monepiskopats." *Jahrbuch für Antike und Christentum* 17:74-90.

Daube, David. 1965. " Τρία μυστήρια κραυγῆς: Ignatius, Ephesians, XIX.1." *JTS* 16:128-29.

Davies, Adelbert. 1973. "Irrtum und Häresie. I Clem–Ignatius von Antiochien–Justinus." *Kairos* 15:165-87.

Davies, Stevan L. 1976. "The Predicament of Ignatius of Antioch." *VC* 30:175-80.

————. 1980. *The Revolt of the Widows. The Social World of the Apocryphal Acts.* Carbondale: Southern Illinois University Press, 1980.

Davies, W. D. 1964. *The Setting of the Sermon on the Mount.* Cambridge: Cambridge University Press.

Dell, August. 1914. "Matthäus 16, 17-19." *ZNW* 15:1-49.

Dibelius, Martin. 1936. *A Fresh Approach to the New Testament and Early Christian Literature.* Hertford: Stephen Austin & Sons.

———. 1923. *Der Hirt des Hermas.* Tübingen: J.C.B. Mohr.

Dibelius, Martin, and Conzelmann, Hans. 1972. *The Pastoral Epistles* (trans. Helmut Koester). Philadephia: Fortress Press.

Dibelius, Martin. 1942. *Rom und die Christen im ersten Jahrhundert.* Sitzungsberichte der Heidelberger Akademie der Wissenschaften. Heidelberg.

———. 1956. *Studies in the Acts of the Apostles* (ed. Heinrich Greeven). London: SCM Press.

Dill, Samuel. 1904. *Roman Society from Nero to Marcus Aurelius.* London: MacMillan.

Dix, G. 1946. "The Ministry in the Early Church." In *The Apostolic Ministry.* (ed. K. K. Kirk). London: Hodder & Stoughton.

———. 1978. *The Shape of the Liturgy.* London: A. & C. Black.

Dobschütz, Ernst von. 1904(a). *Christian Life in the Primitive Church* (trans. George Bremner). London: Williams and Norgate.

——— 1904(b). *Probleme des Apostolischen Zeitalters.* Leipzig.

Dodds, E.R. 1965. *Pagan and Christian in an Age of Anxiety.* Cambridge: Cambridge University Press.

Dölger, Franz Joseph. 1933. "Christophorus als Ehrentitel für Martyrer und Heilige im christlichen Altertum." *Antike und Christentum, Kultur und Religionsgeschichtliche Studien* 4:73-80.

———. 1936. "Theou Phone." *Antike und Christentum, Kultur- und Religionsgeschichte Studien* 5:218-23.

Donahue, P. J. 1978. "Jewish Christianity in Ignatius' Letters." *VC* 32:81-93.

Donfried, Karl P. (ed.). 1977. *The Romans Debate.* Minneapolis: Augsburg Publishing House.

———. 1974. *The Setting of Second Clement in Early Christianity.* Leiden: E.J. Brill.

Douglas, Mary. 1973. *Natural Symbols. Explorations in Cosmology.* London: Barrie and Jenkins.

———. 1966. *Purity and Danger. An Analysis of Concepts of Pollution and Taboo.* London: Routledge and Kegan Paul.

Downey, Glanville. 1961. *A History of Antioch in Syria.* Princeton: Princeton University Press.

Drews, Paul. 1904. "Untersuchungen zur Didache." *ZNW* 5:53-79.

Duchesne, Louis. 1909. *The Early History of the Christian Church from its Foundation to the End of the Third Century.* London: John Murray.

———. 1886. *Le Liber Pontificalis.* 2 vols. Paris: E. Thorin.

Duff, A. M. 1958. *Freedmen in the Early Roman Empire.* Cambridge: W. Heffer & Sons.

Duverger, Maurice. 1964. *Introduction to the Social Sciences.* London: George Allen and Unwin.

Easton, Burton Scott. 1948. *The Pastoral Epistles. London: SCM Press.*

Edersheim, Alfred. 1985. *Sketches of Jewish Social Life.* Grand Rapids: William B. Eerdmanns (reprint of 1876 edition).

Edmundson, George. 1913. *The Church in Rome in the First Century* Bampton Lectures, 1913. London: Longmans, Green and Co.

Eggenberger, Chr. 1951. *Die Quellen der politischen Ethik des I. Klemensbriefes.* Zurich.

Eisenstadt, S.N. (ed.) 1968a. *Max Weber. On Charisma and Institution Building.* Chicago: The University of Chicago Press.

——— 1968b. "Social Institutions." *International Encyclopedia of the Social Sciences.* New York: Cromwell Collier and MacMillan. Vol. 14:409-29.

———. 1965. "The Study of Processes of Institutionalization, Institutional Change, and Comparative Institutionalization." *Essays on Comparative Institutions*. New York: John Wiley and Sons.

Elliott, John H. 1985. "Criticism of the New Testament" *Semeia* 35:1-34.

————. 1981. *A Home for the Homeless. A Sociological Exegesis of I Peter, Its Situation and Strategy*. London: SCM Press.

Ellis, E. Earle. 1971. "Paul and His Co-workers." *NTS* 17:437-52.

————. 1974. " 'Spiritual' Gifts in the Pauline Community." *NTS* 20:128-44.

Esler, P.F. 1984. "Community and Gospel in Luke-Acts: The Social and Political Motivations of Lucan Theology." D.Phil. thesis. Oxford.

Farrer, A.M. 1946. "The Ministry in the New Testament." In *The Apostolic Ministry* (ed. K.E. Kirk). London: Hodder and Stoughton.

Filson, Floyd V. 1950. *The New Testament Against Its Environment. The Gospel of Christ the Risen Lord*. London: SCM Press.

————. 1939. "The Significance of the Early House Churches." *JBL* 58:105-12.

————. 1964. *Three Crucial Decades. Studies in the Book of Acts*. London: The Epworth Press.

Finley, M. I. 1973. *The Ancient Economy*. London: Chatto & Windus.

————. 1977. *The World of Odysseus*. London: Chatto & Windus.

Fiorenza, Elisabeth Schüssler. 1983. *In Memory of Her. A Feminist Theological Reconstruction of Christian Origins*. London: SCM Press.

Fornberg, Tord. 1972. *An Early Church in a Pluralistic Society. A Study of II Peter* (trans. Jean Gray). London: Gluk Gleerup.

Foucart, P. 1873. *Des associations religieuses chez les Grecs. Thiases, Eranes, Orgéons*. Paris: Klincksieck.

Frend, W. H. C. 1954. "The Gnostic Sects and the Roman Empire." *Journal of Ecclesiastical History* 5:25-37.

————. 1984. *The Rise of Christianity*. London: Darton, Longman and Todd.

Frey, P. Jean-Baptiste. 1936 and 1952. *Corpus Inscriptionum Iudaicarum. Recueil des Inscriptions, Juives qui vont du IIIe siècle avant Jésus-Christ au VIIesiècle de Notre Ére*. 2 vols. Rome: Seminaire Francais.

Friedrich, Carl J. 1961. "Political Leadership and the Problem of the Charismatic Power." *The Journal of Politics* 23:3-24.

Fuellenbach, J. 1980. *Ecclesiastical Office and the Primacy of Rome. An Evaluation of Recent Theological Discussion of First Clement*. Washington, D.C.: The Catholic University of America Press.

Funk, Robert W. 1967. "The Form and Structure of II and III John." *JBL* 86:424-30.

————. 1976. "The Watershed of the American Biblical Tradition:The Chicago School, First Phase, 1892-1920." *JBL* 95:4-22.

Funk, F.X. 1901. *Die Apostolischen Väter*. Tübingen and Leipzig: Laupp.

Gager, John G. 1975. *Kingdom and Community: The Social World of Early Christianity*. Englewood Cliffs: Prentice Hall.

Gamber, K. 1967. "Die frühchristliche Hauskirche nach Didascalia Apostolorum II,57,1-58,6." *Studia Patristica* 10.1:337-44.

Gaudemet, J. 1969. "Familie I (Familienrecht)." *RAC* 7:286-358.

Gealy, Fred D., and Noyer, Morgan D. 1955. "The First & Second Epistles to Timothy and The Epistle to Titus." In *The Interpreter's Bible II*. New York: Abingdon Press, pp. 343-51.

Geertz, Clifford. 1958. "Ethos, World-View and the Analysis of Sacred Symbols." *Antioch Review* 17:421-37.

————. 1964. "Ideology as a Cultural System." In *Ideology and Discontent* (ed. by David E. Apter). London: Collier-MacMillan, pp. 47-76.

————. 1973. *The Interpretation of Cultures.* New York: Basic Books.

————. 1966. "Religion as a Cultural System." In *Anthropological Approaches to the Study of Religion.* (ed. M. Banton). London: Tavistock Publications, pp. 1-46.

Gerkan, A. von. 1934. "Die frühchristliche Kirchenanlage von Dura." *Römische Quartelschrift* 42:219-32.

————. 1964. "Zur Hauskirche von Dura-Europas." *Mullus, Festschrift Theodor Klausner, Reallexion zur byzantinischen Kunst* Ergänzungsband I: 143-49.

Gerke, F. 1931. *Die Stellung des I Clemensbrief innerhalb der Entwicklung der altchristl. Gemeindeverfassung und des Kirchenrechts. TU* 47.

Gerth, H.H., and Mills, C. Wright. 1979. *From Max Weber: Essays in Sociology.* New York: Oxford University Press.

Gielen, Marlis. 1986. "Zur Interpretation der paulinischen Formel ἡ κατ' οἶκον ἐκκλησία." *ZNW* 77:109-25.

Giet, Stanislas. 1963. *Hermas et les pasteurs: les trois auteurs du Pasteur d'Hermas.* Paris: Editions du Cerf.

Gill, Robin. 1977. *Theology and Social Structure.* Oxford: A.R. Mowbray.

Gnilka, Joachim. 1969. "Geistliches Amt und Gemeinde nach Paulus." *Kairos* 11:95-104.

————. 1971. "Das Kirchenmodell der Epheserbriefen." *BZNF* 15:161-84.

————. 1982. *Der Philemonbrief.* Freiburg: Herder.

————. 1968. *Der Philipperbrief.* Freiburg: Herder.

Goltz, Eduard Freiherrn von der. 1894. "Ignatius von Antiochien als Christ und Theologe." *TU* 12,3.

————. 1905. "Tischgebete und Abendsmahlgebete in den altchristlichen und in der griechischen Kirche." *TU* 29.

Goodspeed, Edgar J. 1933. *The Meaning of Ephesians.* Chicago.

Goppelt, Leonhard. 1970. *Apostolic and Post-apostolic Times.* London: Adam and Charles Black.

————. 1968. "Kirchenleitung und Bischofsamt in den ersten drei Jahrhunderten." In *Kirchenpräsident oder Bischof?* (ed. Ivar Asheim and Victor R. Gold). Göttingen: Bertelsmann, pp. 9-35.

Gore, Charles. 1900. *The Church and the Ministry[4].* London: Longmans, Green, and Co.

Graham, Walter J. 1966. "Origins and Interrelations of the Greek House and the Roman House." *Phoenix* 20:3-31.

Grant, Robert M. 1964. *The Apostolic Fathers: A New Translation and Commentary.* Vol. 1: *An Introduction.* New York: Thomas Nelson & Sons.

Grant, Robert M., and Graham, Holt H. 1965. *The Apostolic Fathers. A New Translation and Commentary.* Vol. 2: *First and Second Clement.* London: Thomas Nelson & Sons.

Grant, Robert M. 1966. *The Apostolic Fathers: A New Translation and Commentary.* Vol. 4: *Ignatius of Antioch.* London: Thomas Nelson & Sons.

————. 1970. *Augustus to Constantine.* London: William Collins Son and Co.

————. 1977. *Early Christianity and Society.* New York, London: Harper & Row.

————. 1946. "Polycarp of Smyrna." *Anglican Theological Review* 28:137-50.

————. 1980. "The Social Setting of Second-Century Christianity." *JCSD I.* pp. 16-29.

Grayston, K., and Herdan, G. 1959-60. "The Authorship of the Pastorals in the Light of Statistical Linguistics." *NTS* 6:1-15.

Green, Henry Alan. 1985. *The Economic and Social Origins of Gnosticism.* Atlanta: Scholars Press.

————. 1977. "Suggested Sociological Themes in the Study of Gnosticism." *VC* 31:169-80.

Greeven, Heinrich. 1935. *Das Hauptproblem der Sozialethik in der neueren Stoa und im Urchristentum.* Gütersloh: Bertelsmann.

———— 1952/53. "Propheten, Lehrer, Vorsteher bei Paulus." *ZNW* 44:1-43.

Grelot, Pierre. 1974. "Le Épîtres de Paul: La mission Apostoliques." In *Le Ministère et les Ministères Selon le Nouveau Testament* (ed. J. Delorme). Paris: Editions du Seuil, pp. 34-56.

————. 1971. "Sur l'origine des ministères dans les Églises Pauliniennes." *Istina* 16:453-69.

Groh, Dennis E. 1971. "Tertullian's Polemic Against Social Co-optation." *Church History* 40:7-14.

————. 1971. "Upper-Class Christians in Tertullian's Africa." *TU* 117:41-7.

Gülzow, Hennecke. 1967. "Kallist von Rom. Ein Beitrag zur Soziologie der römischen Gemeinde." *ZNW* 58:102-121.

————. 1974. "Die sozialen Gegebenheiten der altchristlichen Mission." In *Kirchengeschichte als Missionsgeschichte* (ed. H. Frohnes and V.W. Knorr). Vol. 1. Munich: Kaiser, pp. 189-226.

Guthrie, Donald. 1957. *The Pastoral Epistles.* London: Tyndale Press.

————. 1963. *The Pauline Epistles. New Testament Introduction.* London: Tyndale Press.

Gutmann, J., ed. 1971. *Ancient Synagogues: The State of Research.* Chico: Scholars Press.

———— ed. 1975. *The Synagogue: Studies in Origins, Archeology, and Architecture.* New York: KTAV.

Hagner, D.A. 1973. *The Use of the Old and New Testaments in Clement of Rome.* Leiden: E.J. Brill.

Haenchen, Ernst. 1971. *The Acts of the Apostles. A Commentary.* Oxford: Basil Blackwell.

Hainz, Josef. 1972. *Ekklesia. Strukturen paulinischer Gemeinde-Theologie und Gemeinde-Ordnung.* Regensburg.

Hall, H. 1644. *The Apostolical Institution of Episcopacy.* Oxford.

Hall, J. 1640. *Episcopacie by Divine Right Asserted.* London.

———— 1628. *The Olde Religion. A Treatise wherein is Laid Downe the True State of the Difference Between the Reformed, and the Romane Church.* London.

Halliday, William Reginald. 1922. *Lectures on the History of Roman Religion.* London: Hodder and Stoughton.

Hammond, Henry. 1651. *Dissertationes quartor, quibus Episcopatus Jura ex S. Scripturis et Antiquitate adstruuntur, Contra sententiam D. Blondelli et aliorum.* London.

Hammond, Mason. 1951. *City-State and World-State in Greek Political Thought until Augustus.* Cambridge: Harvard University Press.

Hands, A.R. 1968. *Charities and Social Aid in Greece and Rome.* London: Thames and Hudson.

Hanson, A. T. 1982. *The Pastoral Epistles.* London: Marshall, Morgan & Scott.

Hardy, E.G. 1906. *Studies in Roman History.* London: Swan Sonnenschein.

Harnack, Adolf. v. 1897. *Die Chronologie der altchristlichen Litteratur bis Eusebius.* Bd. I. Leipzig: J.C. Henrichs.

————. 1910. *The Constitution and Law of the Church in the First Two Centuries.* London: Williams and Norgate.

————. 1929. *Einführung in die alte Kirchengeschichte. Das Schreiben der römischen Kirche an die Korintische aus der Zeit Domitians (I. Clemensbrief).* Leipzig: J.C. Henrichs.

————. 1920. *Entstehung und Entwickelung der Kirchenverfassung und Kirchenrecht in den zwei ersten Jahrhunderten.* Leipzig: J.C. Henrichs.

————. 1909. "Der Erste Klemensbrief. Eine Studie zur Bestimmung des Charakters des ältesten Heidenschristentum." *Sitzungsberichte der königlich Preussischen Akademie der Wissenschaften,* 38-63.

———. 1907. *Essays on the Social Gospel* (trans. G.M. Craik). London: Williams and Norgate.

———. 1893. *Geschichte der altchristlichen Litteratur bis Eusebius.* Ersten Teil. Leipzig: J.C. Henrichs.

Harnack, Adolph, and De Gebhardt, Oscar. 1877. *Hermae Pastor.* Lipsiae: J.C. Henrichs.

Harnack, Adolf v. 1976. *History of Dogma.* 5 vols. Gloucester: Peter Smith.

———. 1884. "Lehre der Zwölf Apostel nebst Untersuchungen zur ältesten Geschichte der Kirchenverfassung und der Kirchenrechts." *TU* 2,1 and 2,2.

———. 1908. *The Mission and Expansion of Christianity in the First Three Centuries* (trans. James Moffatt). 2 vols. London: Williams and Norgate.

———. 1886. "Die Quellen der sogenannten Apostolischen Kirchenordnung." *TU* 3,5.

———. 1908. "Das Urchristentum und die Sozialen Fragen." *Preussische Jahrbücher* 131:443-59.

———. 1904. *What is Christianity?* London: Williams and Norgate.

Harrison, P. N. 1956. "The Authorship of the Pastoral Epistles." *Expository Times* 67:77-81.

———. 1936. *Polycarp's Two Epistles to the Philippians.* Cambridge: Cambridge University Press.

———. 1921. *The Problem of the Pastoral Epistles.* Oxford: Oxford University Press.

Harvey, A. E. 1974. "Elders." *JTS* 23:318-32.

Hatch, Edwin. 1888. *The Organization of the Early Christian Churches³.* London: Longmans and Green.

Hauck, A. 1901. "Kirchenbau." *Realenzyklopädie für protestantische Theologie und Kirche³.* Vol 10 (ed. J.J. Herzog). Leipzig:J.C. Henrichs: pp. 774-94.

Headlam, Arthur C. 1920. *The Doctrine of the Church and Christian Reunion.* London: John Murray.

———. "The Epistle of Polycarp to the Philippians." *The Church Quarterly Review.* 181:1-25.

Hefele, Charles Joseph. 1876. *A History of the Councils of the Church* (trans. Henry Nutcombe Oxenham). 7 vols. Edinburgh: T. and T. Clark.

Heinrici, G. 1876. "Die Christengemeinde Korinths und die religiösen benossenschaften der Griechen." *Zeitschrift für Wissentschaftliche Theologie* 19:465-521.

———. 1880. *Das erste Sendschreiben des Apostel Paulus and die Korinthier.* Berlin: Hertz.

———. 1877. "Zur Geschichte der Anfänge paulinischer Gemeinden." *Zeitschrift für Wisseneschaftliche Theologie* 20:89-130.

———. 1887. *Das Zweite Sendschreiben des Apostel Paulus an die Korinthier.* Berlin: Hertz.

Heintze, W. 1914. "Der Clemensroman und seine griechischen Quellen." *TU* 40.

Helm, Rudolf. 1956. *Eusebius Werke. Siebenter Band. Die Chronik des Hieronymus.* Leipzig: J.C. Henrichs.

Hemer, Colin J. 1986. *The Letters to the Seven Churches of Asia in Their Local Setting.* Sheffield: JSOT Press.

Hengel, Martin. 1974. *Property and Riches in the Early Church. Aspects of a Social History of Early Christianity* (trans. John Bowden). Philadelphia: Fortress Press.

———. 1966. "Die synagogen Inschrift von Stobi." *ZNW* 57:145-83.

Hennecke, E. 1963 & 1965. *New Testament Apocrypha* (ed. W. Schneemelcher, trans. R. Mcl. Wilson). 2 vols. London: Lutterworth Press.

Herrmann, Peter, et. al. 1978. "Genossenschaft." *RAC* 10:83-155.

Hertling, L. 1939. "I Kor 16,15 und I Clem 42." *Biblica* 20:276-83.

Hildebrand, J. 1745. *Commentationem de Episcopis et Iuribus Episcopalibus.* Helmstadt.

Hill, Clifford Stanley. 1982. "The Sociology of the New Testament Church to A.D. 62: An Examination of the Early New Testament Church in Relation to its Contemporary Social Setting." Ph.D. thesis, University of Nottingham.

Hilhorst, A. 1976. *Sémitismes et latismes dans le Pasteur d'Hermas.* Nijmegen.

Hinson, Glenn E. 1981. *The Evangelization of the Roman Empire.* Macon: Mercer University Press.

Hitchcock, F. R. Montgomery. 1928-29. "Tests for the Pastorals." *JTS* 30:272-79.

Hitchcock, Roswell D., and Brown, Francis. 1885. *The Teaching of the Twelve Apostles.* London: John C. Nimmo.

Hock, Ronald F. 1978. "Paul's Tentmaking and the Problem of His Social Class." *JBL* 97:555-64.

_____. 1976. "Simon the Shoemaker an Ideal Cynic." *Greek, Roman and Byzantine Studies* 17:41-53.

_____. 1980. *The Social Context of Paul's Ministry — Tentmaking and Apostleship.* Philadelphia: Fortress Press.

Hoebel, E. Adamson. 1954. *The Law of Primitive Man. A Study in Comparative Legal Dynamics.* Cambridge: Harvard University Press.

_____. 1958. *Man in the Primitive World. An Introduction to Anthropology.* London: McGraw-Hill.

Hoffmann, R. Joseph. 1984. *Marcion: On the Restitution of Christianity. An Essay on the Development of Radical Paulinist Theology in the Second Century.* Chico: Scholars Press.

Hofstadter, Richard. 1968. "History and Sociology in the United States." In *Sociology and History: Methods.* New York: Basic Books, pp. 3-19.

Hoh, J. 1932. *Die kirchliche Busse im zweiten Jahrhundert.* Breslau.

Holmberg, Bengt. 1980a. *Paul and Power: The Structure of Authority in the Primitive Church as Reflected in the Pauline Epistles.* Lund: GWK Gleerup.

_____ 1980b. "Sociological versus Theological Analysis of the Question Concerning a Pauline Church Order." In *Die paulinische Literatur und Theologie* (ed. Sigfred Pedersen). Göttingen: Vanderhoeck and Ruprecht, pp. 187-200.

Holtzmann, H.J. 1893. *Hand-Commentar zum Neuen Testament. Dritte Band. Die Briefe an die Kolosser, Epheser, Philemon, die Pastoralbriefe.* Leipzig: J.C. Henrichs.

_____. 1880. *Die Pastoral, Kritisch und exegitisch bearbeitet.* Leipzig: J.C. Henrichs.

Hopkins, Clark. 1979. *The Discovery of Dura Europas* (ed. Bernard Goldman). New Haven: Yale University Press.

Hornschuh, M. "Acts of Andrew." *ANT* 2:390-403.

Hort, Fenton John Anthony. 1914. *The Christian Ecclesia. A Course of Lectures on the Early History of and Early Conceptions of the Ecclesia.* London: MacMillan.

Jaeger, Werner. 1961. *Early Christianity and Greek Paideia.* London: Oxford University Press.

James, M.R. 1980. *The Apocryphal New Testament.* Oxford: Clarendon Press.

Jastrow, Marcus. 1903. *A Dictionary of the Targomim, the Talmud Babli and Yerushalmi, and the Midrashic Literature.* London: Luzuc.

Jaubert, Annie. 1971. *Clément de Rome. Épître aux Corinthiens.* Paris: Editions du Cerf.

_____. 1974. "Les Épîtres de Paul: Le Fait Communautaire." in *Le Ministère et les ministères selon le Nouveau Testament* (ed. Jean Delorme). Paris, pp. 16-33.

Jay, Eric G. 1981. "From Presbyter-Bishops to Bishops and Presbyters." *The Second Century* 1:125-72.

Jervell, Jacob. 1972. *Luke and the People of God. A New Look at Luke Acts.* Minneapolis: Augsburg Publishing House.

————. 1976. "Die schwache Charismatiker." In *Rechtfertigung. Festschrift für Ernst Käsemann zum 70. Geburtstag* (ed. Johannes Friedrich, Wolfgang Pöhlmann, and Peter Stuhlmacher). Tübingen: pp. 189-98.

Johnson, Harry M. 1968. "Ideology II, Ideology and the Social System." Vol. 7, *International Encyclopedia of Social Sciences* New York: Cromwell Collier and MacMillan, pp. 76-85.

Johnson, Sherman E. 1975. "Asia Minor and Early Christianity." In *Christianity, Judaism, and Other Graeco-Roman Cults — Studies for Morton Smith at Sixty*. (ed. J. Neusner). Part Two. Leiden: E.J. Brill. pp. 77-145.

————. 1981. "Christianity in Sardis." In *Early Christian Origins. Studies in Honour of Harold R. Willoughby* (ed. Allen Wilkgren). Chicago: Quadrangle Books, pp. 81-90.

Joly, Robert. 1958. *Hermas le Pasteur.* Paris: Editions du Cerf.

Jones, A.H.M. 1940. *The Greek City from Alexander to Justinian.* Oxford: Clarendon Press.

Jones, F. Stanley. 1982. "The Pseudo-Clementines: A History of Research." *Second Century* 2:2-33, 63-96.

Judge, E.A. 1984. "Cultural Conformity and Innovation in Paul: Some Clues from Contemporary Documents." *Tyndale Bulletin* 35:1-35.

———— 1960a. "The Early Christians as a Scholastic Community." *Journal of Religious History* 1:4-15, 125-137.

Judge, E. A., and Thomas, G. S. R. 1966. "The Origin of the Church at Rome: A New Solution?" *The Reformed Theological Review* 25:81-94.

————. 1980. "The Social Identity of the First Christians: A Question of Method in Religious History." *The Journal of Religious History* 11:201-18.

———— 1960b. *The Social Pattern of the Christian Groups in the First Century. Some Prolegomena to the Study of New Testament Ideas of Social Obligation.* London: Tyndale Press.

————. 1972. "St. Paul and Classical Society." *Jahrbuch für Antike und Christentum* 15:19-36.

Juel, Donald. 1983. *Luke Acts. The Promise of History.* Atlanta: John Knox Press.

Karris, Robert J. 1973. "The Background & Significance of the Polemic of the Pastoral Epistles." *JBL* 92:549-64.

————. 1979. *The Pastoral Epistles.* Dublin: Veritas Publications.

Käsemann, E. 1965. *Essays on New Testament Themes.* London: SCM Press Ltd.

————. 1969. *New Testament Questions of Today* (trans. W. J. Montague). London: SCM Press.

Kautsky, Karl. 1925. *Foundations of Christianity: A Study in Christian Origins.* London: Orbach.

Kearsley, R.A. 1985. "Women in Public Life in the Roman East: Iunia Theodora, Claudia Metrodora and Phoebe, Benefactress of Paul." *Ancient Society: Resources for Teachers* 15:124-37.

Keating, J.F. 1901. *The Agapé and the Eucharist in the Early Church. Studies in the History of the Christian Love-Feasts.* London: Methuen.

Keck, L.E. 1974. "On the Ethos of Early Christians." *Journal of the American Academy of Religion* 42:435-52.

Kee, Howard Clark. 1980. *Christian Origins in Sociological Perspective.* London: SCM Press.

————. 1982. *Miracle in the Early Christian World. A Study in Sociohistorical Method.* New Haven: Yale University Press.

Kee, Howard Clark, and Young, Franklin W., and Froelich, Karlfried. 1973. *Understanding the New Testament.* New Jersey: Prentice-Hall.

Kelly, J. N. D. 1963. *A Commentary on the Pastoral Epistles*. London: Adam & Charles Black.

————. 1983. *Early Christian Creeds³*. New York: Longman.

Keresztes, Paul. 1973. "The Jews, the Christians, and Emperor Domitian." *VC* 27:1-28.

Kertelge, Karl. 1972. *Gemeinde und Amt im Neuen Testament*. Munich: Sankt Benno.

Kidd, B. J. 1922. *A History of the Church to A.D. 461*. Vol. 1. Oxford: The Clarendon Press.

Kiley, Mark. 1986. *Colossians as Pseudepigraphy*. Sheffield: JSOT Press.

Kilpatrick, G.D. 1946. *The Origins of the Gospel According to St. Matthew*. Oxford: Clarendon Press.

Kim, Chan-Hie. 1972. *Form and Structure of the Familiar Greek Letter of Recommendation*. Missoula: Society of Biblical Literarture.

Kippenberg, Hans G. 1970. "Soziologische Verortung des antiken Gnostizismus." *Numen* 17:211-231.

Kirk, E. K. 1946. *The Apostolic Ministry: Essays on the History and Doctrine of Episcopacy*. London: Hodder and Stoughton.

Kirsch, J.P. 1897. "Die christlichen Cultusgebäude in der vorkonstantinischen Zeit." In *Festschrift zum elfhundertjährigen Jubiläum des deutschen Campo Santo in Rom* (ed. Stephan Ehses). Freiburg in Breisgau: Herder, pp. 6-20.

Kist, Nicolaus Christian. 1832. "Über den Ursprung der bischöflichen Gewalt in der christlichen Kirche in Verbindung mit der Bildung und dem Zustande der frühesten Christengemeinden." *Zeitschrift für historische Theologie* 2:47-90.

Klauck, Hans-Joseph. 1985. "Gemeinde ohne Amt? Erfuhrungen mit der kirche in die johannischen Schriften." *Biblische Zeitschrift (NF)* 29:193-220.

————. 1981a. *Hausgemeinde und Hauskirche im frühen Christentum*. Stuttgart: Verlag katholisches Bibelwerk.

————. 1981b. *Herrenmahl und Hellenistischer Kult. Eine religionsgeschichtliche Untersuchung zum ersten Korintherbrief*. Münster: Aschendorff.

Kleist, J. 1946. *The Epistles of St. Clement of Rome and St. Ignatius of Antioch*. Westminster: Newman.

Knopf, R. 1920. *Die Apostolischen Väter. Handbuch zum Neuen Testament*. Ergänzungsband I. Tübingen: J.C.B. Mohr.

————. 1899. "Der Erste Klemensbrief." *TU* 20.

————. 1900. "Über die sociale Zusammensetzung der ältesten heidenchristlichen Gemeinden." *ZThK* 10:325-47.

Koch H. 1926. "Zu A. v. Harnacks Beweis für den amtlichen römischen Ursprung des Muratorischen Fragments." *ZNW* 25:154-60.

Kornemann, E. 1901. "Collegium." *PW* 4:380-480.

Koschorcke, Klaus. 1977. "Die Polemik der Gnostiker gegen das kirchliche Christentum." *Gnosis and Gnosticism. Papers read at the 7th International Conference on Patristic Studies* (Oxford, September 8-13, 1975), ed. Martin Krause. NHS VIII. Leiden: E.J. Brill, pp. 43-49.

Kraabel, A. Thomas. 1981. "Social Systems of Six Diaspora Synagogues." In *Ancient Synagogues. The State of Research* (ed. Joseph Gutmann). Chico: Scholars Press, pp. 79-92.

Kraeling, C.H. 1967. *The Christian Building in the Excavation at Dura-Europas*. Final Report VIII, Part II (ed. C. Bradford Welles). New Haven: Dura-Europas Publications.

————. 1967. *Dura Report. Final Report (VIII) The Synagogue, Mithraeum, and Christian Chapel*. New Haven: Dura-Europas Publications.

————. 1934. "The Earliest Synagogue Architecture." *Bulletin of the Amercian Schools of Oriental Research*. 54:18-20.

————. 1932. "The Jewish Community at Antioch." *JBL* 33:130-60.

————. 1956. The Synagogue. *Final Report VIII, Part I of The Excavation at Dura Europas* (ed. A.R. Bellinger, F.E. Brown, A. Perkins, C.B. Welles). New Haven: Yale University Press.

Kraft, Robert A. 1972. "Judaism on the World Scene." *ECH* 81-98.

Kretschmar, G. 1972. "Christliches Passa im 2. Jahrhundert und die Ausbildung der Christlichen Theologie." *Recherches de Science Religieuse* 60:287-323.

Krodel, Gerhard. 1972. "Persecution and Toleration of Christianity until Hadrian." *ECH* 255-67.

Kümmel, W.G. 1975. *Introduction to the New Testament* (trans. Howard Kee). London: SCM Press.

Kurfess, A. 1965. "Christian Sibyllines." *NTA* II 703-45.

Kyrtatas, Dimitris J. 1982. "Social Status and Conversion. The Structure of the Early Christian Communities." Ph.D. dissertation, Brunel University.

Lacey, W.K. 1968. *The Family in Classical Greece*. London: Thames and Hudson.

————. 1986. "Patria Potestas" *The Family in Ancient Rome. New Perspectives*. London: Croom Helm, 1986.

Lake, Kirsopp. 1920. *Landmarks in the History of Early Christianity*. London: MacMillan.

————. 1933. "Proselytes and God-fearers." *The Beginnings of Christianity*, Part I, Vol. V (eds. Kirsopp Lake and Henry J. Cadbury). London: MacMillan, pp. 74-96.

————. 1925. "The Shepherd of Hermas." *HThR* 38:279-80.

Lampe, G.W.H. 1968. *A Patristic Greek Lexicon*. Oxford: Clarendon Press.

La Piana, George. 1927. "Foreign Groups in Rome During the First Centuries of the Empire." *HThR* 20:183-240.

————. 1925. "The Roman Church at the End of the Second Century." *HThR* 38:201-77.

Laub, Franz. 1976. "Paulus als Gemeindegründer (I Thess.)." In *Kirche im Werden* (ed. J. Hainz). München: pp. 17-38.

Leaney, A. R. C. 1984. *The Jewish and Christian World 200 B.C. to A.D. 200*. Cambridge: Cambridge University Press.

Leclerq, H. 1921. "Églises." *Dictionnaire d'Archéologie Chretienne et de Liturgie*. 4:2279-349.

Lee, Clarence L. 1972. "Social Unrest and Primitive Christianity." *ECH* 121-38.

Lemaire, André. 1974. "Les Épîtres de Paul: La Diversité des Ministères." *Le Ministère et les Ministères selon le Nouveau Testament* (ed. Jean Delorme). Paris: Editions du Seuil, pp. 57-73.

Leon, Harry J. 1960. *The Jews of Ancient Rome*. Philadelphia: Jewish Publication Society of America.

Lewis, Naphtali, and Reinhold, Meyer. 1966. *Roman Civilization. Sourcebook II: The Empire*. London, New York: Harper & Row.

Liebenam, W. 1890. *Zur Geschichte und Organisation des römischen Vereinswesens*. Leipzig: J.C. Henrichs.

Lietzmann, Hans. 1914. "Zur altchristlichen Verfassungsgeschichte." *ZNW* 55:97-153.

————. 1961. *A History of the Early Church* (trans. Bertram Lee Woolf). London: Lutterworth Press.

————. 1927. *Petrus und Paulus in Rom*. Berlin, Leipzig.

Lieu, Judith. 1986. *The Second and Third Epistles of John: History and Background*. Edinburgh: T. and T. Clark.

Lightfoot, J. B. 1890. *The Apostolic Fathers. S. Clement of Rome.* Part I, Vols. I & II. London: Macmillan.

———. 1885. *The Apostolic Fathers. S. Ignatius, S. Polycarp.* Part II, Vols. I & II. London: Macmillan.

———. 1888. *Saint Paul's Epistle to the Philippians.* London: Macmillan.

Lilje, Hanns. 1956. *Die Lehre der zwölf Apostel.* Hamburg.

Linton, O. 1932. *Das Problem der Urkirche.* Uppsala: Uppsala University Press.

Lipset, Seymour Martin. 1968. "History and Sociology: Some Methodological Considerations." In *Sociology and History: Methods* (ed. Seymour Martin Lipset and Richard Hofstadter). New York: Basic Books Inc., pp. 20-58.

Lipsius, R.A. 1855. *De Clementis Romani Epistula ad Corinthios.* (no place specified).

Little, A. M. G. 1972. *Roman Bridal Drama at the Villa of the Mysteries.* Leiden: E.J. Brill.

Loening, E. 1889. *Die Gemeindeverfassung des Urchristentums. Eine kirchenrechtliche Untersuchung.* Halle: Niemeyer.

Loewenich, W. von. 1932. "Das Johannes — Verständnis im zweiten Jahrhundert." *Beihefte zur Zeitschrift für die Neutestamentiche Wissenschaft* 13.

Lohfink, Gerhard. 1977. "Die Normativität der Amtvorstellungen in den Pastoralbriefen." *Theologische Quartalschrift* 157:93-106.

Lohse, Eduard. 1971. *Colossians and Philemon* (trans. William R. Poehlmann and Robert J. Karris; ed. Helmut Koester). Philadelphia: Fortress Press.

———. 1977. "Die Ordination im Spätjudentum und im Neuen Testament." *Das kirchliche Amt im Neuen Testament* (ed. K. Kertelge). Darmstadt: Wissenschaftliches Buchgesellschaft, pp. 501-23.

Lüdemann, Gerd. 1980. "The Successors of Pre-70 Jerusalem Christianity: A Critical Evaluation of the Pella Tradition." *JCSD* I 161-73.

Lüders, Otto. 1873. *Die dionysischen Künstler.* Berlin: Weidmann.

Lührmann, Dieter. 1981. "Neutestamentsliche Haustafeln und antike Ökonomie." *NTS* 27:83-97.

MacDonald, Dennis Ronald. 1983. *The Legend and the Apostle. The Battle for Paul in Story and Canon.* Philadelphia: Fortress Press.

MacDonald, Margaret. 1986. "Institutionalization of Pauline Communities: A Sociohistorical Investigation of the Pauline and Deutero-Pauline Writings." D.Phil.dissertation, University of Oxford.

MacMullen, Ramsay. 1984. *Christianizing the Roman Empire (A.D. 100-400).* London and New York: Yale University Press.

———. 1981. *Paganism in the Roman Empire.* London and New Haven: Yale University Press.

———. 1974. *Roman Social Relations 50 B.C. to A.D. 284.* New Haven, London: Yale University Press.

Macrae, George W. 1980. "Why the Church Rejected Gnosticism." *JCSD* I 126-33.

Maddox, Robert. 1982. *The Purpose of Luke Acts.* Edinburgh: T. & T. Clark.

Magie, David. 1950. *Roman Rule in Asia Minor to the End of the Third Century After Christ.* Princeton: Princeton University Press.

Malherbe, Abraham J. 1986. *Moral Exhortation. A Graeco-Roman Sourcebook.* Philadelphia; The Westminster Press.

———. 1982. "Self-Definition Among Epicureans and Cynics." In *Jewish and Christian Self-Definition.* Vol. 3: *Self-Definition in the Graeco-Roman World.* London: SCM Press.

———. 1983. *Social Aspects of Early Christianity.* Philadelphia: Fortress Press.

Malina, Bruce J. 1981. *The New Testament World. Insights from Cultural Anthropology.* London: SCM Press.

————. 1978. "The Social World Implied in the Letters of the Christian Bishop-Martyr (Named Ignatius of Antioch)." *Society of Biblical Literature 1978 Seminar Papers*, vol. 2 (ed. Paul J. Achtemeier). Missoula: Scholars Press.

Mantle, Igna Catharine. 1978. "Roman Household Religion." Ph.D. dissertation, University of Edinburgh.

Markus, R. A. 1980. "The Problem of Self-Definition: From Sect to Church." *JCSD* I London: SCM Press, pp. 1-15.

Marrou, H. I. 1981. *A History of Education in Antiquity³*. London: Sheed and Ward.

Martin, Jochen. 1972. *Der priesterliche Dienst III. Die Genese des Amtspriestertums in der frühen kirche*. Freiburg: Herder.

Martin, R.P. 1974. *Colossians and Philemon*. London: Oliphants.

Martin, T.M. 1986. "Eschatology, History and Mission in the Social Experience of Lucan Christians. A Sociological Study of the Development between Ideas and Social Realities in Luke-Acts." D.Phil. dissertation, University of Oxford.

Martindale, Don. 1959. "Sociological Theory and the Ideal Type." in *Symposium on Sociological Theory* (ed. Llewellyn Gross). Evanston: Row, Peterson and Company, pp. 57-91.

Maurer, Christian. 1949. *Ignatius von Antiochien und das Johannesevangelium*. Freiburg: Herder.

————. πραγματεία, πρᾶξις *TWNT* 6:641-42, 643-45.

Meeks, Wayne A. 1983. *The First Urban Christians: The Social World of the Apostle Paul*. London: Yale University Press.

————. 1977. "In One Body: The Unity of Humankind in Colossians and Ephesians." In *God's Christ and His People* (ed. Jacob Jervell and Wayne A. Meeks). Oslo, Bergen, Tromsö.

Meeks, Wayne A., and Wilken, Robert L. 1978. *Jews and Christians in Antioch in the First Four Centuries of the Common Era*. Missoula: Scholars Press.

Meeks, Wayne A. 1972. "The Man From Heaven in Johannine Sectarianism." *JBL* 91:44-72.

————. 1986. *The Moral World of the First Christians*. Philadelphia: The Westminster Press.

Meinhold, Peter. 1939. "Geschehen und Deutung im Ersten Klemensbrief." *Zeitschrift für Kirchengeschichte* 58:82-129.

————. 1979. *Studien zu Ignatius von Antiochien*. Wiesbaden.

Menard, Jacques E. 1980. "Normative Self-Definition in Gnosticism." JCSD I pp. 134-150.

Merrill, E. T. 1924. *Essays in Early Christian History*. London: Macmillan.

Metzger, Bruce M. 1958. "A Reconsideration of Certain Arguments Against the Pauline Authorship of the Pastoral Epistles." *The Expository Times* 70:91-94.

Metzner, Emil. 1920. *Die Verfassung der Kirche in den zwei ersten Jahrhunderten unter besonderer Berücksichtigung der Schriften Harnacks*. Danzig: Westpreussischer Verlag.

Michaelis, Wilhelm. 1930. *Die Pastoralbriefe und Gefangenschaftbriefe zur Echtheitsfrage den Pastoralbriefe*. Göttingen: Bertelsmann.

Mikat, Paul. 1969. *Die Bedeutung der Begriffe Stasis und Aponoia für das Verständnis des I. Clemensbriefes*. Cologne.

Mills, C. Wright. 1981. *The Sociological Imagination*. London: Oxford University Press.

Milton, John. 1641. *Of Prelatical Episcopacy and whither it may be deduced from the Apostolical time by vertue of those Testimonies which are alleged to that Purpose in some late Treatises*. London.

————1641. *Of Reformation Touching Church-Discipline in England and the Causes that hitherto have hindred it*. London.

Mitton, C. Leslie. 1976. *Ephesians*. New Century Bible. London: Marshall, Morgan & Scott.

———. 1951. *The Epistle to the Ephesians. Its Authorship, Origin, and Purpose*. Oxford: Clarendon Press.

Moberg, David O. 1962. *The Church as a Social Institution*. Englewood Cliffs: Prentice-Hall.

Moffatt, James. 1930. "An Approach to Ignatius." *HThR* 29:1-38.

———. 1930. "Ignatius of Antioch – A Study in Personal Religion." *The Journal of Religion* 10:169-86.

Molland, Einer. "Clemensbriefe." *RGG³* 1836-38.

———. 1954. "The Heretics Combatted by Ignatius of Antioch." *Journal of Ecclesiastical History* 5:1-6.

——— "Hermas." *RGG³* 242.

Moore, C.H. 1920. "Life in the Roman Empire at the Beginning of the Christian Era." In Vol 1: *The Beginnings of Christianity*, 5 vols. (ed. E.T. Foakes Jackson and Kirsopp Lake). London: MacMillan.

Morton, A.Q. 1964. *Christianity and the Computer*. London.

Mosheim, J.L. 1835. *Commentaries on the Affairs of the Christians Before the Time of Constantine the Great*, 3 vols. (trans. R.S. Vidal). London.

——— 1753. *De Rebus Christianorum ante Constantinum magnum Commentarii*. Helmstadt.

Müller, Albert. 1905. "Sterbkassen und Vereine mit Begräbnisfürsorge in der römischen Kaiserzeit." *Neue Jahrbücher für das klassische Altertum* 8:183-201.

Munz, Peter. 1972. "The Problem of 'Die Soziologische Verortung der antiken Gnostizismus'." *Numen* 19:41-51.

Murphy-O'Connor, Jerome. 1984. "The Corinth that Saint Paul Saw." *Biblical Archaeologist* 47:147-59.

Musurillo, Herbert. 1972. *The Acts of the Christian Martyrs*. Oxford: Clarendon Press.

Natalis, Alexander et.al. 1762. *Thesaurus Logicus*, vol. 1.

Nauck, Wolfgang. 1957. "Probleme der frühchristlichen Amtsverständnis." *ZNW* 48:200-20.

The New Testament in the Apostolic Fathers. 1905. A Committee of the Oxford Society of Historical Theology. Oxford: Clarendon Press.

Nickelsburg, George W.E. 1985. "Revealed Wisdom as a Criterion for Inclusion and Exclusion: From Jewish Sectarianism to Early Christianity." In *"To See Ourselves as Others See Us" Christians, Jews, "Others" in Late Antiquity* (ed. Jacob Neusner and Ernest S. Frerichs). Chico: Scholars Press pp. 73-91.

Niebuhr, H. R. 1972. *The Social Sources of Denominationalism*. New York: Holt.

Nilsson, Martin P. 1940. *Greek Popular Religion*. New York: Columbia University Press.

Nisbet, Robert A. 1968. "Kinship and Power in First Century Rome." In *Tradition and Revolt*. New York: Random House, pp. 203-24.

Nock, A.D. 1933. *Conversion. The Old and the New in Religion from Alexander the Great to Augustine of Hippo*. Oxford: Clarendon Press.

———. 1964. *Early Gentile Christianity and its Hellenistic Background*. London: Harper and Row.

———. 1930. Book review of *Religionsgeschichtliche Untersuchungen zu den Ignatius Briefen* by Heinrich Schlier. *JTS* 31:308-13.

Norden, Eduard. 1909. *Die antike Kuntsprosa vom VI. Jahrhundert v. Chr. bis in die Zeit der Renaissance*. 2 vols. Leipzig: J.B. Teubner.

Norris, Frederick W. 1976. "Ignatius, Polycarp and I Clement: Walter Bauer Reconsidered." *VC* 30:23-44.

Oborn, G. T. 1970. "Economic Factors in the Persecution of the Christians to A.D. 260." In *Environmental Factors in Christian History* (ed. J. T. McNeill, M. Spinka, H. R. Willoughby). New York, London: Kennikat Press, pp. 131-48.

Ogilvie, R.M. 1986. *The Romans and Their Gods*. London: Hogarth Press.

Ogletree, Thomas W. 1984. *The Use of the Bible in Christian Ethics*. Oxford: Basil Blackwell.

O'Neill, J. C. 1961. *The Theology of Acts in its Historical Setting*. London: SPCK Press.

Opelt, I. "Epitome." *RAC* 944-73.

Orr, James. 1899. *Neglected Factors in the Study of the Early Progress of Christianity*. London: Hodder and Stoughton.

Osers, E. 1975. *The Delian Aretalogy of Sarapis*. Leiden: E.J. Brill.

Osiek, Carolyn. 1983. *Rich and Poor in the Shepherd of Hermas. An Exegetical-Social Investigation*. Washington: The Catholic Biblical Association of America.

Padgett, Alan. 1987. "Wealthy Woman at Ephesus – I Timothy 2:8-15 in Social Context." *Interpretation* 4:19-31.

Pagels, Elaine. 1976. "The Demiurge and His Archons' – A Gnostic View of the Bishop and Presbyters?" *HThR* 69:301-24.

――――. 1979. *The Gnostic Gospels*. London: Weidenfeld and Nicholson.

Paulsen, Henning. 1977. *Studien zur Theologie des Ignatius von Antiochien*. Göttingen: Vandenhoeck und Ruprecht.

Pearson, Birger A. 1975. "Anti-heretical Warnings in Codex IX from Nag Hammadi." In *Essays on the Nag Hammadi Texts in Honour of Pahor Labib* (ed. Martin Krause) NHS VI. Leiden: E.J. Brill, pp. 145-54.

――――. 1980. "Jewish Elements in Gnosticism and the Development of Gnostic Self-Definition." *JCSD* I 151-60.

Pearson, John. 1672. *Vindiciae Epistolarum S. Ignati*. Cambridge.

Pelham, Henry F. 1911. *Essays on Roman History*. Oxford: Clarendon Press.

Pelikan, Jaroslav. 1980. "The Two Sees of Peter, Reflections on the Pace of Normative Self-Definition in East and West." *JCSD* I 57-73.

Perler, Othmar. 1944. "Ignatius von Antiochien und die römische Christengemeinde." *Divus Thomas* 22:413-51.

――――. 1949. "Das vierte Makkabaeerbuck, Ignatius von Antiochien und die aeltesten Martyrerberichten." *Rivista di Archeologia Cristiana* 25:47-72.

Pervo, Richard I. 1985. "Wisdom and Power: Petronius' Satyricon and the Social World of Early Christianity." *Anglican Theological Review* 67:307-29.

Pesch, Rudolph. 1971. "Structures du ministère dans le Nouveau Testament." *Istina* 16:437-52.

Petersen, Joan M. 1969. "House-Churches in Rome." *VC* 23:264-72.

Petersen, Norman R. 1985. *Rediscovering Paul: Philemon and the Sociology of Paul's Narrative World*. Philadelphia: Fortress Press.

Pfaff, C.M. 1770. *Dissertatio Polemica de Sucessione Episcopali*. Tübingen.

――――1727. *Institutiones Historiae Ecclesiasticae*. Tübingen.

Planck, D.G.F. 1803. *Geschichte der christlich-kirchlichen Gesellschafts-Verfassung*, vol. 1. Hannover: Hahn.

Plumpe, Joseph C. 1943. *Mater Ecclesia. An Inquiry into the Concept of the Church as Mother in Early Christianity*. Washington: Catholic University of America Press.

Poland, Franz. 1909. *Geschichte des griechischen Vereinswesens*. Leipzig.

Porter, Livingstone. 1939. "The Word ἐπίσκοπος in Pre-Christian Usage." *Anglican Theological Review* 21:103-12.

Poschmann, Bernhard. 1940. *Paenitentia Secunda. Die kirchliche Busse im ältesten Christentum bis Cyprian und Origenes.* Bonn: Haustein.

Powell, Douglas. 1981. "Clemens von Rom." *Theologische Realenzyklopädie* 8:113-23.

Preiss, T. 1938. "La mystique de l'imitation du Christ et de l'unité chez Ignace d'Antioche." *Revue d'Histoire et de Philosophie Religieuses* 18:197-41.

Preisedanz, Karl. 1973. *Papyri Magicae. Die Griechischen Zauberpapyri.* 2 vols. Stuttgart.

Prigent, P. 1977. "L'Hérésie Asiate et L'Église Confessante de L'Apocalypse à Ignace." *VC* 31:1-22.

Quasten, Johannes. 1983. *Patrology,* Vol 1. Westminister, Maryland: Christian Classics.

Rahner, Hugo. 1943. *Abendländische Kirchenfreiheit. Dokumente über Kirche und Staat im frühen Christentum.* Cologne: A. Benzinger.

Ramsay, W. A. 1893. *The Church in the Roman Empire before A.D. 170.* London: Hodder and Stoughton.

―――. 1932. "The Date of St. Polycarp's Martyrdom." *Jahresheftes der Österreichischen archaelogischen Institute* 27:245-58.

―――. 1904. *The Letters to the Seven Churches of Asia and Their Place in the Plan of the Apocalypse.* London, 1904.

Rawson, Beryl. 1986. "The Roman Family." In *The Family in Ancient Rome* (ed. Beryl Rawson). London: Croom Helm.

Rehm, B. 1957. "Clemens Romanus II." *Reallexikon für Antike und Christentum* 3:197-206.

Reiling, J. 1973. *Hermas and Christian Prophecy.* Leiden: E.J. Brill.

Reinach, S. 1923. "Ignatius, Bishop of Antioch, and the ΑΡΧΕΙΑ." *Anatolian Studies Presented to Sir William Mitchell Ramsay* (ed. W. H. Buckler, W. M. Calder). Manchester: The University Press, pp. 339-40.

Renan, Ernst. 1866. *Les Apôtres. Histoire des Origines du Christianisme,* Vol. 2. Paris.

Reumann, John. 1959. "OIKONOMIA = 'Covenant' Terms for Heilsgeschichte in Early Christian Usage." *NovT* 3:282-91.

―――. 1958. "'Stewards of God' – Pre-Christian Religious Application of OIKONOMOS in Greek." *JBL* 77:339-49.

Reuning, Wilhelm. 1917. *Zur Erklärung des Polykarpmartyriums.* Darmstadt: Winter.

Rex, John. 1969. *Key Problems of Sociological Theory.* London: Routledge and Kegan Paul.

Richardson, Cyril C. 1935. *The Christianity of Ignatius of Antioch.* New York: AMS Press.

―――. 1937. "The Church in Ignatius of Antioch." *Journal of Religion* 17:428-43.

―――. 1953. *Early Christian Fathers,* Vol. 1. London: SCM Press.

Riddle, Donald W. 1938. "Early Christian Hospitality: A Factor in the Gospel Transmission." *JBL* 57:141-54.

―――. 1927. "Environment as a Factor in the Achievement of Self-consciousness in Early Christianity." *Journal of Religion* 7:146-63.

―――. 1931. *The Martyrs. A Study in Social Control.* Chicago: University of Chicago Press.

―――. 1927. "The Messages of the Shepherd of Hermas: A Study in Social Control." *Journal of Religion* 7:561-77.

Riesenfeld, H. 1961. "Reflections on the Style and the Theology of St. Ignatius of Antioch." *Studia Patristica* IV *TU* 79:312-22.

Rife, J. Merle. 1943. "Hermas and the Shepherd." *Classical Weekly* 37:81.

Rigaux, Beda. 1977. "Die 'Zwölf' in Geschichte und Kerygma." *Das Kirchliche Amt im Neuen Testament* (ed. K. Kertelge). Darmstadt: Wissentschaftliche Buchgesellschaft, pp. 279-304.

Ritschl, A. 1857. *Enstehung der altkatholischen kirche².* Bonn: Marcus.

Robinson, David M. (ed.). 1938. *Excavations at Olynthus. Part VIII. The Hellenic House.* London: Oxford University Press.

———. 1946. *Excavations at Olynthus. Part XII. Domestic and Public Architecture.* London: Oxford University Press.

Robinson, J. Armitage. 1920. *Barnabas, Hermas, and the Didache.* London: SPCK.

Robinson, J.A.T. 1976. *Redating the New Testament.* London: SCM Press.

Robinson, James M. (ed.) 1981. *The Nag Hammadi Library.* New York: Harper & Row.

Robinson, James M., Koester, Helmut. 1971. *Trajectories Through Early Christianity.* Philadelphia: Fortress Press.

Roggs, Joachim. 1964. " Ἐνωσις und verwandte Begriffe in den Ignatiusbriefen." In ... *Und Fragten nach Jesus Festschrift Ernst Barnikol* Berlin: pp. 45-51.

Roloff, Jürgen. 1965. *Apostolat–Verkündigung–Kirche.* Gütersloh: Bertelsmann.

Rordorf, D. Willy. 1964. "Was wissen wir über die christlichen Gottesdiensträume der vorkonstantinischen Zeit?" *ZNW* 55:110-28.

Rostovtzeff, Michael. 1957. *The Social and Economic History of the Roman Empire.* 2 vols. Oxford: Clarendon Press.

———. 1934. "Die Synagoge von Dura." *Römische Quartalschrift* 42:203-18.

Roth, Guenther. 1971. "Max Weber's Comparative Approach and Historical Typology." In *Comparative Methods in Sociology — Essays on Trends and Applications* (ed. Ivan Gallier). Berkeley: University of California Press, pp. 75-93.

Rothe, Richard. 1837. *Die Anfängs der christlichen Kirche und ihrer Verfassung,* vol. 1. Wittenberg.

Rowland, Christopher. 1985. *Christian Origins.* London: SPCK.

Rudolph, Kurt. 1983. *Gnosis. The Nature & History of an Ancient Religion* (trans. P.W. Coxen, K.H. Kuhn, R.M. Wilson). Edinburgh: T. & T. Clark.

———. 1977. "Das Problem einer Soziologie und 'sozialen Verortung' der Gnosis." *Kairos* 19:35-44.

Sampley, J. Paul. 1971. *"And the Two Shall Become One Flesh": A Study of Traditions in Ephesians 5:21-33.* Cambridge: Cambridge University Press.

Sanders, E. P. (ed.) 1980-85. *Jewish and Christian Self-Definition.* 3 vols. London: SCM Press.

Sanders, J. N. 1956. "The Case for the Pauline Authorship." in *Studies in Ephesians* (ed. F. L. Cross). London: A.R. Mowbray.

Sanders, Louis. 1943. *L'Hellénisme de Saint Clément de Rome et le Paulinisme.* Lovan.

Saumaise, Claude de. 1641. *De Episcopis et Presbyteris.* Lyons.

———1645. *Librorum de Primatu Papae.* (no place specified).

Schäferdick, K. 1965. "The Acts of John." *NTA* II:188-215.

Scheel, Otto. 1912. "Zum urchristlichen Kirchen und Verfassungsproblem." *Theologische Studien und Kritiken* 85:403-57.

Schermann, T. 1909. "Griechische Zauberpapyri und das Gemeinde-und Dankgebet im I. Klemensbriefe." *TU* 34.

Schiller, A. "Lex Poppia Poppaea." *PW* Suppl. VI:227-32.

Schlatter, A. 1898. "Die Kirche Jerusalems vom Jahre 70 bis 130." *Beitrage für Förderung christlichen Theologie* II, 3. Gütersloh: Bertelsmann.

Schlatter, Frederic W. 1984. "The Restoration of Peace in Ignatius' Antioch." *JTS* 35:465-69.

Schlier, H. 1929. *Religionsgeschichtliche Untersuchungen zu den Ignatiusbriefen.* Giessen.

———. "αἵρεσις κτλ" *TDNT* 1:180-85.

Schmidt, C. 1885. *The Social Results of Early Christianity* (trans. Mrs. Thorpe). London.

Schmidt, C. 1929. "Studien zu den Pseudo-Clementinen." *TU* 46.

Schnackenburg, Rudolph. 1977. "Episkopos und Hirtamt (Zu Apg. 20, 28)." In *Das Kirchliche Amt im Neuen Testament* (ed. K. Kertelge). Darmstadt: Wissentschaftliche Buchgesellschaft, pp. 418-41.

Schneemelcher, W. 1965. "Acts of Paul." *NTA* II:322-81.

———. 1965. "Acts of Peter." *NTA* II:259-75.

———. 1965. "The Kerygma Petrou." *NTA* II:94-102.

Schneemelcher, W., and Schäferdik, K. 1965. "Second and Third Century Acts of the Apostles, Introduction." *NTA* II:167-88.

Schoedel, William R. 1967. *The Apostolic Fathers. A New Translation and Commentary.* Vol. 5: *Polycarp, Martyrdom of Polycarp, Fragments of Papias* (ed. Robert M. Grant). London: Thomas Nelson & Sons.

———. 1985. *Ignatius of Antioch. A Commentary on the Letters of Ignatius of Antioch.* Philadelphia: Fortress Press.

———. 1980. "Theological Norms and Social Perspectives in Ignatius of Antioch." *JCSD* I: 30-56.

Schöllgen, Georg. 1986. "Monepiskopat und monarchischer Episkopat. Eine Bemerkung zur Terminologie." *ZNW* 77:146-51.

Schulz, Fritz. 1954. *Classical Roman Law.* Oxford: Clarendon Press.

Schürer, E. 1879. "Die Gemeindeverfassung der Juden in Rom in der Kaiserzeit." *Theologische Literaturzeitung* 23:542-46.

———. 1973 – . *The History of the Jewish People in the Age of Jesus Christ (175 B.C.-A.D. 135)* (trans., rev. and ed. Geza Vermes, Fergus Millar, Matthew Black, and Martin Goodman). Edinburgh: T. & T. Clark. (3 vols. to date).

Schürmann, Heinz. 1968. *Traditionsgeschichtliche Untersuchungen zu den synoptischen Evangelien.* Düsseldorf: Patmos pp. 310-40.

———. 1970. *Ursprung und Gestalt. Erörterungen und Businnungen zum Neuen Testament.* Düsseldorf: Patmos, pp. 236-67.

Schütz, John Howard. 1975. *Paul and the Anatomy of Apostolic Authority.* Cambridge: Cambridge University Press.

Schwahn, T. 1932. "Tamiai." *PW* 8:2099-38.

Schweisser, V. 1904. "Der Pastor Hermas und die Opera Supererogatoria." *Theologische Quartalschrift* 86:539-56.

Schweizer, E. 1961. *Church Order in the New Testament.* London: SCM Press.

———. 1959. "The Concept of the Church in the Gospel and Epistles of St. John." *New Testament Essays. Studies in Memory of Thomas Walter Manson* (ed. A. J. B. Higgins). Manchester: Manchester University Press, pp. 230-245.

———. 1976. *The Good News According to Matthew.* London: SPCK.

———. 1982. *The Letter to the Colossians. A Commentary* (trans. Andrew Chester). London: SPCK.

Scott, E.F. 1958. *The Epistles of Paul to the Colossians, to Philemon and to the Ephesians.* London: Hodder and Stoughton.

———. 1957. *The Pastoral Epistles.* London: Hodder & Stoughton.

Scott, Walter. 1924. *Hermetica. The Ancient Greek and Latin Writings which contain Religious or Philosophic Teachings Ascribed to Hermes Trismegistos.* Oxford: Clarendon Press.

Scroggs, Robin. 1975. "The Earliest Christians Communities as Sectarian Movement." In *Christianity, Judaism, and Other Graeco-Roman Cults Studies for Morton Smith at Sixty* (ed. J. Neusner). Leiden: E.J. Brill. Part Two, pp. 1-23.

———. 1980. "The Sociological Interpretation of the New Testament: The Present State of Research." *NTS* 26:164-79.

Seitz, O.J.F. 1947. "Antecedents and Signification of the Term 'Δίψυχος.'" *JBL* 46:211-19.

———. 1944. "Relationship of the Shepherd of Hermas to the Epistle of James." *JBL* 63:131-40.

Shepherd, Massey Hamilton. 1940. "Smyrna in the Ignatian Letters. A Study in Church Order." *Journal of Religion* 20:141-59.

Shils, Edward. 1968. "Charisma." *International Encyclopedia of the Social Sciences,* vol. 2. New York: Cromwell Collier and MacMillan, pp. 386-90.

———. 1965. "Charisma, Order and Status." *American Sociological Review* 30:199-213.

———. 1968. "Ideology I – The Concept and Function of Ideology." *International Encyclopedia of the Social Sciences,* vol. 7. New York: Cromwell Collier and Mac-Millan Inc., pp.66-76.

Shotwell, James T., and Loomis, Louise Roper. 1927. *The See of Peter.* New York: Columbia University Press.

Simmel, Georg. 1955. *Conflict* (trans. Kurt H. Wolff). Glencoe: The Free Press.

Simon, Marcel. 1979. "From Greek Haeresis to Christian Heresy." in *Early Christian Literature and the Classical Intellectual Tradition* (eds. William R. Schoedel and Robert L. Wilkin). Paris: pp. 101-17.

Sjoberg, Gideon. 1960. *The Preindustrial City Past and Present.* Glencoe: The Free Press.

Smith, Dennis Edwin. 1977. "The Egyptian Cults at Corinth." *HThR* 70:201-31.

Smith Jonathan Z. 1975. "The Social Description of Early Christianity." *Religious Studies Review* I:19-25.

Snyder, Graydon E. 1985. *Ante Pacem: Archeological Evidence of Church Life Before Constantine.* Macon: Mercer University Press.

———. 1968. *The Shepherd of Hermas.* Camden: T. Nelson.

Sohm, Rudolph. 1892. *Kirchenrecht I. Die geschichtlichen Grundlagen.* Leipzig: J.C. Henrich.

———. 1895. *Outlines of Church History* (trans. Mary Sinclair). London, New York: MacMillan.

Staats, Reinhart. 1986. "Die katholische Kirche des Ignatius von Antiochien und das Problem ihrer Normitivität im zweiten Jahrhundert." *ZNW* 77:242-54.

Stählin, P. "Ξένος, κτλ." *TDNT* 5:1-36.

Stambaugh, John, and Balch, David. 1986. *The Social World of the First Christians.* London: SPCK.

Stark, Werner. 1966. *The Sociology of Religion. A Study of Christendom.* Vol. 1: *Established Religion.* London: Routledge and Kegan Paul.

———. 1967. *The Sociology of Religion. A Study of Christendom.* Vol. 2: *Sectarian Religion.* London: Routledge and Kegan Paul.

———1967(b). *The Sociology of Religion. A Study of Christendom.* Vol. 3: *The Universal Church.* London: Routledge and Kegan Paul.

———. 1969. *The Sociology of Religion. A Study of Christendom.* Vol. 4: *Types of Religious Man.* London: Routledge and Kegan Paul.

Stauffer, E. 1943. "Zur Vor-und Frühgeschichte des Primatus Petri." *Zeitschrift für Kirchengeschichte* 62:3-34.

Stempel, Hermann A. "Der Lehrer in der 'Lehre der zwölf Apostle'." *VC* 34:209-17.

Stendahl, Krister. 1954. *The School of St. Matthew.* Uppsala.

Stenger, W. 1974. "Timotheus und Titus als literarische Gestalten." *Kairos* 16:67.

Sternberger, D. 1968. "Legitimacy." In *The International Encyclopedia of the Social Sciences,* vol. 9 (ed. David S. Sills). New York: Cromwell Collier and MacMillan, pp. 244-48.

Stevenson, G.H. 1970. "Clubs, Roman." In *The Oxford Classical Dictionary* (ed. N.G.L. Hammond, H.H. Scullard). Oxford: Clarendon Press.

Stevenson, J. 1978. *The Catacombs. Rediscovered Monuments of Early Christianity.* London:

Thames and Hudson.

Stommel, E. 1969. "Domus Aeterna." *RAC* 4:109-28.

Strathmann. 1967. "Λειτουργέω, κτλ." *TDNT* 4. Grand Rapids: Wm. B. Eerdmanns.

Streeter, Burnett Hillman. 1936. *The Four Gospels. A Study of Origins.* London: Macmillan.

_____. 1936. "The Much-Belaboured Didache." *JTS* 37:369-74.

_____. 1929. *The Primitive Church.* London: Macmillan.

Strobel, August. 1965. "Der Begriff des 'Hauses' im griechischen und römischen Privatrecht." *ZNW* 55:91-100.

Stuhlmacher, Peter. 1975. *Der Brief an Philemon.* Zürich.

Stuiber, A. "Clemens Romanus I." *RGG³* 188-97.

Sturdy. J.M. 1979. Review of *Redating the New Testament. JTS* 30:255-62.

Suerre, Aalen. 1962. "'Reign' and 'House' in the Kingdom of God in the Gospels." *NTS* 8:215-40.

Sundberg Jr., Albert C. 1973. "Canon Muratori: A Fourth Century List." *HThR* 66:1-41.

Surkau, Hans-Werner. 1938. *Martyrien in jüdischer und frühchristlicher Zeit.* Göttingen: Bertelsmann.

Swartley, W.M. 1973. "The Imitatio Christi in the Ignatian Letters." *VC* 27:81-103.

Swete, H. B. (ed.) 1921. *Essays on the Early History of the Church and the Ministry.* London: Macmillan.

Syme, Ronald. 1939. *The Roman Revolution.* Oxford: Clarendon Press.

Telfer, W. 1952. "The Date of the Martyrdom of Polycarp." *JTS* 3:79-83.

_____. 1962. *The Office of a Bishop.* London: Darton, Longman & Todd.

Theissen, Gerd. 1982. *The Social Setting of Pauline Christianity* (trans. and ed. John A. Schütz). Edinburgh: T. & T. Clark.

_____. 1978. *Sociology of Early Palestinian Christianity* (trans. by John Bowden). Philadelphia: Fortress Press.

Thomas, G. S. R. 1979. Review of *Kingdom and Community. The Journal of Religious History* 10:95-6.

Thomassin, D. Louis. 1703. *Traité Dogmatique et Historique des Edits . . . pour Maintenir l'Unité de l'Église Catholique.* 3 vols. Paris.

Thompson, W. G. 1970. *Matthew's Advice to a Divided Community.* Rome: Biblical Institute Press.

Thraede, K. "Frau." *RAC* 197-269.

Tidball, Derek. 1983. *An Introduction to the Sociology of the New Testament.* Exeter: Paternoster Press.

Tiede, David L. 1980. *Prophecy and History in Luke-Acts.* Philadelphia: Fortress Press.

Tinh, Tran Tam. 1982. "Sarapis and Isis." In *Jewish and Christian Self-Definition in the Graeco-Roman World,* Vol. 3. London: SCM Press.

Tinsley, E.J. 1957. "The imitatio Christi in the Mysticism of St. Ignatius of Antioch." *Studia Patristica 2 TU* 64:553-60.

Trevett, Christine. 1981. "Ignatius and his opponents in the divided church of Antioch in relation to some aspects of the early Syrian Christian tradition: a study based on the text of the Middle Recension of the Ignatian letters." Ph.D. dissertation, University of Sheffield.

_____. 1983. "Prophecy and Anti-Episcopal Activity: a Third Error Combatted by Ignatius?" *Journal of Ecclesiastical History* 34:1-18.

Trilling, Wolfgang. 1977. "Amt un Amtverständnis bei Matthäus." *Das Kirchliche Amt im Neuen Testament* (ed. K. Kertelge). Darmstadt: Wissentschaftliche Buchhandlung, pp. 524-42.

Troeltsch, E. 1931. *The Social Teaching of the Christian Churches* (trans. O. Wyon). 2 vols. London.

Tröger, Karl Wolfgang. 1977. "Doketische Christologie in Nag-Hammadi-Texten." *Kairos* 19:44-52.

Tuckett, Christopher. 1987. *Reading the New Testament*. London: SPCK.

Turner, Cuthbert Hamilton. 1921. "Apostolic Succession." In *Essays on the Early History of the Church and the Ministry²*. (ed. H.B. Swete) London: Macmillan.

———. 1920. "The Sheperd of Hermas and the Problem of its Text." *JTS* 21:193-209.

———. 1912. *Studies in Early Church History*. Oxford: Clarendon Press.

Unnik, W.C. van. 1977. "The Authority of the Presbyters in Irenaeus' Works." In *God's Christ and His People* (ed. Jacob Jervell and Wayne A. Meeks). Oslo, Bergen, Trömso.

———. 1950. "Is I Clement 20 Purely Stoic?" *VC* 4:181-89.

———. 1951. "I Clement 34 and the 'Sanctus'." *VC* 5:204-45.

Ussher, J. et. al. 1641. *The Original of Bishops and Metropolitans*. Oxford.

Ussher, J. 1644. *Polycarpi et Ignati Epistolae*. Oxford.

Vallée, Gérard. 1981. *A Study in Anti-Gnostic Polemics: Irenaeus, Hippolytus, and Epiphanius*. Waterloo: Wilfred Laurier Press.

———. 1980. "Theological and Non-Theological motives in Irenaeus's Refutation of the Gnostics." *JCSD* I, pp. 174-85.

Vermaseren, M.J. 1960. *Corpus Inscriptionum et Monumentorum Religionis Mithriacae*. 2 vols. The Hague: Martinus Nijhoff.

Vermaseren, M.J., and Essen, C.C. van. 1965. *The Excavations in the Mithraeum of Church of Santa Brisca in Rome*. Leiden: E.J. Brill.

Vermaseren, M.J. 1963. *Mithras the Secret God*. London: Chatto and Windus.

Vermes, G. 1975. *The Dead Sea Scrolls in English*. Harmondsworth: Penguin.

Verner, David C. 1983. *The Household of God: The Social World of the Pastoral Epistles*. Chico: Scholars Press.

Vielhauer, P. 1965. "The Shepherd of Hermas." *NTA* II, pp. 629-42.

Vitringa, Campegii. 1696. *De Synagoga Vetere Libri Tres*. (no place specified)

———. 1842. *The Synagogue and the Church. Condensed from the original Latin work by Vitringa by Joshua L. Bernard*. London.

Vogliano, A. 1933. "La grande iscrizione Bacchica del Metropolitan Museum: I." *American Journal of Archeology*, 2d. ser., 37:215-31.

Vokes, F.E. 1938. *The Riddle of the Didache*. London: SPCK.

Wachsmuth, Dietrich. 1980. "Aspekte des Antiken Mediterranen Hauskults." *Numen* 27:34-75.

Wagner, Johannes. 1949. "Altchristliche Eucharistiefeier im kleinen Kreis. Ein Beitrag zur ältesten Geschichte der Messe." PhD dissertation, rheinischen Friedrich-Wilhelms Universität, Bonn.

Waitz, Hans. 1904. "Die Pseudoklementinen Homilien und Rekognitionen eine Quellenkritische Untersuchung." *TU* 25.

———. 1929. "Die Pseudoklementinen und ihre Quellenschriften." *ZNW* 28:242-72.

———. 1931. "Pseudoklementinische Probleme." *ZKG* 50:186-194.

Waltzing, J.P. 1895-99. *Etude Historique sur les Corporations Professionelles chez les Romains depuis les origines jusqu'à la chute de l'Empire d'Occident*. 4 vols. Louvain: F. Hayez.

Weber, Max. 1968. *Basic Concepts in Sociology* (trans. H.P. Secher). London: Peter Owen.

———. 1968. *Economy and Society. An Outline of Interpretive Sociology*. 3 vols. (ed. Guenther Roth and Claus Wittich). New York: Bedminster Press.

———. 1949. *The Methodology of the Social Sciences* (trans. B.A. Shils and H.A. Finch). Glencoe, Ill: The Free Press.

———. 1965. *The Sociology of Religion* (trans. Ephraim Fishoff). London: Methuen.

———. 1947. *The Theory of Social and Economic Organization.* New York: Oxford University Press.

Weigandt, P. 1963. "Zur sogenannten in 'Oikosformel'." *NovT* 6:49-74.

Weingarten, Hermann. 1881. "Die Umwandlung der ursprünglichen christlichen Gemeindeorganisation zur katholischen Kirche." *Historische Zeitschrift* 9:441-67.

Weizsäker, Carl. 1891. *Das apostolische Zeitalter der christlichen Kirche².* Freiburg i. B.

Welburn, L.L. 1984. "On the Date of First Clement." *Biblical Research* 29:35-54.

Wengst, Klaus. 1987. *Pax Romana and the Peace of Jesus Christ.* London: SCM Press.

White, Lloyd Michael. 1985/86. "Adolf Harnack and the 'Expansion' of Early Christianity: A Reappraisal of Social History" *The Second Century* 5: 97-127.

———. 1982. "Domus Ecclesiae — Domus Dei: Adaptation and Development in the Setting for Early Christian Assembly." PhD dissertation, Yale University.

Whittaker, Molly. 1967. *Der Hirt des Hermas. Die Apostolischen Väter I.* Berlin: J.C. Henrichs.

Wiefel, Wolfgang. 1970. "Die jüdische Gemeinschaft im antiken Rom und die Anfänge des römischen Christentums." *Judaica* 26:65-88.

Wiegand, Theodor. 1920. *Priene. Ein Begleitwort zur Rekonstruktion von A. Zippelius.* Leipzig, Berlin.

Wiegand, Theodor, and Schrader, Hans. 1904. *Priene. Ergebnisse den Ausgrabungen und Untersuchungen in den Jahren 1895-1898.* Berlin: G. Reimer.

Wilde, James A. 1978. "The Social World of Mark's Gospel: A Word About Method." *Society of Biblical Literature 1978 Seminar Papers*, vol 2 (ed. Paul J. Achtemeier). Missoula: Scholars Press.

Wilder, Amos N. 1981. "Social Factors in Early Christian Apology." In *Early Christian Origins. Studies in Honor of Harold R. Willoughby* (ed. Allen Wilkgren). Chicago: Quadrangle Books, pp. 67-76.

Wilken, Robert L. 1980. "The Christians as the Romans (and Greeks) Saw Them." *JCSD* I 100-25.

———. 1972. "Collegia, Philosophical Schools, and Theology." *ECH* 268-91.

———. 1981. "Diversity & Unity in Early Christianity." *The Second Century* I:101-10.

———. 1971. *The Myth of Christian Origins.* New York: Doubleday.

———. 1970. "Toward a Social Interpretation of Early Christian Apologetics." *Church History* 39:1-22.

Willer, David. 1967. *Scientific Sociology. Theory and Method.* Englewood Cliffs: Prentice-Hall.

Williams, S. R. 1978. "The Household in the Early Church, with Comparative Selective Reference to the Roman Pagan Culture of the Roman World." B.Litt. dissertation, University of Oxford.

Wilson, Bryan R. 1959. "An Analysis of Sect Development." *American Sociological Review* 24:3-15.

Wilson, Bryan R. 1973. *Magic and the Millenium: A Sociological Study of Religious Movements of Protest Among Tribal and Third-World Peoples.* New York: Harper and Row, 1973.

———. 1975. *Noble Savages:The Primitive Origins of Charisma and its Contemporary Survival.* London: University of California Press.

———. 1967. *Patterns of Sectarianism. Organization and Ideology in Social and Religious Movements.* London: Heinemann Educational Books.

———. 1982. *Religion in Sociological Perspective.* Oxford: Oxford University Press, 1982.

————. 1970. *Religious Sects: A Sociological Study.* London: World University Library.

————. 1961. *Sects and Society. A Sociological Study of Three Religious Groups in Britain.* London: William Heinemann.

————. 1984. "A Typology of Sects in a Dynamic and Comparative Prospective" (trans. Jenny M. Robertson). in *Sociology of Religion* (ed. Roland Robertson). Middlesex: Penguin, pp. 361-83.

Wilson, William Jerome. 1927. "The Career of the Prophet Hermas." *HThR* 20:21-62.

Workman, Herbert B. 1980. *Persecution in the Early Church.* Oxford: Oxford University Press.

Wrede, W. 1891. *Untersuchungen zum Ersten Klemensbriefe.* Göttingen: Vandenhoeck and Ruprecht.

Wycherley, R.E. 1959. "The Garden of Epicurus." *Phoenix* 13:73-7.

————. 1961. "Peripatos: The Athenian Philosophical Scene - I." *Greece and Rome* 8:152-63.

————. 1962. "Peripatos: The Athenian Philosophical Scene - II." *Greece and Rome* 9:2-21.

Yinger, J. M. 1961. *Religion and the Struggle for Power.* New York: Russell and Russell.

Zahn, T. 1899. *The Articles of the Apostles' Creed.* London: Hodder and Stoughton.

————. 1873. *Ignatius von Antiochien.* Gotha: F.U. Berthes.

Ziebarth, Erich. 1896. *Das griechische Vereinswesen.* Leipzig: S. Hirzel.

Ziegler, A. W. 1958. *Neue Studien zum I Clemensbrief.* Munich: Kaiser.

SR SUPPLEMENTS

Note: Nos. 1, 3, 4, 5, 6, 7, 8, 10, 15 and 20 in this series are out of print.

EDITIONS SR

Note: Nos. 1, 3 and 9 in this series are out of print.

DISSERTATIONS SR

1. *The Social Setting of the Ministry as Reflected in the Writings of Hermas, Clement and Ignatius*
   Harry O. Maier
   1991 / viii + 230 pp.

STUDIES IN CHRISTIANITY AND JUDAISM / ÉTUDES SUR LE CHRISTIANISME ET LE JUDAÏSME

Note: No. 1 in this series is out of print.

2. *Anti-Judaism in Early Christianity*
   Vol. 1, *Paul and the Gospels*
   Edited by Peter Richardson with David Granskou
   1986 / x + 232 pp.
   Vol. 2, *Separation and Polemic*
   Edited by Stephen G. Wilson
   1986 / xii + 185 pp.
3. *Society, the Sacred, and Scripture in Ancient Judaism: A Sociology of Knowledge*
   Jack N. Lightstone
   1988 / xiv + 126 pp.
4. *Law in Religious Communities in the Roman Period: The Debate Over Torah and Nomos in Post-Biblical Judaism and Early Christianity*
   Peter Richardson and Stephen Westerholm
   with A. I. Baumgarten, Michael Pettem and Cecilia Wassén
   1991 / x + 164 pp.

THE STUDY OF RELIGION IN CANADA / SCIENCES RELIGIEUSES AU CANADA

1. *Religious Studies in Alberta: A State-of-the-Art Review*
   Ronald W. Neufeldt
   1983 / xiv + 145 pp.
2. *Les sciences religieuses au Québec depuis 1972*
   Louis Rousseau et Michel Despland
   1988 / 158 p.

COMPARATIVE ETHICS SERIES / COLLECTION D'ÉTHIQUE COMPARÉE

Note: No. 1 in this series is out of print.

2. *Methodist Education in Peru: Social Gospel, Politics, and American Ideological and Economic Penetration, 1888-1930*
   Rosa del Carmen Bruno-Jofré
   1988 / xiv + 223 pp.

Available from / en vente chez:
Wilfrid Laurier University Press
Waterloo, Ontario, Canada   N2L 3C5

Published for the
Canadian Corporation for Studies in Religion/
Corporation Canadienne des Sciences Religieuses
by Wilfrid Laurier University Press